The Crisis in
Youth Mental Health

Recent Titles in Child Psychology and Mental Health

THE CRISIS IN
YOUTH MENTAL HEALTH

Critical Issues and Effective Programs

Volume 2

Disorders in Adolescence

Francisco A. Villarruel and Tom Luster

Volume Editors

Hiram E. Fitzgerald, Robert Zucker, and Kristine Freeark

Editors in Chief

Praeger Perspectives
Child Psychology and Mental Health

Hiram E. Fitzgerald and Susanne Ayres Denham, Series Editors

PRAEGER

Westport, Connecticut
London

KH

Library of Congress Cataloging-in-Publication Data

The crisis in youth mental health : understanding the critical issues and effective programs / editors Hiram E. Fitzgerald, Robert Zucker, and Kristine Freeark.
  p. cm.—(Child psychology and mental health)
  Includes bibliographical references and index.
  ISBN 0-275-98480-X (set : alk. paper)—ISBN 0-275-98481-8 (v.1 : alk. paper)—
  ISBN 0-275-98482-6 (v.2 : alk. paper)—ISBN 0-275-98483-4 (v.3 : alk. paper)—
  ISBN 0-275-98484-2 (v.4 : alk. paper) 1. Adolescent psychopathology. 2. Child psychotherapy. 3. Youth—Counseling of. 4. Community mental health services.
  I. Fitzgerald, Hiram E. II. Zucker, Robert A. III. Freeark, Kristine. IV. Series.

RJ503.C76   2006
618.92'8914—dc22   2005030767

British Library Cataloguing in Publication Data is available.

Library of Congress Catalog Card Number: 2005030767
ISBN: 0–275–98480–X (set)
       0–275–98481–8 (vol. 1)
       0–275–98482–6 (vol. 2)
       0–275–98483–4 (vol. 3)
       0–275–98484–2 (vol. 4)
ISSN: 1538–8883

First published in 2006

Praeger Publishers, 88 Post Road West, Westport, CT 06881
An imprint of Greenwood Publishing Group, Inc.
www.praeger.com

Printed in the United States of America

The paper used in this book complies with the Permanent Paper Standard issued by the National Information Standards Organization (Z39.48–1984).

10 9 8 7 6 5 4 3 2 1

2|8|07

CONTENTS

SERIES FOREWORD

The twentieth century closed with a decade devoted to the study of brain structure, function, and development that in parallel with studies of the human genome has revealed the extraordinary plasticity of biobehavioral organization and development. The twenty-first century opens with a decade focusing on behavior, but the linkages between brain and behavior are as dynamic as the linkages between parents and children, and children and environment.

The Child Psychology and Mental Health series is designed to capture much of this dynamic interplay by advocating for strengthening the science of child development and linking that science to issues related to mental health, child care, parenting, and public policy.

The series consists of individual monographs, each dealing with a subject that advanced knowledge related to the interplay between normal developmental process and developmental psychopathology. The books are intended to reflect the diverse methodologies and content areas encompassed by an age period ranging from conception to late adolescence. Topics of contemporary interest include studies of socioemotional development, behavioral undercontrol, aggression, attachment disorders, and substance abuse.

Investigators involved with prospective longitudinal studies, large epidemiologic cross-sectional samples, intensely followed clinical cases or those wishing to report a systematic sequence of connected experiments are invited to submit manuscripts. Investigators from all fields in social and behavioral sciences, neurobiological sciences, medical and clinical sciences, and education are invited to submit manuscripts with implications for child and adolescent mental health.

Hiram E. Fitzgerald
Susanne Ayres Denham
Series Editors

ACKNOWLEDGMENTS

This project began at a lunch meeting when Norman Watt, Robert Bradley, Catherine Ayoub, Jini Puma and Hi Fitzgerald concluded that there was a great need for a book that summarized the benefits of early intervention. Shortly after agreeing to pursue such a book, Deborah Carvalko, acquisitions editor at Greenwood Publishing Group, contacted Hi to inquire if he knew anyone who would be interested in editing a series on the Crisis in Youth Mental Health. Bingo! This four-volume set is the result and volume 4 is that original lunch time project. The volumes represent a product forged from the labor and energy of an editorial team composed of long-time and current research and professional colleagues: Catherine Ayoub, Robert Bradley, William Davidson, Hiram Fitzgerald, Kristine Freeark, Whitney LeBoeuf, Barry Lester, Tom Luster, Jini Puma, Francisco Villarruel, Norman Watt, Robert Zucker, and Barry Zuckerman. Each editorial team drafted an extraordinary set of researchers who collectively frame the parameters of the crisis in youth mental health, provide cogent analyses of effective evidence-based preventive-intervention programs, and draw attention to policy implications of their work. Volumes such as these are labors of professional and personal love because the rewards to be gained are only those realized by the impact that words and ideas have on current and future generations of scientists, parents, and policy makers. No one has more passion for bringing science to bear on the problems of society than Lou Anna K. Simon, President of Michigan State University. In her commentary, she eloquently and forcefully articulates the need to forge campus–community partnerships, using evidence-based practices to both understand and resolve community-based problems.

Editors and authors provide the grist for anthologies, but there are many millers that grind the grain and bake it into a final loaf. First to thank is Deborah Carvalko who provided the opportunity to even imagine the project. Lisa Pierce, senior development editor at Praeger Press made sure that this host of contributors met their deadlines. Apex Publishing, assisted by four extremely meticulous and energetic copy editors (Ellie Amico [vol. 1], Bruce Owens [vol. 2], Caryl Knutsen [vol. 3], and Carol Burwash [vol. 4]), moved everyone through a tight time frame for copy editing and page proofs, assured cross-volume uniformity in format and style, removed split infinitives, identified missing references, and translated academic language into a more common prose. Finally, at Michigan State University, Vasiliki Mousouli was the diligent project manager who maintained contact with more than 60 editors, authors, and publishers, organized and tracked all of the manuscript activity, and made final format corrections for APA style. In her spare time she managed to complete her doctoral program requirements in school psychology and successfully defend her doctoral dissertation.

What began as lunchtime table talk, resulted in four volumes that collectively summarize much about the crisis in youth mental health. All involved have our deepest respect and thanks for their contributions.

Hiram E. Fitzgerald
Kristine Freeark
Robert A. Zucker

SPECIAL COMMENTARY: UNIVERSITIES AND THE CRISIS IN YOUTH MENTAL HEALTH

Lou Anna Kimsey Simon
President, Michigan State University

There are at least two key reasons why universities are concerned about the crisis in youth mental health. First, increasing numbers of students matriculating at colleges and universities have mental health problems. Because social and emotional well-being is paramount to academic success and to the ability to negotiate the demands of the workplace, universities must be concerned about student socioemotional health. Second, understanding the causes and life course progression of mental health problems relates directly to the scholarship mission of the university, especially those with historical ties to the land grant system of higher education. Land grant universities, established by the Morrill Act of 1862, were founded to allow all citizens access to higher education and to bind together the scholarships of discovery and application. Thus, land grant universities are about values and beliefs regarding the social role and social responsibility of universities with respect to ameliorating the problems of society.

In 2005, Michigan State University celebrates its 150th anniversary as an academic institution, and in 2012 it will celebrate its 150th anniversary as the first land grant university. We have been actively engaged in a campus conversation concerning the role of land grant institutions in the twenty-first century, and much of that conversation has focused on renewing the covenant between higher education and the public that higher education serves. When land grant institutions were founded, the focus of that covenant was on agricultural production and the mechanical arts. Today, the covenant extends to the broad range of problems in contemporary society, not the least of which are those associated with the causes, treatments, and prevention of mental health problems.

Professional and public documents increasingly draw attention to the pervasive problems affecting children throughout the United States and the world. Considering all forms of mental illness, recent studies indicate that half the population will experience a mental health problem sometime during the life course. In the United States, 1 in 10 children and adolescents suffer from mental illness severe enough to cause some level of impairment, but only 1 in 5 receive treatment. Most mental health problems are transitory and relatively easily resolved by brief interventions, including support from mental health professionals, friends, family members, or other individuals in one's social support network. Epidemiologists report that approximately 6 percent of the population experiences profound mental health problems and may require psychotrophic medications and intense psychotherapy to maintain manageable levels of adaptive behavior. However, there is an increasing number of individuals who deal with mental health problems at a level of severity that lies between the ordinary and the profound. The number of children with learning disabilities, speech and language handicaps, mental retardation, emotional disturbances, poor self-regulatory skills, aggressive behavior, substance abuse disorders, and poor school achievement is increasing at alarming rates. Seventeen percent of all children in the United States have one or more developmental disabilities, 20 percent of all school-age children have attention problems, and the age of onset of first drug use, smoking, and sexual activity continues to spiral downward (Fitzgerald, Lester, & Zuckerman, 2000; Koger, Schettler, & Weiss, 2005).

Collectively, students enrolled in higher education represent the rich spectrum of America's ethnic, racial, political, gender, religious, and physical diversity. If higher education does its job well, students will be challenged to examine their personal beliefs and values against this diversity, arriving at deeper understanding of their own values as well as those of others, both of which are implicit to sustaining a free, democratic, and diverse society. For many students, such free-ranging discussion and debate is exciting, provocative, and enriching. Other students may encounter diversity that is beyond their prior experience, and public discourse and challenge to their personal beliefs may provoke anxiety and distress. The mental health crisis among America's youth directly translates to a mental health crisis on America's college and university campuses. Increasing numbers of students report suicide ideation, feelings of hopelessness, depression, anxiety, and a sense of being overwhelmed (Kadison & DiGeronimo, 2004). Increasing numbers of these students come from broken families, and many come from stressful neighborhoods and communities. The crisis in youth mental health contributes to the crisis in college student mental health, and both challenge university capacity to provide the depth of support necessary to help students maintain psychological and behavioral health in the context of pressures for academic success.

The good news is that prevention specialists from many different disciplines have developed evidence-based programs that have positive impacts not only on child behavior but also on families and communities. This four-volume set was designed to affirm principles underlying the importance of prevention and the view that individual development is best understood within the framework of systems theory. Systems theory begins with the premise that from the moment of conception, the organism is embedded within an increasingly complex array of systems (family, neighborhood, school, community, and society) and that all components mutually transact to shape development over the life course. The contextual embeddedness of mental health problems, therefore, requires perspectives from a broad range of social, behavioral, economic, and biomedical sciences as well as the arts and humanities in order to understand behavior in context. Thus, universities are uniquely positioned to make significant contributions to the understanding and remediation of mental health problems because universities are the repositories of all the disciplines and can provide the means for interdisciplinary, systemic research and the development and assessment of prevention and treatment approaches. Moreover, from a land grant perspective, such research and development activities gain even greater authenticity when conducted within the context of campus–community partnerships for health and well-being.

Resolving the crisis in youth mental health is essential for the maintenance of a mentally healthy society because youth constitute society's future policy and political leadership. Universities contribute to the resolution by providing a range of wraparound supportive structures and services and by building stronger campus–community partnerships in health. Equally important for universities is a commitment to search for causal factors that shape developmental pathways that generate mental health problems, to develop biomedical and behavior treatments, and to discover successful ways to prevent or ameliorate mental health problems early in development. The chapters in this volume focus attention to each of these objectives.

REFERENCES

Fitzgerald, H. E., Lester, B. M., & Zuckerman, B. (Eds.). (2000). *Children of addiction: Research, health, and policy issues.* New York: Garland.

Kadison, R. D., & DiGeronimo, T. F. (2004). *College of the overwhelmed: The campus mental health crisis and what to do about it.* Boston: Jossey-Bass.

Koger, S. M., Schettler, T., & Weiss, B. (2005). Environmental toxicants and developmental disabilities. *American Psychologist, 60,* 243–255.

Chapter 1

THE ROLE OF THE FAMILY IN PROMOTING ADOLESCENT HEALTH AND DEVELOPMENT: CRITICAL QUESTIONS AND NEW UNDERSTANDINGS

Stephen Small and Brandon Covalt

Adults are prone to create myths about the meaning of adolescence. Whatever their political or personal inclinations, whether they glorify nature or revere society, whether they are identified with youth or they are detractors of youth, most adults find it imperative to defuse the awesome vitalities of these monsters, saints and heroes. (Kaplan, 1984, p. 50)

Over the past several decades, a great deal has been written about adolescents and their families in both popular and scientific literature. At the same time, the characterization of adolescents and their relationships with parents has been changing. Sometimes life with teens is portrayed as easier than in the past; sometimes as more difficult. Sometimes the teen years are depicted as tumultuous and stressful; at other times they are viewed as tranquil and uneventful. Sometimes parents are viewed as their teen's most important source of guidance and protection; at other times the role of parents is downplayed, and other sources, such as peers and the media, are considered the primary influences.

In this chapter, we examine some of the common conceptions of families with adolescent children and review what the current scientific literature says about them. We attempt to discern the myths from the realities, the oversimplifications from the complexities, and the old from the new. Our approach is somewhat eclectic, addressing a wide range of questions and dissecting issues that we feel have been the most misunderstood or over-simplified. Beginning with the broader social context in which adolescents and their families operate, the focus of this chapter then moves inward to some of the more relational, social, and psychological issues that are important during the adolescent years.

What has led to prevailing misunderstandings about adolescence? Sometimes they result from the poor dissemination of knowledge. While our scientific understanding of adolescent development and family life has grown exponentially over the past two decades, this information has not always made its way to parents, professionals, and the public in a user-friendly manner. Consequently, misinformation, outdated stereotypes, and oversimplifications have endured. Another reason for the persistence of popular misconceptions is that the experience of adolescence itself has changed in recent years. What may have been true in the past may no longer hold true in the present. As we discuss in the next section, the pace and number of changes that have occurred over the past generation are unprecedented in human history and have important implications for teens and their parents.

IS RAISING A TEENAGER TODAY EASIER OR MORE DIFFICULT THAN IT WAS IN THE PAST?

Because of rapid advances in technology and the growth in affluence among American families, it is sometimes assumed that raising teenagers is less difficult than it was for past generations. Like the Chinese symbol for crisis—which is composed of two characters, danger and opportunity—the world that today's teens face is full of great promise as well as the potential for problems. Contemporary American teens have opportunities and benefits that never before existed, but they also face difficulties that previous generations never even imagined. Progress and change bring with them perils and possibilities that make growing up both easier and more difficult than in the past (Larson, Wilson, Brown, Furstenberg, & Verma, 2002). These changes also have implications for parents who are trying to raise their children in this increasingly complex and changing world. Understanding how progress can lead to both new opportunities and new dangers is important if professionals are to better help today's youth and their families successfully cope with and adapt to the demands of contemporary life.

Contemporary American adolescents are healthier, are physically bigger and taller, and live longer lives than any previous generation. The diseases that once crippled or took the lives of many youth are much rarer today (Call et al., 2002; Papalia, Olds, & Feldman, 2004). However, affluence has its costs. Adolescents today reach physical maturity earlier than in the past (Lee, Guo, & Kulin, 2001), and this can mean that young people are sometimes introduced to the social and environmental hazards of adolescence and adulthood before they are socially and emotionally prepared

(Orr & Ingersoll, 1995). For instance, adolescent girls who mature physically earlier than their peers are at greater risk of sexual activity and drug use because of their tendency to hang out with an older social crowd (Hayward, Killen, Wilson, & Hammer, 1997). Affluence has also resulted in an epidemic number young people being overweight or obese, significantly threatening their current and future health (U.S. Department of Health and Human Services, 2001).

Even though the overall physical health and life expectancy of today's adolescents has improved (Call et al., 2002; Centers for Disease Control and Prevention [CDC], 2000), contemporary teens are more likely to experience psychological and social problems than in the past (Smith & Rutter, 1995). The incidence of teen depression, suicide, violence, and drug use are generally much higher than the rates for previous generations. For instance, between 1970 and 1994, both the suicide and the homicide rates for American adolescents doubled (CDC, 2002). Similarly, illicit drug use has increased over the past decade after a period of decline in the late 1980s (Johnston, O'Malley, & Bachman, 2002), and most adolescent drug use rates are much higher than they were prior to the 1970s. The reasons for the increase in psychosocial problems among youth in recent decades are not entirely clear. However, some scholars have speculated that they result from greater stress and anxiety, the presence of fewer adults in the lives of teens, less stable families and social relationships, and greater uncertainty about what the future holds (Easterbrook, 2003; Rutter & Smith, 1995).

As a result of technological and social progress, the number of informational sources available to young people has grown astronomically. Easy access to hundreds of television channels, movies, computer games, and the Internet can be double-edged. On the one hand, young people have access to a nearly unlimited world of ideas and images, making them arguably the most informed, knowledgeable, and aware generation in human history (Roberts, Foehr, Rideout, & Brodie, 1999). At the same time, there is the danger that they will be exposed to ideas and images that can be harmful, that may run counter to the values and beliefs that their parents wish to instill, or for which they do not yet have the skills or psychosocial maturity to handle (Cantor, 2000).

Like other aspects of progress and social change, the expansion of social, educational, and vocational choices can be a mixed blessing for young people. On the positive side, there are more academic and vocational opportunities for young people than ever before. This is especially true for women and traditional minorities who have overcome many barriers in the past 25 years. For instance, more than half of all college students are now women, and the number of minorities enrolled in college has risen 122 percent over the past 20 years (American Council on Education, 2003).

When it comes to choices in lifestyle and career, the opportunities for today's youth often seems limitless. Marriage, for example, has become only one of many relationship options, and vocational opportunities for women have begun to approach those traditionally available to men. Moreover, having children outside of marriage or being in a same-sex relationship are no longer unusual and are gaining social acceptance. On the other hand, there is emerging evidence that more choices can lead to greater stress and anxiety (Schwartz, 2004). The availability of more choices requires that more effort and time be devoted to selecting among them (Easterbrook, 2003; Schwartz, 2004). For instance, when students have only a few options about what high school courses they might take, the decision is likely to be fairly straightforward. However, when faced with numerous choices, the decision becomes more complicated, more time consuming, and potentially more anxiety producing (Schwartz, 2004). Consequently, while the expansion of the number of opportunities and choices available to young people today is a generally positive phenomenon, it can be accompanied by potential psychological costs.

The contemporary changes that produce both possibilities and perils for youth can also make raising teens more complicated and challenging for today's parents. While raising teens has traditionally been considered a demanding task, it appears to be even more difficult for parents as the world becomes more complicated and dangerous and there is less certainty about what the future holds. Because a lot of the options currently available to their children did not exist when they were growing up, many parents today are unsure about what they need to do to adequately prepare their teens for future success.

Further complicating matters is the changing environment in which families raise children. With most adults employed outside the home, there are fewer adults available to supervise teens, leaving teens with more time to spend on their own. Smaller families and greater mobility means that families have smaller kin networks and fewer nearby family members on whom to rely for support, assistance, and knowledge about raising children (Halfon, McLearn, & Schuster, 2002; Small & Eastman, 1991). Finally, parental authority and influence must compete with many powerful external pressures. With the increasing diversity of American society and the growth of all forms of electronic media including the Internet, parents have become a smaller voice in an ever more diverse sea of role models and ideas (Larson et al., 2002). Today's youth are exposed to all types of ideas and images, both healthy and harmful. This not only undermines the influence of parents, making it more difficult for parents to pass on their own values and behavior, but also makes it more difficult for parents to know what the right or best choices are for their teen. Clearly, the world in which we live is changing rapidly. These changes present both perils and possibilities for young people as well as challenges for parents and others who share the responsibility of guiding their development.

IS ADOLESCENCE A MORE DIFFICULT TIME FOR TEENS OR FOR PARENTS?

For many years, both professionals and scholars portrayed adolescence as a time of storm and stress. It was considered a psychologically and socially difficult time for most teenagers. Research over the past 25 years, however, has failed to provide strong support for the conception of adolescence as a tumultuous period for teens; at the same time, there is an emerging literature suggesting that the adolescent years may be a difficult and stressful time for parents (Steinberg, 2001).

Many of the developmental changes that adolescents experience are likely to have implications for the entire family system, especially parents. In addition, parents of adolescents are typically in midlife and experiencing developmental changes of their own. These issues not only may have an influence on the midlife parent's own mental health but can also affect the way they relate to and raise their teenager (Small & Eastman, 1991). In a few developmental domains, it sometimes appears that middle-aged parents and their teenage offspring are encountering very different, sometimes divergent developmental experiences.

In their study of midlife parents of teenagers, Steinberg and Steinberg (1994) identify several facets of adolescent development that can serve as "triggers" for psychological difficulties and distress in parents. These triggers arise from the psychological, emotional, social, and biological changes that are occurring in the adolescent and the interaction of these changes with those that parents themselves may be experiencing.

One of the most obvious developmental changes of adolescence is the onset of puberty and the significant physical transformation that the emerging teen undergoes. These physical changes not only make it clear to parents that their child is growing up and entering a new phase of life but may also serve to remind them that they themselves are growing older (Steinberg & Steinberg, 1994). As teens become physically stronger and more adultlike in their appearance, midlife parents are usually beginning to experience signs of aging. Their child's enhanced physical appearance, stamina, and strength may remind parents that they themselves are no longer the young, vigorous, and physically attractive person they once were. Parents may also experience feelings of loss as their child grows into an increasingly independent young person who seems to need them less and less (Silverberg & Steinberg, 1990).

According to Steinberg and Steinberg (1994), the budding teen's sexuality is another developmental transformation that can be psychologically difficult for parents, especially if the child is a daughter. A teen's sexual maturation can lead parents to worry about their own sexuality and physical attractiveness. In addition, some parents may become envious of their child's attractiveness and sexual potential while also experiencing feelings of loss regarding their own youth. In families where the parents are married, a teen's emerging sexuality can lead to parents becoming dissatisfied with both their spouse and their marriage (Koski & Steinberg, 1990).

An adolescent's striving for independence and autonomy from parents is a normal and necessary part of development. However, as teens push for more control over decisions affecting their own lives, parents may experience a loss of control and perceive a decrease in their parental authority. This can lead to feelings of powerlessness and stress, further contributing to parental anxieties about midlife changes and losses (Small, Eastman, & Cornelius, 1988).

Another typical transformation in the parent–adolescent relationship involves a change in the adolescent's emotional attachment to parents (Wong, Wiest, & Cusick, 2002). Emotional relationships between parents and teens usually remain warm throughout adolescence (Arnett, 1999), but the nature of the relationship is renegotiated (Larson, Richards, Moneta, Holmbeck, & Duckett, 1996). For instance, adolescents often spend more time with friends and less time with parents (Engels, Dekovic, & Meeus, 2002). They may also become more private and less willing to talk with their parents about their personal lives (Finkenauer, Engels, & Meeus, 2002). Emotional energy and attention that was once directed at parents may be redirected toward friends and new intimate relationships (Larson, Richards, Moneta, Holmbeck, & Duckett, 1996). Although this emotional distancing from parents by the adolescent is typical, parents may feel rejected and regret the change in emotional closeness that they once had with their child (Ungar, 2004). There is some evidence to suggest that mothers of adolescent daughters are the most likely to be affected by this emotional distancing, given that mothers and daughters typically have the closest and warmest parent–child relationship (Steinberg & Steinberg, 1994).

A parent's mental health may be adversely affected by the developing teen's tendency to deidealize the parent (Silverberg & Steinberg, 1990). This means that parents are no longer viewed by the child as perfect and all-knowing. Or, as Steinberg and Steinberg (1994) put it, "most children remove their parents from a pedestal and attempt to place them underneath it" (p. 73). Teens may point out parental faults and inconsistencies while at the same time idealizing other adults and making it a point to let their parents know where they fail to measure up. An adolescent's deidealization of parents is a normal part of the individuation process and necessary if he or she is to separate from parents and develop his or her own unique identity. This fall from grace in the eyes of their adolescent can result in lower parental self-esteem, higher levels of depression, and more time spent thinking about midlife concerns (Silverberg & Steinberg, 1990; Steinberg & Steinberg, 1994).

Finally, it has long been known that the frequency and intensity of conflict between parents and children increases during the early adolescent years (Laursen, Coy, & Collins, 1998). Because most of these conflicts are over fairly mundane matters such as curfew, appearance, and keeping one's bedroom clean, it has often been concluded that these squabbles are unimportant and have little effect on the well-being of either parents or teens. Though such conflicts may be relatively insignificant for teens, there is evidence that they are a significant source of stress and strain for parents (Steinberg, 2001).

Insight into why parents and teens experience conflicts differently can be found in the work of Smetana (1989, 1995), who observed that conflicts between parents and teens often arise because they frame and define the issues about which they disagree quite differently. Conflicts arise not just from differences of opinion but also from deeper disagreements about how each party perceives issues as well as disagreements about who has the legitimate right to make final decisions. From the parents' perspective, many conflicts are the result of teens breaking codes of conduct based on moral rules or social conventions. For instance, parents may view their child's messy room as a sanitary issue with moral implications or as a social norm that all people in the house are expected to follow. However, from a teen's perspective, whether they keep their room clean is likely to be perceived as a personal choice or as a way to express personal identity or autonomy, not as a moral-ethical issue or social convention. Consequently, not only might teens see little reason to keep their rooms clean, but they are also likely to believe that the choice is legitimately theirs, not their parents. Parents are more likely to be upset by such disagreements because they see the issues as more complex and important, having to do with matters of ethics, responsibility, and social conventions, matters that have long-term lessons and implications.

In sum, raising teenagers can be a difficult time for parents. Like their adolescent children, they too are experiencing significant developmental changes. These changes, along with those confronting their adolescent children, can have important implications for the mental health of parents and the quality of the parent–teen relationship.

ARE LOVE AND COMMUNICATION REALLY THE MOST IMPORTANT INGREDIENTS IN SUCCESSFUL PARENT–TEEN RELATIONSHIPS?

It is almost a cliché to say that the most important thing that children need is love and that the best way to ensure good relationships is to encourage clear and open communication. Though love and communication are certainly essential to good parent–adolescent relationships (Ben-Zur, 2003), a great deal more is also necessary (Baer, 2002). In fact, parental love and support without clear expectations and limits can be detrimental to teens (Steinberg, 2001). And when it to comes to communication, what matters most is the manner in which communication occurs and what it is that parents are communicating (Kelly, Comello, & Hunn, 2002).

Over the past 25 years, a solid, consistent body of research has emerged about the types of parenting practices that are most optimal for raising teens in contemporary American society. This configuration of parenting practices is known as authoritative parenting (Baumrind, 1991). The authoritative parenting style is characterized by parents who are warm, loving, and supportive of their child while also being firm and clear about their expectations. These expectations are developmentally appropriate and are clearly and consistently communicated to teens (Steinberg, 2001).

The research on authoritative parenting makes apparent that loving parenting that lacks firm limits, structure, and developmentally appropriate expectations is not very effective and is even potentially detrimental (Fisher & Feldman, 1998). Scholars refer to such a parenting style as permissive or indulgent parenting and have found strong evidence that teens with permissive parents do less well academically, are lower in psychosocial maturity, and are more likely to engage in potentially risky behavior like alcohol and drug use and high-risk sexual activity (Small & Luster, 1994; Steinberg & Morris, 2001; Stice & Barrera, 1995).

Similarly, one of the most important aspects of communication is the message that is communicated by parents and the quality of the relationship in which the communication takes place. Authoritative parents establish clear limits and rules about what is permissible and what is not and clearly communicate these expectations to their child (Smetana, 1995). They talk about family rules and expectations before problems occur and also discuss with their teens the consequences of not meeting these expectations and rules.

Another aspect of communication that is highlighted by the research on authoritative parenting is the need to increasingly involve children in meaningful discussions about family rules, expectations, and decisions. Ideally, parents provide a supportive, safe, and respectful environment where teens and parents can talk about important issues and decisions (Steinberg, 2001). In authoritative families, parents allow their teen to present his or her point of view, even when it may be different from their own perspective. This provides a safe place for the child to try out new ideas and practice decision making while also allowing parents a chance to hear their child's point of view, to ask questions, and to provide constructive feedback and suggestions. Communication in authoritative families does not mean that children have the final word but rather that children are heard and that their perspective is taken into account in decisions affecting their lives. Thus, as adolescents mature and demonstrate their ability to make responsible and wise decisions, the balance of power increasingly shifts from parents to teens. Parents gradually become more like advisers and sounding boards to their teens, supporting them as they learn to make good choices more autonomously (Larson et al., 1996).

Authoritative parenting is an effective approach to raising adolescents because it provides a loving, supportive context where good communication can occur and where guidance and structure are provided. However, a balanced interplay of each of these components is the key to successful authoritative parenting. Because authoritative parents are warm and involved, teens are more receptive to parental influence and more apt to abide by the rules that parents set down. Similarly, when youth are provided with age- and context-appropriate opportunities, support, and structure to discuss and make decisions affecting their lives, they are more likely to develop the cognitive and psychosocial skills needed to become responsible and competent individuals (McElhaney & Allen, 2001).

WHAT ROLE DO PARENTS PLAY IN PREVENTION DURING THE ADOLESCENT YEARS?

Because adolescents become increasingly independent and influenced by a growing number of people and sources, parents sometimes believe that there is little they can do to influence their teen, especially when it comes to preventing the many problems associated with the adolescent years. However, the potential of parents to be powerful and important preventers of a myriad of risky youth behaviors has been well documented (Jacobson, 2000). There are a number of parental practices that have been found to help protect adolescents from harm as well as to promote their well-being, including monitoring teen activity, providing structure and rules for appropriate behavior, and spending time together. These parenting practices do not exist independently from one another and are much more effective if they occur within the context of a warm and supportive parent–child relationship (Kerr & Stattin, 2000).

Monitoring

Of the parenting practices associated with reducing problematic teen behaviors, parental monitoring has been found to be one of the most powerful tools that parents have at their disposal. Commonly defined as parents' knowledge of their youngster's whereabouts, activities, and friends (Jacobson, 2000), parental monitoring has consistently emerged as a highly salient factor in empirical investigations of risky youth behavior. A sizable body of research exists that demonstrates the importance of parental monitoring in preventing adolescent alcohol use (Dishion, Nelson, & Kavanaugh, 2003), risky sexual behavior (Small & Luster, 1994), and various forms of delinquency (Jacobson, 2000). Furthermore, teens who are closely monitored by their parents are less likely to be victims of sexual violence by peers (Small & Kerns, 1993). The value of parental monitoring is even greater in high-risk neighborhoods where the opportunities for youth to engage in potentially dangerous behaviors tends to be high and where there are fewer adults in the community to keep an eye on neighborhood teens (Covalt, Park, Tiwari, & Small, 2004). In addition to helping prevent youth problems, there is strong evidence showing that higher levels of parental monitoring are also related to positive outcomes, such as school success (Jacobson, 2000). The important ingredient in parental monitoring is parents' ongoing acquisition of information about the "who, what, where, when, and why" of their adolescent child's daily activities, especially when parents themselves are not present for behavioral supervision.

Structure and Consistency

Another important set of parenting practices associated with the prevention of adolescent problems involves providing adolescents with a family environment that has structure and consistency. This entails parents establishing clear, reasonable, and developmentally appropriate rules and standards that adolescents are expected to follow (Engels et al., 2002). It also involves parents having and applying reasonable and developmentally appropriate sanctions when the teen misbehaves or fails to follow family rules (McElhaney & Allen, 2001). For example, family environments with clear structure and consistent rules can be especially important for preventing drug use. This is what Kosterman, Hawkins, Guo, Catalano, and Abbott (2000) found in their study of adolescent initiation of drug and alcohol use:

> Establishing clear family norms and practicing good family management can inhibit alcohol and marijuana initiation, regardless of how close young people feel to their mothers during this time of adolescent individuation,

separation, and identity formation. Our findings underscore the importance of not giving up on clear standards and good parenting, even if teenagers express anger, antipathy, or distance in response to their parents' efforts to influence them toward healthy behaviors. (p. 9)

Time Spent Together

Another body of research suggests that mothers and fathers who spend more time doing things with and talking with their adolescents are more successful in their parenting roles than their counterparts who spend less time with their youngsters (Fallon, 2001). These authors contend that the more time parents spend with their adolescent children, the more opportunity they have to engage in those parenting practices that have been associated with the prevention of risky youth behaviors. For example, Strom and colleagues (2002, 2003) found that the more time parents spend with their adolescent children, the more opportunity they have for communication, support, guidance, information gathering, expression of positive regard, and practicing relationship skills as well as for helping youth in practical ways, such as homework completion and practicing athletic and other skills.

In their longitudinal study of adolescents, Miller and Volk (2002) found a significant inverse relationship between time adolescents spend with their families and risky behavior. For example, spending few weekday evenings together was a strong predictor of tobacco use. Another study found that the more time teens spent with their parents, the less likely they were to report educational problems (Fallon, 2001). Findings such as these suggest that family time may serve to either prevent or alleviate school-related problems and various forms of deviant behavior.

In sum, parents can play an important role in preventing risky adolescent behavior. When parents are knowledgeable about their teen's whereabouts and activities, are actively involved in their lives, provide structure and consistency, and have clear, enforceable rules, they can be an important and powerful influence for preventing problematic behaviors. However, as we discuss here, parents are not the only important people in their teenager's life, and they alone are not solely responsible for problems if they do occur.

ARE PARENTS THE BEST SOURCES OF COUNSEL FOR THEIR TEENS?

Parents may be the best source of prevention, but they are not always the most skilled at intervention when serious problems emerge. This is where professionals and other caring adults may come in. There are often limits to what parents can do and to what teens will allow them to do. Other important, nonparental adults can be a safe source of guidance and assistance for teens. Parents should not be disheartened or distressed if they discover they are occasionally "left out of the loop."

Parents can be very effective listeners, advice givers, and guidance providers on a number of issues for their teen if given the chance and if they have a good relationship with their child (Kerr & Stattin, 2000; Otto, 2000). Research has demonstrated that youth often turn to their parents for help with problems and to receive a sympathetic ear (Fallon, 2001). On the other hand, the need for emotional boundaries between parent and child, along with the parents' responsibility for enforcing rules and the consequences for breaking them, mean that even when parents are willing to be their teen's first avenue for counsel and assistance, their child may sometimes avoid them. For example, data from community surveys indicate that teens are often uncomfortable going to their parents with some types of problems. In one large, representative sample of youth, only about 25% of teens indicated that they talked to their parents about birth control issues, and less than half reported discussing the risks associated with drinking alcohol or taking drugs (Memmo, Park, & Small, 2000). Findings such as these indicate that parents may not always be viewed by their adolescent children as safe sources of support or guidance when it comes to some of the high-risk choices with which they are confronted (Kerr & Stattin, 2000).

Furthermore, because most teens desire their parents' approval, they may feel the need to evade parents and seek out other adults or friends when some types of problems or difficult decisions arise. From the teen's perspective, telling their parents about a problem might threaten this approval by changing their parents' opinion of them (Kerr & Stattin, 2000). Even the closest teens and parents cannot talk about everything in a teen's life. In order to develop into independent, healthy adults, boundaries need to exist between youth and parents (Baer, 2002). In addition, because parents have the responsibility and authority for disciplining teens, this may preclude them from being able to have unlimited access to adolescents' deepest thoughts and secrets in the way that a someone from outside the family— who won't discipline a child for breaking a rule, for example—might.

It is important for parents to know that the need to involve outside sources of assistance for an issue affecting their teen does not indicate a failure on their part. It can be a sign of positive development when teens seek out and use sources of support and guidance outside the family. In fact, extrafamilial social support has been found to serve as a protective factor during the teen years. Studies have shown that extended family and nonfamilial adults often fulfill important attachment functions in supporting adolescent adjustment (Kenny, Gallagher, Alvarez-Salvat, & Silsby, 2002). Furthermore, resilience research indicates that close and supportive relationships with extended family members or nonfamilial adults can be important in helping youth who are exposed to high levels of risk and stress to overcome these challenges and develop competence (Conger & Conger, 2002; Dumont & Provost, 1999).

The bottom line is that it is important for teens to have multiple sources of support and counsel available to them, including but not limited to their parents (Fallon, 2001). Teachers, school counselors, coaches, activity sponsors, clergy members, friends' parents, older siblings, other relatives, and sometimes trained professionals can all serve as important sources of support and guidance for teens.

Which situations can be handled by a parent, and which are best addressed by a professional? There are a number of important issues to consider, beginning with the seriousness of the issue. Many parents can effectively counsel their teen on normative developmental issues (e.g., what classes to take this semester) and with day-to-day emotional distresses. However, more serious, "nonnormative" problems, such as sexual assault or drug abuse, may be best left to professionals (Hall & Torres, 2002). Another point to consider is whether the parent's counsel is solicited or desired by the teen. In addition, although counselors and other professionals working with adolescents usually strive to promote positive parent–child relations, sometimes this is not fully possible. For youth who have abusive or seriously strained relationships with their parents or whose parents are not available, mental health professionals can help adolescents identify other adults in their lives who have the potential to play a supportive role in promoting positive outcomes (Kenny et al., 2002).

HOW MUCH SHOULD PARENTS FOCUS ON DEVELOPING HIGH SELF-ESTEEM IN THEIR TEEN?

For many years, self-esteem has been touted as one of the most important things that children and teens need in order to be healthy, happy, and successful and to avoid problems such as drugs and delinquency (National Association for Self-Esteem, 2004). Feeling that one is a worthwhile and capable person appears to have some advantages, which is why numerous prevention programs have focused on raising self-esteem as a way to prevent problems. For instance, many drug and alcohol prevention programs make an effort to build self-esteem on the basis of the theory that when youth feel good about themselves, the desire to use alcohol and other drugs will not be as strong (Komro & Toomey, 2002). The same theory has served as the basis for programs aimed at reducing teen pregnancy and delinquency (Durlak, 1997). However, emerging research over the past decade has found that having high self-esteem is not necessarily the panacea that it has often been made out to be (Hewitt, 1998).

Although thousands of studies have linked self-esteem to numerous outcomes, almost all these studies have been correlational (Baumeister, Campbell, Krueger, & Vohs, 2003). Consequently, it is unclear whether low self-esteem is the cause or the consequence of the behavior or outcome in question. Low self-esteem and deleterious outcomes are usually not strongly or directly linked, indicating that while low self-esteem may be a contributing factor in some adolescent problems, it is probably not the primary explanation for undesirable outcomes (Baumeister et al., 2003; Hewitt, 1998).

In addition, there is much research to suggest that high self-esteem is not in and of itself a strong predictor of health, responsible behavior (Baumeister et al., 2003). For instance, many criminals and juvenile delinquents have high self-esteem, especially if they are successful in their criminal or delinquent activities and their accomplishments are recognized and reinforced by peers (Scheff, Retzinger, & Ryan, 1989). Similarly, there is no evidence that teens with low self-esteem are any more likely than their high-self-esteem peers to be sexually active or become pregnant, although there is some data to suggest that higher-self-esteem girls are slightly more likely than lower-self-esteem girls to use birth control (Crockenberg & Soby, 1989). Overall, there is very little evidence that improving a person's self-image will translate into better behavior (Baumeister et al., 2003). While it is probably advantageous to feel positively about oneself, such feelings are not necessary for success. According to Bandura (1987), self-esteem affects neither personal goals nor performance.

Another problem with advancing self-esteem as a developmental panacea is that giving young people false praise for routine behavior or accomplishments is not likely to be very effective (Katz, 1993). Most young people are not fooled by the suggestion that everyone is special or that everyone is a winner. It is doubtful that anyone's self-esteem is going to be raised when everyone in the class receives a certificate for being "outstanding." This does not mean that we should never praise young people or acknowledge their accomplishments. Teens need to be encouraged and recognized for their merits, especially by their parents. But such encouragement needs to be authentic and closely connected to actual accomplishments or demonstrations of character, not just empty praise for simply showing up.

Finally, what is increasingly obvious from the research on self-esteem is that self-esteem typically follows, not precedes, real accomplishment (Bandura, 1997; Baumeister et al., 2003). This means that if we want young people to feel good about themselves, they need to be given real opportunities for successful experiences, along with adequate training and preparation so that they do not fail in their endeavors. When such opportunities for success are provided, young people will not only feel good about themselves but also have good reason to.

ARE MOODINESS AND DEPRESSION A NORMAL PART OF ADOLESCENCE?

Until relatively recently, adolescent "moodiness" was viewed as an inevitable consequence of the hormonal changes associated with normative pubertal development, fortifying the popular perception that adolescence is a sort of "necessary evil" to be tolerated, a storm for parents of teens to ride out (Arnett, 1999; Buchanan & Holmbeck, 1998). Over the past few decades, however, scientists have offered new explanations for adolescent moodiness. These new perspectives challenge traditional stereotypes rooted in conventional wisdom and have important implications for how parents should think about and respond to mood fluctuations in their adolescent children. For many years, parents were told that the fluctuations in adolescent moods resulted from pubertal hormonal activity, such that teenage moodiness was thought to be the province of biology and minimally amenable to environmental influence (Buchanan, Eccles, & Becker, 1992; Steinberg & Morris, 2001). Consequently, most parents accepted the popular misconception that with regard to adolescent moodiness, "nature" was more powerful than "nurture" and that any influence they might have as parents paled in comparison to the power of adolescent hormones. Recent advances in developmental science have revealed, however, that the causes and correlates of adolescent moodiness are much more complex than previously believed, reflecting the influence of both nature and nurture.

Parents need to know that moodiness and depression represent related but distinct constructs that lie on a continuum of well-being. Consequently, it is essential that parents use caution when considering whether their child's moodiness and depression are a normal (and therefore presumably dismissible) part of being an adolescent. Though it may be true that moodiness and periods of depressed mood are common among adolescents (Arnett, 1999), it is dangerous to make the assumption that *depression* is a normal part of adolescence (National Mental Health Association [NMHA], 2004). When parents buy into the popular assumption that depression is normal for adolescents, it increases the likelihood that they will overlook signs of potentially serious psychological distress in their teenage child (Fallon, 2001). Unfortunately for parents, the symptoms of serious clinical depression often mimic the normal moodiness and situational depression common during the adolescent years (NMHA, 2004). This is problematic not only in its own right but also because parents are the first line of defense in obtaining professional help for children when it is needed. Current estimates indicate that as many as one in five adolescents have experienced a serious episode of depression by the time they reach young adulthood (NMHA, 2004), but only a fraction of youth receive professional help or treatment for clinical depression (Talbott & Fleming, 2003).

Parents need to know that the disparity between estimated rates of clinically significant depression among youth and rates of professional assistance leave many young people at risk for very serious, potentially life-threatening consequences. For example, depression has consistently been linked to higher rates of substance abuse, violence, poor academic performance, risky sexual behavior, and numerous other health-threatening problems (Dumont & Provost, 1999; NMHA, 2004). Even worse, thousands of adolescents commit suicide each year, nearly always preceded by serious depression-related warning signs (Hazler & Denham, 2002). Research has also clearly demonstrated the link between adolescent and adult depression, with long-term depressive illness most often having its onset in the teen or young adult years (Walker & Townsend, 1998). Without effective detection, diagnosis, and intervention, far too many seriously depressed adolescents go on to suffer lifelong battles with the misery of clinical depression (Hazler & Denham, 2002). Given the prevalence of serious depressive episodes among today's youth and the potentially grave consequences of allowing depression to go unchecked, the importance of distinguishing between developmentally normative moodiness and serious depression among youth cannot be overestimated. In those cases when a teen does develop clinically significant depression, it is important for parents to be proactive in obtaining good professional help.

Parents may be reassured to know that in addition to enlisting the help of professionals, there are ways in which they themselves can more directly help their teen cope with depression Two recent developments in this relatively new area of research may help inform parents who are concerned about their adolescent's mental health (Beam, Gil-Rivas, Greenberger, & Chen, 2002). First, research has found that young people who use ineffective coping strategies, especially an avoidant style of coping, are at greater risk for serious clinical depression and suicide (Dumont & Provost, 1999). Parents therefore have an opportunity to enhance resiliency in their teen by helping them develop healthy ways of coping with the normative and nonnormative stressors they encounter. Second, research has found that social isolation and inadequate social support place youth at higher risk for depression, suicide, and other deleterious outcomes (Dumont & Provost, 1999). Thus, parents should be made aware of their importance as a source of social support to their teen and their potential role in helping their adolescent build strong and healthy systems of support in their lives (Beam et al., 2002; Hazler & Denham, 2002). This should include helping their children develop and maintain positive peer relationships and relationships with other responsible adults because peers and nonfamilial adults emerge as increasingly important sources of support and assistance for youth during the adolescent years.

ARE PARENTS OR PEERS MORE IMPORTANT DURING ADOLESCENCE?

Stereotypical representations of adolescence have led to the widely held belief that peer relationships become more important than parent–child relationships during the teen years. In actuality, it is not that peers are *more important* than parents but rather that peers become more important *than they previously were* and come to serve teens' needs in different ways during the years of adolescence (Fuligni & Eccles, 1993; Scholte, van Lieshout, & van Aken, 2001). Some of the socialization functions previously served by parents are increasingly shifted to the peer domain during the teen years. This may sometimes leave parents feeling alienated from—and even rejected by—their adolescent children (Ungar, 2004).

It is essential for parents to know that while the importance of peers does increase during adolescence, parents still remain a primary and vital influence (van Wel, te Bogt, & Raaijmakers, 2002). The weight of empirical evidence does not support the common misconception that adolescent development involves a significant emotional withdrawal between parents and teens. Rather, research suggests more stability and continuity in family cohesion throughout adolescence, with changes in the parent–child relationship reflecting a transformation that ultimately results in a more equal balance of power (Baer, 2002; Larson et al., 1996). This transformation can be anxiety provoking for parents of teens, especially when considered in light of the increase in time that adolescents spend with peers outside the direct purview of parents (Fuligni & Eccles, 1993; Larson et al., 1996).

Several aspects of adolescent development are promoted through teens' spending time with age-mates. Peers provide a forum for youth to explore new social relationships and try out new competencies and ways of being (Aseltine, Gore, & Colten, 1994). Adolescent identity development requires experimenting with a variety of new behaviors, skills, roles, and selves across a range of social contexts, especially those where peers are present (Sartor & Youniss, 2004).

Parents sometimes have difficulty determining how to best respond to their teens' social experimentation in the peer context and may be inclined to express disapproval or provide unwanted feedback. But because teens usually choose friends who are like themselves, parents should exercise caution when attempting to directly influence their children's friendships by conveying disapproval. In spite of a parent's best intentions, teens may interpret parental criticism of their friends as a personal criticism (Curran, Stice, & Chassin, 1997).

For many parents, the frustration of learning to cope with the transformation in the parent–child relationship can be exacerbated when they do not feel good about the friends their child chooses to spend time with. These concerns are not unwarranted; research has demonstrated that many forms of adolescent deviant behavior are influenced by the peer group and take place in the presence of peers (Bradley & Wildman, 2002; Garnier & Stein, 2002). However, stereotypical conceptions of "peer pressure" as causing deviance in otherwise innocent youth are not supported by research. Rather, it appears that when it comes to deviant adolescent behavior, the old adage that "birds of a feather flock together" holds remarkably true (Curran et al., 1997). Teens tend to gravitate toward peers whose involvement in problem behavior is similar to their own (Adamczyk-Robinette, Fletcher, & Wright, 2002), and peer pressure is not necessarily a unidirectional process involving the corruption of innocent youth at the hands of deviant peers (Curran et al., 1997).

Research derived from an asset-focused perspective has indicated that peers can also be a positive influence during the adolescent years (Steinberg & Morris, 2001). Friends and other age-mates can promote academic performance, encourage involvement in health-promoting extracurricular activities, and deter teens from risky behavior (Kenny et al., 2002; Maxwell, 2002). In addition, friendships with age-mates are a much-needed source of social support during adolescence and can serve as a protective factor for a number of deleterious outcomes, such as depression and suicide (Hazler & Denham, 2002).

Parents have an important opportunity to focus some of their energy on supporting the development of positive peer relations for their adolescent children. Parents can exert both a direct and an indirect influence on their children's friendship choices, starting well before adolescence begins (Garnier & Stein, 2002; Steinberg, 2001). For example, parents can have an influence on their children's friendship choices through where they choose to live, the schools they choose for their children to attend, the parenting practices they utilize, and the values they instill in their children from the earliest stages of life. All these parental choices can have a powerful and lasting (albeit indirect) influence on the friends that their children choose during the adolescent years.

In sum, it appears that both parents and peers are powerful and important during the adolescent years. In order for critical developmental tasks to be successfully navigated by teens, relationships with parents must be transformed and new social relationships with peers established. Nevertheless, parents continue to have significant influence on many aspects of their teen's development, including the establishment and maintenance of positive peer relationships.

CONCLUSION

Adolescence is an exciting and challenging period in the life cycle. There is a great deal of change and transformation taking place that can have important implications for the development, health, and well-being of both teens and their parents. As we have discussed in this chapter, there exist many misunderstandings about this developmental period that can confuse parents and potentially mislead professionals who work with adolescents and their families. Some of these misconceptions result from old stereotypes, others from a lag in scientific knowledge. However, many seem to be a result of oversimplifications. There is a tendency to view adolescence and family life in simplistic terms and a failure to recognize the nuances and variations that make human development and family relationships rich, challenging, and complex.

Allowing these misunderstandings to persevere unchallenged in the public venue has the potential to result in serious social and human costs. The tendency to oversimplify our understanding of teens and their families may contribute to low expectations and standards for young people, along with negative stereotypes that can limit their access to important resources and opportunities. For example, while it may be true that some emotional distancing and conflict between parents and children is normal during adolescence, teens are often portrayed in the media as overtly hostile and rebellious toward their parents. This may lead parents to withdraw from their adolescent child at the first hint of friction or rejection, removing themselves as an important source of support and guidance. Similarly, parents who buy in to the popular notion that their most important task is to promote self-esteem in their teen may overindulge their child and fail to provide proper regulation and discipline out of fear of stifling their child's growth or self-expression. As professionals and scholars who are concerned about the well-being of adolescents and their families, it is our responsibility to be more vigilant about the sources of knowledge we draw from and more sophisticated in our interpretation of them. The future of teens and their families depends on it.

REFERENCES

Adamczyk-Robinette, S. L., Fletcher, A. C., & Wright, K. (2002). Understanding the authoritative parenting-early adolescent tobacco use link: The mediating role of peer tobacco use. *Journal of Youth and Adolescence, 31,* 311–319.

American Council on Education. (2003). *20th Anniversary Minorities in Higher Education Annual Status Report.* Washington, DC: Author.

Arnett, J. J. (1999). Adolescent storm and stress, reconsidered. *American Psychologist, 54,* 317–326.

Aseltine, R. H., Gore, S., & Colten, M. E. (1994). Depression and the social developmental context of adolescence. *Journal of Personality and Social Psychology, 67,* 252–263.

Baer, J. (2002). Is family cohesion a risk or protective factor during adolescent development? *Journal of Marriage and Family, 64,* 668–676.

Bandura, A. (1987). *Self-efficacy: The exercise of control.* New York: W. H. Freeman.

Baumeister, R. F., Campbell, J., Krueger, J., & Vohs, K. D. (2003). Does high self-esteem cause better performance, interpersonal success, happiness, or healthier lifestyles? *Psychological Science in the Public Interest, 4,* 1–44.

Baumrind, D. (1991). Parenting styles and adolescent adjustment. In J. Brooks-Gunn, R. Lerner & A. C. Peterson (Eds.), *The encyclopedia of adolescence* (pp. 746–758). New York: Garland.

Beam, M. R., Gil-Rivas, V., Greenberger, E., & Chen, C. (2002). Adolescent problem behavior and depressed mood: Risk and protection within and across social contexts. *Journal of Youth and Adolescence, 31,* 343–358.

Ben-Zur, H. (2003). Happy adolescents: The link between subjective well-being, internal resources, and parental factors. *Journal of Youth and Adolescence, 32,* 67–80.

Bradley, G., & Wildman, K. (2002). Psychosocial predictors of emerging adults' risk and reckless behaviors. *Journal of Youth and Adolescence, 31,* 253–266.

Buchanan, C. M., Eccles, J. S., & Becker, J. B. (1992). Are adolescents the victims of raging hormones: Evidence for activational effects of hormones on moods and behavior at adolescence. *Psychological Bulletin, 111,* 62–107.

Buchanan, C. M., & Holmbeck, G. N. (1998). Measuring beliefs about adolescent personality and behavior. *Journal of Youth and Adolescence, 27,* 609–629.

Call, K., Reidel, A., Hein, K., McLoyd, V., Peterson, A., & Kipke, M. (2002). Adolescent health and well-being in the twenty-first century: A global perspective. *Journal of Adolescent Research, 12,* 69–98.

Cantor, J. (2000). Media violence. *Journal of Adolescent Health, 27,* 30–34.

Centers for Disease Control and Prevention. (2000). CDC's guidelines for school and community programs: Promoting lifelong physical activity. Available: http://www.cdc.gov/nccdphp/dash/phactagg.htm

Centers for Disease Control and Prevention. (2002). Suicide in the United States. Available: http://www.cdc.gov/ncipc/factsheets/suifacts.htm

Conger, R. D., & Conger, K. J. (2002). Resilience in midwestern families: Selected findings from the first decade of a prospective, longitudinal study. *Journal of Marriage and Family, 64,* 361–374.

Covalt, B. M., Park, J. K., Tiwari, G., & Small, S. A. (2004, November). *When does parental monitoring matter the most? A person-process-context analysis of risky youth behavior.* Poster Presentation, National Council on Family Relations Annual Conference, Orlando, FL.

Crockenberg, S., & Soby, B. (1989). Self-esteem and teenage pregnancy. In A. Mecca, N. Smelser, & J. Vasconcellos (Eds.), *The social importance of self-esteem* (pp. 125–164). Berkeley: University of California Press.

Curran, P. J., Stice, E., & Chassin, L. (1997). The relation between adolescent alcohol use and peer alcohol use: A longitudinal random coefficients model. *Journal of Consulting and Clinical Psychology, 65,* 130–140.

Dishion, T. J., Nelson, S. E., & Kavanaugh, K. (2003). The family check-up with high-risk young adolescents: Preventing early-onset substance use by parent monitoring. *Behavior Therapy, 34,* 553—563.

Dumont, M., & Provost, M. A. (1999). Resilience in adolescents: Protective role of social support, coping strategies, self-esteem, and social activities on experience of stress and depression. *Journal of Youth and Adolescence, 28,* 343–364.

Durlak, J. A. (1997). *Successful intervention programs for children and adolescents.* New York: Plenum Press.

Easterbrook, G. (2003). *The progress paradox: How life gets better while people feel worse.* New York: Random House.

Engels, R. C. M. E., Dekovic, M., & Meeus, W. (2002). Parenting practices, social skills and peer relationships in adolescence. *Social Behavior and Personality, 30,* 3–18.

Fallon, B. J. (2001). Family functioning and adolescent help-seeking behavior. *Family Relations, 50,* 239–246.

Finkenauer, C., Engels, R. C. M. E., & Meeus, W. (2002). Keeping secrets from parents: Advantages and disadvantages of secrecy in adolescence. *Journal of Youth and Adolescence, 31,* 123–137.

Fisher, L., & Feldman, S. S. (1998). Familial antecedents of young adult risk behavior: A longitudinal study. *Journal of Family Psychology, 12,* 66–80.

Fuligni, A. J., & Eccles, J. S. (1993). Perceived parent-child relationships and early adolescents' orientation toward peers. *Developmental Psychology, 29,* 622–632.

Garnier, H. E., & Stein, J. A. (2002). An 18-year model of family and peer effects on adolescent drug use and delinquency. *Journal of Youth and Adolescence, 31,* 45–57.

Halfon, N., McLearn, K. T., & Schuster, M. (2002). *Childrearing in America.* New York: Cambridge University Press.

Hall, A. S., & Torres, I. (2002). Partnerships in preventing adolescent stress: Increasing self-esteem, coping, and support through effective counseling. *Journal of Mental Health Counseling, 24,* 97–110.

Hayward, C., Killen, J., Wilson, D., & Hammer, L. (1997). Psychiatric risk associated with early puberty in adolescent girls. *Journal of the American Academy of Child and Adolescent Psychiatry, 36,* 255–262.

Hazler, R. J., & Denham, S. A. (2002). Social isolation of youth at risk: Conceptualizations and practical implications. *Journal of Counseling and Development, 80,* 403–410.

Hewitt, J. P. (1998). *The myth of self-esteem: Finding happiness and solving problems in America.* New York: St. Martin's Press.

Jacobson, K. C. (2000). Parental monitoring and adolescent adjustment: An ecological perspective. *Journal of Research on Adolescence, 10,* 65–98.

Johnston, L. D., O'Malley, P. M., & Bachman, J. G. (2002). *Monitoring the future national results on adolescent drug use: Overview of key findings, 2001* (NIH Publication No. 02–5105). Bethesda, MD: National Institute on Drug Abuse.

Kaplan, L. (1984). *Adolescence: The farewell to childhood.* New York: Touchstone.

Katz, L. (1993). *Self-esteem and narcissism: Implications for practice.* Champaign-Urbana, IL: Clearinghouse on Early Education and Parenting. Retrieved from http://ceep.crc.uiuc.edu/eecearchive/digests/1993/lk-sel93.html

Kelly, M. E., Comello, M. L. G., & Hunn, L. C. P. (2002). Parent-child communication, perceived sanctions against drug use, and youth drug involvement. *Adolescence, 37,* 775–788.

Kenny, M. E., Gallagher, L. A., Alvarez-Salvat, R., & Silsby, J. (2002). Sources of support and psychological distress among academically successful inner-city youth. *Adolescence, 37,* 161–183.

Kerr, M., & Stattin, H. (2000). What parents know, how they know it, and several forms of adolescent adjustment: Further support for a reinterpretation of monitoring. *Developmental Psychology, 36,* 366–380.

Komro, K. A., & Toomey, T. L. (2002). Strategies to prevent underage drinking. *Alcohol Research and Health, 26,* 5–14.

Koski, K., & Steinberg, L. (1990). Parenting satisfaction of mothers during midlife. *Journal of Youth and Adolescence, 19,* 465–474.

Kosterman, R., Hawkins, J. D., Guo, J., Catalano, R. F., & Abbott, R. D. (2000). The dynamics of alcohol and marijuana initiation: Patterns and predictors of first use in adolescence. *American Journal of Public Health, 90,* 360–376.

Larson, R. W., Richards, M. H., Moneta, G., Holmbeck, G., & Duckett, E. (1996). Changes in adolescents' daily interactions with their families from ages 10 to 18: Disengagement and transformation. *Developmental Psychology, 32,* 744–754.

Larson, R. W., Wilson, S., Brown, B. Furstenberg, F., & Verma, S. (2002). Changes in adolescents' interpersonal experiences: Are they being prepared for adult relationships in the twenty-first century? *Journal of Adolescent Research, 12*, 31–68.

Laursen, B., Coy, K., & Collins, W. A. (1998). Reconsidering changes in parent-child conflict across adolescence: A meta-analysis. *Child Development, 69*, 817–832.

Lee P., Guo S., & Kulin H. (2001). Age of puberty: data from the United States of America. *Acta Pathologica, Microbiologica et Immunologica Scandinavica, 109*, 81–88.

Maxwell, K. A. (2002). Friends: The role of peer influence across adolescent risk behaviors. *Journal of Youth and Adolescence, 31*, 267–278.

McElhaney, B. K., & Allen, J. P. (2001). Autonomy and adolescent social functioning: The moderating effect of risk. *Child Development, 72*, 220–235.

Memmo, M., Park, J., & Small, S. (2000). *The Dane County youth assessment 2000: Final report.* Madison: Teen Assessment Project, School of Human Ecology, University of Wisconsin.

Miller, T. Q., & Volk, R. J. (2002). Family relationships and adolescent cigarette smoking: Results from a national longitudinal survey. *Journal of Drug Issues, 32*, 945–973.

National Association for Self-Esteem. (2004). *Review of self-esteem research.* Retrieved from http://www.self-esteem-nase.org/research.shtml

National Mental Health Association. (2004). *Adolescent depression: Helping depressed teens.* Retrieved from www.nmha.org/infoctr/factsheets/24.cfm

Orr, D. P., & Ingersoll, G. M. (1995). The contribution of level of cognitive complexity and pubertal timing to behavioral risk in young adolescents. *Pediatrics, 95*, 528–533.

Otto, L. B. (2000). Youth perspectives on parental career influence. *Journal of Career Development, 27*, 111–118.

Papalia, D. E., Olds, S. W., & Feldman, R. D. (2004). *Human development* (9th ed.). New York: McGraw-Hill.

Roberts, D., Foehr, U., Rideout, V., & Brodie, M. (1999). *Kids and media @ the new millennium.* Menlo Park, CA: Kaiser Family Foundation.

Rutter, M., & Smith, D. (1995). Toward causal explanations of time trends in psychosocial disorders of young people. In M. Rutter & D. Smith (Eds.), *Psychological disorders in young people: Time trends and their causes* (pp. 782–808). New York: Wiley.

Sartor, C. E., & Youniss, J. (2002). The relationship between positive parental involvement and identity achievement during adolescence. *Adolescence, 37*, 221–235.

Scheff, T., Retzinger, S., & Ryan, M. (1989). Crime, violence and self-esteem: Review and proposals. In A. Mecca, N. Smelser, & J. Vasconcellos (Eds.), *The social importance of self-esteem* (pp. 125–164). Berkeley: University of California Press.

Scholte, R. H. J., van Lieshout, F. M., & van Aken, M. A. G. (2001). Perceived relational support in adolescence: Dimensions, configurations, and adolescent adjustment. *Journal of Research on Adolescence, 11*, 71–94.

Schwartz, B. (2004). *The paradox of choice: Why more is less.* New York: HarperCollins.

Silverberg, S., & Steinberg, L. (1990). Psychological well-being of parents at midlife: The impact of early adolescent children. *Developmental Psychology, 26,* 658–666.

Small, S. A., & Eastman, G. (1991). Rearing adolescents in contemporary society: A conceptual framework for understanding the responsibilities and needs of parents. *Family Relations, 40,* 455–462.

Small, S. A., Eastman, G., & Cornelius, S. (1988). Adolescent autonomy and parental stress. *Journal of Youth and Adolescence, 17,* 377–391.

Small, S. A., & Kerns, D. (1993). Unwanted sexual activity among peers during early and middle adolescence: Incidence and risk factors. *Journal of Marriage and the Family, 55,* 941–952.

Small, S. A., & Luster, T. (1994). Adolescent sexual activity: An ecological, risk-factor approach. *Journal of Marriage and Family, 56,* 181–192.

Smetana, J. G. (1989). Adolescents' and parents' reasoning about actual family conflict. *Child Development, 60,* 1052–1067.

Smetana, J. G. (1995). Parenting styles and conceptions of parental authority during adolescence. *Child Development, 66,* 299–316.

Smith, D., & Rutter, M. (1995). Time trends in psychosocial disorders. In M. Rutter & D. Smith (Eds.), *Psychological disorders in young people: Time trends and their causes* (pp. 763–781). New York: Wiley.

Steinberg, L. (2001). We know some things: Parent-adolescent relationships in retrospect and prospect. *Journal of Research on Adolescence, 11,* 1–19.

Steinberg, L., & Morris, A. S. (2001). Adolescent development. *Annual Reviews in Psychology, 52,* 83–110.

Steinberg, L., & Steinberg, W. (1994). *Crossing paths: How your child's adolescence triggers your own crisis.* New York: Simon & Schuster.

Stice, E., & Barrera, M. (1995). A longitudinal examination of the reciprocal relations between perceived parenting and adolescents' substance use and externalizing behaviors. *Developmental Psychology, 31,* 322–334.

Strom, R. D., Beckert, T. E., Strom, P. S., Strom, S. K., & Griswold, D. L. (2002). Evaluating the success of Caucasian fathers in guiding adolescents. *Adolescence, 37,* 131–150.

Strom, P. S., Van Marche, D., Beckert, T. E., Strom, R. D., & Griswold, D. L. (2003). The success of Caucasian mothers in guiding adolescents. *Adolescence, 38,* 501–518.

Talbott, E., & Fleming, J. (2003). The role of social contexts and special education in the mental health problems of urban adolescents. *Journal of Special Education, 37,* 111–123.

Ungar, M. (2004). The importance of parents and other caregivers to the resilience of high-risk adolescents. *Family Process, 43,* 23–52.

van Wel, F., ter Bogt, T., & Raaijmakers, Q. (2002). Changes in the parental bond and the well-being of adolescents and young adults. *Adolescence, 37,* 317–334.

Walker, Z., & Townsend, J. (1998). Promoting adolescent mental health in primary care: A review of the literature. *Journal of Adolescence, 21,* 621–634.

Wong, E. H., Wiest, D. J., & Cusick, L. B. (2002). Perceptions of autonomy support, parent attachment, competence and self-worth as predictors of motivational orientation and academic achievement: An examination of sixth- and ninth-grade regular education students. *Adolescence, 37,* 255–267.

Chapter 2

RISK AND RESILIENCE

Tom Luster, Laura Bates, and Deborah J. Johnson

We would like to thank the Michigan Agricultural Experiment Station, Family and Communities Together Coalition, and Michigan State University Outreach Partnerships for providing funding for our research. We would also like to acknowledge the agencies that have worked with us on the Sudanese refugee research—Lutheran Social Services of Michigan and Refugee Services of Catholic Social Services of Lansing/St. Vincent Home, Inc. We would like to thank the Sudanese refugees, agency caseworkers, and foster parents for participating in our research. Finally, we would like to thank Kate Burdick for providing valuable feedback on an earlier draft of this chapter.

Researchers in the social sciences and psychiatry have a long history of studying problem behaviors among children and adolescents. Much of the early research was retrospective, studying the histories of youth with diagnosed problems to identify possible causes of problematic outcomes (Werner & Smith, 1992). This approach yielded insights into the types of individual characteristics, family dynamics, and contextual factors that were the antecedents of problem outcomes and suggested a strong link between exposure to adversity and poor outcomes. However, data from prospective, longitudinal studies demonstrated that many children and adolescents who were exposed to similar challenging circumstances were doing well in spite of the adversity they experienced (Werner & Smith, 1982). By the 1970s, researchers were beginning to systematically study these children, who were doing better than expected; they were described with terms such as invulnerable, stress resistant, and resilient (Masten, 2001). Since that time, research on individuals demonstrating resilience has burgeoned. In this chapter, we review studies that help us understand why some adolescents succumb to the risks they face while others manage to develop competently in difficult circumstances.

The chapter is divided into four sections. In the first section, we define key concepts used by researchers to study individual differences in the developmental outcomes of children and adolescents who experience varying levels of adversity, including risk factors, resilience, protective factors, and vulnerability. We also provide examples from studies that have utilized these concepts.

In the second section, we consider the work of researchers who view resilience in adolescence as an outcome of developmental processes that start in infancy (Masten, 2001; Yates, Egeland, & Sroufe, 2003). Competent adolescents, including those who deal effectively with adversity, have had to successfully negotiate age-salient developmental tasks (e.g., attachment, emotion regulation, peer relationships, and academic achievement) at prior stages of development. Researchers using this perspective are concerned with how developmental processes from infancy through middle childhood set the stage for negotiating the tasks of adolescence.

In the third section, we review the work of therapists who have done case studies of individuals who grew up in abusive or neglectful homes but became well-functioning adults. Using qualitative research methods, clinicians have explored how these individuals managed to achieve success, focusing on characteristics of the individuals, environmental supports they drew on during childhood and adolescence, and the way they processed and came to terms with their experiences of maltreatment.

In the final section, we discuss our research with a group of refugees known in the media as "The Lost Boys of Sudan." This group of adolescents and young adults (which includes a small number of females) were victims of the civil war in Sudan and experienced a series of horrific events and chronic adversity. As children, they experienced extreme trauma, such as separation from parents and exposure to violence, and they endured enormous hardship over a prolonged period. Yet those who work with the Lost Boys who have been resettled in the United States are struck by how many of them seem to be doing well despite growing up in harsh conditions. Drawing on the work of resilience researchers and the insights of the refugees, we are studying how they managed to cope successfully with adversity in Africa and adapt to life in a very different culture. We also share some preliminary findings from our research.

KEY CONCEPTS AND ILLUSTRATIVE FINDINGS

As noted previously, we begin by defining key concepts used by researchers to study individual differences among adolescents within a risk-and-resilience framework.

Risk Factors

A risk factor can be defined as a characteristic of the person or of the context that increases the likelihood of a negative developmental outcome (Werner & Smith, 1992). In other words, the presence of this factor is statistically associated with or predictive of a problematic outcome, such as behavioral problems or academic failure. Characteristics of the individual that are predictive of later difficulties include factors such as low birth weight, attention-deficit/hyperactivity disorder, or a specific learning disability. Contextual risk factors are found in many of the key environments where children and adolescents spend time, including the family (poverty, abuse, neglect), peer group (associating with peers who engage in risky behavior), neighborhood (violence, high concentrations of poverty, absence of resources for youth), and school (lack of safety, a negative school climate) as well as in the larger cultural and historical context (availability of guns, the threat of terrorist attacks). The relevant risk factors are likely to depend on the outcome of interest, although some risk factors (e.g., poverty, a history of physical abuse) are associated with a host of problematic outcomes. Moreover, some conditions that are not normally thought of as risk factors, such as the culture of affluence, may contribute to problem outcomes such as depression, anxiety, and substance abuse among some adolescents if youth feel burdened by pressures to succeed or are disconnected from their career-minded parents (Luthar, 2003a).

Others have categorized risk factors by dividing them into chronic stressors and acute stressors or traumatic events (Norman Garmezy in an interview with Rolf, 1999). Chronic stressors occur over long periods and include circumstances such as parental neglect or long-term poverty. Traumatic events are extreme experiences that occur once or over a relatively short period, including living in a community that is attacked during a war or devastated by an earthquake, being kidnapped, held hostage or raped, or being present during a school shooting. Both chronic and acute stressors place youth at greater risk for adjustment problems, and youth exposed to both types of stressors may be at particularly high risk.

Rutter (2001) has emphasized the importance of making a distinction between risk factors and risk mechanisms. Risk factors are variables that are simply associated with an undesirable outcome; risk mechanisms refer to the direct experiences of the youth that may account for the problematic outcome. For example, being born to a teenage mother is a risk factor for academic and behavioral problems. However, it is usually not the age of the mother per se that causes the poor outcome. The experiences of the children that account for the problem outcomes may be explained by factors frequently associated with adolescent motherhood, including poor parenting, maternal depression and substance abuse, stressful life events such as frequent changes of residence or domestic violence, lack of paternal involvement and financial support, poverty, and living in a dangerous neighborhood (Luster, Bates, Vandenbelt, & Nievar, 2004; Whitman, Borkowski, Keogh, & Weed, 2001).

Another key concept to come out of the risk research is cumulative risk. The probability of poor developmental outcomes among youth increases with exposure to greater numbers of risk factors (Sameroff, Gutman, & Peck, 2003). Many youth can cope successfully with a single risk factor, but as more risks "pile up," the youth's capacity to cope effectively may be overwhelmed. The cumulative effect of multiple risk factors has been demonstrated in studies of adolescents' psychological adjustment and academic performance (Sameroff et al., 2003), behavioral adjustment (Fergusson & Horwood, 2003), and early sexual activity (Small & Luster, 1994). For example, in a study of high school students in the Midwest, we found that 1 percent of females exposed to zero risk factors were sexually active compared to 80 percent of those who were exposed to eight or more risk factors; the findings for males were consistent with those of the females (Small & Luster, 1994). Similarly, Fergusson and Horwood (2003) showed that the rate of illicit drug dependence was 6.4 percent for youth with scores of 0 or 1 on an adversity index, but it was 23.9 percent for those with scores of 6 or more.

Resilience

Studies examining the relation between risk factors and development have consistently demonstrated that a substantial number of people fare well in spite of adverse circumstances. Resilience is defined as "patterns of positive adaptation in the context of significant risk or adversity" (Masten & Powell, 2003, p. 4). According to Masten and Powell, a determination of resilience requires making two judgments: (1) that the person is "doing okay" and (2) that the person has experienced significant risks or adversity that could undermine the successful negotiation of age-salient developmental tasks.

One of the challenges of doing research on resilience involves making each of these judgments (Luthar & Zelazo, 2003). Does "doing okay" mean functioning at a relatively high level in all domains of development, or does it mean simply doing reasonably well in the domain that is most likely to be negatively affected by the risk factors of interest? For people with a long history of physical and emotional abuse by their parents, "doing okay" may mean developing positive, enduring relationships with significant others (Higgins, 1994). Masten and Powell (2003) proposed that competence is judged in terms of how well the child is accomplishing developmental tasks that are salient for people of a given age, society or context, and historical period. One's definition of "doing okay" will affect how many people meet the criteria for resilient adaptation at a given time. Judgments about positive adaptation may also need to be based on what can reasonably be expected given the severity of the adversity that was experienced. Our expectations for The Lost Boys of Sudan, who experienced an extraordinary number of traumatic events and chronic stressors, may be different from those for adolescents who have experienced a single risk factor, such as the divorce of their parents.

Determining if a person has experienced significant adversity can also be challenging, particularly if the researcher must rely on a few survey questions to assess risk. As Luthar and Zelazo (2003) pointed out, adolescents with quite different experiences may be treated as a homogeneous group; those who have been maltreated by their parents continuously over several years may be coded the same way (i.e., risk present) as an adolescent who experienced a single incident of physical maltreatment in an otherwise positive home environment. Likewise, assessment of risk is sometimes based largely on demographic characteristics (father absence, born to a teenage mother, or living in poverty) with no further information about what the child actually experienced. If a child is born to a teenage mother but lives in a well-functioning and supportive household that meets all the needs for normal development, should we consider that child to be showing resilient adaptation if he or she is relatively competent and well adjusted? The individual demonstrating exceptional coping skills may actually be the young but effective mother or the grandmother who holds everything together in the household. Although assessing resilience is challenging, numerous studies confirm that a significant number of adolescents demonstrate positive adaptation despite a history of significant adversity (Luthar, 2003b).

Protective Factors

Protective factor is a useful concept for understanding why some adolescents are doing well despite experiencing significant adversity. Protective factors have been defined as aspects of the person or environment that buffer or ameliorate the effects of adversity, thus allowing the person to be more successful than he or she would be without the protective factors (Werner & Smith, 2001). Garmezy and Masten have identified three major categories of protective factors: (1) personality dispositions and other characteristics of the individual, (2) a supportive family milieu or supportive relationships more generally, and (3) extrafamilial support systems/community resources and opportunities (Masten & Coatsworth, 1998; Masten & Powell, 2003; Rolf, 1999). Characteristics of adolescents that have been linked with resilient adaptation include good intellectual functioning, an internal locus of control orientation, an optimistic outlook on the future, and planful competence—the ability to plan ahead, make good choices, and follow through on plans (Clausen, 1993; Masten & Coatsworth, 1998; Werner & Smith, 2001). Resilient adolescents tend to have appealing characteristics and talents that elicit positive reactions from others (Werner & Smith, 2001). Werner and Smith (2001) found that nearly every resilient adolescent had a positive relationship with a caring and prosocial adult who conveyed the message that "You count." Typically, this caring adult was a parent or extended family member, but in some cases the relationship was with an extrafamilial adult, such as the parents of a close friend, a teacher, or mentor. Resilient adolescents also tended to have positive relationships with prosocial peers. In the community, resilient adolescents had opportunities to discover and develop their talents, engage in prosocial activities, and develop a sense of self-efficacy and a hopeful outlook on the future. Other protective factors identified in various studies will be noted in later sections of this chapter.

Following Rutter's (1987) conceptualization, protective factors have generally been viewed as moderator variables whose effects are evident only in the context of high risk or are more influential in high-risk groups than in low-risk groups. In other words, there is an interaction between risk factors and protective factors such that the effect of the risk factor on the outcome is neutralized or greatly reduced by the presence of the protective factor. However, a number of researchers have suggested that many of the variables identified as protective factors are useful for predicting developmental outcomes in both high-risk and low-risk groups (Fergusson & Horwood, 2003; Luthar, Cicchetti, & Becker, 2000; Luthar & Zelazo, 2003; Masten & Coatsworth, 1998; Sameroff et al., 2003). In fact, the protective factors may be equally beneficial for low- and high-risk youth. Because of these findings, some researchers have proposed that new terms be used to label factors that contribute to positive outcomes in high- and low-risk groups; the terms that have been suggested include promotive factors (Sameroff et al., 2003) and compensatory factors (Fergusson & Horwood, 2003; Garmezy, Masten, & Tellegen, 1984, cited in Luthar & Zelazo, 2003).

The Search Institute uses the term "developmental assets" to label factors that contribute to positive developmental outcomes or thriving at each stage of development. Developmental assets are viewed as important for all children and adolescents regardless of risk status. Assets can be internal (characteristics of the person) or external (contextual factors). Not surprisingly, there is considerable overlap between the 40 developmental assets identified by the Search Institute as important for adolescents and the protective factors that have been identified in various studies of at-risk adolescents (Masten & Coatsworth, 1998; Scales, Benson, Leffert, & Blyth, 2000; Werner & Smith, 2001). As with risk factors, research needs to move beyond simply generating lists of protective factors that are correlated with positive outcomes to increasing our understanding of the processes involved. This is particularly important if the goal is to use knowledge generated from research for purposes of intervention (Luthar et al., 2000; Masten & Powell, 2003).

Vulnerability

Vulnerability is another concept important to understanding problem outcomes and resilience. Vulnerability refers to one's susceptibility to develop problems or a disorder (Werner & Smith, 1992) and can be based in genetics or on prior experiences. For example, some people seem less prone to the ill effects of stressors or environmental agents such as smoking or poor diet, while others are more sensitive to the risk factors they experience, including psychosocial hazards (Rutter, 2001, 2003).

Studies in behavioral genetics indicate that some people are more vulnerable than others for developing certain disorders for genetic reasons. These studies compared the concordance rate for various disorders among monozygotic and dizygotic twins and found significantly greater similarity among monozygotic twins for depression, schizophrenia, criminality, alcoholism, and anorexia (Plomin, 1990). For example, eight twin studies of adult criminality showed a concordance rate of 69 percent for monozygotic twins and 33 percent for dizygotic twins. Behavioral genetic studies also suggest that those who are genetically vulnerable for developing disorders are most likely to actually develop the disorder if they are reared in a high-risk environment (Mednick, Gabrielle, & Hutchings, 1984). Although we often think of genetic factors as contributing to vulnerability, inheritance also plays a role in the development of individual characteristics viewed as protective factors such as intelligence, sociability, physical attractiveness, and optimism (Plomin, 1990; Seligman, 1995).

In addition to genetic vulnerability, Rutter (2001) has pointed out that variation in sensitivity to environmental risks may also depend on prior experiences. Quinton and Rutter (1976) examined the relation between hospital admissions and emotional disturbance among children from low- and high-disadvantage backgrounds. The effects of multiple hospital admissions were more deleterious for children who experienced chronic psychosocial adversity than for those from low-risk backgrounds. Rutter proposed that the experience of psychosocial adversity may have made the high-risk children more vulnerable to the effects of stressful events, such as multiple hospital admissions.

In contrast, youth who are successful in dealing with moderate adversity over time may deal more effectively with subsequent stressors than youth who have little experience coping with stressors or who have been unsuccessful in coping with past stressors. Rutter (2001) refers to this as a "steeling effect." Much like steel is made stronger by exposure to extreme heat, children may become hardened to the effects of adversity by demonstrating that they can overcome adverse circumstances again and again. Thus, experiences that enhance feelings of self-efficacy and self-confidence may make children less vulnerable to subsequent stressors.

RESILIENCE: A DEVELOPMENTAL PROCESS

As we have seen, the number and severity of the risk factors to which a person is exposed, the level of vulnerability, and the availability of protective factors or developmental assets all play a role in developmental outcomes, including the adolescent's competence in stressful circumstances. However, as some researchers have pointed out, one needs to consider how these factors interact over time as children develop (Yates et al., 2003). Those adopting a developmental perspective believe that transactional processes occur between the person and the environment during each period of development, with outcomes in one period of development setting the stage for subsequent periods of development. Dealing successfully with the developmental tasks of an earlier stage provides a foundation for negotiating the developmental tasks of the next stage. Yates and colleagues (2003) proposed that "resilience reflects the developmental process by which children acquire the ability to use both internal and external resources to achieve positive adaptation despite prior or concomitant adversity. Developmental history plays a key role in resilience; it is relevant for the acquisition of coping capacity as well as the ability to draw upon resources from the environment" (p. 250). Thus, successful adaptation at any given time depends on current circumstances, the person's developmental history, and the person's characteristics, competencies, and ability to utilize resources.

Sroufe and his colleagues emphasized the importance of a secure attachment in infancy for setting children on a positive developmental course (Sroufe, Carlson, Levy, & Egeland, 1999). They followed children in impoverished families from infancy to adulthood and found that through positive interactions with caregivers during infancy and early childhood, children develop competencies and attitudes that are important for understanding resilience. Among the characteristics that children acquired are social skills, emotional self-regulation, a capacity for autonomy, flexible problem-solving skills, and an expectation that adults will offer support, guidance, and nurturance (Yates et al., 2003). Children with these skills and orientations are likely to have more positive interactions with peers and adults outside the home.

Success within the peer group and in the school setting, along with a positive sense of self and positive relationships with family members, are key indicators of competence during middle childhood and adolescence. Well-adjusted adolescents have typically dealt with the developmental tasks of earlier periods successfully and have learned how to use both internal and external resources. Moreover, their characteristics tend to elicit positive reactions from others, and they can benefit from the protective factors available in their context. Thus, even if they experience adverse circumstances during adolescence, they are equipped to maintain positive adaptation by drawing on their internal and external resources.

In contrast, troubled adolescents tend to follow a different developmental trajectory with poor experiences in infancy and early childhood leading to a downward spiral of events (Rutter, 2001; Sroufe et al., 1999). This is not to suggest that early experience determines outcomes in adolescence. Early experience only makes some later events and outcomes more or less likely to occur. Some children who experience extremely difficult circumstances early in life show marked improvement when their circumstances improve; clear examples of turning points can be found in children who moved from institutional care to adoptive homes (Hodges & Tizard, 1989), from the Romanian orphanages to family environments (Rutter, 2001), and from Hitler's concentration camps to supportive group homes and adoptive homes (Freud & Dann, 1952; Moskovitz, 1983). Most children show marked improvements in developmental outcomes when they move from adverse circumstances to supportive environments (Clarke & Clarke, 2000).

Unfortunately, relatively few studies of resilience have examined development from infancy to adulthood. The pioneering study of resilience by Werner and Smith (2001) with children of the Hawaiian island of Kauai is one of the exceptions. Werner and Smith (1982) studied adolescents exposed to multiple risk factors during childhood, comparing those who were resilient (i.e., no serious learning or behavioral problems in the first 18 years of life) with those who developed academic, behavioral, or mental health problems. They were able to identify individual and contextual factors at each stage of development that distinguished between the resilient and the troubled adolescents. Table 2.1 provides a summary of those factors.

Consistent with the work of Sroufe and his colleagues in Minnesota, Werner and Smith showed that resilient adolescents tended to have dealt successfully with the tasks of each developmental stage. Using Erikson's (1950) psychosocial stages of development, they found that resilient individuals had dealt successfully with the developmental issues that his theory proposed. For example, in infancy, resilient adolescents tended to have positive relationships with their primary caregivers that led to the development of a sense of trust, the primary issue of this psychosocial stage. To some extent, the positive relationships they enjoyed with their caregivers resulted from their own characteristics; for example, as infants, they tended to be healthy, to have easy temperaments, and to be free of eating and sleeping problems.

Resilient adolescents also differed from troubled adolescents during middle childhood. As school-age children, they were less likely to have reading difficulties than those who eventually developed problems, and they tended to score higher on tests of verbal and reasoning skills. Although not particularly gifted students, they used their talents effectively and were viewed favorably by their teachers. Many developed close relationships with at least one teacher. These relationships were particularly important if relationships at home were strained. Similarly, schools provided predictable, structured, and relatively calm settings for children who came from chaotic home environments. Resilient adolescents also tended to be socially competent with peers and often shared a special interest or a hobby with a friend. Many in the resilient group acquired a sense of pride from developing a special talent even though they might not stand out in the classroom. For example, one child raised guide dogs for the blind, and another excelled at hula dancing. Others developed skills and satisfaction from caring for others (i.e., required helpfulness) (Werner, 1995; Werner & Smith, 1982, 1992, 2001).

Having successfully navigated the developmental tasks of earlier periods, during adolescence the resilient youth developed a strong sense of identity that included a positive self-concept, an internal locus of control orientation, and a belief that they could be successful in their future endeavors. They developed realistic plans for the future, while their struggling peers seemed to have at best only vague plans for the future.

Table 2.1
Protective Factors at Each Stage of Development in Werner and Smith's Kauai Study

Infancy	Toddler	School age	Adolescence
Temperament elicited positive attention —very active —girls were affectionate and cuddly —boys were good natured, easy to deal with	Alertness Autonomy Meets world on own terms Seeks out novel experience Advanced communication, locomotion, and self-help skills	Good peer relations Reading skills by grade 4 Used whatever skills they had effectively Many interests and hobbies; not narrowly sex-typed interests	Positive self-concept/ self-esteem Internal locus of control orientation; self-efficacy Personality inventory —nurturant —responsible
Few eating and sleeping habits that distressed adults	Positive caregiving Erikson— development of a sense of autonomy	Close bond with at least one caregiver	—achievement oriented
Good health Many boys firstborn Availability of alternate caregivers (e.g., grandparents) and support of friends and relatives for the primary caregiver		Good relationship with a teacher Required helpfulness (caring for younger children or elderly) Good verbal and reasoning skills No prolonged separation from parent Structures, rules, and chores in home Erikson—initiative and industry	Girls assertive and independent Outside adult support, such as coach or teacher or clergy member; mentor or confidant Involvement in prosocial activities and organizations— 4-H, YMCA, YWCA, church group
Erikson— development of a sense of trust; close relationship with a parent or other caregiver			Faith that life had meaning Boys—male role model Talent—good at something Erikson—strong sense of identity

37

Although about two-thirds of the Kauai youth exposed to four or more risk factors developed problems during childhood or adolescence, many rebounded as young adults. This suggests that resilience is not a characteristic of the person that is evident at all times and for all outcomes and may depend on when the assessment is made (Luthar & Zelazo, 2003). Werner and Smith's (1992, 2001) follow-up study into adulthood also shows that development continues. Factors that contributed to improved outcomes in adulthood varied from individual to individual but included (1) a supportive marriage or relationship with a significant other, (2) educational advancement in community colleges, (3) participation in a church community, and (4) service in the military. Those who overcame problems evident in adolescence were able to detach from their troubled families and select niches that were compatible with their individual dispositions and talents. They also tended to be hopeful, determined people who persevered despite occasional setbacks.

Based on a review of research, Masten (2001) concluded that resilience is a common phenomenon that typically arises from the operation of basic human adaptational systems rather than from extraordinary qualities of individuals who are competent despite adversity. She noted that studies have consistently shown that resilience is related to "connections to competent and caring adults in the family and community, cognitive and self-regulation skills, positive views of self, and motivation to be effective in the environment" (p. 234). Children who have opportunities to develop and maintain these positive relationships, skills, attitudes, and motivations over the course of development are likely to fare reasonably well despite encountering some obstacles along the way. The children who develop problems experience the types of deprivation that undermine these basic human adaptational systems, leaving the children with impaired cognitive skills, an inability to regulate their emotions, and a lack of motivation to learn and engage their environments.

CLINICAL PERSPECTIVES ON CHILDREN WHO SUCCEED IN SPITE OF THEIR FAMILIES

Although "ordinary magic" may explain resilience for most individuals who cope well with adversity (Masten, 2001), in some cases extraordinary qualities may be required to overcome deplorable circumstances, such as years of emotional, physical, and/or sexual abuse in the home. The risks associated with abuse are well established (Trickett, 1997). Outcomes associated with abuse during adolescence include poor school performance, behavior problems, delinquency, and substance abuse. The extent to which adolescents exhibit these outcomes is likely to depend on their experiences prior to the abuse, the nature and duration of the abuse they experience, and their experiences after the abuse ends. Some therapists have focused on case studies of individuals who have been successful in spite of their troubled families (Higgins, 1994; Rubin, 1996). These qualitative approaches add to the depth of our understanding regarding how resilient individuals process adverse experiences, enlist support from others, and use internal and external resources to lead productive and satisfying lives despite extraordinary hardship.

In the book *The Transcendent Child,* Rubin (1996) presents case studies of adults who turned out well in spite of their families. A successful therapist and writer, her own experiences of growing up in a harsh family environment provided the impetus for studying why some children in troubled families "make it" and others succumb.

Rubin concluded that a common characteristic of resilient individuals was an ability to disidentify with their tormentors quite early in childhood. They recognized that the problems they experienced were because of their "crazy" families, and they did not feel responsible for the mistreatment they endured. The resilient individuals viewed themselves as marginal members of their family. One person referred to feeling like a dog in a cat family when he was growing up. They also vowed that they would be different from their abusers.

In addition to putting psychological distance between themselves and their abusive parents, many found ways to maintain physical distance from their parents once they were old enough to spend time away from home. Many found satisfaction in time spent at school, at the library, practicing music, in sports, at work, or developing other talents. They typically found caring adults in these other settings who confirmed for them that they themselves were likable people outside their homes and that good people exist in the world.

The resilient individuals also had a quality Rubin called adoptability, or the ability to elicit support from mentors and surrogate parents outside their families at key times in their lives. Some of these relationships were long term and others fleeting, but the resilient individuals made good use of the opportunities these helpful people made available to them.

Determination was another quality of those who overcame the effects of abusive homes. The importance of determination is evident in the title of Rubin's opening chapter—"Fall Down Seven Times, Get Up Eight." Although these individuals had periods of their lives when they might not have be viewed as resilient, they always managed to pick themselves up again and move forward. They refused to define themselves as victims and believed that they could make a better life through their own efforts. One adult looking back on her abusive childhood proclaimed, "That is what happened to me; it's not who I am" (Rubin, 1996, p. 228).

They also tended to be intelligent and "street-smart" people. Rubin noted that the resilient individuals showed multiple forms of intelligence as described by Howard Gardner (1993). They stood out in terms of their linguistic, interpersonal, and intrapersonal intelligences; many were creative and had special talents, such as musical ability. Their intelligence helped them to deal with the problems they faced and to process what was happening to them. Rubin emphasized that it is not only what happens to individuals that is important but also how they process these events.

Higgins (1994) came to similar conclusions regarding resilient adults who grew up in abusive homes. Consistent with Rubin's description, surrogate caregivers or caring adults played key roles in the lives of resilient individuals during childhood. Although contact with supportive adults might be limited, resilient individuals seemed to get a lot of emotional mileage out of any acts of kindness they experienced. In other cases, resilient adults had experienced positive caregiving from a parent in the years before their parents changed as a result of alcoholism, depression, or psychosis, or the nonafflicted parent provided some support despite failing to provide adequate protection from the abuse. During adolescence, many of the resilient individuals found support in the homes of friends who had more harmonious families and incorporated the best aspects of family life they witnessed into a model that guided their behavior in adulthood. Positive experiences with peers also helped them to believe in their normality, reinforcing their belief that the problems they experienced were caused by their parents. In general, experiences outside the family helped them to gain insights into their troubled families.

By the end of adolescence, most resilient individuals had a vision of a better future. They had a sense of being "made for more" or being "chosen" to do something important with their lives. In adulthood, they tended to be social activists who selected professions that involved helping those in need and were optimistic about what they could accomplish. Having survived abusive childhoods, they were confident in their ability to deal with challenging circumstances.

Although many of the resilient individuals have admirable qualities, Higgins warns against viewing them as near saints. Each one had made mistakes and struggled with limitations. Moreover, they "pointedly reminded me that they would not have met all (or even most) of the resilient criteria during earlier chapters in their lives" (Higgins, 1994, p. 4). The route to resilience sometimes included missteps, wrong turns, or a temporary lack of direction before individuals find their way.

RESILIENCE AMONG CHILDREN AND ADOLESCENTS EXPOSED TO WAR: SUDANESE REFUGEE YOUTH RESETTLED WITHOUT PARENTS

Sometimes tragic world events provide unique opportunities for learning about human resilience and adaptation. Because of their history, the refugees known in the media as the Lost Boys of Sudan (although a small proportion are girls) represent such a case. Civil war separated them from their families during childhood (typically in the 4–12 age range) and forced them to flee to refugee camps in Ethiopia and eventually Kenya. Many were separated from their parents and fled in groups across Sudan to the refugee camps. Some children—particularly the youngest—died or were lost during the arduous trek; of the 25,000 unaccompanied children who left Ethiopian camps in 1991, only 10,000 to 12,000 reached Kakuma (Duncan, 2000). There, most of them lived in peer groups with limited adult support and supervision for nearly a decade until the United Nations resettled a number of youth, whose parents were deceased or untraceable, in the United States and other Western countries. Girls were more likely to be absorbed into other families or married off to men for the dowries they brought, so they were less likely to be resettled. Some 3,600 youth were eventually recommended for resettlement in the United States (Corbett, 2001).

Children exposed to war are known to experience a number of losses and stresses that place them at much higher risk of psychological disorders and adjustment problems. Studies of refugee children, who experience displacement and possibly separation from parents, reveal that they may suffer from psychiatric disorders such as posttraumatic stress disorder (PTSD), anxiety, disruptive behavior, and psychosomatic symptoms (Shaw, 2003). As with other risks, the likelihood of having adverse psychological effects is greater for those who have experienced more traumatic events over a longer period of time (Shaw, 2003). Nevertheless, many show impressive resilience in the face of significant adversity (Duncan, 2000). What factors have enabled them to overcome horrors and hardships, and what are the successful adaptive strategies that they have employed to meet these challenges?

The case of the Lost Boys offered an opportunity to learn more about these processes. Between November 2000 and September 2001, approximately 135 refugees—84 youth, 12 of whom were girls, and 50 young adults (those 18 and over)—were resettled in Lansing, Michigan. Our interactions with this group during their first two years after resettlement has allowed us not only to document their strengths and problems but also to better understand the coping strategies they have employed to meet a variety of evolving adjustment challenges. In this section, we will present information from our preliminary analysis of information gathered from youth, foster parents, and resettlement agency caseworkers.

Although individual experiences may differ, there is no question that as a group they experienced multiple acute and chronic stressors during most of their developmental years. In her report on Sudanese unaccompanied children in Kakuma being considered for resettlement, Duncan (2000) identified a number of traumatic events and chronic stressors that were the common experience of the group. These same experiences have been described to us by the Lansing group.

After their abrupt separation from parents, the children fled, alone or with siblings or other relatives, to Ethiopia, experiencing continuing attacks from government troops. Many died along the way from hunger, thirst, disease, or attacks by lions and hyenas that followed the groups and picked off the most vulnerable. In 1991, they were expelled from Ethiopia by government troops who attacked suddenly and drove them into the Gilo River during a flood. Some youth relate vivid memories of seeing people drowned or shot by soldiers as they attempted to swim to safety in Sudan. One youth who was about six years of age at the time told us of watching people walk over the bodies of others to get across the river. In Sudan, they were not attacked at first, but there was insufficient food. Later, during the long trek across Sudan to Kenya, they were attacked by the Sudanese air force and snipers from tribal militias; many more died from hunger, thirst, and disease. So many died that the youth were unable to bury them and had to leave their bodies in the bush.

Once they reached Kakuma, the level of danger abated, but the youth experienced many problems based on the lack of resources and support. Hunger and malnutrition were common, and schools had minimal resources to offer for education. Access to education was a particular problem for girls who often were taken in by families to do domestic chores. Youth had few adult protectors to help them navigate the complexities of refugee life, and although limited medical care was available, many were not sufficiently experienced to effectively carry out treatments or advocate for themselves (Duncan, 2000).

At the time of their assessment for resettlement, Duncan (2000) found the youth to be experiencing a high degree of unresolved trauma. Virtually all reported frequent nightmares and feared being attacked suddenly and forced to flee again. Thus, they did not feel that Kakuma was a place of safety. Most were also experiencing anxiety or depression, particularly about finding their place in the adult world. Girls were more likely to be experiencing depression than were boys. Duncan concluded that as a group they were resilient and functioning on a daily level but that "their emotional issues are a drag on their abilities" (p. 6).

On the other hand, Duncan (2001) found considerable evidence of resilience among these children. The coping strategies that she found during their experience in Africa are quite similar to those that we observed in the United States.

The youth who entered the United States in 2000–2001 were moving from adolescence to adulthood with the complicating factor of making this transition in a new and unfamiliar culture. The tasks of adolescence as defined in the United States include establishing an adult identity, forming close relationships with peers of the same sex and the opposite sex, and establishing self-reliance. To make this transition smoothly, youth must develop skills such as emotional self-regulation, the ability to delay gratification, establishing realistic goals and follow-through, good decision making, and good work habits. As mentioned previously, youth who are successful tend to have an internal locus of control and believe that they can be successful. Relevant education and work are key to a successful transition to adulthood in Western culture.

Although the general tasks of this transition may be similar in many cultures, the definition of "success" may vary widely. The challenge for youth from another culture is to adjust to the necessities of life in the culture in which they live while meeting the demands of the culture of origin. In the following pages, we will discuss what we have learned about this transition among the Lost Boys and Girls who resettled in Lansing.

In the two years following their resettlement, our research team collected information to learn about their adjustment, their successes and challenges, and coping strategies they used to overcome problems. Our description is based on information from 70 youth—24 young adult males, 41 minor males (under 18), and five females—as well as 10 foster parents and five agency caseworkers.

During this early period, the youth were demonstrating evidence of considerable strength as measured by their progress in education and employment:

- 77 percent were enrolled in school (95% of minors vs. 48% of young adults).
- 93 percent expected to obtain at least a four-year college degree.
- 73 percent were employed (63% of minors working 17 hours per week, on average, vs. 89% of adults working 35 hours per week, on average).

In addition, they had already developed strong support systems for themselves, by their own report:

- 96 percent had joined a church.
- 74 percent attended church at least twice a month.

- 87 percent had someone to help them solve problems.
- 60 percent talked about their feelings with someone at least twice a month.

In focus groups, they described many of the challenges they faced in adjusting to a new culture and the strategies they used to make these transitions. In the initial stages, they focused on practical concerns, such as getting appropriate identification, opening a bank account, or signing up for classes at the community college. As with many resilient youth, they were effective in enlisting foster families, caseworkers, and other community volunteers to act as cultural brokers (Pipher, 2002). As noted by one focus group participant,

[name of mentor] and the family, they helped me a lot. He took me to [the local community college].... He talked to several people about financial aid.

Another challenge for those placed in foster care (youth under 18 years) was learning to negotiate complex relations in an unfamiliar family structure. In addition, being responsible to a family after years of living on their own was difficult for many youth. The Sudanese youth reported difficulty dealing with limitations placed on how long they could talk with fellow refugees on the phone or rules about visiting each other in their foster homes. In Africa, they had visited with each other for as long and as often as it suited them. Although all adolescents want to spend time talking with their peers, for the Sudanese refugees maintaining these contacts was especially important.

Negotiating the world of work was a challenge, particularly for the young adults who were required to achieve economic self-sufficiency within a few months of entry. Understanding work expectations, forming relations with coworkers, and balancing work with their educational expectations were issues that placed stress on many.

After an initial period of euphoria at having arrived and dealt with the immediate problems of survival, some youth faced more long-term challenges to adjustment. Duncan (2001) noted that six months after resettlement, youth in the Seattle area, although an exceptionally strong and resilient group, were beginning to exhibit increased signs of PTSD, anxiety, and guilt. Our own group had scores on a measure of PTSD that were twice as high as those reported by children experiencing a single traumatic event. They also had higher PTSD scores than Bosnian and Cuban refugees resettled in Michigan (Cusack, 2001). On a measure of behavior strengths and problems (Lambert & Rowan, 1999), they rated themselves as having fewer strengths than did African American youth or youth from the Kingdom of Lesotho in southern Africa. Youth, foster families, and caseworkers reported continuing symptoms, including nightmares, emotional outbursts, fighting, depression, and several suicide attempts. In America, they were encouraged to tell their story, and many found that sharing their story kept it alive and helped them to cope with the past:

> Ya, it's good to talk about it; sometimes it takes the stinging away from my mind.

A major challenge in this later period was to negotiate American culture while maintaining a Sudanese cultural identity. This adjustment is complicated by the fact that many of them have lived not in traditional Sudanese culture for many years but rather in refugee camps. According to Duncan (2001), Sudanese adults view them as noticeably different from traditional Sudanese—for example, having a much greater sense of their "rights." Among the Lansing group, maintaining a Sudanese cultural identity is a salient issue. Many are active with a variety of Sudanese refugee assistance or cultural groups. Many hope to return to Sudan someday to help the country rebuild. As we have seen, this desire to help others is a characteristic of resilient people.

In spite of setbacks, the group as a whole are making a remarkable adjustment with limited support from elders. As reported by Duncan (2001), the coping strategies they developed in the camps are standing them in good stead here. We have found this to be the case among the youth in Lansing.

Like many resilient people, the Lost Boys possessed personal characteristics that have helped them cope with adversity. People who have worked with them describe them as pleasant, friendly, likable youth who have a positive outlook on life. These personality characteristics make it rewarding for others to help them and allow them to accept and use the help that is offered. Duncan (2001) describes their approach as "a long-term belief in the kindness of strangers" (p. 5) that allows them to make use of resources offered to them. Their open acceptance of others, combined with the drama of their story, has touched Americans and has brought benefits that assist in their adjustment. In the United States, the use of cultural interpreters has aided their adjustment:

> We think we are going to stay alone, but when we came, we found that we are not alone. And up to now, we have been here for almost 5 months and we still have help from the Americans. So, we are not alone.

High levels of sociability and peer support are other protective factors that the Lost Boys possessed. A relief agency worker who was involved in the best-interest determinations for resettled youth, observed that it would have been very difficult for a person with a "lone wolf" mentality to have survived their ordeal in Africa. People needed to pool their resources and help each other through difficult times in order to survive. In the United States, youth have continued to "hang together" and help each other. After leaving foster care, many live together in groups, sharing expenses and providing each other with social support. They stay in contact not only with youth in the area but also with refugees scattered throughout the United States and those remaining in Africa.

Another salient personal characteristic is intelligence in the sense of good problem-solving ability. When asked about the importance of intelligence to survival in Africa, one young adult said that he felt that intelligence in the sense of resourcefulness or "street smarts" was more important than academic intelligence. The ability to make good decisions is crucial to survival in such dangerous circumstances. As an example of resourcefulness, one boy related how he devised a plan to cross the flooded Gilo River when they had to evacuate the refugee camp in Ethiopia. The youth, who was six or seven years old at the time, ran to the river with several other boys. He knew he could not swim and observed others jumping into the river and being swept away by the current. He ran back to the camp, got some remnant plastic sheeting, and devised a raft that they used to float across the river. Successfully solving such problems may build a sense of self-efficacy that helps the individual confront the next challenge. Now 21 years old, this young man has continued to demonstrate this resourcefulness in his life in the United States.

In the focus groups, youth described several important protective factors that help them cope with psychological distress and lend meaning to their experience.

Spirituality and Deep Religiosity

Belief in God and their relationship with Him brings a sense of order and purpose to many youth. Some have reported that they prayed regularly and that God gave them signs that their survival meant something. In the words of one young man,

> If God had wanted me to be dead, I would be dead now. But I am not, so he must have other plans for me.

Others spoke of having participated in church youth groups in the refugee camps.

Belief in Education

Duncan (2000) reported that almost all youth being interviewed for resettlement equated education with safety. Youth have a common saying, "Education is my mother and my father," which Duncan interpreted to mean that without family to provide for them, they will need education to provide for themselves. The youth in our group also believe that by getting a good education, they will be able to help others here and those left in the refugee camps. Despite the challenges of becoming self-supporting while trying to get an education, most continue to attend school.

The Sudanese refugee youth, now in their late teens and twenties, are moving through another set of life challenges with some notable successes. No doubt there will be many surprises, but we anticipate that a few issues may be of concern in the future.

Developing an Adult Identity in Two Cultures

These youth tend to identify themselves as Sudanese, although their culture (that of the refugee camp) is not quite familiar to adult Sudanese. Many express a desire to return to Sudan someday to help the country. These youth may take a "when in Rome" approach to living in the United States—complying with the expectations of American culture but not changing the core values they view as Sudanese. Some youth have related to us that elders in the camps were a primary source of support and moral education for them and continue to be a guiding force in their lives. Other youth have embraced American culture, adopting the dress, music, and other accoutrements of American youth culture.

Dealing with Residual Psychological Issues and Survivor's Guilt

These youth—though resilient—are not without symptoms of psychological distress. Traditional counseling was useful to some, but others tended to reject it, as treatment for mental health problems by licensed therapists was not a part of their culture. Some were advised by Sudanese elders that the best way to handle sad memories was to focus on the present and their future; dwelling on what they lost was not viewed as helpful. Groups support seemed a more useful model for some.

Duncan (2001) noted that six months after resettlement, survivor's guilt was beginning to emerge as an issue. Lansing youth express similar feelings of guilt about doing well while others either died or still suffer:

> Sometimes when you talk about it you will not smile. We are not comfortable to talk about it because it is something our people are still now in.... So,

sometimes I don't feel comfortable because they have lost their lives and you
know that if one of you pass away you don't feel good.

Youth and foster families reported receiving calls from individuals
in African asking for assistance. Youth are very conflicted about their
obligations to help, and many send money in response to these requests,
sometimes stretching beyond their capacity to pay.

Unrealized Expectations

Youth have high hopes about the perceived opportunities of America,
but the realities of work and school may not meet their expectations. Some
have been diagnosed with learning disabilities, and others, particularly the
girls, are far behind, and schools have not always done a good job of getting them the supports they will need to succeed. Those who were 18 and
older when they entered the United States had to become economically
self-sufficient within a few months after arriving; working long hours at
low-paying jobs has made it difficult to take college courses or complete
a GED program. In addition, sending money to friends and relatives in
Africa results in having insufficient money to pay for college tuition.
(Financial aid offices do not consider these friends and relatives to be
dependents because the Lost Boys are not legally responsible for them.)

One journalist who wrote about the Lost Boys' resettlement experience in North Dakota titled her article "From Hell to Fargo: The Lost
Boys of Sudan in America" (Corbett, 2001). As young people who have,
in a sense, been to hell and survived, all have demonstrated aspects of
resilience. Many of the coping mechanisms they developed in Africa are
serving them well in this new environment, and we anticipate that, with
support, many will continue to adapt to new challenges, survive, and perhaps even thrive in their new environment.

SUMMARY AND CONCLUSIONS

Research has revealed marked differences in outcomes among individuals exposed to significant risks, and both researchers and practitioners hope to better understand why some people growing up in adverse
circumstances turn out to be competent, productive, and well-adjusted
individuals. We have seen that the developmental trajectories of at-risk
individuals can be influenced by several factors, including the number and
severity of risks to which they are exposed, individual vulnerability, and
the availability of protective factors that mitigate the effects of risk factors
on development. We have also seen that resilience can be viewed as the

outcome of a process in which successfully accomplishing the tasks of each developmental stage provides a foundation for negotiating the tasks of the next stage.

Although our understanding of the processes by which protective factors promote resilience is far from complete, many practitioners are beginning to apply resilience concepts to programs for at-risk children and youth. Using strength-based models, practitioners are demonstrating some success with interventions that focus on building individual, family, school, and community assets for at-risk children and adolescents (Tableman, 2002). In her review of effective interventions and the assets they promoted, Tableman concludes that asset building occurs along the developmental continuum and that the types of assets that interventions focus on change with different developmental stages.

In the early years, maximizing the positive impact of parents and caregivers may be most important, whereas for older children and adolescents, school-based interventions can be significant. However, few intervention studies have followed individuals beyond a few months or years, so research to determine the long-term outcomes of these programs is needed.

In the case of the Sudanese refugee youth, the challenges of developing programs to support healthy development is complicated by vast cultural differences and the cumulative impact of adaptive strategies developed for the diverse settings they experienced before arriving in the United States. The accumulated research on resilience is useful for understanding their resilience. However, some of the protective processes that contributed to their success may be specific to their culture and not noted in the resilience literature, which is based mostly on samples from North America and Europe. In addition, their experience of growing up essentially without parental support is rather unique. Agencies charged with assisting in their resettlement faced many challenges in finding effective ways to support them. Educational placement and counseling to deal with the effects of trauma were particularly challenging, as noted earlier in this chapter. Recognizing the importance of peer group support for these youth, the agencies obtained funding to conduct a group social support/educational program during the first 18 months after resettlement. The group was attended by 25 to 30 youth each week and became a venue where many could maintain peer relationships from Africa. However, attempts to adapt traditional counseling methods to be more acceptable to the youth met with only partial success. Educational systems were ill prepared to address the unique needs of this group, particularly the girls and others who had very limited English proficiency or access to education in the refugee camps. Although those who entered in foster care had access to a number of asset-building services, those who entered as young adults were very limited in the services that they could access. The development of strength-based services for youth from different cultures requires flexibility and sensitivity to the concerns and needs expressed by adults from the culture of origin and the youth themselves.

REFERENCES

Clarke, A., & Clarke, A. (2000). *Early experience and the life path.* London: Jessica Kingsley Publishers.

Clausen, J. A. (1993). *American lives: Looking back at the children of the Great Depression.* New York: Free Press.

Corbett, S. (2001, April 1). From Hell to Fargo: The Lost Boys of Sudan in America. *New York Times Magazine,* 48–55, 75, 80, 84–85.

Cusack, K. J. (2001). *Refugee experiences of trauma and posttraumatic stress disorder (PTSD): Effects on psychological, physical, and financial well-being.* Unpublished doctoral dissertation, Western Michigan University, Kalamazoo, Michigan.

Duncan, J. (2000, February 26). *Sudanese unaccompanied children best interest determination.* Washington, DC: United States Catholic Conference.

Duncan, J. (2001, May 30). *Sudanese "Lost Boys" in the United States: Adjustment after six months.* Washington, DC: United States Catholic Conference.

Erikson, E. H. (1950). *Childhood and society.* New York: Norton.

Fergusson, D. M., & Horwood, L. J. (2003). Resilience to childhood adversity: Results of a 21-year study. In S. S. Luthar (Ed.), *Resilience and vulnerability: Adaptation in the context of childhood adversities* (pp. 130–155). New York: Cambridge University Press.

Freud, A., & Dann, S. (1952). An experiment in group upbringing. *Psychoanalytic Study of the Child, 6,* 127–168.

Gardner, H. (1993). *Multiple intelligences: The theory in practice.* New York: Basic Books.

Garmezy, N., Masten, A. S., & Tellegen, A. (1984). The study of stress and competence in children: A building block for developmental psychopathology. *Child Development, 55,* 97–111.

Higgins, G. O. (1994). *Resilient adults: Overcoming a cruel past.* San Francisco: Jossey-Bass.

Hodges, J., & Tizard, B. (1989). IQ and behavioral adjustment of ex-institutional adolescents. *Journal of Child Psychology and Psychiatry, 30,* 53–75.

Lambert, M. C., & Rowan, G. T. (1999). *Behavioral assessment for children of African descent: Self-report for ages 12 to 18.* East Lansing: Michigan State University Press.

Luster, T., Bates, L., Vandenbelt, M., & Nievar, A. (2004). Family advocates perspectives on the early academic success of children born to low-income adolescent mothers. *Family Relations, 53,* 68–77.

Luthar, S. S. (2003a). The culture of affluence: Psychological costs of material wealth. *Child Development, 75,* 1581–1593.

Luthar, S. S. (2003b). *Resilience and vulnerability: Adaptation in the context of childhood adversities.* New York: Cambridge University Press.

Luthar, S. S., Cicchetti, D., & Becker, B. (2000). The construct of resilience: A critical evaluation and guideline for future work. *Child Development, 71,* 543–562.

Luthar, S. S., & Zelazo, L. B. (2003). Research on resilience: An integrative review. In S. S. Luthar (Ed.), *Resilience and vulnerability: Adaptation in the context of childhood adversities* (pp. 510–549). New York: Cambridge University Press.

Masten, A. S. (2001). Ordinary magic: Resilience processes in development. *American Psychologist, 56,* 227–238.

Masten, A. S., & Coatsworth, J. D. (1998). The development of competence in favorable and unfavorable environments: Lessons from research on successful children. *American Psychologist, 53,* 205–200.

Masten, A. S., & Powell, J. L. (2003). A resilience framework for research, policy, and practice. In S. S. Luthar (Ed.), *Resilience and vulnerability: Adaptation in the context of childhood adversities* (pp. 1–25). New York: Cambridge University Press.

Mednick, S. A., Gabrielle, W. F., & Hutchings, B. (1984). Genetic influences in criminal convictions: Evidence from an adoption cohort. *Science, 224,* 891–894.

Moskovitz, S. (1983). *Love despite hate: Child survivors of the Holocaust and their adult lives.* New York: Schocken Books.

O'Connor, T. G., Rutter, M., Beckett, C., Keaveney, L., Kreppner, J. M., & the English and Romanian Adoptees Study Team. (2000). The effects of severe privation on cognitive competence: Extension and longitudinal follow-up. *Child Development, 71,* 376–390.

Pipher, M. (2002). *The middle of everywhere: The world's refugees come to our town.* New York: Harcourt.

Plomin, R. (1990). *Nature and nurture: An introduction to human behavioral genetics.* Pacific Grove, CA: Brooks/Cole.

Quinton, D., & Rutter, M. (1976). Early hospital admissions and later disturbances of behaviour. An attempted replication of Douglas' findings. *Developmental Medicine and Child Neurology, 18,* 447–459.

Rolf, J. E. (1999). Resilience: An interview with Norman Garmezy. In M. D. Glantz & J. L. Johnson (Eds.), *Resilience and development: Positive life adaptations* (pp. 5–14). New York: Kluwer.

Rubin, L. B. (1996). *The transcendent child: Tales of triumph over the past.* New York: HarperPerennial.

Rutter, M. (1987). Psychosocial resilience and protective mechanisms. *American Journal of Orthopsychiatry, 57,* 316–331.

Rutter, M. (2001). Psychosocial adversity: Risk, resilience and recovery. In J. R. Richman & M. W. Fraser (Eds.), *The context of youth violence: Resilience, risk, and protection* (pp. 14–41). Westport, CT: Praeger.

Rutter, M. (2003). Genetic influences on risk and protection: Implications for understanding resilience. In S. S. Luthar (Ed.), *Resilience and vulnerability: Adaptation in the context of childhood adversities* (pp. 489–509). New York: Cambridge University Press.

Sameroff, A., Gutman, L. M., & Peck, S. C. (2003). Adaptation among youth facing multiple risks. In S. S. Luthar (Ed.), *Resilience and vulnerability: Adaptation in the context of childhood adversities* (pp. 364–391). New York: Cambridge University Press.

Scales, P. C., Benson, P. L., Leffert, N., & Blyth, D. A. (2000). Contribution of developmental assets to the prediction of thriving among adolescents. *Applied Developmental Science, 4,* 27–46.

Seligman, M. (1995). *The optimistic child.* New York: Houghton Mifflin.

Shaw, J. (2003). Children exposed to war/terrorism. *Clinical Child and Family Psychology Review, 6,* 237–246.

Small, S. A., & Luster, T. (1994). Adolescent sexual activity: An ecological, risk-factor approach. *Journal of Marriage and Family, 56,* 181–192.

Sroufe, L. A., Carlson, E. A., Levy, A. K., & Egeland, B. (1999). Implications of attachment theory for developmental psychopathology. *Development and Psychopathology, 11,* 1–13.

Tableman, B. (2002). Validating the assets approach to achieving outcomes for children and youth (Best Practice Brief No. 25). East Lansing: Outreach Partnerships at Michigan State University. Retrieved September 2, 2004, from http://outreach.msu.edu/bpbriefs/issues/brief25.pdf

Trickett, P. K. (1997). Sexual and physical abuse and the development of social competence. In S. S. Luthar et al. (Eds.), *Developmental psychopathology: Perspectives on adjustment, risk, and disorder* (pp. 390–415). New York: Cambridge University Press.

Werner, E. E. (1995). Resilience in development. *Current Directions in Psychological Science, 4,* 81–85.

Werner, E. E., & Smith, R. S. (1982). *Vulnerable but invincible: A longitudinal study of resilient children and youth.* New York: McGraw-Hill.

Werner, E. E., & Smith, R. S. (1992). *Overcoming the odds.* Ithaca, NY: Cornell University Press.

Werner, E. E., & Smith, R. S. (2001). *Journeys from childhood to midlife: Risk, resilience, and recovery.* Ithaca, NY: Cornell University Press.

Whitman, T. L., Borkowski, J. G., Keogh, D. A., & Weed, K. (2001). *Interwoven lives: Adolescent mothers and their children.* Mahwah, NJ: Lawrence Erlbaum Associates.

Yates, T. M., Egeland, B., & Sroufe, L. A. (2003). Rethinking resilience: A developmental process perspective. In S. S. Luthar (Ed.), *Resilience and vulnerability: Adaptation in the context of childhood adversities* (pp. 243–266). New York: Cambridge University Press.

Chapter 3

THE WELL-BEING OF IMMIGRANT ADOLESCENTS: A LONGITUDINAL PERSPECTIVE ON RISK AND PROTECTIVE FACTORS

Carola Suárez-Orozco, Irina Todorova, and Desirée Baolian Qin

Globalization is transforming the United States and, with it, its youth population. At the new millennium, 20 percent of the nation's youth are the children of immigrants. Immigrants are arriving in unprecedented numbers and are reshaping urban, suburban, and rural settings throughout the nation. Their presence is now being felt not only in the traditional immigrant regions of the eastern seaboard and the Southwest but also throughout the South and Midwest—regions of the country that in the recent past rarely have encountered new immigrants in large numbers.

Immigrant youth are extraordinarily diverse, with nearly 80 percent being youth of color, coming from Latin America, Asia, and the Caribbean. They bring with them an astonishingly wide array of linguistic, religious, and cultural beliefs and practices. Some are the children of highly educated professional parents, and others have parents who are illiterate, low skilled, and struggling in the lowest-paid sectors of the service economy (C. Suárez-Orozco, 2000; M. Suárez-Orozco, 2000). Some families are escaping political, religious, or ethnic persecution; others are lured by the promise of better jobs and the hope for better educational opportunities. Some immigrant youth come to settle permanently; others follow their parents from one migrant work camp to another. Some are documented, and others are not. Some engage in transnational strategies living both "here and there," that is, shuttling between their country of birth and their country of choice (Suárez-Orozco, 2004).

While much research has been done on educational adaptation, immigrant students' psychological well-being has received less attention. In this chapter, we offer a framework for understanding in broad psychosocial terms the diverse adaptations and outcomes of immigrant youth, identifying both potential risk factors as well as factors that can be protective for their mental and physical health. We structure this discussion around several conceptual domains, taking into consideration those of utmost importance in terms of impairing or promoting well-being. We begin by outlining some general longitudinal trends in the well-being of immigrant adolescents and the explanations that have been offered for them. We then discuss the psychosocial processes of adaptation that are common to most immigrants regardless of point of origin or destination. These nearly universal processes are related to the experience of uprooting as well as the rites of passage and settlement in the new locale. We go on to examine the social contexts and structures that are highly relevant to well-being—socioeconomic status, immigrant neighborhood characteristics such as poverty and segregation, and the schools that immigrant youth are able to attend. We illustrate how networks of social relations mediate the immigration process. Taken together, these factors will mold the experiences of immigrant youth and impact their mental and physical health as they journey to their varied American destinies. These psychosocial formations are at the heart of any understanding of the complexities of the immigrant adolescent experience. Finally, we offer some suggestions for further research and implications for practice of this burgeoning field of scholarship. In the discussion of the issues, we use examples from existing literature as well as the findings from our research in the Longitudinal Immigrant Student Adaptations (LISA) study.[1]

A LONGITUDINAL PERSPECTIVE ON IMMIGRANT ADOLESCENTS' WELL-BEING

A counterintuitive trend is emerging from a number of studies in immigration conducted in a variety of disciplines. Specifically, though recently arrived immigrants often face poverty and discrimination and have taxing occupations and fewer years of schooling (Morales, Lara, Kington, Valdez, & Escarce, 2002), they are nonetheless healthier than their counterparts staying in the country of origin as well as the population born in the United States. This pattern is most widely studied for immigrants of Latino origin to the United States but has also been identified for people emigrating from Asia to the United States (Hernandez & Charney, 1998; Voelker, 1994), from Turkey to Germany, from China to Canada, and from Vietnam to England (Razum & Twardella, 2002).

This phenomenon is known as the "immigrant health paradox" or the "epidemiological paradox" (Abraido-Lanza, Dohrenwend, Ng-Mak, &

Turner, 1999; Morales et al., 2002; Palloni & Morenoff, 2001; Scribner, 1996; Voelker, 1994). While the significance of the paradox has been challenged as an artifact of statistical bias (Morales et al., 2002) or methodological problems, such limitations do not invalidate the phenomenon, as the evidence that confirms its existence is overwhelming (Palloni & Morenoff, 2001; Razum & Twardella, 2002). This pattern is supported by a broad range of measures of psychological and physical health as well as health behaviors, including overall adult mortality, life expectancy, infant mortality, birth weight, and certain disease outcomes (Iannotta, 2003).

As far as the immigrant children are concerned, according to the report, children of Latino origin, with the exception of those from Puerto Rico, have lower incidences of developmental delays, attention deficit disorders, learning disabilities, and asthma than non-Latino white children (Iannotta, 2003). Another large-scale National Research Council (NRC) study also considered a variety of measures of physical health and risk behaviors among children and adolescents from immigrant families—including general health, learning disabilities, obesity, and emotional difficulties (Hernandez & Charney, 1998)—and showed health advantages for recent immigrant youth on several dimensions. The NRC researchers found that immigrant youth were less likely than their U.S.-born counterparts to evidence acute and chronic conditions, including asthma, anemia, and injuries. Differences between immigrants and nonimmigrants are also apparent when we look at various manifestations of mental health. Immigrant adolescents report less drug use, less delinquency, less misconduct in school, fewer psychosocial problems, and lower level of psychological distress than do American-born youngsters.

Overall, the previously cited findings on immigrant health are counterintuitive in light of the racial and ethnic minority status, lower educational level, and higher poverty rates that characterize many immigrant children and families. Disconcertingly, however, the data suggest an unsettling pattern that needs empirical and theoretical explanation: despite the initial advantage in terms of health, in nearly all immigrant groups today, length of residence in the United States appears associated with *declining* health indicators as well as school achievement and aspirations (Kao & Tienda, 1995; Portes & Rumbaut, 2001; Steinberg, Brown, & Dornbusch, 1996; Suárez-Orozco & Suárez-Orozco, 1995; Vernez, Abrahamse, & Quigley, 1996). Recent immigrants have better health indicators than those who have lived longer in the United States, and foreign-born members of the ethnic group are generally healthier than those of the second and third generation (Iannotta, 2003; Morales et al., 2002). This is in direct violation of the prediction of assimilation theories of adaptation that hypothesizes that immigrant origin youth would do better over time and across generations.

For example, lifetime prevalence of psychiatric disorders is 18.4 percent for Mexican immigrants who have been in the United States less than 13 years, 32.3 percent for those who have been in the United States for more than 13 years, and 48.7 percent for U.S.-born Mexican Americans (Alderet, Vega, Kolody, & Aguilar-Gaxiola, 2000). The NRC study cited earlier also found that the longer immigrant youth are in the United States, the poorer their overall physical and psychological health (Hernandez & Charney, 1998). Furthermore, the more "Americanized" they became, the more likely they were to engage in risky behaviors such as substance abuse, unprotected sex, and delinquency. Ultimately, they face multiple challenges for their health, including injuries, tuberculosis, limited access to health care, and other health disparities (Flores, Bauchner, Feinstein, & Nguyen, 1999; Flores et al., 2002; Williams & Collins, 1995).

In addition to declining health, another aspect of this phenomenon relates to the fact that, according to a number of studies, newly arrived students from Central America (Suárez-Orozco, 1989), Mexico (Suárez-Orozco & Suárez-Orozco, 1995), the Caribbean (Waters, 1996), and Asia (Gibson, 1988; Helweg & Helweg, 1990; Maira, 1998; Rumbaut & Cornelius, 1995; Sue & Okazaki, 1990; Tuan, 1995; Zhou & Bankston, 1998) display highly adaptive attitudes and behaviors to succeed in school. Yet the longer immigrant youth are in the United States, the more negative they become in terms of school attitudes and adaptations. Sociologists Ruben Rumbaut and Alejandro Portes surveyed more than 5,000 high school students in San Diego, California, and Dade County, Florida, comparing grade-point averages and aspirations of first- and second-generation students (Portes & Rumbaut, 2001). They found that length of residence in the United States was associated with declining academic achievement and aspirations. A similar pattern was established in a large-scale study conducted of Canadian immigrants families. Research by Laurence Steinberg, B. Bradford Brown, and Sanford Dornbusch (Steinberg et al., 1996) based on a national study of more than 20,000 teenagers attending nine high schools uncovered a similar trend.

Most of the data to date demonstrating this declining pattern of academic performance have compared first-, second-, and third-generation immigrant-origin students. Data from the LISA study (see note 1) assessed the academic performance and engagement of recently arrived immigrant youth from five sending countries and then examined whether there was a shift in these indicators over time (Figure 3.1). The decline in the grade-point average of students coming from Mexico, Central America, the Dominican Republic, and Haiti all reached statistical significance. Only the grade-point average of the Chinese-origin students did not reach statistical significance, though a similar trend emerged. Strikingly, the grade-point

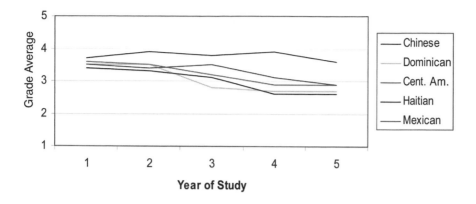

p < .01 (for all groups except Chinese)

Figure 3.1 Group pattern of grade average

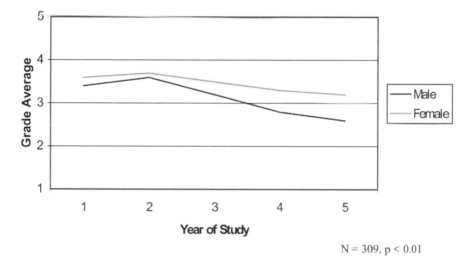

N = 309, p < 0.01

Figure 3.2 Gendered patterns of grade average

average of immigrant boys declined significantly more than that of girls for all groups (Figure 3.2). For both girls and boys, their grades in the first two years are considerably higher than their grades in the last three years. The second year, both girls' and boys' grade-point averages peaked, and from the third year on, both girls and boys experienced steady decrease in their grade-point averages. And girls consistently have statistically significant higher grade-point averages than boys throughout the five-year period (Qin-Hilliard, 2003). (We will return later to an examination of the factors that contribute to this pattern.)

57

In summary, the data suggest that the new immigrant experience subverts the predictions of "assimilation" models that argue that each new generation in the United States tends to do substantially better than the previous one, eventually reaching parity with the mainstream population (Chavez, 1991). Exposure to certain aspects of American socioeconomic structure and culture today appears to be negatively associated with well-being.

Explanations of the "Immigrant Health Paradox"

Several models have been proposed to explain this paradox. The most widely used explanations are that of the "cultural hypothesis" and the "healthy migrant hypothesis." The cultural hypothesis proposes that immigrants bring with them cultural values and behaviors that are health enhancing, while acculturation to the host country leads to the loss of these patterns. The healthy migrant hypothesis, or "selectivity hypothesis," assumes that individuals who undertake the migration journey are selectively healthier than those who remain in the country of origin (Palloni & Morenoff, 2001). Other explanations have also been proposed, such as a "moribund migrant effect" or the "salmon bias hypothesis." These assume that particularly Latinos return to their countries of origin near the end of life and that this affects morbidity and mortality statistics in the United States (Morales et al., 2002). Both the selectivity hypothesis and the salmon bias hypothesis have been tested and have not been able to fully account for the paradox (Abraido-Lanza et al., 1999). These hypotheses may better account for immigrants who arrive voluntarily rather than involuntarily (Ogbu & Herbert, 1998).

One pathway through which the cultural hypothesis accounts for the worsening of health indicators with time is the adoption of high-risk behaviors, which predominate in the host country, while relinquishing those behaviors more typical for the culture of origin (Morales et al., 2002). The research has shown this to be true for alcohol consumption, drug abuse, and smoking and also applies to dietary practices such as a drastic increase in "supersized" high-calorie fast-food meals. Adjusting to the neighborhoods in which the immigrants reside, which are usually characterized by fewer socioeconomic resources and the associated stressors of poverty, may also contribute to poorer health outcomes (Luthar, 1999; Scribner, 1996). It is important to note that these relationships are not unidirectional since they could also include adopting health-protective behaviors from the new context, and the acculturation effects have been shown to vary with gender and ethnicity. The stress of ethnic and racial minority status and the concomitant experience of discrimination—in terms of both structural obstacles and negative social mirroring—are also likely contributors (Coll García & Magnuson, 1997; C. Suárez-Orozco, 2000).

Other cultural characteristics can contribute to explaining the initial health advantages, these being specific cultural practices, greater family cohesion, and the availability of social support for recent immigrants from countries with collectivistic orientations (Abraido-Lanza et al., 1999; Fuligni, Tseng, & Lam, 1999). Immigrants can have extended support networks and multiple communal strategies for dealing with economic hardships and emotional stress and for sharing child care and household responsibilities (Iannotta, 2003). Well-being among immigrants may also be linked to the patterns of social capital that immigrants are able to deploy in their new settings (Portes & Rumbaut, 2001; Zhou & Bankston, 1998).

Thus, a number of social scientists have explored the issues of variability and decline in schooling performance and psychosocial adaptation of immigrant children, some of which we will discuss in this chapter. Social scientists have argued that the "capital" that the immigrant families bring with them—including financial resources, social class and educational background, psychological and physical health, and social supports—have a clear influence on the immigrant experience. Legal status, race, color, and language also mediate how children adapt to the upheavals of immigration. Economic opportunities and neighborhood characteristics—including the quality of schools where immigrants settle, racial and class segregation, neighborhood decay, and violence—all contribute significantly to the adaptation process. Anti-immigrant sentiment and racism also play a role. These factors combine in ways that lead to very different outcomes.

THE ADOLESCENT PSYCHOSOCIAL EXPERIENCE OF IMMIGRATION

For many families, immigration results in growth, opportunity, and the dawning of new horizons. But there are costs involved in all immigrant journeys. Immigration is a transformative process with profound implications for the family. Immigrant youth undergo a constellation of changes that have a lasting impact on their development. Yet surprisingly little systematic research has focused on the psychological experiences of immigrant youth (Coll García & Magnuson, 1997; Suárez-Orozco & Suárez-Orozco, 2001). What do we know about what it is like to be a child of immigration, and what implications can this experience have for well-being?

Transitions

Transitions, while pregnant with possibility, are always stressful. Transitions can trigger a variety of reactions, including excitement, anticipation, and hope as well as anxiety, anger, depression, somatic complaints, and illness (Dohrenwend, 1986). By any measure, immigration is one of the most stressful events a family can undergo (Falicov, 1998). It removes family members from many of their relationships and predictable contexts—community ties, jobs, customs, and (often) language. Immigrants are stripped of many of their significant relationships—extended family members, best friends, and neighbors. They also lose the social roles that provide them with culturally scripted notions of how they fit into the world. Initially, without a sense of competence, control, and belonging, many immigrants will feel marginalized. These changes in relationships, contexts, and roles are highly disorienting and nearly inevitably lead to a keen sense of loss (Ainslie, 1998).

At the most dramatic end of the stress spectrum are the events that result in Post-posttraumatic stress disorder. Asylum seekers from all over the world escape from highly traumatic situations in which they may have witnessed killing and experienced rape or torture, which lead to transient as well as long-term symptoms (including recurrent traumatic memories, a general numbing of responses, and a persistent sense of increased arousal leading to intense anxiety, irritability, outbursts of anger, difficulty concentrating, and insomnia) (Somach, 1995). Other immigrants face a different form of violence as they cross the border. Border crossing can often be a traumatic event for adults and youth alike. It can involve a variety of dangers, including exposure to heat exhaustion as well as violence at the hands of border agents, "coyotes" (paid crossing guides), and others. Undocumented women and girls are particularly at risk of being raped, robbed, or murdered during the migratory process (Amnesty International, 1998; Eschbach, Hagan, & Rodriguez, 1997). New arrivals who experienced trauma will often suffer recurring waves of symptoms over a period of time and will remain preoccupied with the violence and may also feel guilty about having escaped when loved ones remained behind. Parents will be relatively less available psychologically to their child, which presents a developmental challenge (Suárez-Orozco & Suárez-Orozco, 2001).

In the many cases where violence is not a defining feature of the immigrant experience, there are nonetheless normative stresses that immigrant adults and children face. While anticipating the migration and the initial period following the arrival, many experience a sense of euphoria, and expectations are high. On arrival, immigrants focus their energies on attending to the immediate needs of settling into the new environment. The priorities include finding a place to live, securing employment, and enrolling the children in schools. There may be little time for the family to process psychologically many aspects of their new experiences.

After taking care of the essential needs, immigrants will begin to confront some unanticipated realities. Many will experience a variety of psychological problems (Ainslie, 1998; Arrendondo-Dowd, 1981; Sluzki, 1979). Most frequently, the cumulative losses of loved ones and familiar contexts will lead to feelings along a spectrum that range from mild sadness to depression to "perpetual mourning." For others, the general dissonance in cultural expectations and the loss of predictable context will trigger anxiety and disorientation. Many immigrants who arrive with exaggerated expectations of opportunity must come to terms with a starker reality. Disappointed aspirations, when coupled with a hostile reception in the new environment, may lead some to feelings of distrust, suspicion, and anger. Although some immigrants will display these symptoms with clinical acuity, others feel only transient discomfort and adapt to their circumstances with relative ease.

The LISA study (see note 1) used multiple methods to understand the changing social and psychological world of immigrant youth. According to the findings of the LISA study, the psychological well-being of the immigrant youth, measured by a composite index,[2] is maintained at a similar level throughout the five years of the study. There are gender differences, however, with the boys improving from year 1 to year 5 of the study, while for the girls there is no change (with a tendency, however, toward increased psychological complaints). For boys, feelings of sadness and hostility were quite strong in the first year of the study, mainly because of the recent separation from their places of origin and family members. However, boys reported lower levels of psychosomatic symptoms in year 5. On the other hand, the data illustrate greater psychological risk for adolescent girls, who have not shown a reduction in psychological symptoms during their five years of adaptation to their new homes. This is consistent with Portes and Rumbaut's (2001) results showing that immigrant girls combine better educational adaptation with a worse psychological profile in their adaptation compared to their male counterparts.

Factors that showed a positive correlation with psychological well-being were the personal resources that a student can employ, such as optimism,[3] self-efficacy,[4] and self-esteem.[5] The level of these personal resources was maintained during the five years of the study. Actually, the youths' conviction that they can be successful in the United States had increased by year 5.[6] Moreover, in the stepwise regression analysis, evaluating the predictive capacity of several psychosocial factors on psychological well-being as the dependent variable, it is the personal resources of self-esteem and optimism (in addition to the negative social contexts of discrimination and fights in the school) that best predict psychological well-being for the youth.[7]

The findings based on the structured interview were further elucidated by a projective narrative task that consisted of asking the children to tell stories about two pictures from the Thematic Apperception Test (McClelland, 1999; Murray, 1943). The analyses of these narratives shows that from year 1 to year 5 of the study, the youth had increased concerns with adequacy, especially in terms of their abilities to master a presented task paralleling their struggles with mastering English-language skills. Concerns with adequacy were certainly relevant in the initial period after immigration and were projected onto the stories; however, at that time, the barriers to success were conceptualized as external. In year 5, in addition to increased concerns, there is also a qualitative shift to invoking internal barriers to success, such as one's capabilities, a "disappointment with self"; that is, intrinsic characteristics of the self have become the prevalent explanation for elusive success (Todorova & Suárez-Orozco, 2002).

In summary, over the five years of our study, while the threats to well-being are substantial, the majority of the youth in the LISA study maintained a level of psychological well-being similar to that which they had in the initial period after their arrival, and the boys improved in terms of psychological functioning. The decline in psychological well-being that has been documented in the literature is more pronounced for longer length of stay in the United States and for subsequent generations than it is in the initial five years after migration. Interestingly, it is the children's resilience, illustrated by personal resources such as self-esteem, self-efficacy, and optimism, that contributes to a great extent to their preserved well-being. While social resources can also be protective of well-being, as we will illustrate in the following sections, it is precisely the social resources that are most at risk and decline with time. Possibly, this decline in social protective resources might be implicated in the longer-term impaired well-being of immigrant youth because the personal resources and resiliency can become exhausted and insufficient to sustain health on their own.

Separations and Reunification

For many new arrivals, the principal motivation for migration is to be reunited with family members who emigrated earlier. Family networks generate—and sustain—substantial migratory flows. For the majority of immigrant youth, the process of family reunification is a long, often painful, and disorienting ordeal. Data derived from the LISA study revealed that 85 percent of the youth underwent separation from one or both parents for periods from six months to more than 10 years (Suárez-Orozco, Todorova, &

Louie, 2002). Hence, separations are normative to the migratory process. If the youth was left with a loving caretaker for an extended period of time, she will become attached to that caretaker. The aunt or grandmother may assume the role of symbolic mother. When the child is called on to join the parents, although she will be happy about the prospect of "regaining" them, she will also "lose" sustaining contact with the caretakers to whom she has become attached.

Once the youth reunites with her parents in the new setting, mutual calibrations are required. If the separation was for a long period of time, the reunited family must first get reacquainted. When the reunification involves youth who were left behind when very young, the process may go beyond becoming reacquainted—the youth will be in essence "meeting" her parents. Further, they often find themselves entering new family constellations that include stepparents, stepsiblings, and siblings they have never met.

Youth respond in a variety of ways to their separations from family members. Not surprisingly, for some it is a painful process, leading to high reports of depressive symptoms (Suárez-Orozco et al., 2002). Of critical importance to the adjustment process is how the youngster makes meaning of the situation of the separation from parents and other loved ones. If children and youth are well prepared for the separation and if the separation is framed as temporary and necessary and undertaken for the good of the family, the separation will be more manageable than if they feel abandoned. The "context and circumstances" of the separation will play a critical role in different outcomes. If parents and caretakers manage the separation cooperatively and if the accompanying losses are minimized, the youth, though changed, may not necessarily be damaged by the experience.

Learning Culture

A form of stress specific to immigration is referred to as "acculturation stress" (Berry, 1995; Flaskerud & Uman, 1996; Smart & Smart, 1995). Acculturation refers to the process whereby immigrants must learn new cultural parameters and interpersonal expectations. Cultural practices are first learned in childhood as part of socially shared repertoires that make the flow of life predictable. The social flow changes in dramatic ways following immigration; without a sense of cultural competence, control, and belonging, immigrants are often left feeling disoriented.

Immigrant children typically come into contact with American culture sooner—and more intensely—than their parents do. Schools represent an important site of cultural change for immigrant youth. It is where they meet teachers (who are often members of the dominant culture) as well as children from other backgrounds. On the other hand, their parents may be more removed from American culture in all its diversity, particularly if they work in jobs with other immigrants and coethnics (as is typically the case for many new immigrants) (M Suárez-Orozco, 2000). The relative rapidness of the child's absorption into the new culture will create predicaments and tensions (Falicov, 1998). Immigrant adolescents may have feelings ranging from vague to intense embarrassment in regard to aspects of their parents' "old country" ways. Immigrant parents often attempt to slow down the process by warning children not to act like American peers in the new setting.

As a result of their greater exposure to the new culture, children frequently learn the new language more quickly than do their parents. Though the youth may continue to speak the home language, the level of fluency is likely to atrophy over time. Without a concerted effort, the vocabulary and literacy level of the language of origin usually lags far behind that of the new language. Although the youth may easily communicate about basic needs in her language of origin, she is likely to have more difficulty communicating subtleties of thought and emotion in that language (Wong-Fillmore, 1991). Often, the opposite is true with the parents. Hence, in complicated communication sequences, one of the parties in the conversation is likely to be at a disadvantage; miscommunication is a frequent outcome.

THE SOCIAL CONTEXTS OF IMMIGRANT YOUTH

The Neighborhoods

Where immigrants settle will have profound implications for the experiences and adaptation of immigrant youth. Immigrants—especially Latino and Caribbean new arrivals—are settling in large numbers in highly segregated, deep-poverty, urban settings (Orfield & Yun, 1999). The degree of segregation and experienced discrimination will have a series of consequences (Massey & Denton, 1993). New immigrants of color who settle in predominantly minority neighborhoods will have virtually no direct, systematic, and intimate contact with middle-class white Americans. This in turn will affect the kinds of English encountered by the youth, the quality of schools they will attend, and the networks that are useful to access desirable colleges and jobs (Orfield, 1995; Portes, 1996).

Perceived discrimination can also significantly impact the adaptation experiences of immigrant youth. The LISA study illustrates the profound implications of discrimination on the psychological well-being of the immigrant youth. As a whole, 39 percent of the youth say that they have been discriminated against in the United States.[8] Analysis shows that frequency of experienced discrimination is correlated with higher levels of psychological symptoms. In the stepwise regression analysis, evaluating the predictive capacity of several psychosocial factors for psychological well-being as the dependent variable, discrimination proves to be one of the best predictors of well-being (along with the personal resources of self-esteem, optimism, and the negative social contexts of fights in the school).[9]

Other social issues inherent in the neighborhood context also impact immigrant youth's adaptation. Concentrated poverty is associated with the "disappearance of meaningful work opportunities"(Wilson, 1997). Youngsters in such neighborhoods are chronically underemployed or unemployed and must search for work elsewhere. In such neighborhoods with few opportunities in the formal economy, underground or informal activities tend to flourish. Exposure to violence in both neighborhoods and schools is an everyday reality for many immigrant youth today (Collier, 1998). Sociologists Alejandro Portes and Rubén Rumbaut have argued that these structural features interact and conspire to generate a pattern they have termed "segmented assimilation," whereby, over time, large numbers of poor immigrant youth of color will tend to assimilate toward the American underclass rather than assimilating to middle-class norms (Portes & Rumbaut, 2001).

Poverty might be a preexisting condition prior to migration, or it may be temporarily accentuated as immigrants experience some downward mobility in the process of settlement. Poverty is a reality for large numbers of immigrant youth. Nearly a quarter of the children of immigrants live below the poverty line—in comparison to 11 percent for non-Hispanic whites. Nationwide, 37 percent of the children of immigrants report difficulties affording food and are more than four times as likely than native-born children to live in crowded housing conditions. They are twice as likely as native-born children to be uninsured and three times less likely to have a source of regular health care (Capps, 2001).

The effects of immigrant poverty have long been recognized as a significant risk factor for youth development (Luthar, 1999). Children raised in circumstances of socioeconomic deprivation are vulnerable to an array of psychological distresses, including difficulties concentrating and sleeping, anxiety, and depression as well as a heightened propensity for delinquency and violence. Those living in poverty often experience major life events stress as well as the stress of daily hassles. Poverty frequently coexists with a variety of other factors that augment risks—such as single-parenthood, residence in neighborhoods plagued with violence, gang activity, and drug trade as well as school environments that are segregated, overcrowded, and poorly funded.

The School Context

The neighborhood characteristics outlined here are reflected in the schools attended by immigrants. The school context impacts students' health and well-being—studies have looked at both school-level characteristics and assessments of students' educational experiences (Currie, Hurrelmann, Settertobulte, Smith, & Todd, 2000; Ma, 2000; Samdal, Nutbeam, Wold, & Kannas, 1998). Undoubtedly, students' experiences in their schools have consequences for health. These experiences shape students' attitudes toward their school and toward the value of education, which in turn can have implications for the extent to which they engage in health-impairing behaviors. A negative attitude toward school may promote oppositional behavior, which can include engaging in violence, smoking, alcohol consumption, and drug use. At the same time, a stressful school climate, characterized by perceptions of academic pressure, danger, discrimination, and absent supportive relationships, can directly affect students' well-being, who might begin to feel that the requirements of the environment tax their abilities to cope (Karatzias, Power, Flemming, & Lennan, 2002). Stress in the school environment is an important contributor to health problems and psychosomatic symptoms in students and exerts its effects through a combination of individual and contextual-level factors (Torseheim & Wold, 2001). On the other hand, the educational context can be a source of salutatory health knowledge, self-esteem (Karatzias et al., 2002), and social support, which can have a protective effect on students' well-being (Samdal et al., 1998).

Current research is directed toward identifying school characteristics and educational experiences that can have detrimental or enhancing effects on health and well-being (Currie et al., 2000; International Planning Committee, 1999; Karatzias et al., 2002; Ma, 2000). The educational context can be perceived differently for students from different cultural backgrounds, and thus the health-enhancing or health-impairing consequences need to be studied with a sensitivity to cross-cultural differences in values and expectations for education (Collier, 1998).

Immigrant youth today enroll in schools that cover the range from well functioning, with a culture of high expectations and a focus on achievement, to dysfunctional institutions characterized by ever-present fear of violence, distrust, low expectations, and institutional anomie. Unfortunately, poor immigrant youth who need the most academic help tend to enroll in inferior schools with "cultures of violence."

These schools typically have limited and outdated resources and offer an inferior education. Buildings are poorly maintained, and, as a rule, classrooms are overcrowded. Textbooks and curriculum are outdated; computers are few and obsolete. Many of the teachers may not have credentials in the subjects they teach. Clearly defined tracks sentence all too many immigrant students to noncollege destinations (Oakes, 1985; Olsen, 1997). Lacking English skills, immigrant students are often enrolled in the least demanding and competitive classes that eventually exclude them from courses needed for college. These schools generally offer few advanced-placement courses that are critical for entry in many of the more competitive colleges. The ratio of guidance counselor to student is impossibly high. Because the settings are so undesirable, teachers and principals routinely transfer out in search of better assignments elsewhere. As a result, in many such schools, there is little continuity or sense of community that would serve to foster academic engagement (Suárez-Orozco & Suárez-Orozco, 2001).

Data suggest that immigrant youth who arrive during adolescence are at a particular disadvantage in their schooling (Ruiz-de-Valasco, Fix, & Clewell, 2001). Although many immigrants arrive during their secondary school years, most school-based programs targeting immigrant youth are designed for needs of primary school students. Many immigrants who arrive in adolescence must overcome several often-insurmountable obstacles. Frequently, they are not awarded credits for previous course work completed in their countries of origin. They may enter settings with high-stakes testing that have not been designed with second-language learners in mind. Older immigrant youth may have had longer gaps in their previous schooling and enter schools far behind their age levels. Therefore, dropout rates among older immigrant youth have reached disconcertingly high levels (Suárez-Orozco, 2001). And even when older immigrant adolescents are able to graduate, if they lack documented status, they will not be able to pursue higher education.

Data from a variety of studies demonstrate that immigrant students enter the United States with highly positive attitudes toward education (Fuligni, 1997; Kao & Tienda, 1995; Portes & Rumbaut, 2001; Steinberg et al., 1996; Suárez-Orozco & Suárez-Orozco, 2001). But these attitudes are difficult to maintain in a climate of insurmountable obstacles, cultural hostilities, identity threats, and psychological disparagement; under such circumstances, most youth will not continue to invest in schools as an avenue for status mobility. Indeed, facing toxic levels of cultural violence, children will tend to invest significant amounts of their psychic energy to "defend" against these assaults on their sense of self.

The data from year 5 of the LISA study illustrate that 25.6 percent of the youth report that they do not feel safe in their schools, 26.5 percent report that their school is badly affected by crime and violence, and 28.5 percent feel unsafe because of gangs in the school.[10] Additionally, 48.2 percent see students getting into fights, 44.7 percent see students bullying each other,

14.2 percent see students carrying weapons, and 17.4 percent see students selling drugs—from several times a month to daily. Note that these figures are higher than the national level (when all students, including nonimmigrants, other minority, and majority youth, are included), less than 10 percent of students reported having been bullied, and about 20 percent students aged 12 to 18 reported gangs being present in their schools according to the Indicators of School Crime and Safety report (U.S. Department of Education, 2004). A situation in which nearly 30 percent of the immigrant children in our sample feel unsafe in their schools for one reason or another is disturbing, particularly considering that the percentages for each of the indicators were much higher in the initial years of the study and that, with time, the students seem to have become hardened to the climate. This is especially true, considering the strong relationship between feelings of safety in schools and psychological outcomes. In the correlation analysis of our data, the school climate, measured by scales assessing feelings of safety[11] and witnessing fights, weapons, and drugs in school,[12] was a predictor of the psychological well-being of the adolescents. In the regression analysis mentioned earlier, which aimed to assess the factors that have the greatest predictive value with psychological well-being as the dependent variable, witnessing fights in school, with its negative impact on well-being, was one of the four factors main predictive factors in the regression model.[13]

Networks of Relations

Social relations help in significant ways to smooth the waters of immigration. The presence of a healthy social support network has long been regarded to be a key protective factor in stress (Cobb, 1988; Cohen & Syme, 1985). The relative absence of social support has been linked to the etiology of disease, mortality, slowed recovery, and mental illness. Interpersonal relationships provide a number of functions (Wills, 1985). Immigrants rely on instrumental social support to provide them with tangible aid (such as running an errand or making a loan) as well as guidance and advice (including information, job, and housing leads), much needed by disoriented newcomers. Social companionship also serves to maintain and enhance self-esteem and to provide acceptance and approval. Quite predictably, a well-functioning social support network is closely linked to better adjustment to the new environment. Of course, in part, the availability of an effective social support structure will be influenced by the individual's preexisting social competence (Heller & Swindle, 1983).

In all social systems, the family is a basic structural unit and as such is the most significant gravitational field in the lives of individuals. This is especially so for immigrants who may not have other social networks immediately available to them in facilitating the flow of life. Family-level factors are indeed most critical for understanding the long-term adaptations of immigrant children (Portes & Rumbaut, 2001); however, in looking at the role of immigrant families, we must proceed with caution. Immigrant families are structured in a variety of culturally relative formations. In some cases, the nuclear family (father, mother, and children) is the ideal type. In other cases, however, matrifocal patterns (where women are at the center of family life) are the norm. Yet in other immigrant families, extended members such as grandparents, aunts, and uncles are integral to the system. Further, the process of immigration may cause families to take new shape (as the stresses of immigration or bureaucratic immigration restrictions tear the family apart). It is therefore always risky to apply mainstream, American middle-class standards in approaching immigrant family dynamics (Falicov, 1998; Smart & Smart, 1995).

Migration creates particular pressures and stresses on the family system. The stresses of immigration may translate into conflict between family members particularly if there were preexisting tensions prior to migration. Once settled in the new land, family members may discover that new obligations and necessities keep them from each other. Many immigrant parents (particularly those coming from poorer backgrounds) work in several jobs. These multiple obligations make them less available to their children than may have been the case prior to migration. Immigrant parents often tell us that they feel that working hard is the best way they can help their children, yet these long work hours leave many youth unsupervised. This physical absence compounds the psychological unavailability that often accompanies parental anxiety and depression (Athey & Ahearn, 1991). These two forms of absence may leave immigrant youth to their own devices. Although in some cases this leads to hyperresponsible children, in other cases it leads to depressed kids who are drawn to the lure of alternative family structures, such as gangs (Vigil, 1988).

Migration creates other changes within the structure of the family. Children who learn English more quickly than their parents are placed in situations where they must advocate for their parents. They may become privy to "family secrets" in their new roles as translators in medical, legal, and other social settings. Roles are often reversed and thus turn upside down the culturally scripted dynamics of parental authority. More than simple issues of relative linguistic competence are at work in the complex mutual familial calibrations that immigration requires. Former family leaders may be "demoted." A wise grandfather who was the source of guidance now may be unable to give meaningful advice to his granddaughter. As immigrant parents have no "map of experience" before them, their self-assurance and authority can be undermined both in the outer world and in the more intimate inner world of the family (Hoffman, 1989).

Patterns of family control and discipline become an arena where these tensions come to the fore. As parents discipline their children in ways accepted in their country of origin, they may come into conflict with American norms. The children, wise to the ways of the new land, may use the threat of reporting their parents to state agencies against them. This further challenges parental authority. Many immigrant parents fear that in the new country, laws and customs prevent them from ensuring that their children behave in ways they deem appropriate.

Family cohesion and the maintenance of a well-functioning system of supervision, authority, and mutuality are perhaps the most powerful factors in shaping the well-being and future outcomes of all children—immigrant and nonimmigrant alike. Because no family is an island, family cohesion and functioning are enhanced when the family is part of a larger community displaying effective forms of what Felton Earls (1997) has termed "community agency." Likewise, anthropologist George DeVos (1980) has argued that culturally constituted patterns of community cohesion and supervision can "immunize" immigrant youth from the more toxic elements in their new settings. This line of research suggests that when communities are cohesive and when adults within the community can monitor youngsters' activities, they will tend to do better. Children who live in such communities are less likely to be involved with gangs and delinquency and are more focused on their academic pursuits.

Min Zhou (2000) has examined how community-based organizations geared to youth can make a difference in the life chances and opportunities of immigrant youth. Connections with nonparent adults—a community leader, a teacher, a member of the church, or a coach—are important in the academic as well as social adaptation of adolescents in general (Hamilton & Darling, 1996; Lynch & Cicchetti, 1997; Rhodes, 2002; Roeser & Eccles, 1998) and appear to be particularly important to immigrant adolescents. These youth are often undergoing profound shifts in their sense of self and are struggling to negotiate changing circumstances in relationships with their parents and peers. Protective relationships with non-parent adults can provide immigrant youth with compensatory attachments, safe contexts for learning new cultural norms and practices, and information that is vital to success in schools (Roffman, Suárez-Orozco, & Rhodes, 2003).

For immigrant youth arriving in the United States at the beginning of and during adolescence, the school context is a major arena for social relations and a source of social support. In the LISA study, we assessed the longitudinal changes in the adolescents' sources of social support. Our findings illustrate a disturbing tendency in that the availability of support-ive relations in schools (measuring adult support) decreases with time for these adolescents.[14] On the other hand, the level of peer support available to the children does increase slightly with time,[15] indicating that peers are becoming more and more the source of important relationships for the youth. It is the adult support, however, that correlates with psychological well-being, though weakly,[16] pointing to the risks associated with having those sources become less available with time.

The previously mentioned findings, based on the structured interview, were confirmed and further elucidated by the narrative task, based on the Thematic Apperception Test (McClelland, 1999; Murray, 1943). In the first years of immigration, the stories of immigrant children reflect a mobiliza-tion of social resources in terms of seeking out help and support in learning. Longitudinally, within the five years of the LISA study, we observe that the narratives of the immigrant children begin to project a greater degree of alienation from sources of social support, including parents and teachers, and a discouragement in the possibility of receiving help in difficult situations. These patterns can be interpreted as indicative of a buffering role of social support, which assumes that its salutary effects are elicited in the context of stress and not otherwise. However, the narratives of the children in year 5 of the LISA study point to an absence of support when it is needed and an increased sense of inadequacy and lowered self-efficacy (Todorova & Suárez-Orozco, 2002).

Academic performance, of course, is a key indicator of both current and future well-being (Mandel & Marcus, 1988). As part of the analyses of the LISA data, we developed a structural equation model to assess the role of a variety of predictors of academic engagement and performance, includ-ing age, gender, parental education, presence or absence of two parental figures in the home, motivation, self-esteem, language skills, school vio-lence, relational engagement (the degree to which students have meaning-ful relationships in school with peers and adults who provide emotional and tangible support), and behavioral engagement (the degree to which students engage in the tasks necessary for school success, including attending class, completing schoolwork as well as homework, and class attendance). We found that while gender, English-language proficiency, motivation, and having two parental figures all significantly predicted fifth-year grade-point average, after controlling for all these variables, behavioral engagement was the strongest predictor of grade-point aver-age. We specifically considered the effect of relational engagement on behavioral engagement. We considered the effect of relational engage-ment on behavioral engagement. Relational engagement significantly predicted behavioral engagement. It also served to mediate the effects of

Structural Equation Model

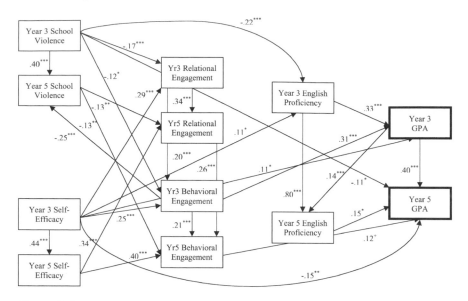

Figure 3.3

school violence and low self-esteem on behavioral engagement. Hence, relational engagement plays an important role in enhancing academic performance. Girls demonstrated significantly higher levels of relational engagement than did boys. In addition to these direct effects, relational engagement mediated the problems of school violence as well as low self-esteem. Hence, this model demonstrates the critical role relations play in immigrant adolescents' academic engagement and consequent performance in school (Figure 3.3).

Networks of relationships with parents, extended family, peers, mentors, and community are crucial to the lives of immigrant youth in multiple ways. They can serve to help immigrant youth develop healthy bicultural identities, engender motivation, and provide specific information about how to successfully navigate schooling pathways (Suárez-Orozco, Suárez-Orozco, & Doucet, 2004). Healthy social support network moderate stress and predict well-being for adults and children alike. When successful, these relationships help immigrant youth and their families overcome some of the barriers associated with poverty and discrimination that prevent full participation in the new country's economic and cultural life (Stanton-Salazar, 2001). The increasingly unavailability of helping relations and/or the motivation to seek support for immigrant children is a phenomenon that needs to be addressed by parents, teachers, and schools.

A large percentage of the students in American schools are currently children of immigrants. They arrive with optimism, a love for learning, and a strong motivation for education, which is often a means of giving back to parents and extended family. Their well-being is entwined in relational networks, which include parents, peers, and community. The well-being of newly arrived immigrant students, including academic achievement, can be fostered through constructing environments that are conducive to multiple forms of relational goals. Over time, while many immigrant youth persist and their mental health and motivation for learning flourish, for many others this optimism is lost and negative academic, psychosocial, and health consequences ensue. Understanding the role of relational networks that promote well-being is an important step toward nurturing immigrant youth's optimism and future health.

FUTURE RESEARCH

Research with immigrant youth necessitates multimodal methodologies. Tools of anthropology, sociology, demography, psychology, and educational research together can illuminate the varieties of the immigrant experience. No single strategy is likely to explain the nuanced interplay of factors at work in immigrant youth's life experiences. The combination of qualitative and quantitative approaches can construct a more intricate picture than would be possible using only one of these methodologies. Immigrant youth must be studied in a variety of contexts, including their neighborhoods, schools, workplaces, and homes. As researchers, theoreticians, and practitioners, we are challenged to synthesize findings that employ a variety of disciplinary strategies and that consider individuals from a myriad of cultural backgrounds (Suárez-Orozco, 2001).

Although cross-sectional research is often the most affordable and practical approach, it remains inherently limited. We concur with Fuligni's (2001) plea for longitudinal research following the same children as they encounter and negotiate differences in the cultural traditions of the motherland and the new society. Cross-sectional studies seem to have established the disconcerting results of acculturation, leading many to conclude that the longer youth of immigrant origin are in the new context, the worse their well-being and academic performance. Only with longitudinal research, however, can acculturative changes be separated from normative developmental shifts. Although longitudinal design is an essential research strategy if we are to understand the assimilation patterns of immigrant youth, only a handful of such studies have been conducted to date (Kasinitz, Mollenkopf, & Waters, 2004; Portes & Rumbaut, 2001; Suárez-Orozco & Suárez-Orozco, 2001).

In addition, there is a need for more comprehensive and ambitious comparative research. Such research can help us better determine the constant shared processes that characterize all immigrant journeys—such as cultural disorientation, family role reversals, tensions about old values and new, and so forth. At the same time, comparative work is necessary to explore group differences in immigrant adaptation. How do the experiences of various groups of origin differ? When differences exist, how can we best account for them? How do background factors in both the motherland (financial resources, parental education, premigration trauma, and so on) and the new society (poverty, community supports, housing quality, neighborhood safety, school characteristics, documented status, and so on) interact to account for specific outcomes? What is the relationship between cultural-level differences versus socioeconomic differences? How are we to account for the fact that after controlling for socioeconomic differences, there are still substantial group differences in outcomes, such as in schooling? What is the role of cultural values, and are they congruent or incongruent with the values of the surrounding community? How does discrimination, negative social mirroring, and low teacher expectations affect student outcomes over time? What is the role of gender in experience, expectations, and outcomes?

Cross-cultural research on immigrants forces us to reexamine the traditional social science assumptions around validity and reliability (McLoyd & Steinberg, 1998). Questions and prompts that are valid for one group may not be valid for another. Hence, it is a challenge to develop single instruments that capture the experiences of individuals from a variety of backgrounds. There is a growing consensus in the field of cross-cultural research that mixed-method designs, linking emic (outsider) and etic (insider) approaches, triangulating data, and embedding emerging findings into an ecological framework, are essential to this kind of endeavor (Doucette-Gates, Brooks-Gunn, & Chase-Lansdale, 1998; Hughes, Seidman, & Edwards, 1993; Sue & Sue, 1987).

The methodological tools and theoretical perspectives afforded by an interdisciplinary approach are most appropriate for research on this population. Ethnography allows us to gain the informants' "point of view" and guides us in the development of systematic strategies of assessment, allowing us to interpret findings in a locally relevant context. Psychological techniques are useful in systematically following up on the tentative theoretical constructions that emerge from the ethnographic process.

Using triangulated data is crucial when faced with the challenges of validity in conducting research with groups of diverse backgrounds. Further, it serves to counteract the inherent limitations of self-report data—a problem we suspect is exaggerated among immigrant youth. By sifting through self-reports, parent reports, teacher reports, and their own observations, researchers are able to establish both concurrence and disconnection in what youth say they do, what others say they do, and what researchers see them do.

Cross-cultural research is best conducted by a diverse team of researchers who include "outsider" and "insider" approaches to data collection and analysis (Cooper, Jackson, Azmitia, & Lopez, 1998). Bicultural and bilingual insiders are essential to establish rapport and trust within the communities and gain entry into immigrant populations that might otherwise be difficult to access. Further, insiders are able to explain and inform their culture in depth. Outsiders can provide a fresh comparative perspective. Careful interpretation of data must take place in diverse interdisciplinary interpretive communities that provide culturally sensitive frameworks to examine causal patterns and conceptual relationships. In making comparisons, however, it is essential to avoid facile assumptions that "cultural differences" or individual agency single-handedly can account for differences in outcomes. Much can be learned from the narratives of highly successful immigrant youth. Of course, the danger to be avoided in such work is to engage in interpretations that "blame the victim" among less successful immigrant youth.

It is essential that we deepen our understanding of this burgeoning youth population. As first- and second-generation immigrant origin youth currently constitute 20 percent of the children growing up in the United States, their healthy development will have fundamental long-term implications for our society. Unfortunately, however, until recently psychologists have largely ignored the particular circumstances of their development. As social scientists, we must recognize the specific strengths and challenges of immigrant youth and strive to conduct culturally sensitive quality research that considers the multiplicity of factors —structural, cultural, familial, and individual—that contribute to differential outcomes.

NOTES

1. The data for this research are part of the Longitudinal Immigrant Student Adaptation Project, directed by Carola Suárez-Orozco with Marcelo Suárez-Orozco while at Harvard University. The project longitudinally followed 400 immigrant children (ages 9 to 14 at the beginning of the study) coming from five major regions (China, Central America, the Dominican Republic, Haiti, and Mexico) to the Boston and San Francisco areas for five years. This interdisciplinary project utilized a variety of methods, including structured student and parent interviews, ethnographic observations, projective and objective measures, reviews of school records, teacher questionnaires, and interviews. This project was made possible by funding provided by the National Science Foundation, the W. T. Grant Foundation, and the Spencer Foundation. The data presented,

the statements made, and the views expressed are solely the responsibility of the authors.

2. As part of the psychosocial measures included in our study, our cross-cultural research team developed a psychological symptom scale, informed by the *DSM-V* of the American Psychiatric Association and the SCL-90 questionnaire (Derogatis, 1977) that included questions determined by our interdisciplinary research team to be developmentally appropriate and cross-culturally relevant. The questions were piloted on informants at the same developmental level as our participants, representing each of the country of origin groups under consideration. This 26-item scale consisted of five subscales—depression, anxiety, cognitive functioning, interpersonal sensitivity, and hostility. The subscales of the Symptom checklist we used included the following items: "Lately, do you": *Depression:* not have much energy, not feel like eating, cry easily, feel sad, feel not interested in much of anything, worry too much. *Interpersonal sensitivity:* feel critical of others, feel shy, feel others do not understand you, feel people do not like you, feel like you are not as good as other people. *Cognitive functioning:* have trouble remembering things, have trouble making decisions, have trouble concentrating. *Anxiety:* feel nervous, feel something terrible is going to happen, feel like your heart is racing, feel tense, keep remembering something frightening. *Hostility:* feel annoyed too easily, lose temper too easily, get into arguments too easily.

3. $r = -0.35$, $P < 0.001$.

4. $r = -0.23$, $P < 0.001$.

5. $r = -0.32$, $P < 0.001$.

6. $t = 2.16$, $P < 0.05$.

7. For self-esteem, beta $= -0.29$, $P < 0.01$; for optimism, beta $= -0.20$, $P < 0.05$.

8. $r = 0.23$, $P < 0.001$.

9. Beta $= 0.13$, $P < 0.05$

10. These are based on responses "Agree" and "Strongly agree" with statements constructed to assess perceptions of safety in schools

11. $r = -0.20$, $P < 0.001$.

12. $r = 0.22$, $P < 0.01$.

13. Beta $= 0.16$, $P < 0.05$.

14. $t = -3.38$, $P < 0.001$.

15. $t = 2.04$, $P < 0.005$.

16. $r = -0.13$, $P < 0.05$.

REFERENCES

Abraido-Lanza, A., Dohrenwend, B., Ng-Mak, D., & Turner, B. (1999). The Latino mortality paradox: A test of the "Salmon bias" and healthy migrant hypothesis. *American Journal of Public Health, 89,* 1543–1548.

Ainslie, R. (1998). Cultural mourning, immigration, and engagement: Vignettes from the Mexican experience. In M. M. Suárez-Orozco (Ed.), *Crossings: Mexican immigration in interdisciplinary perspectives* (pp. 283–306).

Cambridge, MA: David Rockefeller Center for Latin American Studies/ Harvard University Press.

Alderet, E., Vega, W. A., Kolody, B., & Aguilar-Gaxiola, S. (2000). Life-time prevalence of the risk factors for psychiatric disorders among Mexican migrant farm-workers. *American Journal of Public Health, 90,* 608–614.

Amnesty International. (1998). *From San Diego to Brownsville: Human rights violations on the USA-Mexico border.* Retrieved September 20, 2005 from http://web.amnesty.org/library/Index/ENGAMR510331998?open&of= ENG-MEX

Arrendondo-Dowd, P. (1981). Personal loss and grief as a result of immigration. *Personnel and Guidance Journal, 59,* 376–378.

Athey, J. L., & Ahearn, F. L. (1991). *Refugee children: Theory, research, and services.* Baltimore: The John Hopkins University Press.

Berry, J. W. (1995). Psychology of acculturation. In N. Goldenberg & J. B. Veroff (Eds.), *The culture and psychology reader* (pp. 457–488). New York: New York University Press.

Capps, R. (2001). *Hardship among children of immigrants: Findings from the 1999 National Survey of America's families.* Washington, DC: Urban Institute.

Chavez, L. (1991). *Out of the Barrio: Toward a new politics of Hispanic assimilation.* New York: Basic Books.

Cobb, S. (1988). Social support as a moderator of life stress. *Psychosomatic Medicine, 3,* 300–314.

Cohen, S., & Syme, S. L. (1985). Issues in the study and application of social support. In S. Cohen & S. L. Syme (Eds.), *Social support and health.* Orlando: Academic Press.

Coll García, C., & Magnuson, K. (1997). The psychological experience of immigration: A developmental perspective. In A. Booth, A. C. Crouter, & N. Landale (Eds.), *Immigration and the family* (pp. 91–132). Mahwah, NJ: Lawrence Erlbaum Associates.

Collier, M. (1998). *Cultures of violence in Miami-Dade public schools.* Working paper no. 2 from the Immigration and Ethnicity Institute,: Florida International University, Miami. Retrieved September 20, 2005 from http://www.fiu.edu/~iei/index/working2.html.

Cooper, C. R., Jackson, J. F., Azmitia, M., & Lopez, E. M. (1998). Multiple selves, multiple worlds: Three useful strategies for research with ethnic minority youth on identity, relationships and opportunity structures. In V. McCloyd & L. Steinberg (Eds.), *Studying minority adolescents: Conceptual, methodological and theoretical issues* (pp. 111–125). Mahwah, NJ: Lawrence Erlbaum Associates.

Currie, C., Hurrelmann, K., Settertobulte, W., Smith, R., & Todd, J. (2000). *Health and health behaviour among young people.* WHO Policy Series: Health policy for children and adolescents. Retrieved March 3, 20003, from http://www.hbsc.org/publications/reports.html

Derogatis, L. R. (1977). The SCL-90. Clinical psychometric research. In *The SCL-90 manual I: Scoring, administration, and procedures for the SCL-90.* Baltimore: Johns Hopkins University School of Medicine.

DeVos, G. (1980). Ethnic adaptation and minority status. *Journal of Cross-Cultural Psychology, 11,* 101–125.

Dohrenwend, B. P. (1986). Theoretical formulation of life stress variables. In A. Eichler, M. M. Silverman, & D. M. Pratt (Eds.), *How to define and research stress* (pp. 31–35). Washington, DC: American Psychiatric Press.

Doucette-Gates, A., Brooks-Gunn, J., & Chase-Lansdale, L. P. (1998). The role of bias and equivalence in the study of race, class, and ethnicity. In V. McCloyd & L. Steinberg (Eds.), *Studying minority adolescents: Conceptual, methodological, and theoretical issues* (pp. 211–236). Mahwah, NJ: Lawrence Erlbaum Associates.

Earls, F. (1997). Tighter, safer neighborhoods. *Harvard Magazine, Nov./Dec.,* 14–15.

Eschbach, K., Hagan, J., & Rodriguez, N. (1997). *Death at the border.* Houston: Center for Immigration Research.

Falicov, C. J. (1998). *Latino families in therapy: A guide to multicultural practices.* New York: Guilford Press.

Flaskerud, J. H., & Uman, R. (1996). Acculturation and its effects on self-esteem among immigrant Latina women. *Behavioral Medicine, 22,* 123–133.

Flores, G., Bauchner, H., Feinstein, A., & Nguyen, U.-S. (1999). The impact of ethnicity, family income and parental education on children's health and use of health services. *American Journal of Public Health, 89,* 1066–1071.

Flores, G., Fuentes-Afflick, E., Barbot, O., Carter-Pokras, O., Claudio, L., Lara, M., McLaurin, J., Pachter, L., Gomez, F. R., Mendoza, F., Valdez, R. B., Villarruel, A., Zambrana, R., Greenberg, R., & Weitzman, M. (2002). The health of Latino children: Urgent priorities, unanswered questions and a research agenda. *Journal of the American Medical Association, 288,* 82–90.

Fuligni, A. (1997). The academic achievement of adolescents from immigrant families: The roles of family background, attitudes, and behavior. *Child Development, 69*(2), 351–363.

Fuligni, A. (2001). A comparative longitudinal approach to acculturation among children from immigrant families. *Harvard Educational Review, 71,* 566–578.

Fuligni, A., Tseng, V., & Lam, M. (1999). Attitudes toward family obligations among American adolescents with Asian, Latin American and European backgrounds. *Child Development, 70,* 1030–1044.

Gibson, M. A. (1988). *Accommodation without assimilation: Sikh immigrants in an American high school.* Ithaca, NY: Cornell University Press.

Hamilton, S. F., & Darling, N. (1996). Mentors in adolescents' lives. In K. Hurrelmann & S. F. Hamilton (Eds.), *Social problems and social contexts in adolescence: Perspectives across boundaries* (pp. 199–215). New York: Aldine de Gruyter.

Heller, K., & Swindle, R. W. (1983). Social networks, perceived social support, and coping with stress. In R. D. Felner (Ed.), *Preventative psychology:*

Theory, research, practice in community intervention (pp. 7–103). New York: Pergamon.

Helweg, A., & Helweg, U. (1990). *An immigrant success story: East Indians in America*. Philadelphia: University of Pennsylvania Press.

Hernandez, D., & Charney, E. (Eds.). (1998). *From generation to generation: The health and well-being of children of immigrant families*. Washington, DC: National Academy Press.

Hoffman, E. (1989). *Lost in translation: A life in a new language*. New York: Penguin.

Hughes, D., Seidman, E., & Edwards, D. (1993). Cultural phenomena and the research enterprise: Toward a culturally anchored methodology. *American Journal of Community Psychology, 21,*1–170.

Iannotta, J. (2003). *Emerging issues in Hispanic health: A summary of a workshop*. Washington, DC: National Research Council.

International Planning Committee. (1999). *The European network of health promoting schools: The alliance of education and health*. Retrieved March 3, 2003, from http://www.who.dk/document/e62361.pdf

Kao, G., & Tienda, M. (1995). Optimism and achievement: The educational performance of immigrant youth. *Social Science Quarterly, 76,* 1–19.

Karatzias, A., Power, K. G., Flemming, J., & Lennan, F. (2002). The role of demographics, personality variables and school stress on predicting school satisfaction/ dissatisfaction: Review of the literature and research findings. *Educational Psychology, 22,* 33–50.

Kasinitz, P., Mollenkopf, J., & Waters, M. (2004). *Becoming New Yorkers: Ethnographies of the new second generation*. New York: Russell Sage Foundation.

Luthar, S. (1999). *Poverty and children's adjustment*. Thousand Oaks, CA: Sage.

Lynch, M., & Cicchetti, D. (1997). Children's relationships with adults and peers: An examination of elementary and junior high school students. *Journal of School Psychology, 35,* 81–99.

Ma, X. (2000). Health outcomes of elementary school students in New Brunswick: The education perspective. *Evaluation Review, 24,* 435–456.

Maira, S. (1998). *The quest for ethnic authenticity: Second-generation Indian Americans in New York City*. Unpublished Ed.D. dissertation, Harvard University, Cambridge, MA.

Mandel, H. P., & Marcus, S. I. (1988). *The psychology of underachievement: Differential diagnosis and differential treatment*. New York: Wiley.

Massey, D., & Denton, N. (1993). *American apartheid*. Cambridge, MA: Harvard University Press.

McClelland, D. (1999). How the test lives on: Extensions of the Thematic Apperception Test approach. In L. Gieser & M. Stein (Eds.), *Evocative images: The thematic apperception test and the art of projection*. Washington, DC: American Psychological Association.

McLoyd, V., & Steinberg, L. (Eds.). (1998). *Studying minority adolescents: Conceptual, methodological, and theoretical issues.* Mahwah, NJ: Lawrence Erlbaum Associates.

Morales, L., Lara, M., Kington, R., Valdez, R., & Escarce, J. (2002). Socioeconomic, cultural and behavioral factors affecting Hispanic health outcomes. *Journal of Healthcare for the Poor and Underserved, 13,* 477–503.

Murray, H. A. (1943). *Thematic Apperception Test.* Cambridge, MA: Harvard University Press.

Oakes, J. (1985). *Keeping track: How schools restructure inequality.* New Haven, CT: Yale University Press.

Ogbu, J. U., & Herbert, S. (1998). Voluntary and involuntary minorities: A cultural-ecological theory of school performance with some implications for education. *Anthropology and Education Quarterly, 29,* 155–188.

Olsen, L. (1997). *Made in America: Immigrant students in our public schools.* New York: New Press.

Orfield, G. (1995). *Latinos in education: Recent trends.* Unpublished manuscript, Harvard Graduate School of Education, Cambridge, MA.

Orfield, G., & Yun, J. T. (1999). *Resegregation in American schools.* Cambridge, MA: Harvard University, Civil Rights Project.

Palloni, A., & Morenoff, J. (2001). Interpreting the paradoxical in the Hispanic paradox: Demographic and epidemiological approaches. *Annals of the New York Academy of Sciences, 954,* 140–174.

Portes, A. (1996). Children of immigrants: Segmented assimilation and its determinants. In A. Portes (Ed.), *The economic sociology of immigration: Essays on networks, ethnicity, and entrepreneurship* (pp. 248–280). New York: Russell Sage Foundation.

Portes, A., & Rumbaut, R. G. (2001). *Legacies: The story of the second generation.* Berkeley: University of California Press.

Qin-Hilliard, D. (2003). Gendered expectations and gendered experiences: Immigrant students' adaptation in schools. In C. Suárez-Orozco & I. Todorova (Eds.), *New directions for youth development: Understanding the social worlds of immigrant youth* (pp. 91–109). San Francisco: Jossey-Bass.

Razum, O., & Twardella, D. (2002). Time travel with Oliver Twist: Toward an explanation for a paradoxically low mortality among recent immigrants. *Tropical Medicine and International Health, 7,* 4–10.

Rhodes, J. (2002). *Stand by me: The risks and rewards of youth mentoring relationships.* Cambridge, MA: Harvard University Press.

Roeser, R. W., & Eccles, J. S. (1998). Adolescents' perception of middle school: Relation to longitudinal changes in academic and psychological adjustment. *Journal of Research on Adolescence, 8,* 123–158.

Roffman, J., Suárez-Orozco, C., & Rhodes, J. (2003). Facilitating positive development in immigrant youth: The role of mentors and community organizations. In F. A. Villarruel, D. F. Perkins, L. M. Borden, & J. R. Keith (Eds.), *Community youth development: Programs, policies, and practices* (pp. 90–117). Thousand Oaks, CA: Sage.

Ruiz-de-Valasco, J., Fix, M., & Clewell, B. C. (2001). *Overlooked and under-served: Immigrant students in U.S. secondary schools.* Washington, DC: Urban Institute.

Rumbaut, R. G., & Cornelius, W. A. (1995). Educating California's immigrant children: Introduction and overview. In R. G. Rumbaut & W. A. Cornelius (Eds.), *California's immigrant children: Theory, research, and implications for educational policy* (pp. 1–16). La Jolla: University of California, San Diego, Center for U.S.-Mexican Studies.

Samdal, O., Nutbeam, D., Wold, B., & Kannas, L. (1998). Achieving health and educational goals through schools: A study of the importance of school climate and the student's satisfaction with school. *Health Education Research, 13,* 383–397.

Scribner, R. (1996). Editorial: Paradox as paradigm: The health outcomes of Mexican Americans. *American Journal of Public Health, 86,* 303–305.

Sluzki, C. (1979). Migration and family conflict. *Family Process, 18,* 379–390.

Smart, J. F., & Smart, D. W. (1995). Acculturation stress of Hispanics: Loss and challenge. *Journal of Counseling and Development, 75,* 390–396.

Somach, S. (1995). *Issues of war trauma and working with refugees: A compilation of resources.* Washington, DC: Center for Applied Linguistics Refugee Service Center.

Stanton-Salazar, R. D. (2001). *Manufacturing hope and despair: The school and kin support networks of U.S.-Mexican youth.* New York: Teachers College Press.

Steinberg, S., Brown, B. B., & Dornbusch, S. M. (1996). *Beyond the classroom.* New York: Simon and Schuster.

Suárez-Orozco, C. (2000). Identities under siege: Immigration stress and social mir-roring among the children of immigrants. In A. Robben & M. Suárez-Orozco (Eds.), *Cultures under siege: Social violence and trauma* (pp. 194–226). Cambridge: Cambridge University Press.

Suárez-Orozco, C. (2001). Afterword: Understanding and Serving the Children of Immigrants. *Harvard Educational Review, 71,* 579–589.

Suárez-Orozco, C. (2004). Formulating identity in a globalized world. In M. Suárez-Orozco & D. B. Qin-Hilliard (Eds.), *Globalization: Culture and education in the new millennium* (pp. 173–202). Berkeley: University of California Press.

Suárez-Orozco, C., & Suárez-Orozco, M. (1995). *Transformations: Immigration, family life, and achievement motivation among Latino adolescents.* Stanford, CA: Stanford University Press.

Suárez-Orozco, C., & Suárez-Orozco, M. (2001). *Children of immigration.* Cambridge, MA: Harvard University Press.

Suárez-Orozco, C., Suárez-Orozco, M., & Doucet, F. (2004). The academic engage-ment and achievement of Latino Youth. In J. A. Banks & C. A. M. Banks (Eds.), *Handbook of research on multicultural education* (2nd ed., pp. 420–437). San Francisco, CA: Jossey-Bass.

Suárez-Orozco, C., Todorova, I., & Louie, J. (2002). "Making up for lost time": The experience of separation and reunification among immigrant families. *Family Process, 41,* 625–643.

Suárez-Orozco, M. (1989). *Central American refugees and U.S. high schools: A psychosocial study of motivation and achievement.* Stanford, CA: Stanford University Press.

Suárez-Orozco, M. (2000). Everything you ever wanted to know about assimilation but were afraid to ask. *Daedalus: Journal of the American Academy of Arts and Sciences, 129*(4), 1–30.

Sue, D., & Sue, S. (1987). Cultural factors in the clinical assessment of Asian Americans. *Journal of Consulting and Clinical Psychology, 55,* 579–487.

Sue, S., & Okazaki, S. (1990). Asian-American educational achievements: A phenomenon in search of an explanation. *American Psychologist, 45,* 913–920.

Todorova, I., & Suárez-Orozco, C. (2002, November). *Changing countries, changing stories: Immigrant children's narratives projected with the Thematic Apperception Test.* Paper presented at the Murray Research Center Lecture Series, Radcliffe Institute for Advanced Study, Cambridge, MA.

Torseheim, T., & Wold, B. (2001). School-related stress, support, and subjective health complaints among early adolescents: A multilevel approach. *Journal of Adolescence, 24,* 701–713.

Tuan, M. (1995). Korean and Russian students in a Los Angeles high school: Exploring the alternative strategies of two high-achieving groups. In R. G. Rumbaut & W. A. Cornelius (Eds.), *California's immigrant children: Theory, research, and implications for educational policy.* (pp. 107–130). La Jolla: University of California, San Diego, Center for U.S.-Mexican Relations.

U.S. Department of Education. (2004). *Indicators of school crime and safety.* Retrieved September 23, 2005, from http://nces.ed.gov/pubs2005/2005002.pdf

Vernez, G., Abrahamse, A., & Quigley, D. (1996). *How immigrants fare in US education.* Santa Monica, CA: Rand.

Vigil, J. D. (1988). *Barrio gangs: Street life and identity in southern California.* Austin: University of Texas Press.

Voelker, R. (1994). Born in the USA: Infant health paradox. *Journal of the American Medical Association, 272,* 1803–1804.

Waters, M. (1996). The intersection of gender, race, and ethnicity in identity development of Caribbean American teens. In B. J. R. Leadbeater & N. Way (Eds.), *Urban girls: Resisting stereotypes, creating identities* (pp. 65–84). New York: New York University Press.

Williams, D. R., & Collins, C. (1995). US socioeconomic and racial difference in health: Patterns and explanations. *Annual Review of Sociology, 21,* 349–386.

Wills, T. A. (1985). Supportive functions of interpersonal relationships. In S. Cohen & S. L. Syme (Eds.), *Social support and health* (pp. 61–82). Orlando: Academic Press.

Wilson, W. (1997). *When work disappears: The world of the new urban poor.* New York: Vintage Books.

Wong-Fillmore, L. (1991). When learning a language means losing the first. *Early Childhood Research Quarterly, 6,* 323–346.

Zhou, M. (2000). *How community matters for immigrant children: Structural constraints and resources in Chinatown, Koreatown, and Pico-Union, Los Angeles.* Berkeley: University of California Press.

Zhou, M., & Bankston, C. I. (1998). *Growing up American: How Vietnamese children adapt to life in the United States.* New York: Russell Sage Foundation.

Chapter 4

LIFE WITH NO HOME: THE PLIGHT OF RUNAWAY YOUTH

Ruby J. Martinez

Each day, homeless and runaway youth face tremendous risks to their health and safety. They struggle to meet their basic emotional, social, and financial needs. Many have extensive histories of trauma, and, indeed, verbal, physical, and sexual abuse in the home are often cited by runaways as a principal reasons for running. Unfortunately, revictimization while living on the streets is common with high rates of rape, sexual exploitation, and physical injury. The grim reality of street life contributes to high levels of substance abuse, depression, and suicidal behavior among runaways. This chapter presents data on why youth run away from home, their experiences on the streets, and the difficulties they endure and comments on community programs attempting to serve this unique and vulnerable population.

It is difficult to estimate the actual size of the homeless youth population. They are highly mobile, live scattered throughout communities, and move in and out of domiciles and public institutions (Ringwalt, Greene, Robertson, & McPheeters, 1998). According to the National Survey on Drug Use and Health conducted by the Office of Applied Studies (OAS), approximately 7 percent of youth between the ages of 12 and 17 (1.6 million) had run away from home and slept on the street in 2002. These youth were primarily male (54.7%) and from metropolitan counties (80.1%). Sixty percent were White, 18.5 percent Black, 14.9 percent Hispanic, 3.2 percent Asian, and 1.8 percent American Indian–Alaska Native (OAS, 2003).

These numbers are similar to those found in another national survey conducted in 1992 that used the Centers for Disease Control and Prevention *Youth Risk Behavior Survey.* Interviews were completed on 6,496 teenagers, with African American and Hispanic youth oversampled. In this nationally representative sample, 7.6 percent reported at least one night of homelessness over the past 12 months; the results were consistent with prior studies that estimated the incidence of youth homelessness in the United States at approximately 1.5 million annually (Ringwalt et al., 1998). The prevalence of homelessness did not vary significantly by race, family poverty, family structure, or residence in any particular region of the country, but males were more likely than females to report homelessness. In any case, this population is one that is difficult to identify because of their desire to be invisible, especially to police or social services professionals, and often is visually indistinguishable from youths in general (Ringwalt et al., 1998).

Teens become homeless for many reasons. Although some choose to leave home seeking independence and the freedom to make their own decisions, most are trying to escape violence or abuse. Others are forced to leave (termed "throwaways") by parents intolerant of their teens' lifestyle (e.g., substance use or sexual orientation). Another group includes teens who are taken away from their home by government agencies and who then subsequently run from their placement either because they are experiencing abuse or because of a desire to return home. Only a small percentage or runaway teens become homeless because of the death of a parent.

PHYSICAL AND SEXUAL ABUSE

Whitbeck, Hoyt, and Ackley (1997) studied the accuracy of runaway and homeless adolescents' depictions of their prior family life. They found that regardless of who provided the information—adult parents/caretakers or the runaway youth—the responses were "strikingly and disturbingly" similar. Both report problematic parent–child relationships with low levels of parental monitoring, warmth, and supportiveness and high levels of parental rejection and family violence and critical levels of physical and sexual abuse.

MacLean, Embry, and Cauce (1999) studied the family characteristics of 356 homeless youths who were runaways or throwaways (parents demanded the child leave home) or were removed from their home by a government agency. Thirty-five percent of runaways, 36 percent of throwaways, and 56 percent of removed children reported sexual abuse, while 47 percent of runaways, 52 percent of throwaway children, and 63 percent of removed children reported physical abuse. Children from all three groups had high rates of revictimization on the streets, including assault, robbery, and rape. In another sample of 219 runaway/homeless youth, half reported sexual abuse, and a little more than half reported physical abuse. The sexually abused youth were more likely to meet criteria for conduct disorder and, in cases where drug use was present, were more likely to have a history of severe aggression (Booth & Zhang, 1996).

Researchers have questioned whether teens with histories of sexual abuse were more likely than nonabused teens to be revictimized on the street (Tyler, Hoyt, & Whitbeck, 2000). It was postulated that the psychological and emotional trauma suffered by sexually abused children renders them vulnerable and easily victimized by others in the harsh and high-risk environment of the street. They found that the early emotional and psychological problems of abused youths left them vulnerable to exploitation and revictimization, with serious and cumulative developmental consequences. As victims of physical and sexual abuse, runaways expressed feeling little or no control in effectively handling current and future sexual encounters, leaving them vulnerable to ongoing exploitation (Kaliski, Rubinson, Lawrance, & Levy, 1990).

Greene and Ringwalt (1998) found that girls who are homeless or runaways are at greater risk of pregnancy than girls living at home and of becoming pregnant during a time in their lives when they are least prepared physically, economically, and emotionally to handle childbirth. Their study compared four groups of youth: 85 street-dwelling youth, 169 shelter-dwelling youth, a household sample of 379 with recent runaway or homelessness experience, and a group of 1,609 household youth with no runaway/homeless experience. The standardized lifetime prevalence of pregnancy was 47.9 percent among street youth, 30.9 percent among shelter youth, 8.8 percent among youth with recent runaway or homeless experience, and 7.2 percent among those living in households with no runaway behavior (Greene & Ringwalt, 1998). In a study that included 219 runaway and homeless teens (54% male), more than 60 percent of the female subjects had been pregnant, and 39 percent of the male subjects knew of someone they had gotten pregnant (Booth & Zhang, 1996).

SURVIVAL ON THE STREETS

Martinez (in press) used an exploratory design to study teens who repeatedly ran from home or placement to learn how teens maintained their personal safety while on the streets. This sample of teens, recruited from a youth detention setting, reported that their ability to run away was a means to escape from undesirable or intolerable situations. Leaving home changed their problem set and gave them a greater sense of control over their lives. Run behavior initially served as an escape from an intolerable situation, but often running evolved into a chronic means of problem solving. As the teens developed street skills (and, for many, gang affiliations), they became more adept at life on the streets, usually surviving by engaging in drug dealing and other antisocial behavior. Gangs often served as surrogate families, but individual safety and survival was critically dependent on learning who to trust and how much.

Boa, Whitbeck, and Hoyt (2000) studied 602 homeless and runaway teens (40% males and 39% ethnic minority) and found that family abuse was positively correlated with depression, run behavior, and peer (as opposed to family) support. As runs became more frequent and prolonged, traditional support systems were replaced by nonconventional peer groups that provided companionship, emotional, and material assistance. The homeless adolescent became socialized to street life, receiving advice, learning survival skills, and affiliating with deviant peers. In this unsupervised, hostile environment interactions were often aggressive and coercive. Exploitation and victimization were common (Bao et al., 2000). Ennett, Bailey, and Federman (1999) examined characteristics of runaway teens' social networks to determine if there was any association with a greater or less likelihood of engaging in substance abuse and unsafe sexual behavior. Their sample was predominantly African American (80.4%), and most (96%) were repeat runners (median of six times). Approximately 25 percent of the sample reported no social relationships, and this was significantly and positively correlated with a greater risk of illicit drug use, having multiple sex partners, and engaging in survival sex. These findings support the concept that social integration has protective risk-deterring effects.

One of the most disturbing behaviors/choices that homeless youth make is "survival sex," the selling of sex to meet subsistence needs (Greene, Ennett, & Ringwalt, 1999). Young, relatively inexperienced runaways with few skills and limited mobility, not initially aware of the street economy, often are compelled to rely on prostitution as a means of obtaining money for the day's food and shelter (Clatts, Davis, Sotheran, & Atillasoy, 1998). Survival sex appears to be more prevalent in street-dwelling youth compared with shelter-dwelling youth and prevalent across all racial and ethnic groups. In a study of survival sex using a nationally representative sample of shelter and street youth ($n = 631$), 2.1 percent of Black and 11.6 percent of White youth residing in a shelter engaged in survival sex, compared to 23.8 percent of Black and 28.8 percent of White youth living on the street. Of all other respondents in this sample, 10.8 percent of shelter-dwelling youth compared with 28.5 percent of youth living on the street engaged in survival sex (Greene et al., 1999). Survival sex was strongly associated with recent substance use indicators and with lifetime injection drug use (Greene et al., 1999).

As the emotional degradation inherent in sexual exploitation becomes progressively debilitating over time, there is increased self-medication through the use of street drugs (Clatts et al., 1998). Sexual conduct and drug use are co-occurring high-risk behaviors with serious short- and long-term consequences. Youth who had been sexually abused were significantly more likely to engage in unprotected sex acts, had more partners, and reported more use of alcohol and illicit drug use than a nonabused sample (Rotheram-Borus, Mahler, Koopman, & Langabeer, 1996).

The extreme sensitivity of discussing one's sexual behaviors, especially trading sex for money or other favors, obscures the accuracy of data on the prevalence of survival sex. Yates, MacKenzie, Pennbridge, and Cohen (1988) found that about 26 percent of their sample engaged in survival sex, and similar findings (28%) occurred in another study of runaway youth by Greene and colleagues (1999), while only 11 percent of youth reported trading sex for money or drugs in another sample (Van Leeuwen et al., 2004). Bailey, Camlin, and Ennett (1998) studied a sample of 327 homeless and runaway youth and found that 44.6 percent reported giving or receiving sex in exchange for money, drugs, food, or shelter and that 45.1 percent reported that they were not motivated to use a condom despite expressing knowledge about how HIV infection is spread (Bailey et al., 1998).

Tragically, a runaway's immediate needs outweigh any concern for the future. This population does not believe they are at risk for HIV infection. because of the long latency period between infection and appearance of symptoms, runaways may not perceive AIDS to occur in adolescents (Kaliski et al., 1990). Efforts to educate and change the sex risk behaviors of homeless youth have been discouraging. Booth, Zhang, and Kwiatkowski (1999) and others have found that the relationship between greater AIDS knowledge and lower-risk behaviors was not supported and that peer intervention models were ineffective. In a collaborative effort with the Center for Disease Control and Prevention, Allen et al. (1994) conducted HIV seroprevalence surveys of homeless populations from 1989 to 1992. Five study sites specifically served runaway youth. In this sample, HIV seroprevalence rates ranged from 0 to 7.3 percent with females having prevalence rates similar to homosexual/bisexual males and African Americans having higher rates than Whites.

SUBSTANCE ABUSE

Substance abuse is multifactorial with genetic, psychosocial, and environmental influences. It was a recurring theme before and during a teen's life on the streets. An estimated one in seven children in the United States live in households with one or more adults who abused or were dependent on alcohol in the past year. Marijuana, cocaine, and heroine are widely available and prices have fallen to record lows (U.S. Department of Health and Human Services [USDHHS], Center for Substance Abuse Research, 2000). Researchers have long reasoned that substance abuse is a coping strategy that allows people to avoid (at least temporarily) unpleasant emotional states by altering awareness and judgment (Denoff, 1987).

In a sample of 432 homeless youth living in both service centers and street hangout sites, Kipke, Montgomery, Simon, and Iverson (1997) found that 71 percent of this sample met criteria from the *Diagnostic and Statistical Manual of Mental Disorders* (3rd ed.; *DSM-III*) for either alcohol or drug abuse disorder and that 43 percent met the criteria for both. These and other researchers found that the length of time youth were homeless was positively associated with both the risk of alcohol abuse and drug abuse disorders (Van Leeuwen et al., 2004).

National studies indicate that youth who had run away reported higher rates of alcohol, marijuana, and illicit drug use than those who did not, and this difference was present across age and gender groups. For example, 50 percent of youth who had run away reported alcohol use in the past year, compared to 33 percent of youth who had not (OAS, 2003). Alcohol and marijuana were the most frequently reported substances of abuse. Van Leeuwen et al. (2004) reported that 69 percent ($n = 109$) of their sample used alcohol and that 75 percent ($n = 119$) used marijuana in the past nine months with 12 percent reporting daily use of alcohol and 52 percent reporting daily marijuana use.

Whitbeck, Johnson, Hoyt, and Cauce (2004) compared a sample of 428 homeless/runaway youth against a national sample of youth living at home. Forty-seven percent of the runaway males and 40 percent of the females met *DSM* criteria for alcohol abuse compared with 9 percent of control group males and 6 percent of females who participated in the National Co-morbidity Survey (NCS). Results for drug abuse were also significantly different for these two samples: 47 percent of homeless males and 35 percent of homeless females met criteria for drug abuse compared to 4 percent of NCS males and 2 percent of NCS females. Males and females did not differ on their likelihood of meeting lifetime prevalence of alcohol abuse; however, males were more like than females to meet the criteria for drug abuse.

Research also suggests significant rates of use of heroine in this population. While daily heroine use was reported in 26 percent ($n = 6$) of the study group, a much higher number (44%, or $n = 10$) reported using heroine one to three times per month in that same sample (Van Leeuwen et al., 2004). When youth inject drugs, they risk infection by blood-borne pathogens such as hepatitis and HIV. In one sample of 186 homeless youth (ages 12 to 23) living in three cities in northern California, almost half the sample reported injecting drug use (IDU), beginning at an average age of 17 (Martinez et al., 1998). Sixty-one percent of the sample had been on the streets longer than one year, 58 percent were male, 82 percent were White, and 76 percent described themselves as heterosexual. Fifty-three percent of IDU youth reported traumatic history events, while only 25 percent of non-IDU youth reported the same. The most commonly reported traumatic events for this sample included being kicked out of their parent's home (20%), forced institutionalization (19.3%), physical abuse (12%), introduction to illicit drug use by their parents (18.1%), parental substance abuse (19.3%), and sexual abuse (6%). Almost half the IDU group reported sharing needles with others.

As expected, street youth report more serious health problems than youth who live in shelters with higher rates of emergency room visits related to alcohol or drug use. Half the street youth and more than a third of the sheltered youth in this study had no routine health care source (Klein et al., 2000).

MENTAL ILLNESS

In a previously mentioned study, Whitbeck and colleagues (2004) compared a sample of 428 runaway/homeless youth living in eight cities across the Midwest to a same-aged population of teens from the NCS sample to compare prevalence rates of mental disorders and co-occurring disorders between the two groups. They found that 89 percent of the homeless/runaway youth met *DSM-III-R* criteria for at least one major mental disorder compared to 33 percent of the NCS sample and that 67.3 percent of the homeless/runaway youth met criteria for two or more disorders compared to 10.3 percent of the NCS sample. Runaway and homeless youth in this sample met *DSM* criteria more often than the NCS sample in all areas of studied mental illnesses. For example, the homeless/runaway teens were more than twice as likely to meet criteria for a major depressive disorder than the NCS sample (30% vs. 14%), four times more likely to meet criteria for conduct disorder (76% vs. 18%), and seven times more likely to meet criteria for posttraumatic stress disorder (PTSD) (36% vs. 5%). Even with the researchers cautioning that the NCS used a probability sample and this research did not, these prevalence rates for both groups are alarming.

The prevalent nature of pre- and in-run trauma experienced by runaways corresponds to high prevalence rates of PTSD in this group. Taylor and Chemtob (2004) reviewed the efficacy of treatments for child and adolescent traumatic stress. Of the 102 reports identified, only eight randomized controlled studies were found. None of these, though, involved the efficacy of pharmacotherapy despite a recent report that 95 percent of child psychiatrists have used pharmacotherapy (primarily selective serotonin reuptake inhibitor and alpha-adrenergic agonists) to treat childhood and adolescent PTSD. On an encouraging note, though, they found that regardless of the treatment choice (cognitive behavioral therapy, eye movement desensitization and reprocessing, or individual/group psychotherapy), all treatment options led to substantial reductions in symptoms and improved functioning in subjects.

"The relationship between familial substance use and suicide attempts by youth suggests that such use has a profound adverse effect on the emotional and behavioral functioning of youth" (Greene & Ringwalt, 1996, p. 1054). Youth with family members who had used substances were twice as likely to have ever attempted suicide—a finding that is independent of the youth's own substance use (though this too was positively correlated with attempted suicide). In a nationally representative sample of youth residing in shelters and a multi-city purposive sample of youth on the streets, Greene and Ringwalt (1996) found that one-fourth of the shelter participants and one-third of the street youths reported suicide attempts. Stiffman (1989) reported that suicide attempters have significantly more behavioral and mental health problems than the nonattempters, particularly in the areas of depression and drug and alcohol use. Thirty percent of runaway youths in her study had attempted suicide (80% of the attempters were female) and had three times the rate of heavy alcohol use and twice the rate of regular illicit drug use compared to nonattempters. The lack of services that might effectively reach these needy youth is emphasized by the finding that half the teenage suicide attempters never received any professional help following their attempt.

Molnar, Shade, Kral, Booth, and Watters (1998) examined the relationship between prior home life risk factors and suicide attempts in three large metropolitan cities ($N = 775$). They found that sexual and physical abuse before leaving home were independent predictors of suicide attempts for females and males. Females reported sexual abuse (70% with a mean age of first incident of 9.0 years) more than physical abuse (35%). Males were more likely to report physical abuse (35%) compared to sexual abuse (24% with a mean age of first incident of 9.9 years). The authors found that of the participants who reported both sexual abuse before leaving home and having attempted suicide, 79 percent reported that their first sexual abuse occurred at a younger age than their first suicide attempt. Their finding that 72 percent of females and 51 percent of males reported suicidal ideation, with 48 percent of females and 27 percent of males reporting previous suicide attempts (34% of the total study population) is consistent with rates from several other studies.

For street youth, "the self devaluation process may play an integral role in adolescent suicide by hampering the adolescent's ability to generate problem solving strategies and by distorting the assessment of required skills necessary for more effective and less self destructive forms of adaptation" (Denoff, 1987, p. 584). Consistent findings of high levels of stress and depression among runaways (Ayerst, 1999) are revealed in the rates of mental illness in this population. Rohr (1996) found that runaways have a distinctive personality profile that is significantly different from a nonrunaway control group but remarkably similar to a known adolescent mental health clinical group in a university-based day treatment program (DTP). A personality inventory for children screening tool was administered to the three groups. Of the 10 measured variables, four were determined to have high predictive value. Low scores on adjustment, achievement, and family relations plus a high score on delinquency identified runaways with 97.5 percent accuracy; conversely, high scores for adjustment, achievement, and family relations and a low delinquency score correctly identified 100 percent of the nonrunaway control group. Disturbingly, similar rates of mental illness were found between the runaway group and the DTP group with known moderate to severe psychopathology. In this runaway sample (80% female), 73 percent met diagnostic criteria for dysthymia or major depression, 59 percent had attempted suicide or experienced suicidal ideation, and 29 percent had a prior mental illness history. In another study, Shelton (2001) examined the rate of emotional disorders in the juvenile justice system and found that 53 percent of the children had a diagnosable mental disorder(s) and that 46 percent had difficulty in their daily functioning. Given the significant overlap between delinquent behavior and mental disorder, Shelton questioned the ability of either the juvenile justice system or the mental health system to adequately provide for the needs of these teens.

Booth and Zhang (1997) administered the Diagnostic Interview Schedule for Children to 219 runaway and homeless adolescents and found that half the males and 60 percent of the females could be given a diagnosis of conduct disorder, while Whitbeck et al. (2004) found that as many as 83 percent of male and 70 percent of female runaways met criteria for conduct disorder. Conduct disorder is characterized by antisocial behaviors in which the basic rights of others and major age-appropriate norms are violated. This includes a diverse set of maladaptive behaviors, including lying, stealing, physical aggression and cruelty, and impaired interpersonal functioning.

Foster Home Placements

In 1994, 502,000 children lived in foster care (USDHHS, Children's Bureau, 1997). This number has more than doubled over the past decade, and the increase is thought to be related to increasing rates of poverty, homelessness, substance abuse, HIV infection within families, and fewer resources for permanent placements (Simms, 1998). When children are removed from their home, they typically experience stress associated with the isolation of being removed from family and friends. This stress is further intensified by frequent placement changes, especially common with older foster children (Pelzer, 1995).

The racial/ethnic distribution of children placed in foster care about a decade ago was 46 percent African American, 42 percent White, and

12 percent Hispanic. African American children were more likely than White children to be placed in foster care (versus in-home care) even when they shared the same problems and characteristics. The majority of White and Hispanic children received in-home services (72% and 60%, respectively), while the majority of African American children were placed in foster care (56%). Children who received in-home services stayed in the child welfare system for an average of three months, versus 26 months for those in foster care (USDHHS, Children's Bureau, 1997).

Taussig (2002) examined protective and vulnerability factors in a longitudinal study of youth placed in foster care. In this study, youth and their caretakers were interviewed and assessed six months following the youth's admission to foster care. The youth were reinterviewed five years later regarding their involvement in four domains of risk behavior (sexual, delinquent/violent, substance use, and suicidal/self-destructive behaviors) and with a unitary construct, the Total Risk Behavior Scale. The participants who completed both the time 1 and the time 2 measures consisted of 110 (from a total of 214 original participants) ethnically diverse youth aged 7 to 12. Sixty percent of these 110 youth were female, 43.6 percent were Caucasian, 36.4 percent were African American, and 20 percent were Hispanic. A little more than 58 percent had substantiated neglect, 41.8 percent experienced caretaker abuse, 22.7 percent experienced physical abuse, 16.4 percent had experienced sexual abuse, and 10.9 percent reported other maltreatment such as emotional abuse. At the time 2 interview, more than half ($n = 57$) of the participants' cases had been closed; most of these ($n = 43$) were closed because of reunification with family. Other closed cases included those who were adopted ($n = 8$) or permanently placed with relatives/guardians; three were incarcerated, two had gone AWOL, and one was emancipated. Of the 53 youth with open cases, about half were in nonrelative foster care, 32.1 percent were in kinship placement, and the remaining 15.1 percent were living in group home or residential treatment centers.

The study concluded that increased age was positively correlated with substance use, sexual behavior, and total risk behavior. Gender was not significantly related to any of the dependent variables. Ethnicity was predictive of self-destructive behavior. African Americans reported the lowest levels, followed by Caucasian youth, with Hispanic youth reporting the highest levels of self-destructive behavior. Further, Caucasian youth were less likely to engage in delinquent behavior than were Hispanic youth. Sexual abuse was not significantly related to any of the dependent variables (the risk domains), but physical abuse predicted more delinquency and total risk behavior scores, while neglect predicted more delinquent and substance use scores (Taussig, 2002).

Researchers have described the existing "systemic abuse and neglect" that occurs with the failure of substitute care arrangement in the child welfare system (Kufeldt & Nimmo, 1987). Shelter-based foster youth (Ensign, 2001) have poor access to care and services, for foster care children are characterized by overutilization of emergency room services and underutilization of nonemergent ambulatory care settings (Rubin, Alessandrini, Feudtner, Localio, & Hadley, 2004). When children enter foster care, a thorough physical examination is often required, but comprehensive mental health and developmental health assessments are much less common (Leslie et al., 2003). The foster care systems are given the enormous task of ensuring the safety and well-being of at-risk children, often without evidence-based guidance or the necessary resources to ensure the safety of the children. Despite the challenges of this system, research indicates that for some youth, functioning improves over time while in foster care placement (Horwitz, Balestracci, & Simms, 2001). Because of such research, the belief that reunification of children in foster care with their family of origin is the most favorable outcome for a child has been challenged. Comparisons between reunified and nonreunified youth suggest that reunified youth had more frequent and serious problems on returning home. Reunified youth reported more self-destructive behavior, substance abuse, and delinquent behavior were more likely to drop out of school or to receive lower grades than those who were not reunified (Taussig, Clyman, & Landsverk, 2001). These authors caution that returning to a home that once had significant stressors does not ensure a positive outcome.

JUVENILE DETENTION

When youth repeatedly run away from home or placement, they may be held in juvenile detention for failure to comply with court orders to reside in placement. In 1996, 141,844 children were arrested for running away from home, and girls represented 57 percent ($n = 81,003$) of this population. In America, children are arrested for running away at 65 times the rate of children arrested for homicides (Schiraldi & Ziedenberg, 1999). Runaway youth who refuse to live in placement are held for "status offenses," which are victimless acts that primarily involve nonviolent crimes. Once in the detention center, the teens can be mixed with other youth populations with more serious charges, such as homicide, rape, or theft.

In a review of the mental health needs of youth in the juvenile justice system, Cocozza and Skowyra (2000) present several disturbing findings. An estimated one in five youth in the juvenile justice system suffers from a serious mental health disorder, often with a co-occurring substance abuse disorder. There is a disturbing trend toward relying on the justice system to care for individuals with mental illness despite a lack of adequate research or known effective treatment models in this setting. Even where programs are available, they are often understaffed, underfunded, and inadequately prepared to work with this specialized population. As part of the "get tough" movement of the 1990s, the juvenile justice system has shifted from treatment and rehabilitation toward retribution and punishment, increasing the confusion about who is responsible for providing mental health services to incarcerated youth.

Cocozza and Skowyra (2000) outlined several potential strategies to meet the growing challenges surrounding the treatment of these youth. Cross-system coordination for strategic planning and budgeting is essential. Utilizing a team approach and staff cross training would allow for a comprehensive screening and continuous assessment of each youth that would be maintained throughout the process of intake, adjudication, disposition, and aftercare. Youth with serious mental disorders should, when possible, be diverted into appropriate community-based services that allow youth to remain in their home, school, and neighborhood.

RESILIENCE

Resilience in youth, including the runaway, is an evolving concept. It was first described as the ability to survive and adapt to adversity or trauma and to bounce back after significant struggles in life. Resiliency has been associated with both internal and external protective factors that contribute to the youth's ability to thrive despite adversity. Internal factors include mental processes such as temperament, intelligence, sense of humor, empathic abilities, and internal locus of control. External factors relate to family cohesion, warmth, and love by at least one parent. Masten (2004) provides insight into factors that can contribute to better outcomes for adolescents who have suffered significant psychosocial adversity. Establishing and maintaining connections to competent and caring parent(s) or adult mentors or to community organizations (school, shelters, and community-based organizations) that provide support, structure, and accountability helps high-risk teens negotiate the stress and confusion in their lives. Teens that are hopeful for their future are motivated to behave in ways that are more likely to positively impact their future. Developing problem-solving skills allows for more effective planning, coordination, and implementation of actions with a greater chance of attaining the desired outcome. Integrating these components with self-awareness and introspection allows teens to make adaptive course corrections when in risky environments. These and other internal and external regulatory processes play key roles in psychosocial growth and the development of resilience.

The literature suggests that resilient behavior differs depending on the individual life circumstances of the teen. For instance, a running child in crisis and struggling to adapt to life on the streets will, of necessity, choose different behaviors than a child living in a stable, supportive, loving environment. Hunter and Chandler (1999) studied resilience in adolescents using a rating scale, free-writing exercises, and focus groups that encouraged adolescents to tell their stories of overcoming adversity in their lives. Their sample consisted of 51 inner-city teens from a vocational high school (22 were Latino, 20 were Black, and 6 were White). Teens who identified themselves as resilient (girls less so than boys) characterized themselves as being insular, disconnected, self-reliant, and self-protective, with no one to depend on or trust but themselves. For them, resilience meant developing a skill set that stressed independence, self-awareness, and a survival strategy that depended on detachment from others. The potential risk of this approach to life is an unhealthy sense of self and self-worth and difficulty trusting and connecting with others. Caucasian teens perceived themselves to be less resilient than their Latino and African American peers. The researchers concluded that resilience in adolescence may not be an adaptive process of overcoming adversity but instead may be a survival process of defense that includes behaviors such as isolation, disconnecting, denial, and aggression that allows them to be self-reliant and not have to trust or depend on others.

Rew, Taylor-Seehafer, Thomas, and Yockey (2001) studied resilience in homeless youth by administering a series of surveys. The sample consisted of 59 homeless youth (ages 15 to 22) recruited from a street outreach program in central Texas. Sixty-four percent of the sample was male, 61 percent Caucasian, 12 percent African American, 19 percent Latino, 2 percent Native American, and 5 percent listed "Other" for ethnicity. Nearly half the sample reported a history of sexual abuse, and more than a third self-identified as homosexual or bisexual in orientation. More than half the sample reported that they were asked to leave home by their parents, and 37 percent left because of disapproval of their alcohol or drug use. Overall, the mean resilience score (using the Resilience Scale) was relatively high at 4.48 for this sample (range of 1 to 7), with 1 being not resilient and 7 being very resilient. These researchers found that resiliency was significantly and negatively correlated with loneliness, hopelessness, and life-threatening behaviors. Surprisingly, they also found resilience to be significantly and negatively correlated with connectedness. They concluded that despite being disconnected from conventional social structures, youth who perceived themselves as resilient (able to cope with adversity) were less lonely and less hopeless and engaged in fewer life-threatening behaviors compared with those who perceived themselves as nonresilient. These researchers questioned whether resilience in homeless youth was a different phenomenon than for youth thriving in traditional family and social connections.

Stefanidis, Pennbridge, MacKenzie, and Pottharst (1992) attempted to correlate past experiences and current behaviors of runaways with their ability to move from crisis intervention into stable living situations. Unfortunately, many homeless youth have often experienced rejection and maltreatment, are mistrustful of close relationships, and are unwilling to allow themselves to rely on others. They deny wanting or needing care from others and exaggerate their feelings of well-being. They often ridicule other young people who are seeking help and refuse help for themselves even when they need it. Some would use threats of violence, disrespect, and vulgar language to disrupt services.

The social network of street youth is characterized by nonconventional relationships and enhanced vulnerability. Bao et al. (2000) identified that when adolescents strike out on their own, they are involved in an age-segregated nonconventional support system made up of young people who have many of the same problems. For these teens, the peer support system becomes an important primary source of social support that provides not only companionship but also material aid, emotional support, and the teaching of survival skills on the streets. However, the more the adolescent becomes separated from family influences and adult supervision, the greater the likelihood that he or she will associate with deviant peers (Fleisher, 1998). Peer networks can both create risk and serve as a protective factor. A teen may engage in deviant behavior with the same peer group that may in one instance provide instrumental and emotional social support and in the next victimize him or her physically, financially, or sexually (Bao et al., 2000). The structure (role relationships) and context (physical/emotional support) of the runaway's social relationships have important behavioral consequences—the behaviors can receive support or sanction, and the social networks' cumulative effect can be contradictory (Ennett et al., 1999).

Street life for most teens is, at least initially, perceived as a viable alternative to their current life circumstances. Denoff (1987) considered this a reflection of the social and developmental limitations on a teenager's ability to conceptualize options in response to stresses in his or her life. Teens view conflict or difficulties at home as unresolvable, beyond their physical or emotional endurance, and unmanageable within the current family circumstances. Thus, despite its inherent danger, running away often provides the teen with a temporary solution to a painful problem (Stefanidis et al., 1992).

PREVENTION AND INTERVENTION

Life for the runaway teen is often simply a new version of the conflicts and abuses that they had hoped to escape by leaving home. The street is a harsh environment, and many of the teens who live there are self-reliant, are untrusting of systems, and engage in antisocial behavior in order to survive. It is unclear whether runaways arrive on the street possessing these attributes or whether life on the street cultivates them. It is clear, however, that while teens are busy "running" and surviving, they are not focused on their education, developing their self-identity, or establishing goals for their young adult years. While many become parents at an early age, few have had positive role models for healthy relationships or parenting.

Resilience in this population appears to be related to the ability to be self-reliant and unattached to others. While the characteristics of self-reliance, aggression, and a general distrust of others were necessary in order to survive the experience of homelessness, these characteristics create significant obstacles when working with these teens in school, placements, and treatment. Adults providing services to this group must be prepared for resistance, testing of limits, and trust to be gained only with time, patience, and understanding. In agencies where teens receive services or care, a stable, consistent, supportive staff is essential to create an atmosphere of acceptance and willingness to help. The abuses, violence, and exploitation suffered before and during their runs require sensitive and compassionate understanding. They may not be willing to disclose their "reality" for fear of disapproval or judgment on poor choices, risky behaviors, and substance abuse.

Existing research on this population has indicated that there are many types of runaway teens, each with unique needs. Some teens left home out of necessity for their safety and may or may not desire to return home, while others would like to live at home but are not welcome to do so. Others were removed from their home by social services, and some of these are running away from placement, still with the hope of eventually getting back to their biological parents. Those who have been removed are often disappointed that the system is unable to help them reunite with family and that their foster home experience and run to the street were no less violent than what had occurred in their home of origin (Martinez, in press). They often hold an idealized view, believing that if they would be able to return home, things would be different than before. They maintain the hope that they will be wanted and welcomed home. We have not yet mastered a plan to care for whole families or whole communities in crisis.

While the social services system removes children from abusive homes with the goal of providing safety for them, that system must examine itself and account for the abuse in foster homes and the multiple failed foster home placements, especially for youth of color. The system could be made more effective using an oversight committee of child advocates (community members, social scientists, health specialists, educators, and juvenile justice advocates) who have sufficient power to order services, shift funding, change assignments of social service workers, and design new services for children with special needs. The system could develop new ways of ensuring safety for children that does not include permanent removal of the child from home. New technology may allow for better monitoring of safety. If children are removed from home, the system must be able to ensure that it can provide a safe and nurturing setting in which they can thrive.

Runaway youth are, as a group, a disenfranchised segment of our society and have little clout in meeting their needs through legal and socially acceptable channels. Overall, they are uneducated, work minimum-wage jobs or are unemployed, and avoid contact with systems that might attempt to confine and control them. Most have few support systems outside their peer group, numerous health risks, and a limited ability to effect change in their lives. They are in many ways an invisible segment of our society, yet their presence reminds us of the social problems of decades past that continue today. Many of their parents, perhaps involving several generations, used some of the same harmful coping strategies.

The availability of mental health services is essential given the prevalence of mental illness and substance abuse disorders within this population. Diagnostic and treatment services should be available in all systems that affiliate with youth, including schools, detention centers, drop-in centers, group homes, foster care, and faith-based systems. Because of the stigma attached to the need for mental health services, these services should be present in primary health clinics, with the mental health and primary care provider in side-by-side offices. In school systems, teachers and nurses must work together to identify at-risk youth and be confident that when abuse is identified, systems are available and ready to deal with the problem with the goal of keeping families together whenever possible. Because these youth often have few positive role models, guidance on healthy relationships with self and others is needed. The complex social and health problems associated with serious emotional disturbance in youth require a systems approach in which multiple service sectors work in an organized, collaborative way (USDHHS, 1999).

Innovative and nontraditional means of educating runaway youth are needed to enable them to join the workforce in gainful employment. While the GED is often viewed as the standard for basic education, this is not always the best path for some of these youth. Runaway teens are among the poorest citizens, and most need to be employed immediately; others are willing to live in a shelter while they pursue their educational needs. For those youth who need to support themselves, on-the-job training may be the best alternative. Job readiness skills may be needed in order for them to learn how to be a responsible employee. For some youth, leaving a lucrative life of crime for a minimum-wage job is difficult from a financial perspective. For these youth, counseling can be useful to explore this decision.

Finally, effective intervention with teens who live on the streets may require changes in current policy. In one study using a diverse sample of runaway youth, those under the age of 18 who did not want their parents to know of their whereabouts reported that they avoided certain shelters that required them to show identification. They avoided health care settings where service providers were required to report cases of assault, abuse, or suicidal/homicidal intent. They viewed drop-in centers more positively than shelters because they were more flexible and required less paperwork and there was less necessity to disclose personal information. Although not all youth in the sample wanted to leave street life, those who did reported wanting help in planning, advice, support, and life skill training from service providers. They noted that providing for their daily survival needs such as food and a place to stay often conflicted with finding and holding a job. They explained that many services (obtaining food) were available only during the business hours. Despite motivation to leave the streets, many found themselves "stuck" on the streets (DeRosa et al., 1999).

REFERENCES

Allen, D., Lehman, S., Green, T., Lindegren, M., Onorato, I., Forrester, W., & Field Services Branch. (1994). HIV infection among homeless adults and runaway youth, United States, 1982–1992. *AIDS, 8,* 1593–1598.

Ayerst, S. (1999). Depression and stress in street youth. *Adolescence, 34*(135), 567–575.

Bailey, S., Camlin, C., & Ennett, S. (1998). Substance use and risky sexual behavior among homeless and runaway youth. *Journal of Adolescent Health, 23,* 378–388.

Bao, W., Whitbeck, L., & Hoyt, D. (2000). Abuse, support and depression among homeless and runaway adolescents. *Journal of Health and Social Behavior, 41,* 408–420.

Booth, R., & Zhang, Y. (1996). Severe aggression and related conduct problems among runaway and homeless adolescents. *Psychiatric Services, 47,* 75–80.

Booth, R., & Zhang, Y. (1997). Conduct disorder and HIV risk behaviors among runaway and homeless adolescents. *Drug and Alcohol Dependence, 48,* 69–76.

Booth, R., Zhang, Y., & Kwiatkowski, C. (1999). The challenge of changing drug and sex risk behaviors of runaway and homeless adolescents, *Child Abuse and Neglect 23,* 1295–1306.

Clatts, M., Davis, W., Sotheran, J., & Atillasoy, A. (1998). Correlates and distri-
    bution of HIV risk behaviors among homeless youths in New York City:
    Implications for prevention and policy. *Child Welfare, 77,* 195–207.
Cocozza, J., & Skowyra, K. (2000). Youth with mental health disorders: Issues
    and emerging responses. *Juvenile Justice, 7,* 3–13.
Denoff, M. (1987). Cognitive appraisal in three forms of adolescent maladjustment.
    Social Casework: The Journal of Contemporary Social Work, 68, 579–588.
De Rosa, C., Montgomery, S., Kipke, M., Iverson, E., Ma, J., & Unger, J. (1999).
    Service utilization among homeless and runaway youth in Los Angeles,
    CA: Rates and reasons. *Journal of Adolescent Health, 24,* 449–458.
Ennett, S., Bailey, S., & Federman, E. (1999). Social network characteristics
    associated with risky behaviors among runaway and homeless youth.
    Journal of Health and Social Behavior, 40, 63–78.
Ensign, J. (2001). The health of shelter-based foster youth. *Public Health Nursing,
    18,* 19–33.
Fleisher, M. S. (1998). *Dead End Kids—Gang girls and the boys they know.*
    Madison: University of Wisconsin Press.
Greene, J., Ennett, S., & Ringwalt, C. (1999). Prevalence and correlates of sur-
    vival sex among runaway and homeless youth. *American Journal of Public
    Health, 89,* 1406–1409.
Greene, J., & Ringwalt, C. (1996). Youth and familial substance use's association
    with suicide attempts among runaway and homeless youth. *Substance Use
    and Misuse, 31,* 1041–1058.
Greene, J., & Ringwalt, C. (1998). Pregnancy among three national samples of
    runaway and homeless youth. *Journal of Adolescent Health, 23,* 370–377.
Horwitz, S., Balestracci, K., & Simms, M. (2001). Foster care placement improves
    children's functioning. *Archives of Pediatric Adolescent Medicine, 155,*
    1255–1260.
Hunter, A., & Chandler, G. (1999). Adolescent resilience. *Image—The Journal of
    Nursing Scholarship, 31,* 243–247.
Kaliski, E., Rubinson, L., Lawrance, L., & Levy, S. (1990). AIDS, runaways, and
    self-efficacy. *Family Community Health, 13,* 65–72.
Kipke, M., Montgomery, S., Simon, T., & Iverson, E. (1997). "Substance abuse"
    disorders among runaway and homeless youth. *Substance Use and Misuse,
    32,* 969–986.
Klein, J., Woods, A., Wilson, K., Prospero, M., Greene, J., & Ringwalt, C.
    (2000). Homeless and runaway youths' access to health care. *Journal of
    Adolescent Health, 27,* 331–339.
Kufeldt, K., & Nimmo, M. (1987). Youth on the street: abuse and neglect in the
    eighties. *Child Abuse and Neglect, 11,* 531–543.
Leslie, L., Hurlburt, M., Landsverk, J., Rolles, J., Wood, P., & Kelleher, K. (2003).
    Comprehensive assessments for children entering foster care: a national
    perspective. *Pediatrics, 112,* 134–142.
MacLean, M., Embry, L., & Cauce, A. (1999). Homeless adolescents' paths to sep-
    aration from family: Comparison of family characteristics, psychological

adjustment, and victimization. *Journal of Community Psychology, 27,* 179–187.

Martinez, R. (in press). Understanding runaway teens. *Journal of Child and Adolescent Psychiatric Nursing.*

Martinez, T., Gleghorn, A., Marx, R., Clements, K., Boman, M., & Katz, M. (1998). Psychosocial histories, social environment, and HIV risk behaviors of injection and noninjection drug using homeless youths. *Journal of Psychoactive Drugs, 30,* 1–10.

Masten, A. (2004). Regulatory processes, risk, and resilience in adolescent development. *Annals of the New York Academy of Science, 1021,* 310–319.

Molnar, B., Shade, S., Kral, A., Booth, R., & Watters, J. (1998). Suicidal behavior and sexual/physical abuse among street youth. *Child Abuse and Neglect, 22,* 213–222.

Office of Applied Studies. (2003). *Results from the 2002 National Survey on Drug Use and Health: National findings* (DHHS Publication No. SMA 03–3836, NHSDA Series H-22). Rockville, MD: Substance Abuse and Mental Health Services Administration.

Pelzer, D. (1993). *A child called "It": One child's courage to survive.* Deerfield Beach, FL: Health Communications, Inc.

Pelzer, D. (1995). *The lost boy: A foster child's search for the love of a family.* Deerfield Beach, FL: Health Communications, Inc.

Rew, L., Taylor-Seehafer, M., Thomas, N., & Yockey, R. (2001). Correlates of resilience in homeless adolescents. *Journal of Nursing Scholarship, 33,* 33–40.

Ringwalt, C., Greene, J., Robertson, M., & McPheeters, M. (1998). The prevalence of homelessness among adolescents in the United States. *American Journal of Public Health, 88,* 1325–1329.

Rohr, M. (1996). Identifying adolescent runaways: The predictive utility of the personality inventory for children. *Adolescence, 31*(123), 605–623.

Rotheram-Borus, M., Mahler, K., Koopman, C., & Langabeer, K. (1996). Sexual abuse history and associated multiple risk behaviors in adolescent runaways. *American Journal of Orthopsychiatry, 66,* 390–400.

Rubin, D., Alessandrini, E., Feudtner, C., Localio, A., & Hadley, T. (2004). *Pediatrics, 114,* 354–360.

Schiraldi, V., & Ziedenberg, J. (1999). Runaway juvenile crime? The context of juvenile arrests in America. Washington, DC: Justice Policy Institute. Retrieved September 19, 2005, from http://www.cjcj.org/jpi/runaway.html

Shelton, D. (2001). Emotional disorders in young offenders. *Journal of Nursing Scholarship, 33,* 259–263.

Simms, M. (1998). Medical care of children who are homeless or in foster care. *Current Opinion in Pediatrics, 10,* 486–490.

Stefanidis, N., Pennbridge, J., MacKenzie, R., & Pottharst, K. (1992). Runaway and homeless youth: The effects of attachment history on stabilization. *American Journal of Orthopsychiatry, 62,* 442–446.

Stiffman, A. (1989). Suicide attempts in runaway youth. *Suicide and Life-Threatening Behavior, 19,* 147–159.

Taussig, H., Clyman, R., & Landsverk, J. (2001). Children who return home from foster care: A 6-year prospective study of behavioral health outcomes in adolescence. *Pediatrics, 108,* E10.

Taussig, H. N. (2002). Risk behaviors in maltreated youth placed in foster care: A longitudinal study of protective and vulnerability factors. *Child Abuse and Neglect, 26,* 1179–1199.

Taylor, T., & Chemtob, C. (2004). Efficacy of treatment of child and adolescent traumatic stress. *Archives of Pediatric Adolescent Medicine, 158,* 786–791.

Tyler, K., Hoyt, D., & Whitbeck, L. (2000). The effects of early sexual abuse on later sexual victimization among female homeless and runaway adolescents. *Journal of Interpersonal Violence, 15,* 235–250.

U.S. Department of Health and Human Services. (1999). *Mental health: A report of the surgeon general.* Substance Abuse and Mental Health Services Administration, Center for Mental Health Services; National Institutes of Health, National Institute of Mental Health. Rockville, MD: Author.

U.S. Department of Health and Human Services, Children's Bureau. (1997). *1994 National Study of Protective, Preventive and Reunification Services Delivered to Children and Their Families.* Washington, DC: U.S. Government Printing Office. Retrieved September 19, 2005, from http://www.acf.dhhs.gov/programs/cb/publications/97natstudy/natstudy.htm.

Van Leeuwen, J., Hopfer, C., Hooks, S., White, R., Petersen, J., & Pirkopf, J. (2004). A snapshot of substance abuse among homeless and runaway youth in Denver, Colorado. *Journal of Community Health, 29,* 217–229.

Whitbeck, L., Hoyt, D., & Ackley, K. (1997). Families of homeless and runaway adolescents: A comparison of parent/caretaker and adolescent perspectives on parenting, family violence, and adolescent conduct. *Child Abuse and Neglect, 21,* 517–528.

Whitbeck, L., Johnson, K., Hoyt, D., & Cauce, A. (2004). Mental disorder and comorbidity among runaway and homeless adolescents. *Journal of Adolescent Health, 35,* 132–140.

Yates, G., MacKenzie, R., Pennbridge, J., & Cohen, E. (1988). A risk profile comparison of runaway and non runaway youth. *American Journal of Public Health, 78,* 820–821.

Chapter 5

EMOTIONAL AND BEHAVIORAL PROBLEMS OF FOSTER YOUTH: EARLY FINDINGS OF A LONGITUDINAL STUDY

Mark E. Courtney and Sherri Terao

The child welfare system has the responsibility for providing out-of-home care[1] to many of society's most vulnerable and troubled youth. Most children and adolescents enter the child welfare system because of abuse and neglect with causes often associated with parent psychopathology, substance abuse, and extreme poverty (Pecora, Whittaker, & Maluccio, 1992). At times, even circumstances associated with placement in foster care may be linked to problematic outcomes. Initial placement in a foster home or residential facility involves separation from family and familiar settings, and many youth subsequently experience inconsistent parenting, institutional settings, school transitions, and other adjustment difficulties (Fein, Maluccio, & Kluger, 1990).

For the child victim, maltreatment is a chronic and stressful life condition, particularly because various forms of child abuse and neglect tend to coexist (McGee, Wolfe, Yuen, & Carnochan, 1995; Widom, 1989, in De Bellis, 2001). Unfavorable experiences while in care (such as extended stays, multiple placements, and exposure to further abuse) potentially contribute to the chronicity of mental health symptoms. Long-term consequences of child maltreatment include aggression and violent behavior, nonviolent criminal behavior, substance abuse, self-injurious and suicidal behavior, emotional problems, interpersonal problems, and academic and vocational difficulties (Malinosky-Rummell & Hansen, 1993).

In this chapter, we briefly review research on the mental health problems faced by adolescents in the child welfare system. We then describe the unique and problematic situation of a subgroup of foster youth, those about to "age out" of foster care because they have reached the age of majority. We present findings from our ongoing longitudinal study of a group of these foster youth to illustrate their need for mental health services. We believe that this is a particularly vulnerable group, given that they are on the brink of being on their own and will likely lose access to many of the supports provided to them by the child welfare system.

FOSTER YOUTH AND MENTAL HEALTH PROBLEMS

Given foster youths' exposure to a multitude of adverse conditions and stressors, reports indicate high rates of mental health problems and psychopathology among youth in foster care. In a review of studies published between 1974 and 1994, Pilowsky (1995) found that one-half to three-fourths of children entering foster care had behavior or social competency problems that warranted treatment. Harman, Childs, and Kelleher (2000) found children in foster care were also more likely to suffer from depression (5.9% vs. 1.1%), anxiety disorder (2.5% vs. .8%), attention-deficit/ hyperactivity disorder (14.7% vs. 3.9%), conduct disorder (4.5% vs. .6%), bipolar disorder (1.0% vs. .1%), and oppositional defiant disorder (9.4% vs. 1.9%) than children eligible for Aid to Families with Dependent Children (AFDC). Similar findings by Landsverk, Garland, and Leslie (2002) indicate as many as 80 percent of youth involved with child welfare had emotional or behavioral disorders or developmental delays or exhibited other indicators of the need for mental health services.

State child welfare systems use a variety of different placement options, ranging from nonrelative foster care, relative foster care placements, and therapeutic and residential treatment centers for youth in out-of-home care. In one study, kinship care youth (youth placed with family members or relatives) were found to have behavior problems at a higher rate (30% to 50%) than youth in the general population (Landsverk et al., 2002). In a similar study, youth in relative placements were found to receive fewer services than those youth placed in nonrelative foster placements (Leslie et al., 2000).

Given the high rates of mental health need among foster youth, over the past decade, researchers have begun examining the patterns of mental health service utilization for this population. Three studies have utilized Medicaid paid claims data to evaluate mental health usage by low-income children, including foster children. State-specific studies of mental health service utilization, such as Halfon, Berkowitz, and Klee (1992), found that although children in foster care represented fewer than 4 percent of Medicaid eligible children in California, they accounted for 41 percent of all mental health claims. In a similar study conducted in Washington, Takayama, Bergman, and Connell (1994) found 25 percent of children in the Washington state foster care system used Medicaid reimbursed mental health services. However, only 3 percent of children eligible through AFDC had used Medicaid mental health services. In another study, Farmer et al. (2001) found higher rates of mental health service utilization among youth who came into contact with the child welfare system than among poor youth with the same level of psychological disturbance. Similarly, in southwestern Pennsylvania, Harman et al. (2000) found children in foster care were 3 to 10 times more likely to receive a mental health diagnosis, had 6.5 times more mental health claims, were 7.5 times more likely to be hospitalized for mental health conditions, and had mental health expenditures that were 11.5 times greater than children in AFDC. The study also found the mental health utilization rates of foster youth were comparable with those of children with disabilities.

While the previously mentioned studies shed light on the concerns related to mental health service needs of youth in foster care, questions about generalizability arise because these data were drawn from state-specific samples. The National Survey of Child and Adolescent Well-Being (NSCAW), the first national longitudinal study focused on the experiences of children and families involved in the child welfare system, provided the first national estimate of mental health need and service use (Leslie, Hurlburt, Landsverk, Barth, & Slymen, 2004).

Investigators used the Achenbach Child Behavior Checklist to estimate emotional and behavioral problems for 462 youth and access to mental health treatment. More than half the sample was accessing mental health services, and among those with scores of 64 or higher (above the 98th percentile in a normative population), approximately one-fourth had not accessed mental health services between the time of initiation of the investigation and the interview with the child's caregiver (indicating a substantial degree of unmet need).

According to the analysis of NSCAW data by Burns et al. (2004), clinical need was related to receipt of mental health care across all age-groups. For young children, sexual abuse (versus neglect) increased access to mental health services, and among latency-age youth, being African American and living at home significantly reduced the likelihood of care. This is consistent with previous studies indicating that youth placed in foster care because of neglect or caregiver absence may be less likely than other maltreated youth (i.e., sexually abused youth) to receive mental health services (Leslie et al., 2000). Adolescents living at home were also less likely to receive services, whereas having a parent with severe mental illness increased the likelihood of service use.

Nearly all research on the mental health of adolescents in foster care has been descriptive in nature, identifying the scope of the problem. While it is important to examine the risks facing children in foster care, it is equally important to understand how protective factors ameliorate the stressors and negative long-term effects associated with the child maltreatment that brings children into care and with the care experience itself. According to Rutter (1987), protective factors may be defined as "individual, family, and community characteristics that positively modify, ameliorate, or alter a person's response to some environmental danger that predisposes that individual to maladaptive outcomes; they enable children to survive and thrive in the face of adversity" (pp. 317–319). Unfortunately, very little research has focused specifically on risk and protective factors associated with the mental and behavioral health of foster youth. Nevertheless, the broader literature on risk and protective factors and a few studies that have examined the correlates of functioning for youth in out-of-home care provide some guidance.

For example, in his earlier work, Rutter (1981) found that many of the stressors contributing to psychiatric disorders were related to a youth's interpersonal relationships. Most often these relationships were characterized by loss, disappointment, and negative interpersonal relations. From this research, we can glean that the interpersonal relationships of youth in care may serve as both risk and protective factors, depending on the quality of the relationships. Later, Rutter (1990) found that a consistent relationship early on with a supportive adult has a protective quality for maltreated youth. Consideration of the potential stressful events in a foster youth's life (i.e., neglect or abuse; disrupted connections to parents, siblings, extended family, and supportive peers; and multiple foster placements) leads naturally to speculation that these youth may require strong corrective interpersonal relationships to overcome the effects of trauma and disrupted familial and social support. Other studies have found that perceived levels of social support have been found to protect against the development of emotional and behavioral problems later in life among children exposed to maltreatment (Testa, Miller, Downs, & Panek, 1992).

The importance of strong interpersonal relationships suggest that the type of out-of-home care to which a child or youth is exposed may affect their development. For example, a study by Roy, Rutter, and Pickles (2000) found that the quality of children's experiences while in care may affect their behavioral outcomes. They found that there was a significantly higher rate of hyperactivity and inattention among institution-reared children than among those placed in family foster care.

Nollan, Pecora, Nurius, and Whittaker (2002) identified protective factors associated with greater self-sufficiency skills among foster youth, including "mastery of decision making" and "social relationships," both important indicators of mental health. The protective factors identified by

Nollan et al. (2002) included positive relationships with the foster mother, positive relationships with peers, a significant relationship with an adult, employment opportunities, and volunteer experiences. In particular, the protective factor of "having an adult with whom to talk" was an important predictor of self-sufficiency skills and associated with a higher skill level. According to Nollan et al. (2002), it is clear that having a relationship with an adult with whom the youth could talk is important because this may be an indicator of the "security a youth feels" (p. 14). The protective factor of volunteer experiences also provides an opportunity for youth to form relationships with other adults.

Taussig (2002) conducted a prospective study examining protective and vulnerability factors of maltreated youth in foster care. The study found that there are some risk and protective factors that present shortly after a youth is placed in foster care (e.g., sexual behavior, delinquent/violent behavior, substance use, and suicidal/self-destructive behaviors) that are predictive of engagement in risk behaviors six years later. For example, low perceived support from classmates and poorer behavioral conduct on the part of classmates predicted greater involvement in later risk behaviors. Taussig (2002) suggests that "it is possible that increasing school achievement and classmate support may reduce engagement in risk behaviors" and "targeting youth ... for intervention efforts designed to increase their association with prosocial peers may also foster more prosocial behaviors" (p. 1193).

THE UNIQUE PLIGHT OF ADOLESCENTS "AGING OUT" OF FOSTER CARE

Each year, 20,000 adolescents leave the foster care system and attempt to live independently (U.S. General Accounting Office, 1999). Current federal child welfare funding provides very limited support to states to allow youth to remain in foster care past their eighteenth birthday. As a result, in all but a few jurisdictions nationally, youth are discharged from foster care at the age of 18 or shortly thereafter; in other words, they "age out" of care, thus leaving foster youth "on their own" at a relatively early stage in the transition to adulthood.

In light of the multiple challenges described previously, it is imperative that we understand the pathways to adulthood for foster youth. Very few studies have focused on the transition to adulthood among foster youth. Keeping in mind the limited research in this area, reviews of the literature have suggested that foster youth aging out of the system have relatively poor mental and physical health, limited education and employment experience, and a relatively high likelihood of experiencing unwanted outcomes, such as homelessness, incarceration, and nonmarital pregnancy (Collins, 2001; McDonald, Allen, Westerfelt, & Piliavin, 1996).

In response to some early studies that described problems faced by youth after leaving care (e.g., Festinger, 1983; Meier, 1965), independent living programs were developed to assist young people aging out of the foster care system. In principle, these programs were designed for teens for whom out-of-home care had become a permanent situation (i.e., they were very unlikely to return home or be adopted). In 1985, the Independent Living Initiative (Public Law 99-272) provided federal funds to states under Title IV-E of the Social Security Act to help adolescents develop skills needed for independent living, though congressional appropriations for the programs were made annually. Funding for the Independent Living Program (ILP) was reauthorized indefinitely in 1993 (Public Law 103-66), allowing states to engage in longer-term planning of their programs. The ILP gave states great flexibility in the kinds of services they could provide to foster youth. Basic services outlined in the law included outreach programs to attract eligible youth, training in daily living skills, education and employment assistance, counseling, case management, and a written transitional independent living plan. The ILP funds could not, however, be used for room and board. The federal government required very little reporting from states about the ILP beyond creation of state ILP plans and had "no established method to review the states' progress in helping youths in the transition from foster care" (U.S. General Accounting Office, 1999, p. 3). The U.S. General Accounting Office (1999) found that at least 42,680 youth in 40 states (only about 60% of all eligible youth) received some type of independent living service in 1998.

The Foster Care Independence Act (FCIA) of 1999 (Public Law 106-169) amended Title IV-E to create the John Chafee Foster Care Independence Program, giving states more funding and greater flexibility in providing support for youth making the transition to independent living. The FCIA doubled federal independent living services funding to $140 million per year, allowed states to use up to 30 percent of these funds for room and board, and enabled states to assist young adults 18 to 21 years old who have left foster care. Importantly, the FCIA permits states to extend Medicaid eligibility to former foster children up to age 21. Given the economic circumstances of youth leaving the foster care system, Medicaid will be in many, if not most, cases their only potential source of health insurance. Thus, states' decisions regarding whether to extend Medicaid to foster youth after the age of 18 will play a large role in determining this population's access to health and mental health services. There is currently a great deal of interest on the part of policymakers in the well-being of youth aging out of foster care, whether they are receiving needed services during care and in the years after they leave care and whether such services are helpful.

FORMER FOSTER YOUTH AND MENTAL HEALTH PROBLEMS

An indication of the success, or lack thereof, of the child welfare system in helping to ameliorate the mental health problems experienced by foster youth can be found by examining the mental health status of former foster youth, including those who age out of the system. Unfortunately, very few studies have assessed the well-being of this population, particularly with respect to their mental health, and most studies that have been done are now quite dated. Nevertheless, previous studies suggest that former foster youth suffer from more mental health problems than the general population (Festinger, 1983; Jones & Moses, 1984). Support for this conclusion comes from data on former foster youth's utilization of mental health services and research assessments of their mental health. For example, in Festinger's (1983) study of youth who had recently left out-of-home care in New York City, 47 percent of subjects had sought help or advice from a mental health professional subsequent to discharge from out-of-home care, a far higher rate of help seeking than found in the general population. In another study, Jones and Moses (1984) reported that 3 percent of their subject population resided in residential or group care facilities, an extremely high rate when compared to the .3 percent admission rate into psychiatric hospitals in the United States in 1983 (McDonald et al., 1996). Former foster youth also suffer from higher levels of depression than the general population (Barth, 1990; Cook, 1992). More recently, to gauge the mental health of former foster youth in Wisconsin assessed at ages 19 and 20, Courtney, Piliavin, Grogan-Kaylor, and Nesmith (2001) had their subjects complete a standardized self-report mental health assessment, the Mental Health Inventory (Veit & Ware, 1983). They found that the overall psychological health of the members of their sample was significantly worse than that of their peers of the same age and race.

BACKGROUND AND OVERVIEW OF THE STUDY

We now turn to a description of our study of a group of youth who are in the process of aging out of the foster care system in three midwestern states. It is by far the largest study of its kind to date. The Midwest Evaluation of the Adult Functioning of Former Foster Youth (hereafter referred to as the Midwest Study) is intended to provide guidance to the participating states in their efforts to help foster youth make the transition to independent living. Based on in-person interviews with the youth themselves, the Midwest Study is following the progress of 732 foster youth in Illinois, Iowa, and Wisconsin through age 21. All these youth had reached the age of 17 years while placed in out-of-home care because of abuse or neglect and had been in care for at least one year prior to their seventeenth birthday.

Before going into the field to conduct interviews, all adolescents in out-of-home care supervised by the public child welfare agency who were between 17 and 17 1/2 years old and had been in state care at least one year prior to their seventeenth birthday were identified for sampling purposes.[2] The only youth excluded from this population were those who could not participate in the survey because of developmental disability, incarceration or psychiatric hospitalization at the time of the interview, or severe mental illness. Additional reasons for youth being deemed ineligible for the study included current runaway or missing person status and current placement out of state. In addition, some eligible youth were not interviewed for the following reasons: care provider refusal to participate, youth refusal to participate, no contact with the youth, or lack of contact information. In Iowa and Wisconsin, all youth who fit the sample selection criteria were included in the survey sample; in Illinois, because of the size of the population and available funds, we drew a sample of approximately 67 percent from the overall population of youth who met the sample criteria. Interviews were conducted between May 2002 and March 2003. Of the 770 adolescents fielded for the study, 732 consented to participate and completed an in-person or telephone interview, for an overall response rate of 95.1 percent. Interviews were conducted with 63 youth in Iowa, 474 youth in Illinois, and 195 youth in Wisconsin. This chapter details the findings of the first wave of the study, focusing on indicators of mental illness.[3] Future reports will cover the information we obtain from in-person interviews with youth after they reach their nineteenth and twenty-first birthdays.

DEMOGRAPHIC CHARACTERISTICS AND FAMILY OF ORIGIN

The study sample was almost evenly split between male ($n = 357$; 48.8%) and female ($n = 375$; 51.2%) youth. The majority ($n = 416$; 56.8%) was African American, 31.1% ($n = 227$) was Caucasian, 9.7% ($n = 71$) were of mixed racial heritage, and the remainder were Native American ($n = 10$; 1.4%) or Asian American/Pacific Islander ($n = 4$; .5%). Just under 1 in 10 ($n = 67$; 8.7%) identified themselves as Hispanic. About three-fifths (59.3%) were 17 years old, with the remainder having reached their eighteenth birthday by the time of the interview.

Just prior to their placement in out-of-home care, most youth ($n = 595$; 81.3%) resided with at least one birth parent, the birth mother in the vast majority of cases. In contrast, just over one-fourth ($n = 200$; 27.3%) reported residing with their birth father, and a slightly higher percentage reported living with grandparents ($n = 229$; 31.2%). About 65% ($n = 474$) reported having a biological sibling present in the home.

TRAUMA PRIOR TO ENTERING
OUT-OF-HOME CARE

Before considering the prevalence of mental health problems exhibited by youth in out-of-home care, it is important to remember that these youth were removed from the care of their parents because a juvenile court determined that their parents were either unwilling or unfit to parent them any longer. Coming from such homes, foster children and youth bring with them experiences that increase the likelihood that they will suffer from mental health problems. Table 5.1 shows the results of a series of questions asked of the youth about the characteristics of their primary caregivers at the time they were removed from home. Respondents were asked if one or more of their primary caregivers (in the vast majority of cases, their mother) exhibited a given characteristic. Table 5.1 shows that youth in foster care come from homes in which their parents exhibit a range of problems that might reasonably be expected to contribute to the development of emotional and behavioral problems on the part of the youth.

The maltreatment that children and youth experience before their placement in out-of-home care, another characteristic of the families they typically come from, can also increase their risk of having poor mental health. In order to obtain a sense of the maltreatment histories of the youth in

Table 5.1
Primary Caregiver Characteristics (N = 729)

Characteristics	Present	
	NOC	%
Abused alcohol	257	35.1
Abused drugs	312	42.6
Had mental illness	140	19.1
Showed inadequate parenting skills	283	38.7
Abused their spouse	171	23.4
Had a criminal record	176	24.0
Had other problems	90	12.3

Table 5.2
Number of Youth Reporting Abuse and Neglect by a Caretaker and Sexual Abuse (N = 730)

	Present	
Responses	*NOC*	*%*
Abuse	257	35.1
Neglect	430	58.7
Sexual abuse	198	27.0

our study, we administered selected items from the Lifetime Experiences Questionnaire (LEQ) (Rose, Abramson, & Kaupie, 2000). The LEQ assesses a broad range of specific examples of maltreatment.[4] The questions we used from the LEQ assess whether the respondent experienced physical abuse or neglect in the home they were removed from prior to entering out-of-home care. In addition to questions from the LEQ, we asked youth if they had ever been "raped" or "sexually molested" as part of a larger set of questions used to assess for the presence of posttraumatic stress disorder. Table 5.2 aggregates reported maltreatment experience into categories of neglect, abuse, and sexual abuse. Once again, the experiences of these youth prior to entering state care provide ample explanation for why they may later experience mental health problems.

EXPERIENCES IN CARE

The primary purpose of the child welfare system is to protect children from the harm they received in their homes, reunite them with their families when that can be done safely, and provide them with "permanency" through adoption or guardianship when they cannot return home. Unfortunately, children in out-of-home care, particularly adolescents, too often suffer further harm because of the instability of their living arrangements once they are removed from home.

One source of instability for some children in out-of-home care—and a potential source of emotional conflict—is failed attempts at family reunification. This occurs when the decision is made by the child welfare agency and juvenile court to return a child to the care of their parent(s), only to have to take the child back into care at a later date because of continuing threats to the child's well-being. Table 5.3 shows that more than one-fifth of youth in the Midwest Study reported reentry into out-of-home care and that one-third of those did so more than once.

Table 5.3
Reentry to Care

	Total (N=732)	
Ever reentered out-of-home care after returning home	NOC	%
Yes	161	22.0
No	567	77.5
Missing	4	0.5

	Total (N=161)	
Number of reentries	NOC	%
1	109	67.7
2	29	18.0
3+	23	14.3

Youth in our study were asked about the number of foster home placements and group homes, residential treatment centers, or child care institutions they had been in since entering the foster care system. Tables 5.4 and 5.5 detail these placement experiences. All but 22 youth had experienced at least one foster home placement, and about two-thirds of all respondents had lived in at least one group home, residential treatment center, or child care institution. With respect to foster home placements, one-quarter of youth report only one placement, whereas more than two-fifths experienced four or more. Less than one-quarter of the youth report only one placement in group care, and about 14% had four or more.

Our respondents were also asked about whether they had ever run away from out-of-home care for at least one night. Nearly half reported having run away from out-of-home care, and nearly two-thirds of those who ran away did so on multiple occasions, with more than 17 percent of the overall group having run away five or more times.

In summary, many foster youth experience an extraordinary level of instability in their living arrangements while in out-of-home care. To be sure, some of this instability may be attributed to their own behavior, such as running away from care. Even much of the placement disruption they experience that is not due to runaway behavior may nevertheless be a reflection of the difficulty child welfare authorities have in finding care providers who can cope over a long period with the emotional and behavioral problems of these youth. In other words, it is very difficult to distinguish the extent to which youths' problems lead to placement instability from the degree to which their problems are a result of inadequate foster care. At any rate, youth experiencing such instability in their living

Table 5.4
Number of Foster Home Placements

	Total (N=732)	
Placements	NOC	%
0	22	3.0
1	184	25.1
2	133	18.2
3	110	15.0
4	70	9.6
5	56	7.7
6	32	4.4
7+	120	16.4
Missing	5	0.7

Table 5.5
Number of Group Home/Residential Treatment/Child Care Institution Placements

	Total (N = 732)	
Responses	NOC	%
0	289	39.5
1	168	23.9
2	98	13.4
3	69	9.4
4	43	5.9
5+	60	8.2
Missing	5	0.7

arrangements are unlikely to be able to maintain the kinds of supportive relationships with adults and peers that are crucial to healthy adolescent development.

MENTAL HEALTH AND MENTAL HEALTH CARE SERVICES

As noted previously, existing research suggests that foster youth suffer from more mental health problems than the general population. Given foster youths' exposure to a multitude of adverse conditions and stressors, adolescents in out-of-home care may also be at elevated risk of developing posttraumatic stress disorder and substance use disorders. Although the Midwest Study is not focused primarily on mental health, the study does involve the collection of some data that speak directly to the prevalence of some affective disorders and alcohol and substance disorders among this population. In addition, the study collects data that speak at least indirectly to the youths' involvement in externalizing problem behaviors that are typical of conduct disorders. Next, we summarize evidence from the Midwest Study suggesting that older foster youth are very likely to suffer from one or more mental health problems.

We collected information on selected mental health diagnoses using the Composite International Diagnostic Interview (CIDI; World Health Organization, 1998). Designed for use by nonclinicians, the CIDI is a highly structured interview that renders both lifetime and current psychiatric diagnoses according to definitions and criteria of the *Diagnostic and Statistical Manual of Mental Disorders* (4th ed.). We used the CIDI to assess major depression and dysthymia, social phobia, generalized anxiety disorder, posttraumatic stress disorder, alcohol abuse, alcohol dependence, and substance abuse and dependence. Baseline data were gathered using the lifetime version of the CIDI, thereby assessing whether the youth had ever met the criteria for a given diagnosis.[5]

Table 5.6 shows CIDI results across all diagnostic categories we assessed. Altogether, 267 (36.5%) of our respondents suffer from one or more of the selected mental or behavioral health disorders. Table 6 also shows the prevalence of diagnoses broken down by the gender of the respondents. In general, females and males in this group reported similar histories of behavioral and mental health disorders, with two notable exceptions. Female foster youth were nearly three times as likely as males to provide responses that generated a CIDI diagnosis of posttraumatic stress disorder and about twice as likely as males to report symptoms characteristics of depression or dysthymia. This explains nearly all the difference between genders in the overall rate of diagnosis, with females being about one-third more likely to have one or more diagnoses.

In addition to questions pertaining to psychiatric diagnoses, we asked the youth a variety of questions about behavior that is indicative of conduct disorder and/or other externalizing behavior disorders. Nearly all these questions come from the National Longitudinal Study of Adolescent Health (hereafter Add Health).[6] Our use of questions from the Add Health survey allows us to compare the responses of foster youth in our study to those of youth of similar ages.

For our study, 15 items from the Add Health survey were employed to assess the frequency of delinquent behaviors among our sample during the year prior to our first interview. As shown in Figure 5.1, our respondents provide fairly similar reports to those of their peers in the Add Health sample when it comes to relatively minor forms of delinquent behavior, such

Table 5.6
CIDI Diagnostic Results by Gender

	Total (N = 732)					
	Total		Female		Male	
Diagnosis	NOC	%	NOC	%	NOC	%
Post traumatic stress disorder	118	16.1	89	23.7	29	8.1
Depression or dysthymia*	73	10.0	50	13.3	23	6.4
Generalized anxiety disorder	10	1.4	5	1.3	5	1.4
Social phobia	3	0.4	3	.8	0	0
Alcohol abuse	72	9.8	30	8.0	42	11.8
Alcohol dependence	32	4.4	19	5.1	13	3.6
Substance abuse	63	8.6	27	7.2	36	10.1
Substance dependence	31	4.2	13	3.5	18	5.0
Any diagnosis*	267	36.5	156	41.6	111	31.1

*Difference between genders is statistically significant at P < .05.

as painting graffiti or being unruly in public. However, the foster youth are consistently more likely than their peers to report having been involved in more serious delinquency. The differences are particularly marked on items regarding theft, serious fighting and causing injury, and running away, all of which are symptoms of externalizing behavior disorders.

We compared our group of foster youth to their age peers in the Add Health national sample on experiences in school that are generally indicative of disruptive behavior. Compared to the national sample, foster youth in the Midwest Study are more than twice as likely to have been suspended ($n = 498$; 66.8%) and nearly four times as likely to have been expelled from school ($n = 121$; 16.5%).

The Midwest Study also asked questions intended to measure involvement with the juvenile justice system. These questions ask respondents about their history of arrest, conviction for committing a crime, and overnight stay in a correctional facility. More than half our sample experienced one or more of these outcomes, with more than half having a history of arrest, more than one-third having spent the night in a correctional facility, and one-fifth reporting being convicted of a crime. Table 5.7 illustrates these findings by gender, indicating that in all categories, males are much more likely than females to experience these kinds of direct involvement with the juvenile justice system.

In summary, based on the initial findings of the Midwest Study, older foster youth are very likely to exhibit emotional and behavioral problems, with females appearing more likely to experience posttraumatic stress

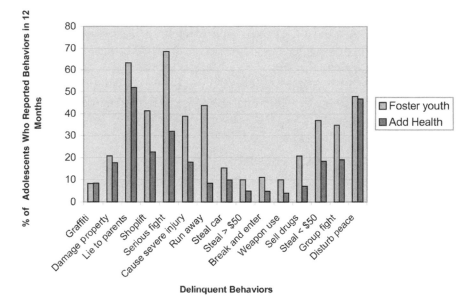

Figure 5.1   Delinquent behaviors: foster youth versus Add Health

Table 5.7
Legal System Involvement by Gender

	Total (N − 732)					
	Male		*Female*		*Total*	
Response	NOC	%	NOC	%	NOC	%
Have you ever been arrested?	217	60.6	155	41.4	372	50.8
Have you ever been convicted of a crime?	99	27.7	57	15.2	156	21.3
Have you ever spent one night or more in jail, prison, juvenile hall, or other correctional facility?	154	43.0	91	24.3	245	33.5
Has youth had any legal involvement? (one or more of the above)	235	65.6	169	45.2	404	55.2

disorder and males being more likely to exhibit behaviors that are indicative of externalizing disorders, such as conduct disorder. We estimated the number of youth in our sample having a potential need for mental health services by combining measures of internalizing and externalizing problems. Specifically, we calculated the number and percentage of the sample, by gender, that either had a diagnosable mental health problem as assessed by the CIDI or reported having spent at least one night in a corrections facility, the latter being a simple but crude indicator of externalizing behavior problems. Interestingly, females ($n = 196$; 52.4%) and males ($n = 197$; 53.7%) appear about equally likely to exhibit behavioral or emotional problems when both internalizing and externalizing problems are taken into account.

RECEIPT OF MENTAL AND BEHAVIORAL HEALTH SERVICES

In addition to gathering information about emotional and behavioral problems, we also asked the foster youth about the kinds of services they received that might have helped with these problems. Many of the foster youth in our study received various forms of mental health services in the year before our interview. More than one-third received some kind of counseling, nearly one-quarter used prescribed drugs for a psychological or psychiatric condition, and 7 percent had spent at least one night in a psychiatric hospital in the past year.

To put these figures into perspective, we compared the responses of foster youth in our study to those of their age peers in the Add Health study on relevant survey items that are common between the two studies. Table 5.8 presents a comparison of foster youths' reported receipt of health care services in comparison with the Add Health sample. Interestingly, the foster youth did not differ from the national sample in the likelihood that they had visited a doctor or dentist, suggesting that they received primary care at about the same rate as their peers. In contrast, foster youth were clearly much more likely than the national sample to have received psychological or emotional counseling and substance abuse counseling, though our

Table 5.8
Comparison of Health and Mental Health Care Utilization, Midwest Study Sample Versus Add Health Sample

| | Total (N = 732) | | |
| | Midwest | | Add Health |
Responses	NOC	%	%
Routine physical examination in the past year	612	83.6	80.0
Routine dental examination in the past year	516	70.5	66.7
Received psychological or emotional counseling	267	36.5	13.0
Received substance abuse counseling in the past year	99	13.5	2.5

data do not allow us to accurately gauge how many of the foster youth who needed mental health services actually received them. Importantly, this accounting of mental health services does not take into account the 18.1 percent ($n = 132$) or our respondents who were living in group care at the time of our interview, a form of out-of-home care that is intended to provide therapeutic care for troubled youth.

RESILIENCE OF FOSTER YOUTH AND SOURCES OF SUPPORT

An exclusive focus on the trauma histories and mental and behavioral health problems of older foster youth could convey the mistaken impression that they have little going for them. On the contrary, this group of youth exhibits a remarkable level of resilience in the face of considerable adversity. Moreover, they have significant sources of interpersonal and institutional support on which to draw.

Their optimism toward the future, for example, reflects the ability of the vast majority of them to maintain a generally positive perspective toward life. Approximately 90 percent of the sample reported they were "fairly" or "very" optimistic about the future. Further evidence of their resiliency can be found in their educational aspirations. For example, in spite of the fact that nearly half ($n = 347$; 47.3%) of the youth had received special education services and more than one-third ($n = 272$; 37.2%) had repeated at least one grade, the vast majority hope to graduate from college ($n = 522$; 71.3%), and more than three-fifths ($n = 440$; 60.2%) expect to do so.

The fact that these youth have been removed from the care of their families might lead one to the conclusion that they have few family connections or other sources of interpersonal support. In fact, the vast majority of the foster youth in our study identified a number of individuals with whom they feel a strong sense of closeness. Table 5.9 shows the number and percentage of our respondents who indicated feeling "very," "somewhat," "not very," or "not at all" close to various people in their lives. Very few of the youth did not feel at least somewhat close to their current foster caregivers, and more than three-fifths felt very close to them.[7] Perhaps surprisingly, almost two-thirds of responding youth reported feeling very close or somewhat close to their biological mothers, with a smaller percentage feeling close to their biological fathers. More than two-fifths of youth reported feeling very close to grandparents, and two-thirds reported feeling very close to siblings. This closeness with family is reflected in the level of contact between the foster youth and their kin. For example, the youth report a median of 15 visits in the previous year with their birth mothers and 12 visits with their grandparent(s).

Table 5.9
Closeness to others

Would you say that you feel very close, somewhat close, not very close, or not at all close to...?	%			
	Very close	*Somewhat close*	*Not very close*	*Not at all close*
Your current foster family	61.9	28.1	4.2	5.8
Relatives you currently live with	68.1	26.3	3.2	2.3
Your biological mother	37.6	26.6	14.7	21.1
Your biological father	19.0	17.6	13.7	49.6
Your grandparents	50.5	22.5	8.0	19.0
Your brothers and sisters	68.7	19.8	6.0	5.5

In addition to questions about relationships to caregivers and family, we also administered the Medical Outcomes Study (MOS) Social Support Survey (Sherbourne & Stewart, 1991), a brief, multidimensional measure of social support survey that was developed for participants in the MOS, a two-year study of patients with chronic conditions. The MOS assesses four dimensions of functional support: emotional/informational, tangible, affectionate, and positive social interaction. Emotional/informational support refers to the expression of positive affect, empathetic understanding, and the encouragement of expressions of feelings. It also measures the offering of advice, information, guidance, or feedback. Tangible support refers to the provision of material aid or behavioral assistance. Positive social interaction refers to the availability of other persons to do enjoyable things with youth. Affectionate support refers to expressions of love and affection. Youth were asked to indicate on a five-point scale how often each type of support was available to them (i.e., 1 = none of the time, 2 = a little of the time, 3 = some of the time, 4 = most of the time, and 5 = all of the time). The foster youth report that, in general, they are receiving social support some or most of the time (mean score across all items of 3.93), with no significant variation across the four dimensions.

Because of their status as wards of the state, foster youth can also rely on the help of the child welfare system, to the extent that such help is made available to them. Our study—and prior research as well (Courtney et al., 2001; Festinger, 1983)—has found that most foster youth and former foster youth have positive views of the system and those adults in the system that are charged with their care. For example, 61.2 percent (*n* = 448) of our respondents agree to strongly agree with the statement that "generally I am satisfied with my experiences in the foster care system." A majority (*n* = 421; 57.4%) agree to strongly agree with the statement that "social workers have been a help to me while I was in the foster care system." Nearly four-fifths of our respondents who were living in a foster home at the time of our interview ($n = 205$; 78.6%) agree to strongly agree with the statement that "all in all foster parents have been a help to me." These findings suggest that many foster youth may see the adults who have supported them while they were in foster care as a source of continuing support during the transition to adulthood.

The generally positive views of the youth toward the foster care system are reflected in their likelihood to seek help from the system after they have aged out of care. We asked the youth a series of questions about how likely they thought it was that they would turn to someone from their foster care agency for help after they left care. Anywhere from two-fifths to one-half of our respondents indicated that they were "likely" or "very likely" to return to someone from their foster care agency for help with finances, employment, housing, and other problems, suggesting that many older foster youth have come to see the system itself as playing the kind of supportive role usually played by family. These responses indicate the potential importance of the child welfare system in serving as a conduit to mental health services for this population *after* they are no longer in state care.

CONCLUSION

Data from our ongoing study of older youth in foster care confirm the findings of earlier research suggesting that members of this population are very likely to have suffered serious trauma prior to entering out-of-home care and too often experience less-than-stable living arrangements while in state care. Older foster youth are also at high risk of emotional and behavioral problems, with females being more likely than males to suffer from posttraumatic stress disorder and depression and males being more likely to exhibit serious externalizing behavior problems indicative of conduct disorder. Not surprisingly, older foster youth are also more likely than their peers to utilize mental health services. While the troubles faced by many of these adolescents are clear, it is also the case that many of them possess considerable optimism and high aspirations, are close to members of their foster families and families of origin, and have positive connections to their foster care agency. These assets could prove very important to them during their transition out of care and toward adulthood.

Our findings provide food for thought for practitioners. Attention to the mental health needs of adolescents in foster care has increased in recent years, and many youth are receiving services to help them with their emotional and behavioral problems. Still, our data suggest that child welfare

authorities would be well advised to assess the mental health of *all* youth
entering the child welfare system and to conduct periodic reassessments.
Too often, the child welfare system waits until a youth has "failed" several
foster placements before recognizing that the youth has problems that
require more help than can be provided by a well-intentioned foster parent
with little or no support from mental health professionals. This is a failure of the adults in these youths' lives rather than the youths themselves.
Services and supports for foster youth and foster parents need to be provided earlier in the youths' care histories in order to attempt to prevent the
kind of placement instability experienced by the participants in our study.

Youths' connections to their caregivers should not be ignored by the
various professionals seeking to address the mental health needs of this
population. Given the overwhelmingly positive views expressed by our
respondents toward their foster parents, these adults should be seen as the
central members of any treatment team seeking to help a troubled foster
youth and provide support accordingly. Foster parents are often seen as
mere adjuncts to professional mental health services providers when in
fact they are arguably as important as any parent would be to the treatment
of an adolescent not in foster care.

Youths' connections to their families of origin call for a reevaluation of
prevailing child welfare practice. There are no reliable data available on
how well child welfare authorities and mental health professionals take
into account these relationships. Still, anecdotal evidence suggests that
professionals too often make the assumption that youth in long-term foster
care do not really have families anymore or that the child welfare system
and the youths' foster care providers have become that family. To be sure,
there is reason for caution when considering whether and how to involve
kin in treatment planning for foster youth because these youth were nearly
always removed from the care of their parents for reasons of abuse or
neglect. Nevertheless, most of these youth were placed in out-of-home care
because of neglect, not abuse, and their parents are not an active threat to
their safety. More important, the youths' relationships with their siblings,
grandparents, and other members of their extended family are clearly
important to them and should not be neglected in treatment planning.

Mental health professionals need to help these youth find ways to maximize the support they can glean from relationships with kin and how to better manage the relationships that are problematic. This may be particularly
important to former foster youth during the transition to adulthood. For
example, in their Wisconsin study of former foster youth who were 19 to
20 years old and 12 to 18 months out of care, Courtney et al. (2001) found
that while youth reported the same kind of closeness to kin as that of the

youth in our study, 25 percent of them also reported that their families were a problem for them "most or all of the time."

This chapter speaks primarily to the mental health problems of foster youth before and during their stays in out-of-home care, but our study's primary purpose is to examine the transition to adulthood for children leaving state care. Thus, we would be remiss in not pointing out a major limitation of current child welfare and mental health policy when it comes to youth aging out of foster care. Currently, Medicaid is the primary source of funding for mental health services for foster youth, particularly outpatient services. Yet, except in states that have extended Medicaid eligibility to foster youth, these youth lose their eligibility for Medicaid when they reach the age of majority and leave care.[8] Few former foster youth are employed in jobs that provide health insurance or enough income to pay for insurance (Courtney et al., 2001). Thus, in the absence of state action to continue their coverage through age 21 as allowed under current federal law (action taken to date by only a few states), many if not most of these youth will lose health insurance and with it access to many mental health services (Eilertson, 2002). The effect of this policy on utilization of mental health services is already clear. Courtney et al. (2001) found that fewer than half as many former foster youth in their study were receiving mental health services after leaving care as had done so while in care, in spite of the fact that there was no change over time in the overall level of psychological distress reported by the study participants. Thus, one of the most important things society can do for foster youth, given their need for access to mental health services, is to make sure that they are not deprived of those services precisely at the moment when society expects them to make the transition to adulthood.

NOTES

1. We use the terms "foster care" and "out-of-home care" interchangeably throughout this chapter. Both terms are meant to include not only traditional foster family care but also court-supervised foster care by adults that are related to the child in question and the various forms of group care utilized by child welfare authorities (e.g., group homes and residential treatment centers).

2. Youth whose primary reason for placement was adjudicated delinquency, in other words, those under the supervision of a probation agency, were not included in the study.

3. Sample sizes in some tables vary from 732 because of missing data for some questions.

4. For example, the following is one of the questions used to identify neglect: "Did you ever have a serious illness or injury or physical disability,

but your caretaker ignored it or failed to obtain necessary medical or remedial treatment for it?" Physical abuse was assessed using questions such as "Did any of your caretakers ever hit you hard with a fist, or kick you or slap you really hard?"

5. Errors in the programming language used for the computer-assisted administration of the CIDI led to interviewers failing to ask some questions needed for the diagnoses of major depression and substance abuse. Specifically, respondents who answered "yes" to screening questions for depression (e.g., "In your lifetime, have you ever had two weeks or longer when nearly every day you felt sad, empty, or depressed for most of the day?") or substance abuse (e.g., "Have you ever used any of the following drugs (marijuana, cocaine...?") were not asked the follow-up questions necessary to make a complete CIDI diagnosis. We attempted to reinterview these study participants. Of the 352 respondents who missed questions needed for the diagnosis of depression, we were able to reinterview 256 (72%). Similarly, we were able to reinterview 247 (72.4%) of the 341 respondents who missed questions necessary for a diagnosis of substance abuse. Nevertheless, we are missing data on 96 respondents with a higher likelihood of diagnosis of depression and 94 with higher likelihood of a diagnosis of substance abuse. Thus, our estimates of the level of depression and substance abuse for this population are likely somewhat lower than they would be if we had complete interview data from all respondents. If the youth we were unable to reinterview experienced depression and substance abuse at the same rates as those we were able to interview, the lifetime prevalence of depression among this population would be 12.4 percent instead of 10 percent, and the lifetime prevalence of substance abuse would be 11.6 percent instead of 8.6 percent.

6. Add Health is a national, longitudinal study of the multiple contexts of adolescents' lives and how these affect health and health-related behaviors (Resnick et al., 1997). Add Health researchers conducted in-home interviews with a nationally representative sample of more than 20,000 students in grades 7 through 12 who have been followed into young adulthood over three waves of interviews.

7. Since the 1980s, child welfare agencies have frequently relied on members of a child's extended family to provide court-supervised foster care. Over one-third of the youth in our study ($n = 261$; 35.7%) were living in so-called kinship foster care at the time of our first interview.

8. Some youth retain eligibility to Medicaid because they have children of their own and meet Medicaid income eligibility requirements.

REFERENCES

Barth, R. (1990). On their own: The experiences of youth after foster care. *Child and Adolescent Social Work, 7,* 419–440.

Burns, B. J., Phillips, S. D., Wagner, H. R., Barth, R. P., Kolko, D. J., Campbell, Y., & Landsverk, J. (2004). Mental health need and access to mental health services by youths involved with child welfare: A national survey. *Journal of the American Academy of Child and Adolescent Psychiatry, 43,* 960–970.

Collins, M. E. (2001). Transition to adulthood for vulnerable youths: A review of research and implications for policy. *Social Service Review, 75,* 271–291.

Cook, S. K. (1992). *Long term consequences of foster care for adult well-being.* Unpublished doctoral dissertation, University of Nebraska, Lincoln.

Courtney, M. E., Piliavin, I., Grogan-Kaylor, A., & Nesmith, A. (2001). Foster youth transitions to adulthood: A longitudinal view of youth leaving care. *Child Welfare, 6,* 685–717.

De Bellis, M. D. (2001). Developmental traumatology: A contributory mechanism for alcohol and substance use disorders. *Psychoneuroendocrinology, 27,* 155–170.

Eilertson, C. (2002). *Independent living for foster youth.* Washington, DC: National Conference of State Legislatures.

Farmer, E. M. Z., Burns, B. J., Chapman, M. V., Phillips, S. D., Angold, A., & Costello, E. J. (2001). Use of mental health services by youth in contact with social services. *Social Service Review, 75,* 605–624.

Fein, E., Maluccio, A. N., & Kluger, M. (1990). *No more partings: An examination of long-term foster family care.* Washington, DC: Child Welfare League of America.

Festinger, T. (1983). *No one ever asked us: A postscript to foster care.* New York: Columbia University Press.

Halfon, N., Berkowitz, G., & Klee, L. (1992). Children in foster care in California: An examination of Medicaid reimbursed health services utilization. *Pediatrics, 89,* 1230–1237.

Harman, J. S., Childs, G. E., & Kelleher, K. J. (2000). Mental health care utilization and expenditures by children in foster care. *Archives of Pediatric Adolescent Medicine, 154,* 1114–1117.

Jones, M. A., & Moses, B. (1984). *West Virginia's former foster children: Their experiences in care and their lives as young adults.* New York: Child Welfare League of America.

Landsverk, J., Garland, A. F., & Leslie, L. K. (2002). Mental health services for children reported to child protective services. In J. E. B. Myers, C. T. Hendrix, L. Berliner, C. Jenny, J. Briere, & T. Reid (Eds.), *APSAC handbook on child maltreatment* (2nd ed., pp. 487–507). Thousand Oaks, CA: Sage.

Leslie, L. K., Hurlburt, M. S., Landsverk, J., Barth, R. P., & Slymen, D. J. (2004). Outpatient mental health services for children in foster care: A national perspective. *Child Abuse and Neglect, 28,* 697–712.

Leslie, L. K., Landsverk, J., Ezzet-Lofstrum, R., Tschann, J. M., Slymen, D. J., & Garland, A. F. (2000). Children in foster care: Factors influencing outpatient mental health service use. *Child Abuse and Neglect, 24,* 465–476.

Malinosky-Rummell, R., & Hansen, D. J. (1993). Long-term consequences of childhood physical abuse. *Psychological Bulletin, 114,* 68–79.

McDonald, T. P., Allen, R. I., Westerfelt, A., & Piliavin, I. (1996). *Assessing the long-term effects of foster care: A research synthesis.* Washington, DC: Child Welfare League of America.

McGee, R., Wolfe, D., Yuen, S., & Carnochan, J. (1995). The measurement of maltreatment. *Child Abuse and Neglect, 19,* 233–249.

Meier, E. G. (1965). Current circumstances of former foster children. *Child Welfare, 44,* 96–206.

Nollan, K. A., Pecora, P. J., Nurius, P. N., & Whittaker, J. K. (2002). Risk and protective factors influencing life skills among youths in long-term foster care. *International Journal of Child and Family Welfare, 1–2,* 5–17.

Pecora, P. J., Whittaker, J. K., & Maluccio, A. N. (1992). *The child welfare challenge: Policy, practice, and research.* New York: Aldine de Gruyter.

Pilowsky, D. (1995). Psychopathology among children placed in family foster care. *Psychiatric Services, 46,* 906–910.

Resnick, M. D., Bearman, P. S., Blum, W.S., Bauman, K.E., Harris, K.M., Jones, J., et al. (1997). Protecting adolescents from harm: Findings from the National Longitudinal Study on Adolescent Health. *Journal of the American Medical Association, 278,* 832–843.

Rose, D. T., Abramson, L. Y., & Kaupie, C. A. (2000). *The Lifetime Experiences Questionnaire: A measure of history of emotional, physical, and sexual maltreatment.* Manuscript in preparation, University of Wisconsin, Madison.

Roy, P., Rutter, M., & Pickles, A. (2000). Institutional care: Risk from family background or pattern of rearing? *Journal of Child Psychology and Psychiatry, 41,* 139–150.

Rutter, M. (1981). Stress, coping and development: Some issues and some questions. *Journal of Child Psychology and Psychiatry, 22,* 323–356.

Rutter, M. (1987). Psychosocial resilience and protective mechanisms. *American Journal of Orthopsychiatry, 57,* 316–331.

Rutter, M. (1990). Psychosocial resilience and protective factors. In J. E. Rolf, A. Masten, D. Cicchetti, K. Nuechterlein, & S. Weintraub (Eds.), *Risk and protective factors in the development of psychopathology* (pp. 181–214). New York: Cambridge University Press.

Sherbourne, C. D., & Stewart, A. L. (1991). The MOS Social Support Survey. *Social Science Medicine, 32,* 705–714.

Takayama, J. I., Bergman, A. B., & Connell, F. A. (1994). Children in foster care in the state of Washington: Health care utilization and expenditures. *Journal of the American Medical Association, 271,* 1850–1855.

Taussig, H. N. (2002). Risk behaviors in maltreated youth placed in foster care: A longitudinal study of protective and vulnerability factors. *Child Abuse and Neglect, 26,* 1179–1199.

Testa, M., Miller, B. A., Downs, W. R., & Panek, D. (1992). The moderating impact of social support following child sexual abuse. *Violence and Victims, 7,* 173–185.

U.S. General Accounting Office. (1999, November). *Foster care: Effectiveness of independent living services unknown* (GAO/HEHS-00-13). Washington DC: Author.

Veit, C. T., & Ware, J. E., Jr. (1983). The structure of psychological distress and well-being in general populations. *Journal of Consulting and Clinical Psychology, 51,* 730–742.

Widom, C. S. (1989). The cycle of violence. *Science, 244,* 160–166.

World Health Organization. (1998). *The Composite International Diagnostic Interview (CIDI).* Geneva: Author.

Chapter 6

HETEROGENEITY OF ADOLESCENT DEVIANCE

Donald R. Lynam

Adolescent deviance (i.e., delinquency, substance use, and risky sex) has serious consequences for individuals, families, communities, and society. It is now recognized that adolescent deviance represents more than "boys being boys" and simple fun. Researchers and laypersons alike understand that most serious and violent crimes are committed by teenagers and that the roots of serious adult offending, adult substance abuse and dependence, and risky sexual behavior are found in childhood and adolescence. This chapter reviews several theories of adolescent deviance from the field of antisocial behavior and outlines implications for intervention. Specifically, I present evidence that the causes of adolescent deviance are heterogeneous, arguing for the presence of two types of offenders. I present a sampling of theories addressing each type and review evidence in support of each. I close this chapter with some straightforward intervention implications drawn from the theories reviewed.

THE GENERALITY OF DEVIANCE

Although I review primarily theories of antisocial behavior, each theory can serve as a theory of general deviance. This is true because adolescent misbehavior is broad. Drinking, problem drinking, illicit drug use, cigarette use, delinquency, and sexual precocity and risk taking tend to be observed in the same persons. It was this observation that served as the centerpiece of Jessor and Jessor's (1977) Problem Behavior Theory. This observation has been supported in several large studies. Donovan and Jessor (1985) used data from six samples and a confirmatory factor analytic approach to document that a single variable underlaid problem drinking, illicit drug use, delinquent-type behavior, and precocious sexual intercourse. Osgood, Johnston, O'Malley, and Bachman (1988) used data from three waves of the Monitoring the Future Study to examine the cross-sectional and longitudinal relations among criminal behavior, heavy alcohol use, marijuana use, other illicit drug use, and dangerous driving. They found that a "single latent variable can account for virtually all of their cross-sectional and longitudinal relationships" (p. 91), although they noted that there also exists reliable unique variance in each specific domain. This observation continues to find support. Zhang, Welte, and Wieczorek (2002) modeled the interrelations among drinking (use, heavy use, and dependence), drug use (use and problems associated with use), and criminal behavior (minor and serious) in the Buffalo Longitudinal Study of Young Men, a sample of 625 men aged 16 to 19. These authors again found evidence that a single latent factor underlies diverse forms of deviance.

This generality of deviance is not restricted to adolescence. Krueger and colleagues have published several papers arguing that a single "externalizing" dimension underlies several common mental disorders. For example, using data from the National Comorbidity Study ($N = 8,098$; age range 15 to 54), Krueger (1999) found that alcohol dependence, drug dependence, and antisocial personality disorder could all be considered indicators of a single underlying dimension. In sum, although I discuss theories built in the area of antisocial behavior, they are applicable to all forms of deviance. Thus, I use "deviance" and "antisocial behavior" interchangeably.

HETEROGENEITY IN THE CAUSES OF ANTISOCIAL BEHAVIOR

Although deviance may be general, its causes are heterogeneous. Two findings support this notion. The first is the robust relation between age and crime. A person is more likely to be arrested in the second decade of life than in any other period. In 1996, individuals between the ages of 10 and 19 accounted for 45.3 percent of all arrests for property crimes and 28 percent of all arrests for violent crimes (Maguire & Pastore, 1998). When crime is plotted against age, the rates are highest during mid- to late adolescence; for all types of crime, there is a dramatic increase in the number of offenders from early to mid-adolescence (ages 13 to 15) that reaches a peak in mid- to late adolescence (ages 16 to 18) and declines thereafter, more slowly than it increased. For example, in 1996 the violent crime rate increased from a low of 0.22 per 1,000 among those under 12 years of age to 9.96 among 16- to 18-year-olds and dropped to 8.78 among 19- to 21-year-olds with a steady decline thereafter. Importantly, this increase across adolescence reflects an increase in individuals joining the ranks of offenders rather than the same set of offenders increasing their rates of offending. The basic form of this age–crime relation is stable across crime type. Additionally, although males are more antisocial than females at all ages, the relation between age and crime is maintained across gender. Finally, the age–crime curve is also found across data sources, countries, and historical periods. The robustness of this relation has led some to assert that the relation between age and crime is one of the "brute facts" of criminology (Hirschi & Gottfredson, 1983). This relation is similar to those observed for other forms of deviance.

The second finding is that tomorrow's antisocial adults are found among today's antisocial children. Childhood conduct problems are a major risk factor for adult disorders characterized by antisocial behavior (Glueck & Glueck, 1950; Robins, 1966; Sampson & Laub, 1990). Aggression, in general, is predictive of antisocial outcomes in adulthood. Huesmann, Eron, Lefkowitz, and Walder (1984) tracked, across 22 years, a group of men and women who were rated as aggressive by their peers in late childhood. They found that aggressive children became aggressive adults; aggressive men were more likely to commit serious criminal acts, abuse their spouses, and drive while intoxicated, whereas the women were likely to punish their children severely. These investigators have also shown that aggression is stable across generations, having tracked its transmission across three generations.

Probably the best-known demonstration of the continuity of antisocial behavior is Robins's (1966) now classic study of the adult outcomes of 524 clinic-referred boys and their controls. When she followed the boys up 30 years after admission, Robins found that "not only were antisocial children more often arrested and imprisoned as adults ... but they were more mobile geographically, had more marital difficulties, poorer occupational and economic histories, impoverished social and organizational relationships, poor Armed Services records, excessive use of alcohol, and to some extent poorer physical health" (p. 68). Most important, only boys who were antisocial in adolescence went on to receive diagnoses of sociopathy in adulthood.

Robins (1978) has since replicated her findings in several different samples. From her work, two cardinal rules of the relation between early antisocial behavior and later chronic antisocial behavior have emerged. First, rarely, if ever, does antisocial behavior arise de novo in adulthood. This implies that to find the antisocial adult of tomorrow, one must look among the antisocial children of today. This continuity has been made explicit in successive versions of the *Diagnostic and Statistical Manual of Mental Disorders* (*DSM-III, DSM-III-R, DSM-IV;* American Psychiatric Association, 1980, 1987, 1994). The criteria sets for diagnoses of antisocial personality disorder require conduct problems to have been evident before the age of 18. The second rule is also important to dwell on: children with severe conduct problems become antisocial adults in fewer than 50 percent of cases. This implies that researchers' ability to identify children who will later go on to be chronic offenders as adults is limited.

Based on these findings, two conclusions are warranted. First, the severely antisocial adult is identifiable in childhood and adolescence. Second, there is much heterogeneity in child and adolescent antisocial behavior. The golden grail of high-risk research has become the identification of the minority of children who are most likely to persist in their antisocial behavior from among the multitude of children who engage in some antisocial acts. In what follows, I review several current attempts at such identification. Following this, I review several theories dealing with the adolescents who offend only temporarily.

THE CHRONIC OFFENDERS

There have been multiple attempts at identifying the chronic offenders—individuals who begin antisocial behavior early in the life course and continue it through adulthood. There are commonalities across the theories. Each specifies a relatively small subgroup. Each uses comorbid characteristics or developmental history to identify the chronic offender. Each theory highlights the role of individual differences as causes. In these theories, chronic offenders possess certain deficits or characteristics that make them more likely to engage in deviant activities. Finally, each theory considers this type of offending to be a form of psychopathology.

Moffitt's Life Course Persistent Offenders

The most comprehensive approach is Moffitt's (1993) dual taxonomy of antisocial behavior. In this theory, Moffitt differentiates two types of offenders based on the age of onset, course of antisocial behavior, and the cause underlying the behaviors. Moffitt (1993) terms the first group life course persistent offenders (LCP) whose antisocial tendencies become apparent early in childhood, who account for a disproportionately large percentage of all crimes, and who are likely to continue offending throughout adulthood. These offenders are characterized by subtle, early-emerging neuropsychological deficits manifest as poor motor coordination, attention problems, hyperactivity, impulsivity, language problems, and learning disabilities. These initial difficulties are translated into undercontrolled and overtly antisocial behavior via interactions with the social environment, primarily through failed parent–child encounters. To explain this, Moffitt draws on the notion of evocative person–environment transactions (Caspi & Bem, 1990), which are evident when an individual's behavior evokes characteristic reactions from the environment that serve to reinforce the original behavior. Difficult children evoke typical reactions from parents that include harsh and erratic parental discipline, reduction of parental efforts at socialization, and increases in permissiveness for later aggression, all of which are likely to exacerbate rather than ameliorate the child's existing tendencies.

These difficult children would challenge the most capable parents. Unfortunately, these children are not randomly assigned to home environments; some of the possible sources of the original neuropsychological difficulties are linked to parental behavior and characteristics (e.g., drug abuse, poor pre- and postnatal nutrition, lack of stimulation/affection, physical abuse and neglect, and the genetic transmission of impulsivity or irritability). Thus, the most difficult children are born to parents who are the least capable of adequately socializing them.

Once a child begins his antisocial journey, he is kept to his path by two types of continuity: contemporary and cumulative. Contemporary continuity arises when an individual carries with him into later life the same traits that got him into trouble earlier. For example, an undercontrolled child may exhibit angry outbursts and aggression toward his peers, resulting in peer rejection and hostile relations with peers. These same angry outbursts as an adult may alienate employers, coworkers, and intimate others, resulting in the inability to maintain a job or a relationship. Cumulative continuity operates when early behavior structures future outcomes and opportunities that "channelize" the individual into his ill-started path. For example, the undercontrolled child who drops out of school may be limited to high-stress, frustrating, low-wage jobs; the resultant frustration and stress may then contribute to the individual's continued participation in criminal behavior. Moffitt identifies two particular sources of cumulative continuity: (1) the development of a restricted behavioral repertoire and (2) the ensnarement by consequences of antisocial behavior. Antisocial and undercontrolled children miss out on opportunities to learn about and practice prosocial alternatives. Similarly, these children are more likely to make poor decisions that diminish the probability of later success (e.g., teenage parenthood, addiction, a criminal record, and a spotty work history).

Moffitt and colleagues have provided evidence in support of the taxonomy, particularly the LCP aspect, in several studies from the Dunedin Multidisciplinary Health and Development Study—a longitudinal study of a birth cohort of more than 1,000 subjects who have been studied extensively from birth to age 27. For example, Bartusch, Lynam, Moffitt, and Silva (1997) identified two factors underlying antisocial behavior from childhood to late adolescence. The first, related to early antisocial behavior (ages 5, 7, 9, and 11), was most strongly correlated with low verbal ability, hyperactivity, and negative/impulsive personality. The second factor, related to adolescent delinquency (ages 13 and 15), was most strongly correlated with peer delinquency. These findings were replicated across parent, self-, and teacher ratings. Moffitt, Caspi, Dickson, Silva, and Stanton (1996) formed five groups of boys using parent, teacher, and self-reports from ages 5 to 18: LCP offenders, adolescence-limited (AL) offenders, abstainers, recoverers, and unclassifieds. The LCP and AL boys differed from each other on a variety of theoretically meaningful measures. For example, at ages three and five, relative to AL boys, LCP boys were rated by observers as more emotionally labile, restless, negative, willful, and rougher in play and as having shorter attention spans; in short, LCP boys were more likely to show difficult temperaments in early childhood. In accord with Moffitt's theorizing, although AL and LCP boys did not differ in general delinquency during adolescence, LCP boys were much more likely to have been convicted of a violent offense by age 18. The LCP boys also self-reported more "psychopathic" personalities, describing themselves as unconventional, impulsive, willing to take advantage of others, suspicious, and callous. Finally, LCP boys tended to have experienced more "snares" than other boys; they were more likely to report feeling distant from their families and were more likely to have dropped out of school. Most recently, Moffitt and Caspi (2001) expanded the variety of variables examined in a comparison between the LCP and AL offenders. They found that the LCP offenders experienced more parental risk (e.g., single parenthood and harsh and inconsistent discipline) and more neurocognitive risk (e.g., neurological abnormalities and impaired neuropsychological functioning) and evidenced a more difficult child temperament (e.g., more difficult to manage and hyperactivity). The one set of factors that did not differentiate LCP from AL offenders were those dealing with peer delinquency. Both LCP and AL offenders had more delinquent peers than unclassified participants.

Other investigators have provided direct and indirect support for this theory, primarily the LCP aspect. For example, multiple studies have documented the relation between serious antisocial behavior and neuropsychological problems (see Dodge, Coie, & Lynam, in press). In a series of studies, Piquero and colleagues found evidence for the interaction of high-risk family environments and neuropsychological difficulties in predicting early-onset antisocial behavior (e.g., Piquero & Tibbetts, 1999). A number of studies have documented the relation between early-onset offending and later adult offending. For example, Fergusson, Horwood, and Ridder (2004) used data from the Christchurch Health and Development Study, a longitudinal study of an unselected birth cohort of 1,265 children followed from birth to age 25, to examine the long-term outcomes of early-onset conduct problems. These authors found that conduct problems between ages seven and nine predicted a wide range of adverse psychosocial outcomes, including crime, substance use, mental disorder, risky sexual behavior, and partner violence. Even after controlling for a variety of potential covariates, the 5 percent of the sample with the highest rates of early conduct problems had rates of these outcomes between 1.5 and 19 times the rates seen in the 50 percent of the sample with the lowest rates of early conduct problems.

HIA+CP Children

Lynam (1996) has proposed a developmental theory of serious adult antisocial behavior, based on the idea that the precursor of the adult psychopath is the child with symptoms of both hyperactive-impulsive-attention problems (HIA) and conduct problems (CP). Lynam proposed that the psychopath-to-be begins with deficient P-constraint (psychopathic constraint), which means that he has difficulty incorporating feedback from the environment and using this information to modulate his responses while pursuing rewards. Lynam suggested that this deficit is manifest initially in signs of the HIA complex. As this child grows older, this deficit in P-constraint will lead to mild symptoms of CP (read oppositional defiant disorder)—difficulty controlling his temper, use of obscene language, and maladaptive responses such as arguing with adults, lying, and blaming others for things he has done. On entering school, with its increased demands for restraint and increasing social contact, additional symptoms of CP will emerge, such as aggression and stealing. Finally, as an adult, Lynam suggested that the individual will manifest many of the signs and symptoms of psychopathy. In this theory, the progression from HIA symptoms to symptoms of CP to symptoms of serious adult antisocial behavior is simply the maturing/evolution over time of the same underlying pathology, a deficiency in P-constraint. That is, the expression of the pathology changes as opportunities for its expression change.

Lynam (1996) reviewed evidence that HIA+CP children were at great risk for later antisocial personality and that they may be at specific risk for later psychopathy. He reviewed longitudinal studies demonstrating that children with both types of symptoms were more likely than their counterparts to have high rates of delinquency in adolescence and to continue their offending into adulthood. He provided evidence from cross-sectional studies demonstrating that children with HIA and CP have the earliest ages of an onset of antisocial behavior and the most frequent, severe, and varied pattern of offending and were the most likely to offend across situations—all of which portend later chronic offending. Lynam also reviewed family studies demonstrating that HIA+CP in the proband was related to more severe antisocial behavior in the relatives of these probands than in the relatives of CP-only probands.

Waschbusch (2002) provided a comprehensive review of the literature on comorbid HIA-CP. He found evidence that the HIA+CP differed from comparison groups in terms of defining features (e.g., conduct problems and antisocial behavior), associated features (e.g., cognitive and social functioning), course (e.g., age at onset and stability), and etiology (e.g., genetic contribution). In each case, the HIA+CP was more disturbed; that is, the HIA+CP group had more conduct problems, higher rates of antisocial behavior, poorer cognitive and social functioning, earlier ages of onset, more stable courses, and distinct genetic underpinnings.

Most recently, Flory and Lynam (2003) reviewed research examining the relations among HIA, CP, and substance use. They reviewed cross-sectional and longitudinal studies showing that the comorbid group is at especially high risk for concurrent and future substance use. For example, in a sample of 481 young adults, Flory, Milich, Lynam, Leukefeld, and Clayton (2003) found that adolescent HIA and CP interacted to predict young adult marijuana dependence, hard-drug use, and hard-drug dependence. In each case, the nature of the interaction was such that individuals with high levels of CP and HIA were at greatest risk.

Fledgling Psychopathy

The term "psychopathy" has been around for well over 100 years, applied mainly to adults. Clinicians and researchers (e.g., Cleckley, 1941; Hare, 2003) have been remarkably consistent in their descriptions of the psychopath. Behaviorally, the psychopath is an impulsive risk taker involved in a variety of criminal activities. Interpersonally, the psychopath has been described as grandiose, egocentric, manipulative, forceful, and coldhearted. Affectively, the psychopath displays shallow emotions, is unable to maintain close relationships, and lacks empathy, anxiety, and remorse. Given this description, it is not surprising that the psychopathic offender is among the most prolific, versatile, and violent of offenders (e.g., Hare, 2003). Recently, several researchers have borrowed the construct of psychopathy from the adult literature in an attempt to discriminate those children with conduct problems who will become chronic offenders from those whose antisocial behavior will remit over time (Frick, Barry, & Bodin, 2000; Lynam 1996, 1997). All this work is predicated on the assumption that early manifestations of psychopathy will resemble later manifestations—a reasonable a priori assumption given the stability of personality. Several instruments have been constructed to assess psychopathic traits in adolescence and childhood, and much research has been aimed at validating these assessments and examining their predictive utility. Most of the work has involved asking if juvenile psychopathy behaves like adult psychopathy in terms of the relations to antisocial outcomes, the patterns of comorbidity, the relation to extraoffending elements of the network, and the relation to underlying processes. With few exceptions, the research has supported the idea that juvenile psychopathy looks like adult psychopathy (for a complete review, see Lynam & Gudonis, 2005).

Psychometrics

Research has provided supportive evidence for the psychometrics of the three leading measures of juvenile psychopathy: Childhood Psychopathy Scale (CPS; Lynam, 1997), Antisocial Process Screening Device (APSD; Frick & Hare, 2001), and Hare Psychopathy Checklist: Youth Version (PCL:YV; Forth, Kosson, & Hare, 2003). Each of the three has been shown to be reliable, particularly at the total score level (e.g., Frick, Cornell, Barry, Bodin, & Dane, 2003; Lynam et al., 2005). There is evidence for adequate convergence among these juvenile psychopathy assessments, particularly for the total score and particularly between the CPS and APSD. In two studies, the correlation between the total scores on the CPS and APSD ranged from .80 in Falkenbach, Poythress, Norman, and Heide (2003) to .86 in Salekin, Leistico, Neumann, DiCicco, and Duros (2004).

Relations to Antisocial Behavior

Most important, there have been more than 20 studies examining the relation between juvenile psychopathy and offending. These studies have found similar relations between psychopathy and antisocial behavior in juveniles as those found in adults. Juvenile psychopathy is moderately strongly related to age at onset (e.g., Corrado, Vincent, Hart, & Cohen, 2004), number and variety of offenses (e.g., Lynam, 1997; Salekin et al., 2004), stability of offending (Lynam, 1997), and quantity and quality of aggression (Brandt, Kennedy, Patrick, & Curtin, 1997; Murrie, Cornell, Kaplan, McConville, & Levy-Elkon, 2004). For example, using the CPS, in a sample of 430 12- to 13-year-old boys from a high-risk study, Lynam (1997) reported that juvenile psychopathy was moderately correlated (r range: .19 to .39) with past and current delinquency and related to serious delinquency that is stable across time.

Moreover, several studies have examined the *predictive* relations between juvenile psychopathy and antisocial behavior. A few have examined the relation between juvenile psychopathy and institutional infractions (e.g., Brandt et al., 1997; Murrie et al., 2004). For example, Spain, Douglas, Poythress, and Epstein (2004) administered three psychopathy instruments to 85 male adolescent offenders aged 11 to 18 in a residential treatment facility. They found significant relations between the total number of infractions and each of the psychopathy indices. Additional studies have examined the predictive relations between juvenile psychopathy measures and recidivism (Catchpole & Gretton, 2003). Falkenbach et al. (2003) examined the predictive utility of both self- and parent reports of the APSD and CPS in predicting recidivism among a group of 69 juveniles in a diversion program. These authors found that rearrest during the one-year follow-up was predicted by both the APSD and the CPS. Most recently, Gretton, Hare, and Catchpole (2004) followed across 10 years a sample of 157 boys who were originally assessed for psychopathy in adolescence using a precursor to the PCL:YV. These authors found that juvenile psychopathy was significantly correlated with violent recidivism and time to first new offense.

Two studies examined the relation between juvenile psychopathy and treatment outcomes. Using the PCL:YV in a sample of 64 adjudicated youth in a substance treatment program, O'Neill, Lidz, and Heilbrun (2003) found that high scorers on the PCL:YV attended the program for fewer days, participated more poorly when they did attend, and showed less clinical improvement across the course of treatment. Spain et al. (2004), in a sample of 85 male adolescent offenders currently in residential treatment, examined the relation between scores on the CPS, APSD, and PCL:YV and two treatment indicators: loss of treatment level due to misbehavior and number of days to promotion to the next treatment level. Only the CPS was significantly related to loss of treatment level, whereas scores on the both the CPS and the APSD were related to the number of days to promotion.

Finally, and importantly, several of these studies have attempted to demonstrate the incremental validity provided by the construct of juvenile psychopathy in predicting antisocial behavior. For example, Lynam (1997) demonstrated that scores on the CPS were related to concurrent serious delinquency above and beyond social class, IQ, impulsivity, and delinquency. Salekin et al. (2004), in a sample of 130 adolescent offenders, found that scores on the PCL:YV predicted concurrent delinquency above and beyond the disruptive behavior disorders. In the strongest demonstrations, three studies showed that psychopathy predicted future antisocial behavior above and beyond current antisocial behavior. Murrie et al. (2004), in a sample of 113 incarcerated adolescents, reported that scores on the PCL:YV predicted institutional violence above and beyond previous violence. Frick et al. (2003), in a community sample of 98 children, found that scores on the callous-unemotional scale of the APSD predicted later delinquency above and beyond contemporary conduct problems, although the relations did not hold for conduct problems or aggression. Most recently, Gretton et al. (2004) found that scores on the PCL:YV predicted violent recidivism across a 10-year follow-up above and beyond a number of criminal history and conduct disorder variables.

Extraoffending Elements of the Nomological Network

Juvenile psychopathy has also been found to relate in predicted ways to constructs that do not involve offending, such as other forms of psychopathology, personality, and several measures of cognitive processing. In each case, the relations replicate those obtained in adults.

Other Forms of Psychopathology. For example, at the adult level, psychopathy has been shown to be positively related to externalizing problems but negatively or unrelated to internalizing problems. These same relations have been observed in juveniles (e.g., Frick et al., 2000; Salekin et al., 2004). For example, Lynam (1997) examined the relations between scores on the mother-reported CPS and self-reported and teacher-reported psychopathology on the Youth Self Report and the Teacher Report Form in a large sample of 12- to 13-year-old boys. He found the predicted positive relations with externalizing problems and negative relations to internalizing problems.

Personality. The relations between psychopathy and personality are also fairly well charted. Lynam and colleagues (e.g., Lynam, 2002; Lynam & Derefinko, in press) have written extensively on the relation between psychopathy and the Five Factor Model of personality, which emphasizes five broad domains, identified as extraversion, agreeableness, conscientiousness, neuroticism, and openness. Using multiple approaches, Lynam and colleagues provided a personality description of the psychopath as interpersonally antagonistic or extremely low in agreeableness (i.e., suspicious, deceptive, exploitative, aggressive, arrogant, and tough-minded), extremely low in conscientiousness or constraint (i.e., having trouble controlling his impulses and endorsing nontraditional values and standards), and tending to experience negative emotions, particularly anger and cravings-related distress.

This description is quite consistent with results obtained using juvenile psychopathy measures. For example, Lynam et al. (2004) examined the relations between psychopathy assessed using the CPS and the Big Five in two separate cohorts of the Pittsburgh Youth Study. Cohort 1 was comprised of 405 12- to 13-year-old boys, and cohort 2 was comprised of 435 17-year-old boys. Psychopathy and personality were assessed using mother reports in both cohorts; additionally, boys reported on their own personalities in cohort 2. Across both cohorts and across raters in cohort 2, juvenile psychopathy was strongly negatively related to agreeableness and conscientiousness and moderately positively related to neuroticism. Additionally, Lynam et al. tested more specific hypotheses drawn from work in adult psychopathy regarding differential relations between personality and subfactors of psychopathy (see also Salekin, Leistico, Trobst, Schrum, & Lochman, 2005).

Relations to Underlying Processes. Within the adult literature, there have been multiple attempts to link psychopathy to disruptions in various hypothetical underlying biological or cognitive processes. Within recent years, several of these models have filtered down to child and adolescent populations. A review of the existing literature in juvenile psychopathy reveals two primary disruptions: (1) problems in emotional processing and (2) deficits in behavioral inhibition or impulsivity. Each of these disruptions is also found in adult psychopaths. For example, Blair and Coles (2000) investigated expression recognition using faces containing six different emotional facial expressions (fear, happiness, surprise, sadness, disgust, and anger). Results indicated that psychopathic children were impaired in their ability to recognize sadness and fear. This is consistent with research demonstrating deficiencies in the recognition of sad vocal tones among psychopathic boys (Stevens, Charman, & Blair, 2001). Similarly, multiple studies have examined the relation between juvenile psychopathy and measures of behavioral inhibition or impulsivity— a deficit frequently identified among adult psychopaths. Two studies have used adaptations of a card-playing task developed originally to measure response modulation in adult psychopaths. This task consists of 100 cards whose rate of reward per 10 trials drops from 100 to 10 percent across the task; participants must decide whether to play another card or quit the task. Both studies found that juvenile psychopaths, like their adult counterparts, play more cards than juvenile nonpsychopaths (Fisher & Blair, 1998; O'Brien & Frick, 1996). Other studies examined different behavioral tasks designed to assess reward dominant response styles. Blair, Colledge, and Mitchell (2001) used the Iowa Gambling task, which consists of four "decks of cards" that differ from one another in terms of their associated rewards and punishments; participants choose from which decks to play. In their sample of 51 juvenile boys, Blair et al. (2001) found that boys with psychopathic tendencies made more selections from the disadvantageous decks across time, paralleling findings in adult psychopaths.

THE TRANSIENT OFFENDERS

Whereas the previously mentioned theories offered accounts of the chronic offender, the following theories offer accounts of the more temporary offenders who constitute the majority of adolescent offenders. These are offenders whose offending begins and ends in adolescence. Although each theory identifies something about the context of adolescence as the causative agent of adolescent offending, they overlap less than the theories of the chronic offender.

Moffitt's AL Offenders

The second group of offenders in Moffitt's dual taxonomy are referred to as AL) offenders. Their antisocial behavior is posited to begin in early to mid-adolescence and to end in late adolescence or early adulthood. These individuals are hypothesized to offend as a result of a felt maturity gap—the difference between their biological maturity following puberty and their social/legal immaturity prior to adulthood. Moffitt argues that while in this gap, adolescents mimic LCP offenders in efforts to obtain autonomy, peers, money, and status. She further argues that because the predelinquent development of these AL offenders was healthy, they are able to desist from crime when they obtain legal adult status (e.g., close the maturity gap). The recovery of some may be delayed or never occur if they are snared by negative consequences such as criminal records or addictions, but nearly all are expected to recover. According to Moffitt, whereas LCP offending is uncommon, persistent, and pathological, AL offending is common, temporary, and nearly normative.

This aspect of Moffitt's theory, in contrast to the LCP aspect, has been less well studied. There is evidence to support a second type of offender. Several studies have empirically identified offenders groups with onsets in adolescence (e.g., Fergusson & Horwood, 2002; White, Bates, & Buyske, 2001). It appears that adolescent delinquency, in contrast to earlier starting antisocial behavior, is less strongly related to individual difference factors and more strongly related to peer delinquency (Bartusch et al., 1997; Moffitt & Caspi, 2001). It has also been found, as predicted, that AL offenders are less violent than their LCP counterparts.

There are, however, aspects of the theory that have not been supported. AL offending does not appear to be normative. In the Dunedin sample (Moffitt & Caspi, 2001), only 22 percent of the cohort were designated as AL offenders (26% of males and 18% of females). In Christchurch (Fergusson & Horwood, 2002), 38 percent of participants were so designated (50% of men and 26% of women). In a large, American prospective longitudinal study of adolescent development White et al. (2001) reported that only 33 percent of their sample were described as AL offenders.

Additionally, research examining the psychological health of AL offenders is mixed. Although Moffitt and Caspi (2001) report few differences on childhood factors between AL offenders and their nonoffending counter-parts, other research suggests that AL offenders are less psychologically well adjusted than their nonoffending counterparts. For example, Fergusson and Horwood (2002) found linear relations between offender groups (LCP, AL, and nonoffenders) and a number of social, familial, and individual level risk factors. White et al. (2001) found few differences between AL and LCP offenders on a variety of individual and familial-level variables. Hints of this are even present in the Dunedin study; Moffitt et al. (1996) compared groups of offenders on the subscales of a broad personality inventory. They reported that AL offenders were lower in traditionalism, harm avoidance, and self-control but higher in aggression, alienation, and stress reactivity than the sample mean.

Similarly, the recovery of AL offenders is not complete. Several stud-ies document the continuing problems of the AL offenders following adolescence. Moffitt, Caspi, Harrington, and Milne (2002) report that at age 26, relative to an unclassified comparison group, AL offenders were more emotionally unstable, less agreeable, and less controlled in terms of personality; received more past-year psychiatric diagnoses; engaged in more partner violence; and obtained less education and occupied lower-status occupations.

Finally, some elements of this theory have not yet been examined. There are very few studies that have tested directly the idea of a felt maturity gap leading to mimicry of antisocial peers. Bukowski, Sippola, and Newcomb (2000) found that aggressive peers became more attractive while prosocial peers became less attractive on entry to middle school; Caspi, Lynam, Moffitt, and Silva (1993) found an interaction between menarcheal timing and school composition in predicting female delinquency such that early-maturing girls in mixed-sex settings were at greatest risk for delinquency. These authors interpreted the interaction in terms of Moffitt's theory. However, both of these tests are relatively indirect.

Routine Activities

Within criminology, a number of authors have examined the relation between deviance and how people spend their time. Whereas most previ-ous research has used this perspective to study victimization and/or aggre-gate crime rates, work by Osgood and colleagues (e.g., Osgood, Wilson, O'Malley, Bachman, & Johnston, 1996) has applied the idea to individual level deviance. The essence of the theory is that "crime is dependent on opportunity" (p. 638). The motivation for deviance is assumed to be inherent in the situation rather than the person; some situations are sim-ply more likely to result in deviant acts. Three specific elements make deviance more likely: being with peers, being in a situation without an authority figure present, and engaging in unstructured activities that carry no agenda. Thus, situations involving a group of peers, gathered without an agenda, in the absence of authority are more likely to give rise to deviant acts. Individuals who spend more time in such situations are more likely to engage in deviant acts. The final corollary of the theory is that there are striking age-related changes in the prevalence of such activities across adolescence and into young adulthood. Thus, offending and deviance increase across adolescence because individuals spend more time in criminogenic situations as they move through adolescence; offending and deviance decrease across young adulthood as individuals spend less time in these unstructured activities. Osgood et al. (1996) tested this idea using data from the Monitoring the Future Study. They examined how four activities that involved unstructured socializing with peers outside the home (e.g., riding around in a car for fun) related to five types of deviance (e.g., criminal behavior, substance use) from ages 18 to 26. They found that participation in these unstructured activities was strongly associated with criminal behavior and substance use; moreover, routine activities accounted for a substantial proportion of the associations between deviance and age, sex, and socioeconomic status.

Age-Graded Informal Social Control Theory

Sampson and Laub (1993) have provided a comprehensive theory of antisocial behavior across the life course that seems well suited to understanding the onset and offset of adolescent delinquency. These authors argue that deviance results when an individual's bond to society, via individuals and institutions, is weak or broken. They argue that social investment or social "capital" in institutional relationships (family, work, or community setting) serves to increase social control and decrease deviance. Individuals' bonds create interdependent systems of obligation and restraint that impose significant costs on engaging in delinquency, drug use, and other problem behaviors. Thus, the more bonded an individual is to these institutional relations, the less free he or she is to deviate. Additionally, Sampson and Laub argue that the important institutions of informal and formal social control vary across the life course. For example, in adolescence the important institutions are the family, school, peers, and the juvenile justice system. In adulthood, the important institutions become higher education, work, marriage, and children. The onset and offset of adolescent deviance then is due to the changing composition and nature of these social bonds. Adolescence is a time when individuals are cutting ties to family and hence losing some of their social capital, becoming freer to deviate. The new social roles of young adulthood bring with them new attachments and bonds (e.g., higher education, work, and marriage), and the individual has more social capital, comes under greater social control, and is therefore less free to deviate.

There are several studies that are consistent with this model. Sampson and Laub (1993) analyzed data from Glueck and Glueck's classic study *Unraveling Juvenile Delinquency* (1950). They demonstrated that the most delinquent adolescents were those with the weakest social bonds. Most convincingly, they demonstrated that desistance from deviance in adulthood was linked with important life course transitions that created greater social capital. Other studies have similarly shown that adult transitions to work, marriage, and parenthood are related to desistance from crime and decreases in substance use. In the area of substance use, Bachman, Wadsworth, O'Malley, Johnston, and Schulenbarg (1997) found that engagement/marriage was related to decreases in smoking, heavy drinking, marijuana, and cocaine use; most interestingly, they reported that divorce was related to subsequent increases in smoking, heavy drinking, marijuana use, and cocaine use in young adulthood.

IMPLICATIONS FOR PREVENTION

There appear to be two types of adolescent offenders who differ in terms of the topography of their antisocial behavior (i.e., course, onset, and violence) and in the causes hypothesized to underlie it. Based on the theories and evidence reviewed, I draw several implications for prevention and intervention. Most concern the early-onset chronic offenders, but several are relevant to the adolescent-onset offender as well. Although I am not the first to draw these implications, they bear repeating.

1. One size does not fit all. As there is heterogeneity in adolescent deviance, there must be heterogeneity in our approach to intervention. The current review suggests the existence of at least two populations of deviant adolescents—early starters and late starters. Moreover, the causes, sequelae, and outcomes differ across the groups. For the early starters, the causes are located within the individual and his or her early environment, the consequences are broad, and the course is chronic. For the later starters, the causes are located in the developmental context of adolescence, the consequences are more focused, and the course is less chronic.

2. Timing is everything. Not only do interventions need to be tailored in content, but they need to differ in timing as well. Although earlier primary prevention efforts are possible, one must necessarily wait until

adolescence to intervene in later-starting deviance. Waiting until adolescence to intervene with the early starters, however, requires battling years of cumulative continuity. The early starters will already have poisoned relations to parents, peers, and teachers. They will already have limited educational and occupational possibilities. They will already have arrest records. They may be addicted to drugs. Early intervention with this group will do several things: (1) prevent or delay the accumulation of some of the negative consequences, (2) allow utilization of multiple change agents, and (3) allow more time for treatment to take hold.

3. Don't hold back. Early-starting antisocial behavior has a number of primary causes that are subject to intervention, including early disruptions in fetal development, poverty, and poor parenting. Each of these primary causes can be influenced. Once manifest, early-starting deviance has a number of negative consequences that serve to stabilize the behavior—disrupted parenting, poor relations with peers and teachers, and school problems. Each one of these secondary causes can be influenced. Interventions targeting multiple areas will be most effective.

4. Settle in for the long haul. Chronic medical conditions like diabetes serve as models for thinking about early-starting antisocial behavior. Diabetes is not cured, only treated. It requires ongoing treatment and monitoring throughout life. The forestalling of consequences rather than their prevention is often the best that can be hoped for.

There are several interventions programs based on these principles, including Henggler's Multisystemic Treatment (e.g., Henggeler, Melton, & Smith, 1992), the RECAP Program (Reaching Educators, Children, and Parents; Weiss, Harris, Catron, & Han, 2003), the Social Development Model (Hawkins, von Cleve, & Catalano, 1991), and the Fast Track program (Conduct Problems Prevention Research Group [CPPRG], 1999). Each program is directed at children who have engaged in or are at risk for engaging in early antisocial behavior. Each includes early, ongoing, multimodal treatment targeting a variety of risk factors. Each has also been shown to be effective.

For example, Fast Track is a 10-year-long intervention that combines family, peer, academic, classroom, and child social-cognitive skill-training components into a cohesive and comprehensive intervention. The program was delivered to 445 first-grade children at high risk for adolescent violence and contrasted with a similar number of randomly assigned control group children. After the first year of intervention, compared with the control group, the intervention group displayed higher levels of targeted skills in parenting, social cognition, and reading and less aggressive behavior (CPPRG, 1999). These effects on aggressive behavior persisted through third grade (CPPRG, 2002) and appeared to hold equally well across gender, ethnic, and severity-level groups. Effects have persisted through fifth grade, with about a 25 percent reduction in cases that could be classified as clinically deviant (CPPRG, 2004).

5. Late-starting offenders are offenders too. Although it is true that the early starters account for a disproportionate number of offenses, up to 50 percent in a given population, the late starters are committing many of the remainder of those offenses. Not surprisingly, the early-starting group gets the most attention when it comes to thinking about intervention. The argument is that successfully intervening with a single one of these offenders yields a high reduction in offending. This reduction, however, comes at a high monetary cost; none of the intervention programs mentioned previously is inexpensive, although each is less expensive in the long-term than "treating" the individual through the criminal justice system. What is not usually mentioned is that it may be possible and equally cost effective to target the later-onset offenders through smaller-scale interventions universally delivered.

Because the theories of the later-onset offender are divergent, the exact nature of that intervention is more difficult to specify. The routine activities perspective suggests providing structured after-school programs, increasing parental monitoring, and increasing the presence of agents of control at adolescent events. Moffitt's theory of offending would suggest finding ways of providing meaningful "adult-like" roles to adolescents to reduce the felt maturity gap.

There are also lessons to be learned from the substance use prevention field, which has successfully used universally delivered, often school-based interventions to reduce adolescent substance use. One intriguing approach has been explored at the University of Kentucky by Palmgreen and colleagues, who have used a known risk factor for substance use, high sensation seeking, to design public service announcements that will appeal specifically to the at-risk group. Using what they have dubbed the SENTAR (sensation-seeking targeting) approach, these investigators have utilized four principles in their design and delivery of prevention messages: (1) use sensation seeking as a major segmentation variable, (2) design prevention messages high in sensation value to reach high-sensation seekers, (3) use formative research with high-sensation-seeking members of the target audience, and (4) place the prevention messages in high-sensation-value contexts (Palmgreen, Donohew, Lorch, Hoyle, & Stephenson, 2001).

This approach has proven successful across several studies. Early laboratory work revealed that high-sensation-value messages were more effective than low-sensation-value messages in attracting attention and changing attitudes among individuals high in sensation seeking (e.g., Palmgreen et al., 1991). A later field project demonstrated that high-sensation-value messages embedded in programming popular among high-sensation seekers were effective at reaching high-sensation seekers and motivating them to call a hotline featuring alternatives to drug abuse (Palmgreen et al., 1995). Most recently, Palmgreen et al. (2001) evaluated the effectiveness of PSA campaigns targeted at high-sensation-seeking adolescents in reducing actual marijuana use. Using a controlled interrupted time-series design in two matched communities, they found that campaigns reversed upward developmental trends in 30-day marijuana use among high-sensation seekers. These investigators have taken a known risk factor for adolescent substance use, high levels of sensation seeking, and used it to design public service announcements that appeal to the individuals most at risk.

6. The ties that bind. The theories of both Moffitt (1993) and Sampson and Laub (1993) suggest that there are risks of incarceration, particularly for the late-onset offenders. In Moffitt's view, arrest and incarceration serve as "snares" that may make desistance less likely. Such snares reduce legitimate opportunities and the possibility of satisfying adult roles. Similarly, for Sampson and Laub, arrest and incarceration delay or eliminate important life transitions like marriage and steady employment and may serve to cut existing important social ties. Such theories argue strongly in favor of alternative sentencing for drug and first-time offenders.

CONCLUSION

In this chapter, I have argued that there exist at least two types of adolescent offenders—those who will persist in their offending and those who will desist. I have reviewed theories dealing with each type of offender and provided evidence relevant to these theories. The theories dealing with the more chronic offender all target individual characteristics and early environmental contexts. The theories dealing with the more temporary offenders target differing aspects of the adolescent context. As offenders are heterogeneous, so must be our interventions. I have suggested that interventions be targeted with the specific type of offender in mind. Toward this end, I offered some straightforward intervention implications drawn from the theories reviewed.

REFERENCES

American Psychiatric Association. (1980). *Diagnostic and statistical manual of mental disorders* (3rd ed.). Washington, DC: Author.

American Psychiatric Association. (1987). *Diagnostic and statistical manual of mental disorders* (3rd ed., rev. ed.). Washington, DC: Author.

American Psychiatric Association. (1994). *Diagnostic and statistical manual of mental disorders* (4th ed.). Washington, DC: Author.

Bachman, J. G., Wadsworth, K. N., O'Malley, P. M., Johnston, L. D., & Schulenbarg, J. E. (1997). *Smoking, drinking, and drug use in young adulthood.* Mahwah, NJ: Lawrence Erlbaum Associates.

Bartusch, D., Lynam, D. R., Moffitt, T. E., & Silva, P. A. (1997). Is age important? Testing a general versus a developmental theory of antisocial behavior. *Criminology, 35,* 13–48.

Blair, R. J. R., & Coles, M. (2000). Expression recognition and behavioural problems in early adolescence. *Cognitive Development, 15,* 421–434.

Blair, R. J. R., Colledge, E., & Mitchell, D. G. V. (2001). Somatic markers and response reversal: Is there orbitofrontal cortex dysfunction in boys with psychopathic tendencies? *Journal of Abnormal Child Psychology, 29,* 499–511.

Brandt, J. R., Kennedy, W. A., Patrick, C. J., & Curtin, J. J. (1997). Assessment of psychopathy in a population of incarcerated adolescent offenders. *Psychological Assessment, 9,* 429–435.

Bukowski, W. M., Sippola, L. K., & Newcomb, A. F. (2000). Variations in patterns of attraction of same- and other-sex peers during early adolescence. *Developmental Psychology, 36,* 147–154.

Caspi, A., & Bem, D. (1990). Personality continuity and change across the life course. In L. Pervin (Ed.), *Handbook of personality: Theory and research.* New York: Guilford Press.

Caspi, A., Lynam, D., Moffitt, T. E., & Silva, P. (1993). Unraveling girls' delinquency: Biological, dispositional, and contextual contributions to adolescent misbehavior. *Developmental Psychology, 29,* 19–30.

Catchpole, R., & Gretton, H. M. (2003). The predictive validity of risk assessment with violent young offenders: A 1-year examination of criminal outcome. *Criminal Justice and Behavior, 30,* 688–708.

Cleckley, H. (1941). *The mask of sanity: An attempt to reinterpret the so-called psychopathic personality.* Oxford: Mosby.

Conduct Problems Prevention Research Group. (1999). Initial impact of the Fast Track Prevention Trial for Conduct Problems: I. The high-risk sample. *Journal of Consulting and Clinical Psychology, 67,* 631–647.

Conduct Problems Prevention Research Group. (2002). Evaluation of the first three years of the Fast Track Prevention Trial with children at high risk for adolescent conduct problems. *Journal of Abnormal Child Psychology, 30,* 19–35.

Conduct Problems Prevention Research Group. (2004). The effects of the Fast Track Program on serious problem outcomes at the end of elementary school. *Journal of Clinical Child and Adolescent Psychology, 35,* 650–661.

Corrado, R. R., Vincent, G. M., Hart, S. D., & Cohen, I. M. (2004). Predictive validity of the Psychopathy Checklist: Youth Version for general and violent recidivism. *Behavioral Sciences and the Law, 22,* 5–22.

Dodge, K. A., Coie, J. D., and Lynam, D. R. (in press). Aggression and antisocial behavior in youth. In W. V. Damon (Series Ed.) & N. Eisenberg (Vol. Ed.), *Handbook of Child Psychology, Fifth Edition, Vol. 3: Social, emotional, and personality development* (pp. 779–861). New York: Wiley.

Donovan, J. E., & Jessor, R. (1985). Structure of problem behavior in adolescence and young adulthood. *Journal of Consulting and Clinical Psychology, 53,* 890–904.

Falkenbach, D. M., Poythress, N. G., Norman, G., & Heide, K. M. (2003). Psychopathic features in a juvenile diversion population: Reliability and predictive validity of two self-report measures. *Behavioral Sciences and the Law, 21,* 787–805.

Fergusson, D. M., & Horwood, L. J. (2002). Male and female offending trajectories. *Development and Psychopathology, 14,* 159–177.

Fergusson, D. M., Horwood, L. J., & Ridder, E. M. (2004). Show me the child at seven: The consequences of conduct problems in childhood for psychosocial functioning in adulthood. *Journal of Child Psychology and Psychiatry, 45,* 1–13.

Fisher, L., & Blair, R. J. R. (1998). Cognitive impairment and its relationship to psychopathic tendencies in children with emotional and behavioral difficulties. *Journal of Abnormal Child Psychology, 26,* 511–519.

Flory, K., & Lynam, D. R. (2003). The relation between attention deficit hyperactivity disorder and substance abuse: What role does conduct disorder play? *Clinical Child and Family Psychology Review, 6,* 1–16.

Flory, K., Milich, R., Lynam, D. R., Leukefeld, C., & Clayton, R. (2003). Relation between childhood disruptive behavior disorders and substance use and dependence symptoms in young adulthood: Individuals with symptoms of attention-deficit/hyperactivity disorder are uniquely at risk. *Psychology of Addictive Behaviors, 17,* 151–158.

Forth, A. E., Kosson, D. S., & Hare, R. (2003). *Hare Psychopathy Checklist: Youth Version.* Toronto: Multi-Health Systems.

Frick, P. J., Barry, C. T., & Bodin, S. D. (2000). Applying the concept of psychopathy to children: Implications for the assessment of antisocial youth. In C. B. Gacono (Ed.), *The clinical and forensic assessment of psychopathy: A practitioner's guide* (pp. 3–24). Mahwah, NJ: Lawrence Erlbaum Associates.

Frick, P. J., Cornell, A. H., Barry, C. T., Bodin, S. D., & Dane, H. E. (2003). Callous-unemotional traits and conduct problems in the prediction of conduct problem severity, aggression, and self-report of delinquency. *Journal of Abnormal Child Psychology, 31,* 457–470.

Frick, P. J., & Hare, R. (2001). *Antisocial Process Screening Device.* Toronto: Multi-Health Systems.

Glueck, S., & Glueck, E. (1950). *Unraveling juvenile delinquency.* New York: Commonwealth Fund.

Gretton, H. M., Hare, R. D., & Catchpole, R. (2004). Psychopathy and offending from adolescence to adulthood: A 10-year follow up. *Journal of Consulting and Clinical Psychology, 72,* 636–645.

Hare, R. (2003). *The Hare PCL-R* (2nd ed.). Toronto: Multi-Health Systems.

Hawkins, J. D., von Cleve, E., & Catalano, R. F. (1991). Reducing early childhood aggression: Results of a primary prevention programme. *Journal of the American Academy of Child and Adolescent Psychiatry, 30,* 208–217.

Henggeler, S. W., Melton, G. B., & Smith, L. A. (1992). Family preservation using multisystemic therapy: An effective alternative to incarcerating serious juvenile offenders. *Journal of Consulting and Clinical Psychology, 60,* 953–961.

Hirschi, T., & Gottfredson, M. (1983). Age and the explanation of crime. *American Journal of Sociology, 89,* 552–584.

Huesmann, L., Eron, L. D., Lefkowitz, M. M., & Walder, L. O. (1984). Stability of aggression over time and generations. *Developmental Psychology, 20,* 1120–1134.

Jessor, R., & Jessor, S. L. (1977). *Problem behavior and psychosocial development: A longitudinal study of youth.* New York: Academic Press.

Krueger, R. F. (1999). Personality traits in late adolescence predict mental disorders in early adulthood: A prospective-epidemiological study. *Journal of Personality, 67,* 39–65.

Loney, B. R., Frick, P. J., Clements, C. B., Ellis, M., & Kerlin, K. (2003). Callous-unemotional traits, impulsivity, and emotional processing in adolescents with antisocial behavior problems. *Journal of Clinical Child and Adolescent Psychology, 32,* 66–80.

Lynam, D. R. (1996). The early identification of chronic offenders: Who is the fledgling psychopath? *Psychological Bulletin, 120,* 209–234.

Lynam, D. R. (1997). Pursuing the psychopath: Capturing the fledgling psychopath in a nomological net. *Journal of Abnormal Psychology, 106,* 425–438.

Lynam, D. R. (2002). Psychopathy from the perspective of the five-factor model of personality. In P. T. Costa, Jr., & T. A. Widiger (Eds.), *Personality disorders and the five factor model of personality* (2nd ed., pp. 325–348). Washington, DC: American Psychological Association.

Lynam, D. R., Caspi, A., Moffitt, T. E., Raine, A., Loeber, R., & Stouthamer-Loeber, M. (2005). Adolescent psychopathy and the Big Five: Results from two samples. *Journal of Abnormal Child Psychology, 33,* 431–443.

Lynam, D. R., & Derefinko, K. (in press). Psychopathy and personality. In C. J. Patrick (Ed.), *Handbook of psychopathy.* New York: Guilford Press.

Lynam, D. R., & Gudonis, L. (2005). The development of psychopathy. *Annual Review of Clinical Psychology, 1,* 381–408.

Maguire, K., & Pastore, A. L. (1998). *Sourcebook of criminal justice statistics 1997.* Washington, DC: U.S. Government Printing Office.

Moffitt, T. E. (1993). Adolescence-limited and life-course persistent antisocial behavior: A developmental taxonomy. *Psychological Review, 100,* 674–701.

Moffitt, T. E., & Caspi, A. (2001). Childhood predictors differentiate-life-course-persistent and adolescencelimited antisocial pathways among males and females. *Development and Psychopathology, 13,* 355–375.

Moffitt, T. E., Caspi, A., Dickson, N., Silva, P. A., & Stanton, W. (1996). Childhood-onset versus adolescent-onset antisocial conduct in males: Natural history from age 3 to 18. *Development and Psychopathology, 8,* 399–424.

Moffitt, T. E., Caspi, A., Harrington, H., & Milne, B. J. (2002). Males on the life-course persistent and adolescence-limited pathways: Follow-up at age 26 years. *Development and Psychopathology, 14,* 179–207.

Murrie, D. C., Cornell, D. G., Kaplan, S., McConville, D., & Levy-Elkon, A. (2004). Psychopathy scores and violence among juvenile offenders: A multi-measure study. *Behavioral Sciences and the Law, 22,* 49–67.

O'Brien, B. S., & Frick, P. J. (1996). Reward dominance: Associations with anxiety, conduct problems, and psychopathy in children. *Journal of Abnormal Child Psychology, 24,* 223–240.

O'Neill, M. L., Lidz, V., & Heilbrun, K. (2003). Predictors and correlates of psychopathic characteristics in substance abusing adolescents. *International Journal of Forensic Mental Health, 2,* 35–46.

Osgood, D. W., Johnston, L. D., O'Malley, P. M., & Bachman, J. G. (1988). The generality of deviance in late adolescence and early adulthood. *American Sociological Review, 53,* 81–93.

Osgood, D. W., Wilson, J. K., O'Malley, P. M., Bachman, J. G., & Johnston, L. D. (1996). Routine activities and individual deviant behavior. *American Sociological Review, 61,* 635–655.

Palmgreen, P., Donohew, L., Lorch, E. P., Hoyle, R., & Stephenson, M. T. (2001). Television campaigns and adolescent marijuana use: Tests of sensation-seeking targeting. *American Journal of Public Health, 91,* 292–296.

Palmgreen, P., Donohew, L., Lorch, E. P., Rogus, M., Helm, D., & Grant N. (1991). Sensation seeking, message sensation value, and drug use as mediators of PSA effectiveness. *Health Communication, 3,* 217–227.

Palmgreen, P., Lorch, E. P., Donohew, R. L., Harrington, N. G., D'Silva, M., & Helm, D. (1995). Reaching at-risk populations in a mass media drug abuse prevention campaign: Sensation seeking as a targeting variable. *Drugs and Society, 8,* 29–45.

Piquero, A. R., & Tibbetts, S. G. (1999). The impact of pre/perinatal disturbances and disadvantaged familial environment in predicting criminal offending. *Studies on Crime and Crime Prevention, 8,* 52–70.

Robins, L. N. (1966). *Deviant children grown up.* Baltimore: Williams and Wilkins.

Robins, L. N. (1978). Sturdy childhood predictors of adult antisocial behaviour: Replications from longitudinal studies. *Psychological Medicine, 8,* 611–622.

Salekin, R. T., Leistico, A.-M. R., Neumann, C. S., DiCicco, T. M., & Duros, R. L. (2004). Psychopathy and comorbidity in a young offender sample: Taking a closer look at psychopathy's potential importance over disruptive behavior disorders. *Journal of Abnormal Psychology, 113,* 416–427.

Salekin, R. T., Leistico, A.-M. R., Trobst, K. K., Schrum, C. L., & Lochman, J. E. (2005). Adolescent psychopathy and the interpersonal circumplex: Expanding evidence of a nomological net. *Journal of Abnormal Child Psychology, 33,* 445–460.

Sampson, R. J., & Laub, J. H. (1990). Crime and deviance over the life course: The salience of adult social bonds. *American Sociological Review, 55,* 609–627.

Sampson, R. J., & Laub, J. H. (1993). *Crime in the making: Pathways and turning points.* Cambridge, MA: Harvard University Press.

Spain, S. E., Douglas, K. S., Poythress, N. G., & Epstein, M. (2004). The relationship between psychopathic features, violence and treatment outcome: The comparison of three youth measures of psychopathic features. *Behavioral Sciences and the Law, 22,* 85–102.

Stevens, D., Charman, T., & Blair, R. J. R. (2001). Recognition of emotion in facial expressions and vocal tones in children with psychopathic tendencies. *Journal of Genetic Psychology, 162,* 201–211.

Waschbusch, D. A. (2002). A meta-analytic examination of comorbid hyperactive-impulsive-attention problems and conduct problems. *Psychological Bulletin, 128,* 118–150.

Weiss, B., Harris, V., Catron, T., & Han, S. S. (2003). Efficacy of the RECAP intervention program for children with concurrent internalizing and externalizing problems. *Journal of Consulting and Clinical Psychology, 71,* 364–374.

White, H., Bates, M. E., & Buyske, S. (2001). Adolescence-limited versus persistent delinquency: Extending Moffitt's hypothesis into adulthood. *Journal of Abnormal Psychology, 110,* 600–609.

Zhang, L., Welte, J. W., & Wieczorek, W. F. (2002). Underlying common factors of adolescent problem behaviors. *Criminal Justice and Behavior, 29,* 161–182.

Chapter 7

YOUTH SUICIDAL BEHAVIOR: A CRISIS IN NEED OF ATTENTION

James J. Mazza

Suicide and suicidal behavior in children and adolescents has been at a crisis stage for the past two decades; however, it has only been recently that it is receiving some of the attention it truly deserves (Gould, Greenberg, Velting, & Shaffer, 2003; U.S. Department of Health and Human Services [DHHS], 2001). Using the most current data from 2001, suicide is currently the third leading cause of death in the United States for youth between the ages of 5 and 19 behind automobile accidents and homicide (Centers for Disease Control and Prevention [CDC], 2004). However, in some states, such as Washington, suicide is ranked second among 15- to 19-year-olds and twice that of the homicide rate (Washington State Youth Suicide Prevention Program, 2004).

SUICIDAL BEHAVIOR

Unfortunately, suicide is only one behavior among a continuum of suicidal behaviors that consists of suicidal ideation at one end, followed by suicidal intent, then suicidal attempt(s), and finally death due to suicide, the far end of the continuum (Reynolds, 1988; Reynolds & Mazza, 1994). These stages or behaviors along the continuum are not independent, nor does every child or adolescent who is suicidal go through all four stages. As one moves up or along the suicidal behavior continuum, the prevalence of each behavior becomes less but increases in suicidal risk and/or lethality. According to the 2003 Youth Risk Behavior Survey (YRBS; CDC, 2004) completed by more than 15,000 high school students nationally, approximately one of out six high school adolescents (16.9%) stated they had thought seriously of attempting suicide, with a similar number (16.5%) stating that they had made a plan to attempt suicide. Regarding suicide attempts, approximately 1 out of 12 had made a suicide attempt in the past year, and 2.9% had made a suicide attempt that required medical attention (CDC, 2004).

Suicidal Ideation

Suicidal ideation is at the beginning of the suicidal behavior continuum and is often viewed as the precursor to other more serious suicidal behaviors (DHHS, 2001; Ladame & Jeanneret, 1982; Mazza, in press; Reynolds, 1988; Reynolds & Mazza, 1994). Suicidal ideation consists of thoughts and cognitions about killing oneself as well as specific thoughts related to suicide. These thoughts and cognitions ranged from general thoughts about killing oneself or wishes of being dead or never being born to more specific and detailed thoughts, including a specific plan to kill oneself with the how, when, and where premeditated (Reynolds, 1988; Reynolds & Mazza, 1994).

In examining gender differences of suicidal ideation, females tend to be thinking about suicide more than males (CDC, 2004; Mazza & Reynolds, 2001; Reynolds, 1988). The results from the YRBS found that 21.3 percent of females had seriously considered attempting suicide within the past year compared to 12.8 percent for males (CDC, 2004). In using the Suicidal Ideation Questionnaire (Reynolds, 1987) to identify current suicidal ideation, Mazza and Reynolds (2001) found that 16 percent of females scored about the clinical cutoff score compared to 7 percent for males.

Suicidal Intent

Suicidal intent is defined as the intentions of the individual at the time of their attempt in regard to their wish to die (Overholser & Spirito, 2003). Suicidal intent is made up of multiple components: expressed intent, planning, communication, and concealment (Kingsbury, 1993). Behaviors that represent these four components include but are not limited to giving away prized or meaningful possessions, writing a will, minor self-destructive behaviors, and subtle and/or overt threats (Reynolds, 1988). Several of these behaviors are overt and may be viewed as a warning sign to friends, family, and significant others that this specific individual is at risk for suicide and that follow-up regarding their current mental health is needed. It is important to note that not all suicidal youth engage in suicidal intent and, likewise, that not all youth who display these behaviors are suicidal.

Suicide Attempts

Suicide attempts are self-injurious behaviors with the intentionality of causing death (Reynolds & Mazza, 1994). Research studies using "psychological autopsies," a method for collecting information about the deceased by interviewing friends and family members about the psychological well-being of the person who committed suicide (Shafii, Carrigan, Whittinghill, & Derrick, 1985), have found that those who died by suicide frequently engaged in prior suicidal behavior, including making multiple suicide attempts (Brent, Baugher, Bridge, Chen, & Chiappetta, 1999). According to the CDC (2004), 1 of out 12 (8.5%) high school adolescents has attempted suicide within the past year (incidence rate). Research findings with middle school adolescents have shown slightly lower rates of 7.7 percent among sixth, seventh, and eighth graders (Reynolds & Mazza, 1999). With the incidence rate hovering around 7 to 8 percent for middle school and high school adolescents, the prevalence rate (lifetime) is considerably higher, ranging from 11 to 14 percent (Mazza & Reynolds, 2001; Riggs & Cheng, 1988), which means that approximately one out of eight to one out of seven high school adolescents attempts suicide before they graduate.

Similar to suicidal ideation, females engage in making a suicide attempt more frequently than males (Gould et al., 1998; Lewinsohn, Rohde, & Seeley, 1996; National Center for Health Statistics [NCHS], 2003; Reynolds & Mazza, 1993). According to the YRBS data, 11.5 percent of females made a suicide attempt in the past year compared to 5.4 percent for males, a ratio of approximately 2:1 (CDC, 2004). Reynolds and Mazza reported a similar 2:1 ratio in a sample of more than 3,400 school-based adolescents (469 suicide attempters) from eight different states. In addition, they found that among suicide attempters females were more likely to have made multiple attempts (35%) compared to males (22%). It should be noted that Garfinkel, Froese, and Hood (1982), who examined the medical records of 505 children and adolescents seen in an emergency room for a suicide attempt, found that most youth (78%) made low lethality attempts, compared to 21 percent of moderate lethality and only 1 percent of high lethality. These results, coupled with the fact that the majority of attempts made by these youth had a high likelihood of being rescued compared to 3.4 percent of low likelihood, suggests that most youth are ambivalent about taking their own lives (Garfinkel et al., 1982).

Suicide

Suicide is defined as an intentional self-injurious behavior that resulted in death (Reynolds & Mazza, 1994). As stated previously, suicide is the third leading cause of death for youth ages 5 to 19 years old (CDC, 2004). Although suicide is the behavior that most frequently grabs the headlines, it is in fact the rarest of the suicidal behavior continuum. According to the latest data (2001), the current rate of suicide is 7.9 per 100,000 for adolescents between the ages of 15 and 19 years and 1.3 per 100,000 for youth between the ages of 10 and 14 years (McIntosh, 2003). The suicide rate for youngsters ages five to nine is a bit more difficult to figure out for multiple reasons, but one primary explanation is that coroners are not likely to categorize a death as suicide unless intentional self-injury is proven, a difficult task among first through fourth graders.

In contrast to suicidal ideation and attempts, males die by suicide approximately five times more often than females (Anderson, 2002; NCHS, 2003). The reason for the large discrepancy in gender differences is twofold. First, males tend to use more lethal means to attempt suicide than females (Anderson, 2002; Reynolds & Mazza, 1993). Second, males are more likely to be substance abusers than females, and research has shown substance abuse to be linked with adolescent suicide (Shaffer et al., 1996; Shafii et al., 1985).

ETHNICITY

The rate of adolescent suicide is not equally dispersed across the different ethnic groups. The highest rates of adolescent suicide are among Native Americans, while the lowest rate tends to be among Asian/Pacific Islanders (NCHS, 2003). Among the other large ethnic groups, Caucasians in general tend to have a higher rate than African Americans, who in turn have a higher rate than Latinos (NCHS, 2003). There are several factors that have been put forth to explain the high rate of suicide among Native Americans; these include a higher prevalence rate of owning firearms, high use of alcohol and/or drugs, and lack of social integration (Middlebrook, LeMaster, Beals, Novins, & Manson, 2001).

METHODS

Fortunately, the suicide attempt methods used by most children and adolescents tend to be of low lethality. As discussed previously in the Garfinkel et al. (1982) findings, children and adolescents tend to use methods of low lethality and allow for a high likelihood of being rescued (rescuability), suggesting that they are ambivalent about taking their own lives. This ambivalence is viewed as a protective factor and allows the youth time to change his or her mind and to seek help. According to the 469 adolescent suicide attempters in the Reynolds and Mazza (1993) study, the two most common methods for male and female adolescents were taking pills (22.5% and 45.1%, respectively) and cutting wrists (18.6% and 30.4%, respectively).

In contrast to adolescent suicide attempts, which are generally of low lethality and high rescuability, the most frequent method of suicide is guns, having high lethality and low rescuability (NCHS, 2003). Fifty-seven percent of all adolescent suicides were from guns, and firearms is the most common method used by both male and female adolescents who commit suicide (NCHS, 2004). Two studies showed that adolescents who died by suicide were three to four times more likely to have guns in their home compared to adolescents who attempted suicide and nonattempting psychiatric adolescents (Brent, Perper, Kolko, & Goldstein, 1988; Brent et al., 1991). Research from other countries has shown that limiting access to lethal means, such as guns or poisonous gases, has been an effective strategy in reducing suicide (DHHS, 2001; Krug, Powell, & Dahlbert, 1998), although further studies investigating this issue are needed.

Critical Issues in Youth Suicidal Behavior

There are several critical issues that are important in helping one understand the complexity of youth suicidal behavior and to help facilitate the implementation of suicide prevention/intervention programs. Identifying warning signs and risk factors that are related to suicidal behavior is an important undertaking in providing accurate risk assessment and determining which strategies to use for intervention. In addition, dispelling myths surrounding adolescent suicidal behavior will provide clinicians and mental health professionals with confidence in working with youth at-risk for suicidal behavior and relieve some anxiety that school administrators have reported about implementing suicide prevention programs in their schools.

RISK FACTORS AND WARNING SIGNS

There are a significant number of warning signs and risk factors that are related to suicide and suicidal behavior (Brent et al., 1999; Cole, 1989, Lewinsohn, Rohde, & Seeley, 1994; Mazza & Reynolds, 2001; Shafii, Stelta-Lenarsky, Derrick, Beckner, & Whittinghill, 1988). Research examining suicidal behavior in adolescents has focused on two specific at-risk populations: those who have died by suicide and those who have attempted suicide. Although these two behaviors are in close proximity on the suicidal behavior continuum, it is important to remember that these groups of adolescents are quite different; suicide attempters tend to be females, who make low-lethality attempts, while those who die by suicide tend to be males, who have made high-lethality attempts. Research studies using psychological autopsies for those who died by suicide and self-report questionnaires and clinical interviews for those who attempted suicide have identified prior suicidal behavior, psychopathology, family history of suicidal behavior and/or psychopathology, and stressful life events (including physical and sexual abuse and relationship problems) as important risk factors and warning signs (Brent et al., 1999; Mazza & Reynolds, 2001; Shafii et al., 1988).

For adolescents, engaging in past suicidal behavior, particularly a past suicide attempt, is one of the strongest predictors of future suicidal behavior (Brent et al., 1999; Groholt, Ekeberg, Wichstrom, & Haldorsen, 1997; McKeown et al., 1998). Groholt and colleagues, who studied children and adolescents who died by suicide, reported that one-fourth to one-third had a history of making a prior suicide attempt. Shaffer and colleagues (1996) reported among children and adolescents who died by suicide that a prior suicide attempt was more predictive for boys than for girls.

A previous history of suicide in the family and/or psychopathology is an important risk factor for adolescent suicidal behavior (Brent, Bridge, Johnson, & Connolly, 1996; Johnson, Brent, Bridge, & Connolly, 1998; Shafii et al., 1985). Based on the results from the studies cited previously, a family history of suicidal behavior significantly increases the likelihood of youth engaging in suicidal behavior. In addition, family history of psychopathology, such as depression, also increases the likelihood of youth suicidal behavior even when the family history of suicidal behavior is negative (Brent et al., 1996). Because some psychopathology has been found to be genetic and these illnesses may include suicidal behavior as part of their symptomatology (i.e., depression, anxiety, and schizophrenia), obtaining a thorough family history becomes an important factor in helping assess and intervene with at-risk youth (Hollenbeck, Dyl, & Spirito, 2003).

Another important risk factor for youth who engage in suicidal behavior is psychopathology (Brent et al., 1999; Marttunen, Aro, & Lonnqvist, 1991; Shafii et al., 1988). Shafii and colleagues (1988), using psychological autopsies, reported that more than 90 percent of youth who died by suicide had at least one psychiatric disorder, such as depression, substance abuse, conduct disorder, and antisocial personality disorder. In fact, most adolescents who have committed suicide have multiple psychiatric disorders occurring simultaneously, a phenomenon called comorbidity (Shafii et al., 1988). The substantial presence of psychopathology and often comorbidity indicates that suicidal behavior does not happen in isolation but rather is related to other mental health difficulties. Depression is the most common psychopathology linked to suicidal behavior, with approximately 50 to 66 percent of those who died by suicide experiencing some type of depressive disorder (Marttunen et al., 1991; Shaffer et al., 1996). However, it is important to note that not all youth who are depressed are suicidal and, likewise, that not all suicidal youth are depressed (Reynolds & Mazza, 1993). Research results from other studies have also identified substance abuse, anxiety disorders, schizophrenia, borderline personality disorder, and adjustment disorder as being related to adolescent suicidal behavior (Brent et al., 1999, Marttunen et al., 1991; Mazza & Reynolds, 2001; Shafii et al., 1988). One important mental health problem is hopelessness, and although it is not a diagnosis in itself, several studies have shown that it is uniquely related to suicidal behavior in adolescents, especially among females (Cole, 1989; Mazza & Reynolds, 1998).

Stressful life events is the last risk factor mentioned in this chapter, although there are many others beyond the few named here. The stress-causing event can happen either to the adolescent or to his or her family. For example, research conducted by Marttunen and colleagues reported events such as parent's divorce, breakup of a romantic relationship, disciplinary or legal action, academic failure, and death of a loved one as being significantly related to youth suicidal behavior (Marttunen, Aro, & Lonnqvist, 1993). In addition, youth who experience physical and/or sexual abuse have been also shown to have higher rates of suicide and attempted suicide compared to peers who have not been abused (Johnson et al., 2002; Silverman, Reinherz, & Giaconai, 1996). However, determining the unique relationship of physical and/or sexual abuse regarding youth suicidal behavior is complicated because frequently the abusive behaviors are accompanied by other risk factors as well, such as family and/or individual psychopathology.

MYTHS

Dispelling myths surrounding youth suicidal behavior is important, so clinicians and mental health workers can feel confident in the questions they ask and the strategies they implement. In addition, these myths have been a barrier for parents and school administrators when talking to their children regarding issues related to suicidal behavior. One of the biggest myths is the belief that talking about suicide will cause or give youth ideas about suicide (Kalafat, 2003; Reynolds, 1988). Unfortunately, this myth is held by many parents, school administrators, school counselors, and mental health workers. Actually, talking about suicide and suicidal behavior with a trusted adult allows youth the opportunity to ask questions and share their feelings about themselves or someone else who may be at risk. The issues of suicidal behavior are frequently on the minds of youth, and there is a high probability that many students know someone who has died by or attempted suicide. Given that most adults are uncomfortable talking about suicidal behavior and the taboo surrounding the subject, providing a bridge of communication that is nonjudgmental is a proactive approach in helping students discuss their beliefs, feelings, and misperceptions. Proactive approaches, such as screening youth for suicidal behavior, have been recommended by the U.S. surgeon general as a primary care strategy (DHHS, 2001).

The second myth regarding suicidal behavior is that those who attempt suicide typically get medical treatment (Smith & Crawford, 1986). Unfortunately, most youth do not tell their parents about their suicide attempts. In a study of 313 adolescent suicide attempters, Smith and Crawford reported that only 12 percent received medical treatment for their attempt, leaving 88 percent untreated. One facet of this behavior is that most youth are not old enough to drive, nor are their friends; thus, transportation for medical treatment would require telling an older sibling or parent about their behavior, an approach that most adolescents do not take.

A third myth is in regard to youth leaving suicide notes if they are suicidal (Garfinkel et al., 1982; Leenaars, 1992). Garfinkel and colleagues (1982) found that only 5 percent of children and adolescents wrote a suicide note before their suicide attempt. Similar to the medical treatment myth, one of the primary reasons they do not write a suicide note is that they do not want their parents finding out what they are thinking or feeling. Adolescents often feel that parents are overly involved or interfering in their lives and that writing a suicide note only increases the likelihood of getting parents more involved.

The last myth surrounds parents' knowledge of their child's suicidal behavior. It is a myth that parents know if their child is suicidal (Kashani, Goddard, & Reid, 1989). The Kashani et al. study found that 86 percent of parents were unaware of their child's suicidal behavior, including suicide attempts. Again, similar to several other myths, adolescents do not communicate their suicidal thinking or behavior to their parents. The importance of this finding is that clinicians, school counselors and psychologists, and youth mental health workers need to ask the youth themselves directly regarding suicidal behavior rather than relying on parents for this information. Remember the first myth: asking about suicidal behavior does not cause or give ideas to youth. Thus, direct questioning regarding suicide is a proactive strategy.

SUMMARY OF BACKGROUND INFORMATION

Thus far, this chapter has provided some background information regarding the different types of suicidal behavior, their definitions, and facts regarding the frequency of each. However, it should be noted that the agreement of standardized nomenclature regarding the definitions of suicidal behaviors remains a contentious issue for researchers and clinicians (Berman & Jobes, 1991). In addition, the previous sections highlighted descriptive information, risk factors, and warning signs and dispelled several myths that are potential barriers for helping mental health professional in working with at-risk youth. It is hoped that the information given thus far has provided a foundational level of knowledge for the subsequent sections.

A Crisis in Need of Attention

Suicidal behavior in youth has been a crisis in need of attention for the past 20 years. The suicide rate for adolescents ages 15 to 19 years tripled from 1955 to 1994 to a rate of 11.2 per 100,000 but has been slowly declining over the past 10 years to its current level of 7.9 per 100,000 (McIntosh, 2003; NCHS, 2003). The rate of increase over the past 25 years for younger adolescents ages 10 to 14 years has been equally alarming. According to the CDC, the suicide rate for 10- to 14-year-olds increased 99 percent from 1980 to 1997 compared to 11 percent for 15- to 19-year-olds during the same period (McIntosh, 2003). Within the past five years, the U.S. surgeon general has recognized this crisis and provided two important documents: "The Surgeon General's Call to Action to Prevent Suicide" and the "National Strategy for Suicide Prevention: Goals and Objectives for Action" (DHHS, 2001; U.S. Public Health Service, 1999). Although these two documents emphasize the problem of suicide in our society in general, they specifically highlight the problem in youth suicide and provide a structure for developing broad-based support systems in communities, workplaces, and schools. In addition, the national strategy calls for the development and implementation of suicide prevention programs that are evidenced based in preventing and/or reducing suicidal behavior in schools, universities, and other environments (DHHS, 2001).

SCHOOL-BASED PREVENTION PROGRAMS

Middle schools and high schools are an ideal place to implement suicide prevention programs. Although a majority of the students at these institutions are not at risk for suicidal behavior, implementing programs at these institutions would maximize the identification of youth who are at risk. Given the myths that were highlighted previously, it is unlikely that teachers, school administrators, and/or parents know if their students or child is at risk for suicidal behavior. In addition, goal 4.2 of the U.S. surgeon general's National Strategy for Suicide Prevention highlighted the need to develop evidence-based suicide prevention programs for schools, universities, and other facilities, while goal 7.2 emphasized the need to incorporate suicide risk screening to identify those at risk for suicide (DHHS, 2001). However, the development and implementation of suicide prevention programs, especially in the school environment, involves numerous factors and resources (Kalafat, 2003). In addition, some suicide prevention programs focus on helping adolescents stay in school, based on research that shows higher rates of suicidal behavior in youth who are at risk for dropping out of school (Eggert, Nicholas, & Owens, 1995; Eggert, Thompson, Herting, & Nicholas, 1995).

One of the first steps is to identify what has been done in the past, what has worked, and what has not worked. Garland, Shaffer, and Whittle (1989) reviewed 115 suicide prevention programs that were designed for youth and developed in the early to mid-1980s. Results of their review found that many programs were problematic with short duration (two hours or less), had subscribed to a stress-model theoretical orientation, and focused on goals of educating staff and students about youth suicidal behavior and raising awareness of the problem. Mazza's (1997) review of 11 school-based suicide prevention programs from 1980 to 1994 found similar problematic structures and was critical of programs not providing empirical support showing the efficacy of their programs in regard to suicidal behavior themselves. Many of the first-generation programs (Kalafat, 2003), those developed in the 1980s and early 1990s, failed to identify their intended audience, lacked clear goals, and provided mixed results (Ciffone, 1993; Kalafat & Elias, 1994; Overholser, Hemstreet, Spirito, & Vyse, 1989; Shaffer, Garland, Gould, Fisher, & Trautman, 1988). With increased research in this area and reviews of multiple programs, several major components were identified that needed to change.

First, Garland and colleagues (1989) reported that 96 percent of the programs they reviewed used a stress-model theoretical orientation. This was quite problematic because it provided the message that anyone could become suicidal if under enough stress. In addition, this theoretical orientation ignored the significant amount of research that links suicidal behavior to psychopathology (Brent et al., 1999; Marttunen et al., 1991; Shaffer et al., 1996). Thus, it was recommended that suicide prevention programs use an empirical-based theoretical orientation, such as mental illness or psychopathology, rather than a stress-related model (DHHS, 2001).

Second, prevention programs were of short duration, ranging from several hours to several days, and were not linked to the education curriculum (Garland et al., 1989). Programs that are implemented in isolation and are not part of a larger school curriculum frequently are viewed as inefficient, strain school resources, and are not well supported. Thus, suicide prevention programs have been recommended to be consistent with school culture, utilize school resources efficiently, and comply with school mandates (Kalafat, 2003).

Third, the goals of most prevention programs were to enhance knowledge of staff and students regarding youth suicidal behavior, change attitudes about seeking help for oneself or a friend who may be at risk for suicide, and raise awareness of the problem of youth suicide (Garland et al., 1989; Mazza, 1997). Although these goals centered on important behaviors within a suicide prevention curriculum, they do not focus on reducing suicidal behavior itself. Thus, when programs provided data on effectiveness in reaching their intended goals, many programs were deemed effective without measuring actual changes in suicidal behavior. Unfortunately, increases in knowledge and attitude changes have not resulted in substantial changes in suicidal behavior (Berman & Jobes, 1995; Ciffone, 1993). Furthermore, although suicide itself has a low-base rate, several other behaviors along the continuum, such as suicidal ideation or suicide attempts, happen at a great enough frequency that they could be used as dependent measures for evaluating program effectiveness (Mazza, 1997; Potter, Powell, & Kachur, 1995). Thus, the implementation of efficacy measures that examine actual suicidal behavior has been recommended as part of the program effectiveness evaluation for second-generation programs (Konick, Brandt, & Gutierrez, 2002; Mazza, 1997; Potter et al., 1995).

This leads to the fourth change, which is program evaluation design. Second-generation evaluation or programs need to not only measure actual suicidal behavior but also provide multiple evaluation periods that examine the short-term and long-term impact of their prevention programs. Most of the first-generation programs used a pretest–posttest design (Ciffone, 1993; Kalafat & Elias, 1994; Overholser et al., 1989; Shaffer, Garland, Vieland, Underwood, & Busner, 1991), and when examining knowledge gains and attitude changes, this design/approach makes logical sense. However, short-term and long-term follow-up are recommended to determine the short- and long-term impact of the program after it has been implemented (Kalafat, 2003; Mazza, 1997). This is especially important when examining suicidal behavior, as it allows time to pass and provides multiple opportunities for students to implement program strategies or procedures and, conversely, for suicidal behavior to occur.

The last component that needs revision is the intended target audience. As stated earlier, many of the first-generation programs were implemented, but it was unclear if they were intended for at-risk suicidal students, friends of those who might be at risk, all students, or school staff (Garland et al., 1989; Kalafat, 2003). Implementing a unilateral approach to address the needs of those who are at risk for suicidal behavior as well as those who are not and trying to educate students, staff, and school administrators at the same time does not work (Kalafat, 2003). Because students have diverse needs regarding mental health and specifically suicidal behavior, it is recommended that school-based suicide prevention programs be multifaceted in addressing the needs of students of varying degrees of risk, staff, administrators, and other caring adults, such as parents and coaches. In addition, second-generation programs need to span beyond the school environment and involve community, parents, and other mental health professionals in order to be successful. For example, once a student is identified as high risk for suicide, most school counselors or psychologists are not trained to provide clinical services to this student; thus, linking with trained community professionals in this case is essential. Likewise, providing opportunities for student involvement in the development and delivery of the program has been shown to be effective as well (Eastgard, 2000) because most suicidal youth confide in their peers rather than adults (Brent et al., 1988; Kalafat & Elias, 1992), and peer-to-peer messages are sometimes more effective than teacher-to-peer messages.

Determining the audience for school-based suicide prevention programs is more complex than it seems, and a one-size-fits-all approach does not work (Kalafat, 2003). The Institute of Medicine has three categories for describing the audiences who receive treatment or intervention/prevention programs:

a) "Universal" programs are intended for everyone or the general audience. For schools, this would include all students as well as teachers, school counselors, administrators, and other adults who are in close contact with students. Specific to suicide prevention programs, universal programs include increasing awareness of youth suicidal behavior, identifying warning signs, teaching appropriate responses to peers who may come in contact with someone who is suicidal, and identifying youth who may be at risk for suicide (Kalafat, 2003). In addition, school procedures and policies for intervention with suicidal youth are also included in universal programs. Most suicide prevention programs target universal populations (Kalafat & Elias, 1994; Overholser et al., 1989; Shaffer et al., 1991).

b) "Selective" programs target those subpopulations that are at greater risk because of predetermined risk factors that have been linked to suicidal behavior through previous research. In this case, adolescents with psychopathology, youth in transition between middle and high school and between high school and higher education, and those who have a history of suicidal behavior in their family would be targeted. Components of a selective program may include developing and teaching coping strategies and skills, identifying different community and school resources to get help, coaching and practicing help-seeking behavior, highlighting peer involvement and how to respond to someone who may be suicidal, and identifying youth who have already engaged in past or are currently engaging in suicidal behavior. In contrast to universal programs, there are no selective suicide prevention programs to date, at least none that have appeared in the suicidology literature base (Kalafat, 2003). One could argue that being an adolescent in general is a subpopulation at risk, given the high prevalence of alcohol and drug use among teens, the transition from grade 8 to grade 9 and again after grade 12, and the change in social support, coupled with the biological changes that are related to numerous psychopathologies. Perhaps most programs in middle and high school are actually "selective universal" suicide prevention programs.

c) "Indicated" programs target a subpopulation that has already been identified as being at risk through screening, usually indicating past or current suicidal behavior, peer or self-referral, or other identification process. Indicated programs focus on helping to resolve the current conflicts or crises and aim to reduce the risk of engaging in more suicidal behavior. Components of an indicated prevention program include developing and teaching adaptive coping strategies that help youth deal with stress and emotional dysregulation; understanding how to access emergency help; providing ongoing support during crisis or emotional times; learning to cope with mental health problems and their relationship to suicidal behavior; identifying caring adults in school, home, and community environments; and learning how to talk about their feelings. There is one indicated program that has provided empirical data regarding the effectiveness of their program called Reconnecting Youth (RY) (Eggert, Nicholas, et al., 1995). This program identifies students who are at risk for school dropout and places them in one of two groups: RY class or controls. Result from this indicated prevention program showed that students who received the RY class engaged in less suicidal behavior than controls (Eggert, Thompson, et al., 1995). Subsequent work using shorter intervention programs have been also shown to be effective in reducing suicidal ideation and attitudes among high-risk adolescents (Randell, Eggert, & Pike, 2001; Thompson, Eggert, Randell, & Pike, 2001). One interesting finding to note was that simply conducting a brief assessment interview showed a reduction in suicidal risk behavior, suggesting that assessment alone may act as an intervention because it allowed students to talk to an adult who simply wanted to know how he or she felt.

There are strengths and challenges to each type of suicide prevention program as there are for each school district and individual school. The program that may fit the best for one school may be the least favorite for another. It is important to view the universal, selective, and indicated programs as complementary rather than competitively. This type of complementary intervention would address the needs of those who have engaged in past and/or current suicidal behavior (indicated) while fulfilling the role of educating nonsuicidal students, school staff, and administrators about the risk factors, warning signs, facts, and myths surrounding youth suicide.

It is important to remember that the development, implementation, and evaluation of school-based suicide prevention programs is an iterative process (Kalafat, 2003). Of equal importance is the ongoing systematic process of evaluating current programs and making revisions where possible and developing new third-generation programs that utilize the strengths of past programs. The first-generation programs, although far from perfect, provided important stepping-stones in developing and implementing more effective second-generation programs. There are several second-generation programs that have addressed the needs of the students, at risk and not at risk for suicide, and have spanned across school, community, and home environments (Kalafat, 2003). The first program, called Lifelines ASAP (Kalafat, Ryerson, & Underwood, 2001), was implemented in New Jersey, and the second one, called Suicide Prevention and School Crisis Management Program (Zenere & Lazarus, 1997), was implemented in Florida. Long-term follow-up results, 10 years and 6 years, respectively, have shown a reduction in youth suicides in those counties where the programs were implemented that was not evident in these states or nationally during the same time period (Kalafat, 2003). With successful programs such as these, it is hoped that second-generation programs will in turn inform third-generation programs and so on, with the goal to develop and implement suicide prevention programs that meet the needs of all students through education, identification, and treatment in a seamless environment across school, community, and home.

PSYCHOTHERAPY TREATMENTS

There have been numerous types of psychotherapy approaches used with children and adolescents, including psychoanalytic, cognitive-behavioral, dialectical behavior, group therapies, and family-focused interventions (Gutstein & Rudd, 1990; Lewinsohn et al., 1996; Miller Rathus, Linehan, Wetzler, & Leigh, 1997; Ottino, 1999; Ross & Motto, 1984; Rotheram-Borus, Piacentini, Miller, Graae, & Castro-Blanco, 1994). Unfortunately, researchers rarely collected any systematic empirical data that examined the outcome of the therapeutic intervention on actual suicidal behavior. Outcomes from these therapeutic approaches were often measured by reduced hospitalization visits, reduction in related psychopathology severity (i.e., depression), and increased family support (Greenfield, Hechtman, & Trembaly, 1995; Gutstein & Rudd, 1990; Millet et al., 1997). There have been a few randomized trials (treatment versus controls—with regard to suicidal behavior it is usually standard care) examining the treatment effects of different interventions among suicidal adolescents (Cotgrove, Zirinsky, Black, & Weston, 1995; Harrington et al., 1998; Rudd et al., 1996). The results from these studies do not provide clear support for any of the different treatment approaches. Several studies failed to show that their approach was significantly better than the standard care. A study by Harrington et al. (1998) did show that adolescents who had attempted suicide but were not depressed had lower levels of suicidal ideation during the six months of follow-up compared to controls; however, the number of suicide attempts after treatment were similar for both groups.

It is important to note one psychotherapy treatment that has shown consistent results in reducing suicidal behavior among adults, particularly women, called Dialectical Behavior Therapy (DBT; Linehan, 1993). Dialectical behavior therapy is a specific type of cognitive-behavioral therapy that focuses on clients' suicidal behavior as a result of emotional dysregulation (Linehan, 1993). There are four sets of skills targeted in DBT: mindfulness, distress-tolerance, emotional regulation, and interpersonal effectiveness. Randomized control studies have shown that clients receiving DBT had substantially fewer suicide attempts during treatment and follow-up and fewer hospitalizations due to suicidal behavior than clients who were placed in the control group (treatment as usual). These strong results have prompted others (Miller, 1999; Miller et al., 1997) to incorporate and utilize these skills in working with suicidal youth. To date, however, this author is unaware of any randomized trials examining the reduction of suicidal behavior in youth using DBT.

PSYCHOPHARMACOLOGY

The issue of using psychopharmacological treatment among suicidal youth has come under strong scrutiny lately because of the recent findings that some of the most popular antidepressant drugs (i.e., Prozac and Paxil) may increase the risk of suicidal behavior among youth (Richwine, 2004). Several selective serotonin reuptake inhibitors (SSRIs) have been banned in the United Kingdom, including Paxil and Effexor, for use with children and adolescents (Alliance for Human Research Protection [AHRP], 2004). The only SSRI not banned by the United Kingdom is Prozac, which has received approval for use in children who suffer from depression (AHRP, 2004). In the United States, the Food and Drug Administration (FDA) advisory panel recently suggested that all SSRIs carry a "black box warning" on their labels stating that these drugs can cause suicidal behavior in children (Elias, 2004). The FDA frequently follows the suggestions of the FDA advisory panel. The FDA officials stated that approximately 2 to 3 percent of children on the SSRIs became more suicidal because of the drugs (Elias, 2004). Although banning drugs or providing warning labels seems like an easy fix to the problem, the flip side is that many physicians may be hesitant to prescribe antidepressants to children and adolescent for other types of mental health problems even if warranted. Remember, psychopathology is one of the key risk factors associated with youth suicidal behavior. The controversy surrounding antidepressants (more specifically SSRIs) will not go away soon; however, raising the public's awareness of the challenges and strengths of psychopharmacological treatments is important for those who prescribe these medications as well as for those whom the medication is prescribed.

HOW CAN I MAKE A DIFFERENCE?

Making a difference to a youth who is suicidal does not require expert training in suicidology, a clinical degree in child and adolescent psychology, or a degree in pediatric medicine. It is important, however, that one recognize his or her limitations and to keep in mind that the ultimate goal in talking to someone who is thinking about suicide is to get him or her to an adult who has professional training in the area of youth suicidal behavior. The Washington State Youth Suicide Prevention Program (2004) suggests three simple but very important steps in talking to someone who is thinking about suicide:

1. Show you care: I am concerned about you and how you are feeling.
2. Ask the question, Are you thinking about suicide? or Are you thinking about killing yourself?
3. Get help from an adult: I know where *we* can get help.

The first step is key and needs to be done with care and concern to establish a trusting relationship that will allow for a smooth transition into steps 2 and 3. Step 1 is designed to show the youth that you are willing to listen to his or her problems or feelings. It is important that this is done in a nonjudgmental way and that you do not negate the severity of the problem the youth is experiencing. Negating statements such as "everything will be better soon," "that is not a big problem," and "you have so much going for you" should be avoided, as they are often viewed as dismissing. It is often hard for youth to talk to an adult because they feel that adults do not listen to them and minimize the importance of significant issues that are on their minds. Thus, showing that you care and being a good listener will help youth feel more comfortable in talking about their true feelings.

The second step, asking the youth directly if they are thinking about suicide, seems to be the hardest for adults. Although distraught youth feel this question is a natural follow-up from what has been said in response to step 1, many adults feel that asking about suicide is too abrasive or personal. Nonetheless, it is an appropriate question and is an extension of step 1, showing concern and listening. If the youth responds "yes" in step 2, don't panic and keep listening intently with the ultimate goal being to get this youngster to an adult who has professional training or knows someone who can access the professional help, which is step 3. If the youth says "no" or "of course I would never do that," simply let him or her know that you are glad and that sometimes youth who are struggling with various issues think about these things but that there are always better strategies than suicide.

Step 3 is getting the youth to a trained professional in the area of youth suicidal behavior or getting him or her connected to someone who can contact the appropriate professional resources. In school settings, school psychologists and school counselors are often the contact person who has the referral list of mental health workers or clinicians who specialize in the area of youth suicidal behavior. As the adult who conducted steps 1 and 2, it is important that you facilitate step 3 to the professional or to the resource person. The transition to another adult whom the youth may not know or feel comfortable with is important so that the youth does not feel abandoned or passed off to someone else. If you identify someone who is at risk for suicide, it is important that caring adults from the school, home, and community environments be identified and in close contact with each other to make sure the youth is safe and being monitored.

SUMMARY

This chapter provided an overview of youth suicidal behavior and the issues surrounding the field today. As can be seen from the chapter, youth suicidal behavior is quite complex and is indeed a crisis that needs to be addressed across multiple environments: school, community, and home. It is only through collaborative efforts, resources, and support that we can make an impact on helping reduce the rate of youth suicide and provide appropriate services for those who are thinking about or who have engaged in suicidal behavior.

RESOURCES FOR YOUTH SUICIDE

Here is a list of important resources to contact regarding information about youth suicide:

1. 1 800-273-TALK—National Suicide Crisis line in case of an emergency
2. American Association of Suicidology (http://www.suicidology.org)
3. American Foundation of Suicide Prevention (http://www.afsp.org)
4. Centers for Disease Control and Prevention (http://www.cdc.gov)

5. Suicide Prevention Resource Center (http://www.sprc.org)

6. Substance Abuse and Mental Health Service Administration (http://www.samhsa.gov)

REFERENCES

Alliance for Human Research Protection. (2004). UK issues ban on second SSRI antidepressant for children. Retrieved October 1, 2004, from http://www.ahrp.org/infomail/03/09/21.html

Anderson, R. N. (2002). Deaths: Leading causes for 2000. *National Vital Statistics Reports, 50*(16). Hyattsville, MD: National Center for Health Statistics.

Berman, A. L., & Jobes, D. A. (1991). *Adolescent suicide assessment and intervention.* Washington, DC: American Psychological Association.

Berman, A. L., & Jobes, D. A. (1995). Suicide prevention in adolescents (ages 12–18). *Suicide and Life-Threatening Behaviors, 25,* 143–154.

Brent, D. A., Baugher, M., Bridge, J., Chen, T., & Chiappetta, L. (1999). Age- and sex-related risk factors for adolescent suicide. *Journal of the American Academy of Child and Adolescent Psychiatry, 38,* 1497–1505.

Brent, D. A., Bridge, J., Johnson, B. A., & Connolly, J. (1996). Suicidal behavior runs in families: A controlled family study of adolescent suicide victims. *Archives of General Psychiatry, 53,* 1145–1152.

Brent, D. A., Perper, J. A., Allman, C. J., Moritz, G. M., Wartella, M., & Zelenak, J. P. (1991). The presence and accessibility of firearms in the homes of adolescent suicides: A case-controlled study. *Journal of the American Medical Association, 266,* 2989–2995.

Brent, D. A., Perper, J., Kolko, D. J., & Goldstein, C. E. (1988). Risk factors for adolescent suicide: A comparison of adolescent suicide victims with suicidal inpatients. *Archives of General Psychiatry, 45,* 581–588.

Centers for Disease Control and Prevention. (2004). Youth risk behavior surveillance—United States, 2003. *Mortality and Morbidity Weekly Review, CDC Surveillance Summaries, 53,* 1–96.

Ciffone, J. (1993). Suicide prevention: A classroom presentation to adolescents. *Social Work, 38,* 196–203.

Cole, D. A. (1989). Psychopathology of adolescent suicide: hopelessness, coping beliefs, and depression. *Journal of Abnormal Psychology, 98,* 248–255.

Cotgrove, A., Zirinsky, L., Black, D., & Weston, D. (1995). Secondary prevention of attempted suicide in adolescence. *Journal of Adolescence, 18,* 569–577.

Eastgard, S. (2000). *Youth suicide prevention toolkit.* Seattle: Youth Suicide Prevention Program.

Eggert, L. L., Nicholas, L. J., & Owens, L. M. (1995). *Reconnecting youth: A peer group approach to building life skills.* Bloomington, IN: National Educational Service.

Eggert, L. L., Thompson, E. A., Herting, J. R., & Nicholas, L. J. (1995). Reducing suicide potential among high-risk youth: Tests of a school-based prevention program. *Suicide and Life-Threatening Behavior, 25,* 276–296.

Elias, M. (2004). FDA advisers: Kids antidepressants need warnings. Retrieved October 1, 2004, from http://www.app.com/app/story/0,21625,1054341,00.html

Garfinkel, B. D., Froese, A., & Hood, J. (1982). Suicide attempts in children and adolescents. *American Journal of Psychiatry, 139,* 1257–1261.

Garland, A. F., Shaffer, D., & Whittle, B. A. (1989).A national survey of school-based adolescent suicide prevention programs. *Journal of the American Academy of Child and Adolescent Psychiatry, 28,* 931–934.

Gould, M. S., Greenberg, T., Velting, D. M., & Shaffer, D. (2003). Youth suicide risk and preventive interventions: A review of the past 10 years. *Journal of the American Academy of Child and Adolescent Psychiatry, 42,* 386–405.

Gould, M. S., King, R., Greenwald, S., Fisher, P., Schwab-Stone, M., Kramer, R., Flisher, A. J., Goodman, S., Canino, G., & Shaffer, D. (1998). Psychopathology associated with suicidal ideation and attempts among children and adolescents. *Journal of the American Academy of Child and Adolescent Psychiatry, 37,* 915–923.

Greenfield, B., Hechtman, I., O., & Tremblay, C. (1995). Short-term efficacy of interventions by a youth crisis team. *Canadian Journal of Psychiatry, 40,* 320–324.

Groholt, B., Ekeberg, O., Wichstrom, L., & Haldorsen, T. (1997). Youth suicide in Norway, 1990–1992: A comparison between children and adolescent completing suicide and age- and gender-matched controls. *Suicide and Life-Threatening Behaviors, 27,* 250–263.

Gutstein, S. E., & Rudd, M. D. (1990). An outpatient treatment alternative for suicidal youth. *Journal of Adolescence, 13,* 265–277.

Harrington, R., Kerfoot, M., Dyer, E., McNivern, E., Gill, J., Harrington, V., Woodham, A., & Byford, S. (1998). Randomized trial of a home-based family intervention for children who have deliberately poisoned themselves. *Journal of the American Academy of Child and Adolescent Psychiatry, 37,* 512–518.

Hollenbeck, J., Dyl, J., & Spirito, A. (2003). Social factors: Family functioning. In A. Spirito & J. Overholser (Eds.), *Evaluating and treating adolescent suicide attempters: From research to practice* (pp. 19–40). San Diego: Academic Press.

Johnson, B. A., Brent, D. A., Bridge, J., & Connolly, J. (1998). The familial aggregation of adolescent suicide attempts. *Acta Psychiatrica Scandinavica, 97,* 18–24.

Johnson, J. G., Cohen, P., Gould, M. S., Kasen, S., Brown, J., & Brook, J. S. (2002). Childhood adversities, interpersonal difficulties, and risk for suicide attempts during late adolescence and early adulthood. *Archives of General Psychiatry, 59,* 741–749.

Kalafat, J. (2003). Suicidal approaches to youth suicide prevention. *American Behavioral Scientist, 46,* 1211–1223.

Kalafat, J., & Elias, M. (1992). Adolescents' experiences with and response to suicidal peers. *Suicide and Life-Threatening Behavior, 22,* 315–321.

Kalafat, J., & Elias, M. (1994). An evaluation of adolescent suicide intervention classes. *Suicide and Life-Threatening Behavior, 24,* 224–233.

Kalafat, J., Ryerson, D., & Underwood, M. (2001). *Lifelines ASAP: Adolescent suicide awareness and response program.* Piscataway, NJ: Rutgers Graduate School of Applied and Professional Psychology.

Kashani, J. H., Goddard, P., & Reid, J. C. (1989). Correlates of suicidal ideation in a community sample of children and adolescents. *Journal of the American Academy of Child and Adolescent Psychiatry, 28,* 912–917.

Kingsbury, S. J. (1993). Clinical components of suicidal intent in adolescent overdoes. *Journal of the American Academy of Child and Adolescent Psychiatry, 32,* 518–520.

Konick, L. C., Brandt, L. A., & Gutierrez, P. M. (2002, April). School-based suicide prevention programs: A meta analysis. Paper presented at the annual conference of the American Association of Suicidology, Bethesda, MD.

Krug, E. G., Powell, K. E., & Dahlbert, L. L. (1998). Firearm-related deaths in the United States and 35 other high- and upper-middle income countries. *International Journal of Epidemiology, 27,* 214–221.

Ladame, F., & Jeanneret, O. (1982). Suicide in adolescence: Some comments on epidemiology and prevention. *Journal of Adolescence, 5,* 355–366.

Leenaars, A. (1992, April). Suicide notes and their implications for intervention. Paper presented at the annual conference of the American Association of Suicidology, Chicago.

Lewinsohn, P. M., Rohde, P., & Seeley, J. R. (1994). Psychosocial risk factors for future adolescent suicide attempts. *Journal of Consulting and Clinical Psychology, 62,* 297–305.

Lewinsohn, P. M., Rohde, P., & Seeley, J. R. (1996). Adolescent suicidal ideation and attempts: Prevalence, risk factors, and clinical implications. *Clinical Psychology Science Practice, 3,* 25–36.

Linehan, M. (1993). *Cognitive behavior therapy of borderline personality disorder.* New York: Guilford Press.

Marttunen, M. J., Aro, H. M., Henriksson, M. M., & Lonnqvist, J. K. (1991). Mental disorders in adolescent suicide. *Archives of General Psychiatry, 48,* 834–839.

Marttunen, M. J., Aro, H. M., & Lonnqvist, J. K. (1993). Precipitant stressors in adolescent suicide. *Journal of the American Academy of Child and Adolescent Psychiatry, 32,* 1178–1183.

Mazza, J. J. (1997). School-based suicide prevention programs: Are they effective? *School Psychology Review, 26,* 382–396.

Mazza, J. J. (in press). Suicidal behavior in children and adolescents. In *Encyclopedia of School Psychology.* Lawrence, KS: Sage.

Mazza, J. J., & Reynolds, W. M. (1998). A longitudinal investigation of depression, hopelessness, social support, major and minor life events and their relation to suicidal ideation in adolescents. *Suicide and Life-Threatening Behavior, 28,* 358–374.

Mazza, J. J., & Reynolds, W. M. (2001). An investigation of psychopathology in nonreferred suicidal and nonsuicidal adolescents. *Suicide and Life-Threatening Behavior, 31,* 282–302.

McIntosh, J. L. (2003). Suicide statistics. Retrieved May 31, 2004, from http://www.suicidology.org/associations/1045/files/2001datapg.pdf

McKeown, R. E., Garrison, C. Z., Cuffe, S. P., Waller, J. L., Jackson, K. L., & Addy, C. L. (1998). Incidence and predictors of suicidal behaviors in a longitudinal sample of young adolescents. *Journal of the American Academy of Child and Adolescent Psychiatry, 37,* 612–619.

Middlebrook, D. L., LeMaster, P. L., Beals, J., Novins, D. K., & Manson, S. M. (2001). Suicide prevention in American Indian and Alaska Native communities: A critical review of programs. *Suicide and Life-Threatening Behaviors, 31,* 132–149.

Miller, A. (1999). Dialectical behavior therapy: A new treatment approach for suicidal adolescents. *American Journal of Psychotherapy, 53,* 413–417.

Miller, A., Rathus, J., Linehan, M., Wetzler, S., & Leigh, E. (1997). Dialectical behavior therapy adopted for suicidal adolescents. *Journal of Practical Psychiatry and Behavioral Health, 3,* 78–86.

National Center for Health Statistics. (2003). Historical tables for 1979–1998. Retrieved May 31, 2004, from http://www.cdc.gov/nchs/data/statab/gm290–98.pdf

National Center for Health Statistics. (2004). Mortality data for 1999—2001. Retrieved October 4, 2004, from http://www.cdc.gov/nchs/datawh/statab/unpubd/mortabs/lcwk1_10.htm

Ottino, J. (1999). Suicide attempts during adolescence: Systematic hospitalization and crisis treatment. *Crisis, 20,* 41–48.

Overholser, J. C., Hemstreet, A. H., Spirito, A., & Vyse, S. (1989). Suicide awareness programs in the schools: Effects of gender and personal experience. *Journal of the American Academy of Child and Adolescent Psychiatry, 28,* 925–930.

Overholser, J., & Spirito, A. (2003). Precursors to adolescent suicide attempts. In A. Spirito & J. Overholser (Eds.), *Evaluating and treating adolescent suicide attempters: From research to practice* (pp. 19–40). San Diego: Academic Press.

Potter, L., Powell, K. E., & Kachur, P. S. (1995). Suicide prevention from a public health perspective. *Suicide and Life-Threatening Behaviors, 25,* 82–91.

Randell, B. P., Eggert, L. L., & Pike, K. C. (2001). Immediate post intervention effects of two brief youth suicide prevention interventions. *Suicide and Life-Threatening Behaviors, 31,* 41–61.

Reynolds, W. M. (1987). *Suicidal Ideation Questionnaire.* Odessa, FL: Psychological Assessment Resources.

Reynolds, W. M. (1988). *Suicidal Ideation Questionnaire: Professional manual.* Odessa, FL: Psychological Assessment Resources.

Reynolds, W. M., & Mazza, J. J. (1993). *Suicidal behavior in adolescents. I. Suicide attempts in school-based youngsters.* Unpublished manuscript.

Reynolds, W. M., & Mazza, J. J. (1994). Suicide and suicidal behavior. In W. M. Reynolds & H. F. Johnston (Eds.), *Handbook of depression in children and adolescents* (pp. 520–580). New York: Plenum Press.

Reynolds, W. M., & Mazza, J. J. (1999). Assessment of suicidal ideation in young inner-city youth: Reliability and validity of the Suicidal Ideation Questionnaire—JR. *School Psychology Review, 28,* 17–30.

Richwine, L. (2004). FDA agrees on antidepressant risks for youth. Retrieved October 4, 2004, from http://news.yahoo.com/news?tmpl=story&u=/ nm/20040916/hl_nm/health_antidepressants_dc_2

Riggs, S., & Cheng, T. (1988). Adolescents' willingness to use a school-based clinic in view of expressed health concerns. *Journal of Adolescent Health Care, 9,* 208–213.

Ross, C. P., & Motto, J. A. (1984). Group counseling for suicidal adolescents. In H. Sudak, A. Ford, & N. Rushforth (Eds.), *Suicide in the young* (pp. 367–392). Boston: John Wright.

Rotheram-Borus, M. J., Piacentini, J., Miller S., Graae, F., & Castro-Blanco, D. (1994). Brief cognitive-behavioral treatment of adolescent suicide attempters and their families. *Journal of the American Academy of Child and Adolescent Psychiatry, 33,* 508–517.

Rudd, M. D., Rajab, M. H., Orman, D. T., Stulman, D. A., Joiner, T., & Dixon, W. (1996). Effectiveness of an outpatient intervention targeting suicidal young adults: Preliminary results. *Journal of Consulting and Clinical Psychology, 64,* 179–190.

Shaffer, D., Garland, A., Gould, M., Fisher, P., & Trautman, P. (1988). Preventing teenage suicide: A critical review. *Journal of the American Academy of Child and Adolescent Psychiatry, 27,* 675–687.

Shaffer, D., Garland, A., Vieland, V., Underwood, M., & Busner, C. (1991). The impact of curriculum based suicide prevention programs for teenagers. *Journal of the American Academy of Child and Adolescent Psychiatry, 30,* 588–596.

Shaffer, D., Gould, M. S., Fisher, P., Trautman, P., Moreau, D., Kleinman, M., & Flory, M. (1996). Psychiatric diagnosis in child and adolescent suicide. *Archives of General Psychiatry, 53,* 339–348.

Shafii, M., Carrigan, S., Whittinghill, J. R., & Derrick, A. M. (1985). Psychological autopsy of completed suicide in children and adolescents. *American Journal of Psychiatry, 142,* 1061–1064.

Shafii, M., Stelta-Lenarsky, J., Derrick, A. M., Beckner, C., & Whittinghill, J. R. (1988). Comorbidity of mental disorders in the post-mortem diagnosis of completed suicide in children and adolescents. *Journal of Affective Disorders, 15,* 227–233.

Silverman, A. B., Reinherz, H. A., & Giaconai, R. M. (1996). The long-term sequelae of child and adolescent abuse: A longitudinal community study. *Child Abuse and Neglect, 20,* 709–723.

Smith, K., & Crawford, S. (1986). Suicidal behavior among "normal" high school students. *Suicide and Life-Threatening Behavior, 16,* 313–325.

Thompson, E. A., Eggert, L. L., Randell, B. P., & Pike, K. C. (2001). Evaluation of indicated suicide risk prevention approaches for potential high school dropouts. *American Journal of Public Health, 91,* 742–752.

U.S. Department of Health and Human Services. (2001). *National strategy for suicide prevention: Goals and objectives for action.* Rockville, MD: Author.

U.S. Public Health Service. (1999). *The surgeon general's call to action to prevent suicide.* Washington, DC: Author.

Washington State Youth Suicide Prevention Program. (2004). Retrieved October 4, 2004, from http://www.yspp.org

Zenere, F. J., III, & Lazarus, P. J. (1997). The decline of youth suicidal behavior in an urban, multicultural public school system following the introduction of a suicide prevention and intervention program. *Suicide and Life-Threatening Behaviors, 27,* 387–403.

Chapter 8

MENTAL HEALTH ISSUES FACING ADOLESCENTS IN THE JUSTICE SYSTEM: CHALLENGES AND OPPORTUNITIES

Marc Schindler

More than 20 years ago, Jane Knitzer commented in her groundbreaking 1982 report *Unclaimed Children: The Failure of Public Responsibility to Children and Adolescents in Need of Mental Health Services* that children who are charged in the juvenile justice system and show a range of emotional or behavioral disorders pose a complex and unsolved challenge for the juvenile justice and mental health systems. Knitzer (1982) concluded that these youth had been consistently neglected and ignored by public service systems. Ten years later, writing in the most comprehensive monograph to date on youth with mental health issues in the juvenile justice system, Joseph Cocozza (1992) unfortunately concluded that the situation had not changed since Knitzer's 1982 report.

In recent years, some two decades after Knitzer's comments, we are now seeing an increasing focus at the national level to mental health issues, generally, including an acknowledgment of serious deficiencies and gaps in services in community-based mental health services. Within this context, the issue of youth with mental health disorders in the juvenile justice system has also received an increasing amount of attention. Thus, researchers and experts in the field have noted that the mental health needs of youth in the juvenile justice system have received more attention at the federal level in the past several years than in the past three decades combined (Cocozza & Skowyra, 2000).

This chapter discusses a review of the data on youth with mental health issues in the justice system, recent attention by Congress and others to the particular issue of youth with mental health disorders being incarcerated while awaiting mental health treatment, and some promising approaches and programs to working with youth with mental health disorders in the justice system.

REVIEW OF THE LITERATURE

The surgeon general's 2002 report on children's mental health found that approximately 20 percent of children and adolescents in the general youth population are experiencing a mental disorder (U.S. Public Health Service, Report of the Surgeon General's Conference on Children's Mental Health, 2002). Further, approximately 10 percent experience mental illness severe enough to cause impairment at home, in school, and in the community (Cocozza, & Skowyra, 2002; U.S. Public Health Service, 2002).[1] The report's findings showed that mental disorders among youth in the general population was significantly higher than previously believed yet also found that less than half of these youth receive the treatment that they need (U.S. Public Health Service, 2002).

Though we know more today than when Knitzer wrote in 1982 and Cocozza commented in 1992, the research on youth in the justice system with mental health needs is still developing. Existing research shows that the majority of youth in the justice system, ranging anywhere from 70 to 100 percent, have some diagnosable mental disorder (Otto, Greenstein, Johnson, & Friedman, 1992). For less serious mental disorders such as conduct disorder, the prevalence is estimated to be 80 percent or more of youthful offenders (Cocozza & Skowyra, 2000). Further, approximately 20 percent have a serious mental disorder, compared with 9–13 percent in the general population (Cocozza & Skowyra, 2000). Goldstrom (2000) has also noted that the estimates of specific disorders prevalent among detained youth include 50 to 95 percent with conduct disorder, approximately 50 percent with attention deficit disorder, 6 to 41 percent with anxiety disorders, 25 to 50 percent with substance abuse or dependence, 32 to 78 percent with affective disorders, and approximately 5 percent with psychotic disorders. Other studies have also reported variable rates of prevalence rates for specific disorders. Whereas Teplin, Abram, McClelland, Dulcan, and Mericle, (2002) report a prevalence rate of approximately 1 percent for schizophrenia, for example, Timmons-Mitchell et al. (1997) report the rate to be closer to 16 percent, whereas Atkins, Pumariega, and Rogers (1999) report a significantly higher rate (45%). Similar disparities are noted for other mental health disorders, including mood disorders (compare Teplin et al., 2002; Timmons-Mitchell et al., 1997; Wasserman et al., 2002), anxiety disorders (compare Garland, Hough, McCabe, Wood, & Aarons, 2001, Teplin et al., 2002; Timmons-Mitchell et al., 1997; Wasserman, McReynolds, Lucas, Fisher, & Santos, 2002), and attention-deficit/hyperactivity disorder (Pliskza, Sherman, Barrow, & Irick, 2000; Teplin et al., 2002; Timmons-Mitchell et al., 1997; Wasserman et al., 2002). Thus, it appears that the prevalence of mental disorders among youth in the juvenile justice system is two to three times higher than youth in the general population (Chino, Personius-Zipoy, & Tanata, 2004; Cocozza & Skowyra, 2000).

Research on these issues goes back to the early 1970s, though unfortunately the bulk of this research has been uneven and the results have varied greatly. The two most comprehensive reviews of the literature in the 1990s both concluded that few well-controlled epidemiological studies existed at the time (Otto et al., 1992; Wierson, Forehand, & Frame, 1992).

Some of the most detailed and promising recent research is being carried out in Chicago by Linda Teplin and her colleagues (Teplin et al., 2002). Teplin has been conducting a comprehensive analysis of a large sample of youth in Cook County's juvenile detention center, using a well-validated and standardized instrument. Participants in the study were nearly 2,000 male and female youth between 10 and 18 years of age who were randomly sampled on intake to Chicago's detention center between 1995 and 1998. Similar to the population in the facility, the sample was primarily male (64.1%) and had a mean age of 15 years. The sample was 54.9 percent African American, 28.7 percent Hispanic, and 16.2 percent White. Participating youth were interviewed over two to three hours using the Diagnostic Interview Schedule for Children (DISC, Version 2.3), which is designed to assess the presence of a diagnosis from the *Diagnostic and Statistical Manual of the American Psychiatric Association* (3rd ed., revised) in the preceding six months.

Teplin's study revealed a high rate of at least one disorder in boys (66.3%) and an even significantly higher rate among girls (73.8%) (Teplin et al., 2002). For both boys and girls, the highest rates of diagnoses were for substance use disorders (50.7% and 46.8%, respectively), disruptive behavior disorders (41.4% and 45.6%, respectively), and anxiety disorders (21.3% and 30.8%, respectively). Females were significantly more likely to have multiple disorders, including any effective disorder, any anxiety disorder, and substance abuse disorders other than alcohol or marijuana use (Teplin et al., 2002).

In addition, generally there has been greater attention in recent years to the fact that many youth in the juvenile justice system who suffer from some mental disorder also are likely to have a co-occurring substance abuse disorder (Cocozza & Skowyra, 2000). Thus, although research in this area is in its initial phases, one study found that "approximately half of all adolescents receiving mental health services" in the general population are reported to have a dual diagnoses (Greenbaum, Foster-Johnson, & Petrila, 1996). Further, while there is limited research on the mental health of delinquent youth in general, there is even less specific research on the mental health needs of girls in the juvenile justice system (Veysey, 2003). Based on her analysis, Vesey asserts that most of the girls in the juvenile justice system meet the criteria for at least one mental disorder.

Finally, despite the recent advances by respected university-based researchers, such as Teplin, clearly there is a need for more comprehensive research in this area in order to fully understand the significance of the challenge facing policymakers and practitioners dealing with these issues.

INCREASED NUMBER OF YOUTH WITH MENTAL HEALTH DISORDERS IN THE JUVENILE JUSTICE SYSTEM

Though the research in this area is still developing, clearly there is a sense in communities and states around the country that the number of youth with mental health issues entering local juvenile justice systems is increasing at significant rates. Thus, according to a report to Congress, the Coalition for Juvenile Justice (2000) concluded that the juvenile justice system has largely become a warehouse for children suffering from mental illness (Hubner & Wolfson, 2000). In addition, the secretary of the Florida Department of Juvenile Justice, in response to the question of what was the most challenging issue facing juvenile corrections at the turn of the century, stated providing specialized services, such as mental health and substance abuse services, within the juvenile correctional continuum (Cocozza & Skowyra, 2000), and the Texas Youth Commission reported a nearly 30 percent increase between 1995 and 2001 in the number of youth with mental disorders entering the state's juvenile justice system (Reyes & Brantley, 2002).

Researchers have attributed this increase to a combination of factors. As Thomas Grisso (2004) wrote, "Beginning in the 1980s, a rising tide of teenage violence led virtually every state to pass laws mandating severe penalties for violent young offenders and reducing the discretion of juvenile court judges to screen out those with mental disorders. At the same time, state after state saw the collapse of public mental health services for children and the closing of residential facilities for disturbed youths" (p. 5). Grisso posits that the results were predictable, "juvenile detention centers began to take the place of psychiatric emergency rooms, and juvenile correctional beds increasingly were occupied by youths who really needed hospital beds. In some cases, parents voluntarily gave custody of their children to the juvenile justice system, or managed to have their children arrested, simply to obtain the mental health services they could no longer find in their communities" (p. 5) Similarly, the President's New Freedom Commission on Mental Health (2003) stated, "As a shrinking public health care system limits access to services, many poor and racial or ethnic minority youth with serious emotional disorders fall through the cracks into the juvenile justice system" (p. 32). The U.S. General Accounting Office (GAO) studied this issue as well. In data from child welfare officials in 19 states and county juvenile justice officials in 30 counties, the GAO (2003) estimated that in 2001, 12,700 children were placed by their parents into the child welfare or juvenile justice systems so that these children could receive mental health services. The President's New Freedom Commission Final Report (2003) found the GAO findings highly disturbing, stating that the report illustrated the "tragic and unacceptable circumstances that result in thousands of parents being forced to place their children into the child welfare or juvenile justice systems each year so that they may obtain the mental health services they need" (p. 33). The commission continued, "Loving and responsible parents who have exhausted their savings and health insurance face the wrenching decision of surrendering their parental rights and tearing apart their families to secure mental health treatment for their troubled children" (p. 33).

This gap in community-based mental health services, combined with stricter juvenile justice codes in states throughout the country, has resulted in inappropriate incarceration for literally thousands of youth in preadjudication (before trial) detention and postadjudication (following sentencing) juvenile facilities. Exacerbating this situation is the reality that juvenile justice systems—and secure juvenile facilities in particular—are woefully unprepared to adequately and appropriately respond to the needs of youth with mental health disorders. Staff in juvenile facilities often lack adequate training to recognize and deal with symptoms of mental health problems, and in many states and counties facilities have significant shortages in qualified mental health professional staff to respond to the special needs of youth with mental health disorders. In addition, youth with mental health disorders often have the most difficulty in adjusting to being incarcerated and tend to demand more attention and time from staff than other youth. These gaps in services have resulted in dangerous and tragic consequences in facilities throughout the country.

The U.S. Department of Justice's Office of Civil Rights, a number of private nonprofit civil rights law offices and state agencies, and international organizations such as Human Rights Watch have investigated conditions of confinement in facilities throughout the country, exposing inhumane treatment and a glaring lack of adequate mental health services for incarcerated youth. Significant deficiencies in mental health services have been identified in investigations in Maryland, Louisiana, Georgia, Maryland, California, and New Jersey. Examples include the following:

- In a Department of Justice (DOJ) investigation of two juvenile facilities in Maryland, DOJ investigators found that youth whose serious mental health needs could not be met at the facilities were being admitted anyway. The DOJ found that security staff was inadequately trained to conduct the intake mental health questionnaire. One example provided by DOJ included the following:

[A] sixteen year old youth with a diagnosis of schizophrenia was discharged from a hospital and admitted to [the facility]. According to the Intake Database Face Sheet for this youth, while the youth was in the intake area, he was yelling "I'm going to hurt myself," and reporting that he was "not mentally stable." Despite this youth's overt symptoms, the admissions officer conducting the screening answered "No" to questions on the intake screening from asking whether the youth was exhibiting bizarre or unusual behavior, whether the youth was thinking about hurting himself, and whether he showed any sign of current suicide risk. Thus, even though the screening instrument provides that "Yes" answers to any of these questions require refusal of admission and transport to a hospital for immediate care, this youth was admitted to [the facility]. (DOJ findings letter to Maryland's governor, April 9, 2004)

- In a DOJ investigation into conditions in the Los Angeles County juvenile detention center, investigators found serious deficiencies in mental health assessment and referrals. For example, investigators commented,

In many instances, youth were referred for assessment but waited days or weeks for evaluations that referring staff thought should be done immediately. For example, youth experiencing suicidal thoughts or even making suicide attempts might wait three days or longer to be seen by a mental health provider. In another example, the medical director requested that a psychiatrist re-evaluate a youth's medication due to side effects including vomiting, dizziness, blurred vision and headache, noting that he should be seen that day. He waited nearly one month to see a psychiatrist. (DOJ findings letter to Los Angeles County supervisor, April 9, 2003)

- In a DOJ investigation of conditions in two of Louisiana's secure juvenile correctional facilities, investigators found that psychotropic medications were managed inadequately. For example, the DOJ wrote,

Both facilities fail to monitor for medication efficacy or side effects adequately. Tallulah has no psychiatrist to monitor the medications. In addition, both facilities fail to document consent for treatment with these medications in the medical record. Moreover, at Jetson, juveniles reported being put in isolation or being beaten for refusing to take psychotropic medications. Bridge City nursing staff abruptly stop all psychotropic medications at intake until a juvenile sees a psychiatrist. For some psychotropic medications, this is a dangerous practice that does not comport with accepted professional standards. (DOJ findings letter to governor of Louisiana, June 18, 1997)

• In a DOJ investigation into conditions in Georgia's secure juvenile facilities, investigators found inappropriate and inadequate responses to suicidal youth. For example, investigators found the following:

At most [facilities], once a youth has been identified as being at immediate risk for suicidal behavior, staff lock the youth alone in a cell, removing the youth's sheets, clothing and personal effects, leaving the depressed youth alone in a paper gown, sometimes for days. Suicidal youth are then monitored more closely, but they are not permitted to leave their rooms to eat with the other youths, attend school or (often) even to obtain exercise or recreation. This practice of isolating depressed youths in demeaning conditions for hours (and sometimes days) usually exacerbates the youth's depression. (DOJ findings letter to the governor of Georgia, February 13, 1998)

• In an investigation into conditions in 17 county-run juvenile detention centers in New Jersey by the state's Office of the Child Advocate, investigators found that approximately 25 percent of the youths held in the state's detention facilities, many of whom suffered from mental health disorders, were detained simply because the state could not find a more appropriate setting, such as a hospital or a foster home (Kaufmann, 2004).

CONGRESSIONAL INVESTIGATIONS

Congress first initiated action to investigate these issues at the request of Senator Jeff Bingaman (D-N.M.). In response to efforts by families, clinicians, and child advocates in New Mexico to draw attention to the crisis in access to mental health services in their state, Senator Bingaman was joined by Representatives Tom Udall (D-N.M.) and Henry Waxman (D-Calif.) in requesting an investigation into what happens to youth with mental health disorders who entered New Mexico's juvenile justice system.

The investigation, conducted by Minority Staff of the U.S. House of Representatives' Committee on Government Reform Special Investigation Division, surveyed administrators from all 14 county juvenile detention centers in New Mexico (Minority Staff, 2002). Key findings from the investigation included the following:

- Thirteen of the 14 juvenile detention centers in New Mexico incarcerated youth for extended periods in 2001 solely to wait for residential treatment, inpatient services, or outpatient care.

- An estimated 718 youth, or approximately one in seven incarcerated youth, in New Mexico's detention centers during the period of the survey was incarcerated because mental health care was not available.

- Detention center administrators were frustrated by shortages of mental health services.

- A major cause of the extended incarceration was attributed to the New Mexico Medicaid program's failure to provide adequate mental health services (Minority Staff, 2002).

Detention center administrators responding to the survey provided detail on the range of problems they faced. For example, reporting that youth were held for many months in detention centers for no reason other than the lack of available services, one administrator commented. "We kept a young fellow 167 days while they looked for a place to put him. He didn't need to be in jail. He needed treatment capabilities and he sat here that long waiting" (Minority Staff, 2002, p. 3). Lack of access to appropriate mental health services was a common theme, with one administrator stating that "detention centers in New Mexico ... have become the largest mental health institutions in the state" (Minority Staff, 2002, p. 3).

The publication of the New Mexico report led to a request by Representative Waxman and Senator Susan Collins (R-Me.) that the Special Investigations Division conduct a national survey of juvenile detention facilities to determine what happens nationwide to youth with mental health disorders when community services are not available (Minority Staff, 2004). The Special Investigations Division revised the instrument designed for the New Mexico study and conducted a national survey covering the period January 1 to June 30, 2003. More than 500 juvenile detention administrators in 49 states, representing three-quarters of all juvenile detention facilities, responded.

The national report concluded that the use of juvenile detention facilities to house youth waiting for community mental health services is widespread and a serious national problem (Minority Staff, 2004). Key findings from the report included the following:

- Two-thirds of juvenile detention facilities hold youth who are waiting for community mental health treatment.

- Over a six-month period, nearly 15,000 incarcerated youth waited for community mental health services.

- Two-thirds of juvenile detention facilities that hold youth waiting for mental health services report that some of these youth have attempted suicide or attacked others.

- Juvenile detention facilities spend an estimated $100 million each year to house youth who are waiting for community mental health services (Minority Staff, 2004).

Detention facility administrators across the country echoed the statements by administrators in New Mexico. For example, one administrator in Louisiana stated, "The availability of mental health services in this area is slim to none. We have to detain and monitor closely juveniles who are acutely depressed/suicidal due to lack of bed/space at the state mental health facilities. We appear to be warehousing youths with mental health illnesses due to lack of mental health services" (Minority Staff, 2004, p. 5). Another detention center administrator from Oklahoma wrote, "To put it simply we are the dumping grounds for the juvenile justice system. Understand this and understand it well: when the system is unable to get youth placed in a treatment facility or a mental health facility, they will be placed in a detention facility. If a youth needs to be detained in a mental health facility it will not happen; they will be placed in a detention center" (Minority Staff, 2004, p. 7).

A number of facility administrators also spoke to the difficulties in dealing with youth with these special needs. For example, a Missouri administrator commented, "Youth who are banging their head or feet into walls or who are otherwise harming themselves must be restrained creating a crisis situation … consequently detention staff have to divert all resources to that one youth for an extended period of time" (Minority Staff, 2004, p. 9).

While the national survey was not designed to determine the reasons why so many youth are incarcerated awaiting mental health services, respondents to the survey did identify gaps in many levels of care that result in youth being placed in detention. For example, youth waited for residential treatment in 337 facilities of those responding to the survey (97%), for inpatient hospitalization in 190 facilities (55%), for outpatient services in 140 facilities (40%), and for foster care placement in 161 facilities (46%). One juvenile facility administrator from Massachusetts commented, "Inpatient hospitalization has become extremely scarce.... Our staff work diligently to stabilize these clients but their illness calls for a multilateral approach towards treatment, which really is not available in a juvenile detention center" (Minority Staff, 2004, p. 7).

National organizations covering a wide spectrum responded to the findings in the congressional report, from the American Correctional Association to groups like the American Academy of Child and Adolescent Psychiatry, the Bazelon Center for Mental Health Law, and the Youth Law Center. In hearings convened by the House Government Reform Committee, witnesses confirmed the findings in the report. Carol Carothers (2004), executive director of the Maine Chapter of the National Alliance for the Mentally Ill, confirmed that Maine was experiencing the same problems as identified in the report and summed up the depth of the problem, stating,

> The sad truth in Maine and nearly every other state in our country is that youth with mental illnesses are being held in juvenile detention for the sole purpose of awaiting mental health treatment and services. It is hard to imagine a worse place to house a child that requires healthcare treatment and services for their mental illness. Surely we would not dream of placing a child with another serious illness, like cancer for example, in a juvenile detention center to await a hospital bed or community based treatment. It is outrageous that we do this to children with mental illnesses. (Carothers, 2004)

Other witnesses from national organizations testified regarding the underlying causes of the problem. For example, the American Academy of Child and Adolescent Psychiatry identified a number of factors, including the lack of parity in insurance coverage for mental illness; the absence of coordinated systems of care across state health, social service, education, and child welfare and juvenile justice systems, particularly in low-income areas; the inability of some low-income families to qualify for Medicaid; and the shortage of child and adolescent psychiatrists and other children's mental health professionals (Rogers, 2004).

Similarly, the Bazelon Center for Mental Health Law identified a number of reasons for youth with mental health disorders being funneled into the juvenile justice system. These included lack of access to services, particularly during evening and nighttime hours when crises occur; lack of accountability by other systems, particularly school systems that have invoked zero-tolerance policies that result in referrals to court for even minor violations of school rules; bias toward law enforcement solutions, including calling police instead of other, more appropriate agencies when youth with mental health disorders act out; lack of insurance for mental health problems; and lack of coordination among public agencies that serve children and families, such as child welfare, education, mental health, and juvenile justice.

PROMISING APPROACHES

Fortunately, in recent years there has been significant progress in identifying promising programs and strategies that are proving effective in responding to the needs of youth with mental health disorders. Advances have been made both in the area of screening and assessment and in developing programs that are specifically designed to work with youth with mental health and substance abuse issues.

In the past, probably the most significant barrier to recognizing and responding to the needs of youth with mental health problems in the juvenile justice system was the absence of reliable screening and assessment tools. Grisso and Barnum (2003), however, have made great progress in recent years in developing a screening instrument that is brief and easily administered. Specifically, Grisso and Barnum's second Massachusetts Youth Screening Instrument (MAYSI-2), a short, easily administered set of questions that has been tested on a number of juvenile justice populations, appears to be effective as an initial screen to identify signs of mental disturbance or distress, including suicide risk. The MAYSI-2 is being used in juvenile justice systems across the country. For example, since 2000, Pennsylvania has been implementing the MAYSI-2 in secure juvenile detention centers throughout the state (Moyer, 2003). The instrument is being used to alert detention staff of potential mental health and/or substance abuse issues that youth may be experiencing.

Researchers are also beginning to identify a number of strategies and programs that are showing great promise in working with this population. A key component of many programs appears to be an intentional effort to work across systems (Cocozza & Skowyra, 2000).

For example, the Wraparound Milwaukee program is a collaborative county-operated health maintenance organization that provides "wraparound" care through a coordinated package of community-based services. According to the Coalition for Juvenile Justice, Wraparound Milwaukee improves public safety while keeping youth close to home and community with an approach that "employs the idea of 'no wrong door'—allowing a troubled youth and his family to receive supportive mental health services from any point of contact including schools, religious institutions, recreation programs, public health facilities and law enforcement agencies" (Coalition for Juvenile Justice, 2000). In addition, delinquent youth served by Wraparound Milwaukee have also been shown to have significantly improved clinical outcomes (Kamradt, 2000). Recidivism rates were also shown to be positively impacted, with one study measuring delinquency "one year prior to enrollment" versus "one year post enrollment" and reporting substantial reductions in sex offenses (from 11% to 1%), assaults (from 14% to 7%), weapons offenses (from 15% to 4%), and property offenses (from 34% to 17%) (Kamradt, 2000).

Another community-based approach that has proven effective is known as Multisystemic Therapy (MST; Cocozza & Skowyra, 2000), which is designed as a family- and community-based model that addresses a range of family, peer, school, and community factors that can lead to delinquency. Developed by Henggeler and his colleagues, MST has shown to be a "successful and cost-effective alternative to out-of-home placements" (Cocozza & Skowyra, 2000, p. 10). The program has been evaluated in multiple clinical trials. For example, studies conducted among seriously delinquent youth in Memphis, Tennessee, and South Carolina have shown that participation in MST can have significant positive effects on behavior problems, family relations, and self-reported offenses immediately after treatment (U.S. Department of Health and Human Services, 2001). Fifty-nine weeks after referral, seriously delinquent youth who participated in MST had almost 50 percent fewer arrests, spent an average of 73 fewer days incarcerated in justice system facilities, and showed reductions in aggression with peers compared to youth who did not participate in MST (see also Henggeler, Mihalic, Rone, Thomas, & Timmons-Mitchell, 1998).

Clearly, these programs and approaches are better alternatives to incarcerating youth in juvenile correctional facilities. As the President's New Freedom Commission on Mental Health commented, programs like Wraparound Milwaukee demonstrate "that the seemingly impossible can be made possible: children's care can be seamlessly integrated. The services provided to children not only produce better clinical results, reduce delinquency, and result in fewer hospitalizations, but are cost-effective" (President's New Freedom Commission Final Report, 2003, p. 36).

NOTE

1. Additional information is available at the Web site of the National Center for Mental Health and Juvenile Justice, available at http://www.ncmhjj.com/publications/default.asp.

REFERENCES

Atkins, D., Pumariega, W., & Rogers, K. (1999). Mental health and incarcerated youth I: Prevalence and nature of psychopathology. *Journal of Child and Family Studies, 8,* 193–204.

Carothers, C. (2004, July). *Juvenile detention centers: Are they warehousing children with mental illness?* Hearing before the Committee on Governmental Affairs, United States Senate, 108th Congress, Washington, DC.

Chino, M., Personius-Zipoy, J., & Tanata, D. (2004). Screening for mental health problems among incarcerated youth in Nevada: Practice and policy. *Journal of the Nevada Public Health Association, 1,* 10–15.

Coalition for Juvenile Justice. (2000). *Handle with care: Serving the mental health needs of young offenders.* Washington, DC: Author.

Cocozza, J. (Ed.). (1992). *Responding to mental health needs of youth in the juvenile justice system.* Seattle: National Coalition for the Mentally Ill in the Criminal Justice System.

Cocozza, J., & Skowyra, K. (2000). *Youth with mental health disorders: Issues and emerging responses.* Washington, DC: Office of Juvenile Justice and Delinquency Prevention.

Garland, A., Hough, R., McCabe, K., M., Wood, P., & Aarons G. (2001). Prevalence of psychiatric disorders in youths across five sectors of care. *Journal of the Academy of Child and Adolescent Psychiatry, 40,* 409–418.

Goldstrom, I. (2000). The availability of mental health services to young people in juvenile justice facilities. In *Mental health, United States, 2000.* Washington, DC: U.S. Department of Health and Human Services, Substance Abuse and Mental Health Services Administration, Center for Mental Health Services. Available from http://www.mentalhealth.samhsa. gov/publications/allpubs/SMA01-3537/Chapter18.asp.

Greenbaum, P. E., Foster-Johnson, L., & Petrila, J. (1996). Co-occurring addictive and mental disorders among adolescents: Prevalence research and future directions. *American Journal of Orthopsychiatry 66,* 52–60.

Grisso T. (2004). *Double jeopardy: Adolescent offenders with mental disorders.* Chicago: University of Chicago Press.

Henggeler, S. W. (1997). *Treating serious anti-social behavior in youth: The MST approach.* Washington, DC: U.S. Department of Justice, Office of Justice Programs, Office of Juvenile Justice and Delinquency Prevention.

Henggeler, S. W., Mihalic, S. F., Rone, L., Thomas, C., & Timmons-Mitchell, J. (1998). Blueprints for violence prevention: Multisystemic therapy. Boulder: University of Colorado at Boulder, Center for the Study and Prevention of Violence, Blueprint Publications.

Hubner, J., & Wolfson, J. (2000). *Handle with care: Serving the mental health needs of young offenders.* Washington, DC: Coalition for Juvenile Justice.

Kamradt, B. (2000). *Wraparound Milwaukee: Aiding youth with mental health needs.* Washington, D.C.: Office of Juvenile Justice.

Kaufman, L. (2004, November 23). Child detention centers criticized in New Jersey. *New York Times,* pp. A1, B9.

Knitzer, J. (1982). *Unclaimed children: The failure of public responsibility to children and adolescents in need of mental health services.* Washington, DC: Children's Defense Fund.

Minority Staff, Government Reform Committee, U.S. House of Representatives. (2002). Incarceration of youth with mental health disorders in New Mexico. Retrieved December 15, 2004, from http://www.democrats. reform.house.gov/Documents/20040827163919–02001.pdf.

Minority Staff, Government Reform Committee, U.S. House of Representatives. (2004). Incarceration of youth who are waiting for community mental health services in the United States. Retrieved December 15, 2004, from http://democrats.reform.house.gov/documents/20040817121901–25170.pdf.

Moyer, M. (2003). Pennsylvania Juvenile Justice: Screening youth within detention: A glance at the mental health issues experienced by Pennsylvania's youth. *Pennsylvania Juvenile Court Judges Commission Newsletter, 11*(9), 4.

Otto, R., Greenstein, J., Johnson, M., & Friedman, R. (1992). Prevalence of mental disorders among youth in the juvenile justice system. In J. Cocozza (Ed.), *Responding to the mental health needs of youth in the juvenile justice system* (pp. 7–49). Seattle: National Coalition for the Mentally Ill in the Criminal Justice System.

Pliszka, S., Sherman, J., Barrow, M., & Irick, S. (2000). Affective disorders in juvenile offenders: A preliminary study. *American Journal of Psychiatry, 157,* 130–132.

President's New Freedom Commission on Mental Health. (2003). *Achieving the promise: Transforming mental health care in America.* Rockville, MD: Author. Retrieved December 1, 2004, from http://www.mentalhealthcommission.gov/.

Reyes, L., & Brantley, D. (2002, January) *Council of Juvenile Justice Correctional Administrators Best Practices Committee.* Presentation to the Texas Youth Commission Mental Health, Austin TX.

Rogers, K. (2004, July). *Juvenile detention centers: Are they warehousing children with mental illness?* Hearing before the Committee on Governmental Affairs, United States Senate, 108th Congress, Washington, DC.

Teplin, L. A., Abram, K. M., McClelland, G. M., Dulcan, M. K., & Mericle, A. M. (2002). Psychiatric disorders in youth in juvenile detention. *Archives of General Psychiatry, 59,* 1133–1143.

Timmons-Mitchell, J., Brown, C., Schulz, C., Webster, S., Undersood, L., & Semple, W. (1997). Comparing the mental health needs of female and male incarcerated juvenile delinquents. *Behavioral Sciences and the Law, 15,* 195–202.

U.S. Department of Health and Human Services. (2001). *Youth violence: A report of the surgeon general.* Washington, DC: Author. Retrieved, December 10, 2004, from http://www.surgeongeneral.gov/library/youthviolence/summary.htm.

U.S. General Accounting Office, Child Welfare and Juvenile Justice. (2003). *Federal agencies could play a stronger role in helping states reduce the number of children placed solely to obtain mental health services.* Washington, DC: Author.

U.S. Public Health Service. (2002). *Report of the surgeon general's Conference on Children's Mental Health: A national action agenda.* Washington, DC: U.S. Department of Health and Human Services. Retrieved December 1, 2004, from http://www.surgeongeneral.gov/topics/cmh/childreport.htm/.

Veysey, B. M. (2003). *Adolescent girls with mental health disorders involved with the juvenile justice system.* Delmar, NY: National Center for Mental Health and Juvenile Justice.

Wasserman, G., McReynolds, L., Lucas, C., Fisher, P., & Santos, L. (2002). The Voice DISC-IV with incarcerated male youths: Prevalence of disorder. *Journal of the American Academy of Child and Adolescent Psychiatry, 41,* 314–321.

Wierson, M., Forehand, R. L., & Frame, C. L. (1992). Epidemiology and treatment of mental health problems in juvenile delinquents. *Advances in Behaviour Research and Therapy, 14,* 93–120.

Chapter 9

ETHNIC IDENTITY AMONG U.S. LATINO ADOLESCENTS: THEORY, MEASUREMENT, AND IMPLICATIONS FOR WELL-BEING

Adriana J. Umaña-Taylor and Edna C. Alfaro

The Latino population in the United States is growing at an unprecedented rate, and it is expected that this ethnic group will constitute more than 25 percent of the U.S. population by the year 2060 (U.S. Census Bureau, 2000). A large segment of the Latino population includes children under the age of 18, who currently constitute 36 percent of the Latino population (Therrien & Ramirez, 2000). However, our existing knowledge on the normative developmental processes and outcomes of Latino youth is limited (Garcia Coll et al., 1996; Vazquez Garcia, Garcia Coll, Erkut, Alarcon, & Tropp, 2000). One normative developmental process that merits attention is ethnic identity formation during adolescence. A critical developmental task that is thought to be prominent during the period of adolescence is identity formation (Erikson, 1968). Adolescents' identities are informed by multiple components, and for Latino adolescents living in the United States, ethnic identity can become a significantly salient component of one's identity because of the emphasis on race and ethnicity in the United States. Although scholars differ in their conceptualizations of ethnic identity, one definition that encompasses most perspectives conceptualizes ethnic identity as a multifaceted construct that consists of (1) the degree to which individuals have explored their ethnicity, (2) the degree to which they have resolved what their ethnic identity means to them, and (3) the positive or negative affect that they associate with their ethnicity (Umaña-Taylor, Yazedjian, & Bámaca-Gómez, 2004). This conceptualization has been driven largely by ego identity (Erikson, 1968) and social identity (Tajfel, 1981) theoretical frameworks.

THEORETICAL BACKGROUND

According to Erikson's (1968) ego identity theory, individuals' identities develop as a result of one's exploration and resolution regarding specific identity components. Individuals who have explored their identities and, as a result of their exploration, have made commitments regarding particular ideologies and roles (e.g., occupation) are thought to have achieved a secure identity. Based on Erikson's theoretical premises, Marcia (1980) proposed a typology with which to operationalize identity achievement. Marcia's typology includes four statuses (i.e., achieved, moratorium, foreclosed, and diffuse) and individuals' placement in each status is dependent on their degree of exploration regarding a particular component identity as well as the extent of their commitment in that particular domain (Marcia, 1994). For example, an individual who has explored various options regarding a career but has not made a firm commitment in choosing a career would be considered to be in moratorium regarding that particular identity component; conversely, an individual who is very committed to a career as an accountant because of a strong family lineage of accountants but has not explored any other career options would be considered to be foreclosed (i.e., commitment with little to no exploration). Phinney furthered both Erikson's and Marcia's contributions by focusing specifically on the domain of ethnicity. Specifically, she posited that individuals explore and make decisions regarding their ethnicity over time and that this comes to define their ethnic identity (Phinney, 1990).

Scholars who have studied ethnic identity have also relied on social identity theory (Tajfel, 1981) to understand ethnic identity formation and outcomes associated with adolescents' ethnic identification. Social identity theory suggests that individuals' self-concepts are informed largely by their membership in particular social groups and, therefore, that individuals strive to achieve and/or maintain a positive social identity (Tajfel & Turner, 1986). Scholars (e.g., Phinney, Lochner, & Murphy, 1990; Roberts et al., 1999) have used social identity theory as a basis with which to understand how ethnic identity may be associated with psychological outcomes (e.g., self-esteem and depression) among minority youth. Specifically, scholars argue that individuals whose ethnic groups are associated with negative images may accept the negative images and consequently have a poor self-concept or reject the negative images perpetuated by society at large and, in turn, protect their self-concept. Thus, while Erikson's theory and its subsequent operationalization focus more explicitly on the *process* of identity formation, social identity theory focuses on the *affective* component of individuals' identities and how the affect associated with one's social identity may be associated with psychological outcomes.

With regard to understanding how ethnic identity is related to important outcome variables such as psychological functioning, it is important to consider the role of social context. Given the diversity in ethnic composition of regional areas in the United States (e.g., Florida vs. California), it is important to espouse a contextual approach when attempting to understand and interpret the meanings individuals attach to their ethnic identity and, in turn, how those meanings are associated with important outcome variables. Bronfenbrenner's (1989) ecological theory provides a contextual framework with which to understand the interrelations among ethnic identity and outcome variables such as psychological well-being. While ego identity and social identity theories may delineate the process of ethnic identity development as well as the importance of the affect associated with one's ethnic identity, ecological theory helps us understand how the relations among ethnic identity and psychological well-being are context dependent.

MEASUREMENT

Because the construct of ethnic identity is relatively novel, having flourished primarily in the past decade, assessment techniques are still in the process of being refined. Phinney (1992) made great strides toward providing scholars with a theoretically based measure of ethnic identity that could be used with multiple ethnic groups. The Multigroup Ethnic Identity Measure (MEIM; Phinney, 1992) is comprised of 14 items are categorized into three subscales: (1) ethnic identity achievement, (2) ethnic behaviors, and (3) affirmation and belonging. The ethnic identity achievement subscale assesses individuals' degree of exploration and commitment regarding their ethnicity. The ethnic behaviors subscale assesses the degree to which individuals participate in cultural activities, and the affirmation and belonging subscale assesses the degree to which individuals feel positively toward their ethnic group. Although the MEIM includes three distinct subscales, a summation of individuals' scores on all items is typically used to assess ethnic identity (e.g., Dubow, Paragament, Boxer, & Tarakeshwar, 2000; Lorenzo-Hernandez & Ouellette, 1998; Phinney, Dupont, Espinosa, Reville, & Sanders, 1994; Umaña-Taylor, 2004). Finally, the MEIM has proven to be highly reliable across diverse ethnic populations (Cuellar, Nyberg, Maldonado, & Roberts, 1997; Mack et al., 1997; Phinney, 1992; Taub, 1995).

Although the development of the MEIM contributed significantly to moving the field forward in the area of ethnic identity, as our conceptual understanding of ethnic identity matures, it is necessary for us to revisit our assessment strategies and make them congruent with our theoretical premises. Given that theoretical notions of identity emphasize the unique contribution of individuals' exploration and commitment regarding particular ideologies, the MEIM is limited in its ability to provide an assessment of each of these unique components. Specifically, if a summation of the items for the ethnic identity achievement subscale of the MEIM is used, we are unable to distinguish individuals who report high levels of exploration and low levels of commitment from those who report high levels of commitment and low levels of exploration. Thus, there is a need to develop assessment tools that are consistent with our theoretical notions.

Recently, Umaña-Taylor et al. (2004) introduced the Ethnic Identity Scale (EIS), which is comprised of three distinct subscales that assess ethnic identity exploration, ethnic identity resolution, and ethnic identity affirmation. Umaña-Taylor and colleagues advise against using a composite score to assess ethnic identity and, rather, recommend that the associations between each ethnic identity component and individual outcome variables be examined independently. In the section that follows, the work that has examined the relation between ethnic identity and Latino adolescents' psychological well-being will be reviewed. First, work in which a composite score of ethnic identity has been used will be presented, followed by work in which the three components of ethnic identity have been examined individually with measures of psychological well-being.

ETHNIC IDENTITY AND ADOLESCENT WELL-BEING

A secure sense of ethnic identity, which often must be achieved within the context of negative images of one's group, is necessary for the successful transition to healthy functioning in adulthood for ethnic minority individuals (Phinney & Kohatsu, 1997). In line with these ideas, existing empirical work with Latino populations has established a positive relation between ethnic identity and measures of psychological well-being (e.g., self-esteem). Theoretically, this relationship is in line with social identity theory, which posits that individuals' self-concepts are informed largely by their ethnic group membership. Given that self-esteem is viewed as a primary component of one's self-concept (Rosenberg, 1979), it follows that individuals who feel positively about their ethnic group membership will exhibit higher levels of self-esteem. Accordingly, a number of studies have examined the relation between Latino adolescents' ethnic identity and self-esteem.

During adolescence, individuals are increasingly preoccupied with others' perceptions of them, which results in an increased self-consciousness during this developmental period (Rosenberg, 1979). Given the increasing salience of ethnicity during adolescence, it is not surprising that numerous studies have found Latinos adolescents' ethnic identity and self-esteem to be related to one another (e.g., Carlson, Uppal, & Prosser, 2000; Lorenzo-Hernandez & Ouellette, 1998; Martinez & Dukes, 1997; Negy, Shreve, Jensen, & Uddin, 2003; Phinney, Cantu, & Kurtz, 1997; Phinney, Chavira, & Tate, 1993; Phinney et al., 1994; Roberts, et al., 1999; Umaña-Taylor, 2004).

For the most part, researchers have found that as adolescents report higher levels of ethnic identity, they also tend to report higher levels of self-esteem. For instance, with a sample including 372 Latino high school students in Los Angeles, California, researchers found that ethnic identity was a significant predictor of self-esteem such that higher levels of ethnic identity predicted higher levels of self-esteem (Phinney & Kohatsu, 1997). Similarly, multiple studies have reported significant and positive correlations between ethnic identity and adolescents' self-esteem (e.g., Lorenzo-Hernandez & Ouellette, 1998; Phinney, 1992; Roberts et al., 1999). Thus, in multiple studies that have used a composite ethnic identity score, a positive relation has emerged between ethnic identity and self-esteem.

In addition to examining a composite ethnic identity score, recent work has examined the relation between ethnic identity and self-esteem by using the individual subscales of the EIS. Findings from this work indicated that ethnic identity exploration, affirmation, and resolution were each significantly positively related to self-esteem in a sample of ethnic minority high school students (Umaña-Taylor et al., 2004); however, in a sample of university students, only exploration and resolution were positively related to self-esteem. Hence, there appears to be a developmental difference for affirmation in that during earlier developmental periods, the degree to which one feels positively or negatively toward one's ethnicity (i.e., affirmation) is related to one's self-esteem, but during later developmental periods, affirmation is unrelated to self-esteem. Umaña-Taylor and colleagues (2004) suggest that perhaps at later developmental periods, individuals' identities are more multifaceted, and, therefore, that their affect toward ethnicity is not as influential toward their self-concept as are other aspects of their identities (e.g., occupational success).

It is noteworthy that throughout early and late adolescence, individuals' exploration of their ethnicity and their resolution regarding their ethnic identity are both significantly and positively associated with self-esteem and that affirmation is related to self-esteem only during earlier developmental periods. It is possible that the process of exploration—and the knowledge and experience that results from this behavior—may help bolster self-esteem by providing individuals with a secure sense of identity. Similarly, it is possible that the confidence that comes with having resolved what your ethnicity means to you and the role that it will play in your life also serves a positive function in establishing your sense of self. Because we have only begun to examine the conceptually distinct components of ethnic identity, these ideas are speculative; however, future work should consider what it is about exploration and resolution that makes it relevant to individuals' sense of self throughout adolescence.

In addition to exploring the individual ethnic identity subscales and their association with self-esteem, it is possible to use individuals' scores on the EIS subscales to categorize them into an eight-status typology classification (see Umaña-Taylor et al., 2004). The eight-status classification is based heavily on Marcia's operationalization of Erikson's ego identity formation theory and also incorporates the affective evaluative component contributed by social identity theory (see Figure 9.1). Individuals are classified into each status based on their scores (high vs. low) on each of the three ethnic identity components. For example, an individual would be classified as Diffuse Positive if scoring low on exploration, low on resolution, and high on affirmation. Using this typology classification system, it is possible to examine variation in self-esteem scores based on ethnic identity status. Furthermore, this typology classification maintains the methodology for assessing ethnic identity consistent with the theoretical framework.

In existing work with Latino high school students, self-esteem scores have been found to vary significantly based on status classification (Umaña-Taylor, 2005). Specifically, Latino adolescents classified as Diffuse Negative reported significantly lower levels of self-esteem than their counterparts who were classified as Foreclosed Positive, Achieved Negative, or Achieved

Identity Achievement Status	Affirmation	
	Low	High
Low exploration/low resolution — Diffuse	Diffuse Negative	Diffuse Positive
Low exploration/high resolution — Foreclosed	Foreclosed Negative	Foreclosed Positive
High exploration/low resolution — Moratorium	Moratorium Negative	Moratorium Positive
High exploration/high resolution — Achieved	Achieved Positive	Achieved Negative

Figure 9.1.   Eight-status ethnic identity typology classification

Positive. In addition, adolescents classified as Diffuse Positive or Foreclosed Negative also scored significantly lower on self-esteem than those classified as Achieved Positive. On careful examination of the means (see Table 9.1), it is interesting to note that self-esteem scores are lowest for adolescents who report low levels of exploration, resolution, and affirmation (i.e., Diffuse Negative); furthermore, self-esteem scores are highest among those who report high levels of all three ethnic identity components (i.e., Achieved Positive). Interestingly, self-esteem scores for individuals in the Diffuse Negative (i.e., low exploration, resolution, and affirmation) and Diffuse Positive (i.e., low exploration and resolution and high affirmation) categories are not significantly different from one another, although there is a trend for Latino adolescents who are Diffuse Positive to report higher levels of self-esteem. Similarly, no significant differences emerge between those classified as Achieved Negative or Achieved Positive. Taken together, these findings suggest that perhaps ethnic identity resolution and exploration may bear more weight on one's self-esteem than individuals' ethnic identity affirmation. However, careful examination of individuals classified as Foreclosed Positive (i.e., low exploration and high resolution and affirmation) and Achieved Negative (i.e., high exploration and resolution and low affirmation) indicates that their self-esteem scores are strikingly similar ($M = 29.42$ vs. $M = 29.26$). Thus, one may conclude that affirmation does indeed matter, as it is associated with high levels of self-esteem when coupled with high resolution.

Table 9.1

Means and Standard Deviations of Self Esteem by EIS Type from Umaña-Taylor (2005)

		Self-esteem	
	n	*M*	*SD*
Diffuse Negative	11	24.00[ade]	6.48
Diffuse Positive	23	26.35[b]	4.26
Foreclosed Negative	22	25.91[c]	4.24
Foreclosed Positive	86	29.42[e]	5.32
Moratorium Negative	0	—	—
Moratorium Positive	4	26.00	3.56
Achieved Negative	34	29.26[d]	4.33
Achieved Positive	145	31.26[abc]	5.23
F	8.72***		
	(6,318)		

Note: Values with same superscripts are significantly different from one another. For example, superscript "a" indicates that the Diffuse Negative group differed significantly from the Achieved Positive group.

While these findings are discussed in terms of ethnic identity influencing self-esteem, this expected causal direction is based purely on theory because existing work has examined the relations only with cross-sectional data; future studies must employ longitudinal and experimental designs in order to claim causality and develop a clearer understanding of this relation. Nevertheless, these findings underscore the importance of examining the three ethnic identity components independently as opposed to using a composite score of ethnic identity. Although this work is a step forward in a necessary direction, our understanding of the ethnic identity components and their unique relations with self-esteem is an area that is ripe for future research.

ETHNIC IDENTITY AS A PROTECTIVE FACTOR

In addition to examining the direct relation between ethnic identity and measures of psychological well-being, researchers have examined the possible protective function that ethnic identity may serve for Latino adolescents' well-being. In one study, researchers found that ethnic identity affirmation buffered the negative effects of discrimination on Latino adolescents' self-esteem (Romero & Roberts, 2003). Specifically, Mexican-origin adolescents who reported high levels of both discrimination and ethnic identity affirmation reported higher levels of self-esteem than their counterparts who reported high levels of discrimination but low levels of ethnic identity affirmation.

Focusing on a different aspect of adolescent adjustment, researchers found that ethnic identity moderated the negative effects of psychosocial risk factors on Latino and Black adolescents' alcohol and marijuana use (Scheier, Botvin, Diaz, & Ifill-Williams, 1997). Specifically, Scheier and colleagues (1997) found that low levels of ethnic identity were associated with increased drug use for adolescents with higher psychosocial risk factors. In a similar line of work, researchers found that ethnic identity protected Puerto Rican adolescents from drug use by strengthening the positive influence of protective factors (e.g., low levels of familial drug use) and weakening the negative influence of risk factors (e.g., drug availability; Brook, Whiteman, Balka, Win, & Gursen, 1998).

Taken together, these findings suggest that ethnic identity may be a protective factor for Latino adolescents. Specifically, having a strong ethnic identity may protect adolescents not only from the negative effects of discrimination but also from becoming involved in substance use. Although this work must be replicated with additional samples in order to determine its generalizability, if we conclude that the findings are broadly generalizable, this will have vast implications for preventive intervention work with

Latino youth. For example, skill-building programs that enhance adolescents' understanding about and pride in their ethnic backgrounds could have far-reaching implications for Latino adolescents' well-being.

ETHNIC IDENTITY: THE ROLE OF SOCIAL CONTEXT

An additional factor that must be considered when attempting to understand adolescents' ethnic identity is social context. Findings from a study of Mexican-origin adolescents indicated that adolescents who were attending a predominantly non-Latino school (i.e., Latino student body was approximately 15%) reported significantly higher levels of ethnic identity (as measured by a composite score of the MEIM) than their counterparts who attended schools that had significantly larger Latino student bodies (i.e., 45% and 96% of the student body was Latino in the comparison schools; Umaña-Taylor, 2004). Interestingly, while salience of ethnic identity seemed to be greater for adolescents in a dissonant context (i.e., adolescents were a significant numerical ethnic minority in their school context), the correlational relation between ethnic identity and self-esteem was essentially identical across the three school contexts. Thus, it appears that although the salience of ethnic identity may vary as a result of social context, its relation to self-esteem may be not be context dependent, at least for Mexican-origin adolescents living in the Southwest.

Interestingly, findings from research with Puerto Ricans living in New York and Puerto Ricans living in Puerto Rico echo the importance of considering social context when examining psychological adjustment, as research indicates that Puerto Ricans in New York reported higher levels of depressive symptoms when compared to Puerto Ricans living in Puerto Rico (Vega & Rumbaut, 1991). Taken together, these findings support Bronfenbrenner's (1989) recommendation to assess and account for multiple settings in which individuals' lives are embedded in order to understand developmental outcomes. Clearly, more work is needed in order to gain a deeper understanding of the possible moderation effect of social context on the relation between the ethnic identity components and Latino adolescents' well-being.

ETHNIC IDENTITY AMONG NON-LATINO ETHNIC MINORITY ADOLESCENTS

Although there has been a vast increase in the number of studies that have examined the relation between Latino adolescents' ethnic identity and psychological adjustment, our existing knowledge is still limited. Nevertheless, we can turn to research with other ethnic minority groups to better inform our understanding. For instance, the positive relation that has emerged between ethnic identity and psychological well-being among Latino adolescents has also emerged among samples of Chinese (Verkuyten & Lay, 1998), Asian American (e.g., Lee, 2003), and African American (Yasui, Dorham, & Dishion, 2004) adolescents. Thus, it appears that the correlational relation between ethnic identity and psychological well-being is consistent across ethnic minority groups in the United States. While the strength of the relation varies across studies, it is clear that the two constructs are interrelated.

Relations that remain unexplored with Latino youth but have been examined with other populations include the relations among ethnic identity, academic success, and risky sexual behaviors. Existing research with Jewish and African American adolescents suggests that ethnic identity is positively associated with school success (Davey, Eaker, Fish, & Klock, 2003; Oyserman, Bybee, & Terry, 2003). Specifically, researchers have found that Jewish adolescents with higher levels of ethnic identity had higher levels of perceived scholastic competence (Davey et al., 2003). Furthermore, in a study of African American, female adolescents, researchers found a negative relation between ethnic identity and attitudes regarding risky sexual behavior (Belgrave, Van Oss Marin, & Chambers, 2000). As adolescents reported higher levels of ethnic identity affiliation, they tended to report less risky attitudes regarding sexual behavior. Given the significant high school dropout rate (U.S. Department of Education, 2003) and the epidemic of sexually transmitted diseases (Centers for Disease Control and Prevention, 2002) among Latino youth, the possible protective function that ethnic identity may serve with regard to these behaviors among Latino youth will be critical to explore in future research.

Similar to findings with Latino adolescents, ethnic identity has also been found to be a protective factor among other groups of ethnic minority adolescents. In a study with Southeast Asians, researchers found that the positive relation between discrimination and depressive symptoms was weaker among adolescents who reported high levels of ethnic identity affirmation (Noh, Beiser, Kaspar, Hou, & Rimmens, 1999). Similarly, findings from research with African American adolescents indicated that the negative relation between discrimination and school achievement was weakened when adolescents reported high levels of ethnic affirmation (Wong, Eccles, & Sameroff, 2003). To our knowledge, researchers have yet to examine the possible protective function of ethnic identity for *Latino* adolescents' depressive symptoms or school achievement; however, it is possible that the relations that have emerged with other ethnic minority groups may apply to Latino adolescents, as ethnic identity has been found to be protective for various indices of adolescent adjustment (e.g., self-esteem and drug use). As such, these are possible venues for future research to explore.

Finally, work with Latino adolescents (described previously) indicated a possible developmental progression for certain ethnic identity components (i.e., affirmation). Interestingly, existing work with African American adolescents suggests that developmental transitions are associated with changes in salience of ethnicity for adolescents. Specifically, researchers found that the transition from junior high to high school served as a race/ethnicity conscious-raising experience for African American adolescents (French, Seidman, Allen, & Aber, 2000). Specifically, African American adolescents' transition into high school was earmarked by an increase in ethnic identity exploration and resulted in ethnicity becoming more salient. Thus, it is possible that common developmental transitions such as these raise adolescents' consciousness and modify the relations among specific ethnic identity components and measures of well-being, as certain components may become more salient than others during the transitions. Although it is likely that similar processes are taking place among Latino adolescents, this will have to be examined with Latino populations before conclusions are drawn.

DIRECTIONS FOR FUTURE RESEARCH

In sum, existing work suggests that ethnic identity is positively associated with Latino adolescents' psychological well-being. Furthermore, findings highlight the importance of considering social context when attempting to understand adolescents' ethnic identity and its relation to important adolescent outcome variables. Finally, as we move forward in this important area, we must be sensitive to the idea that measurement techniques should be consistent with our theoretical arguments. Prior to closing, it is important to note important considerations for future research on this topic with Latino populations.

First, specific to working with Latino populations, a methodological limitation that is prevalent in this work involves the homogenization of Latinos (Umaña-Taylor, Diversi, & Fine, 2002). In a comprehensive review of studies that examined ethnic identity and self-esteem among Latino adolescents, less than half of the studies reviewed focused on a specific Latino population (e.g., Cuban and Salvadoran; Umaña-Taylor et al., 2002). Given the diverse experiences of Latinos in the United States (e.g., nationality, immigration, legal status, language, and traditions), it is critical that future work on ethnic identity account for important demographic variables (e.g., national origin, generational status, geographical context, immigration history, and socioeconomic status) that contribute to this variability. Without such attention, our understanding of the influence of ethnic identity on Latino adolescents' lives will remain incomplete. In addition, the existing work represents a possible restricted range, as the majority of studies that have focused on one Latino group have focused on individuals of Mexican origin (Umaña-Taylor et al., 2002). Thus, the experiences of minority groups within the Latino populations (i.e., groups that do not represent the numerical majority of Latinos, such as Salvadorans) have remained relatively unexamined. In addition, researchers must also consider geographical context and gather data from Latinos who represent the numerical majority or minority in specific areas. For example, a study of Puerto Ricans in New York City could be conducted in tandem with a study of Puerto Ricans in California.

Additionally, while a robust relation has been evidenced between ethnic identity and self-esteem, it will be important to explore additional indices of well-being. Examining the relation between adolescents' ethnic identity and self-esteem poses a possible challenge of shared method variance because both ethnic identity and self-esteem are aspects of self-concept. In order to move this area forward, it will be important to assess aspects of adolescents' well-being that are conceptually less similar to ethnic identity. For example, the relation between ethnic identity and depression will be important to understand, as Latino adolescents (particularly females) are at increased risk for depression (Joiner, Perez, Wagner, Berenson, & Marquina, 2001; Roberts, Roberts, & Chen, 1997).

With regard to methodology and study design, although existing work demonstrates a correlational relation between ethnic identity and psychological well-being, it will be important to understand the underlying mechanisms by which these variables are associated. One possibility is described by Crocker and Major (1989) in their discussion of self-protective strategies. Specifically, it is possible that individuals who have explored and resolved issues regarding their ethnic identity are aware of discrimination and oppression toward their group and that, when confronted with negative remarks, they attribute those remarks to prejudiced attitudes of others as opposed to some internal characteristic of themselves (Umaña-Taylor et al., 2002), which in turn may protect their self-esteem and any subsequent depression that could result from these negative experiences. In line with this idea, existing work suggests that individuals' ethnic identity is significantly related to their strategies for coping with discrimination and that those strategies are, in turn, associated with adolescents' self-esteem (Phinney & Chavira, 1995). Future studies must employ experimental and longitudinal methods in order to begin to decipher the relations among these important constructs.

Finally, in addition to gathering data from Latino adolescents, we need to design studies in a manner such that multiple informants' voices are heard. Given the central focus of families within Latino populations, the influence of significant others (e.g., mothers, fathers, siblings, and extended family) on the process of ethnic identity formation must be explored. Moreover, in order to develop effective intervention and prevention programs, we must espouse a systems approach in which multiple family members are involved in affecting change.

IMPLICATIONS FOR APPLICATION AND PRACTICE

Although this area of research is relatively novel and our knowledge has only recently begun to grow with regard to understanding the influence of ethnic identity on adolescents' lives, the robust relation that has emerged between ethnic identity and psychological well-being must be considered for intervention and prevention programs. Scholars posit that it is possible that, among ethnic minority children, ethnic-specific coping mechanisms or cultural influences may serve a protective function against the negative effects of stress (Gonzales & Kim, 1997). As evidenced by findings presented in this chapter, it seems likely that ethnic identity does serve a protective function for Latino youth, and if so, we must develop preventive intervention programs in which we empower youth regarding their ethnicity and, in turn, increase their psychological adjustment. In order to develop these programs, we must develop a more complete understanding of the differential influence of the distinct ethnic identity components in order to appropriately design and implement intervention strategies. For instance, if we find that adolescents' exploration is most influential in terms of developing successful coping strategies or protecting individuals' self-esteem, then we must target intervention efforts toward this ethnic identity component. Finally, as we develop preventive intervention programs that focus on ethnic identity, it will be imperative that we involve multiple family members in all stages of this process, as families have proven to be critical for the process of ethnic identity formation (Umaña-Taylor & Fine, 2001). Furthermore, consistent with an ecological perspective (Bronfenbrenner, 1989), we must include service providers and professionals who have daily contact with Latino adolescents (e.g., schoolteachers, administrators, counselors, and psychologists) in these programs. Professionals must become equipped to work effectively with Latino populations, given the rapid growth of the Latino population across all areas of the United States and the increased likelihood that they will serve Latino populations in some capacity at some point in their careers.

REFERENCES

Belgrave, F. Z., Van Oss Marin, B., & Chambers, D. B. (2000). Cultural, contextual, and intrapersonal predictors of risky sexual attitudes among urban African American girls in early adolescence. *Cultural Diversity and Ethnic Minority Psychology, 6,* 309–322.

Bronfenbrenner, U. (1989). Ecological systems theory. *Annals of Child Development, 6, 187*–249.

Brook, J. S., Whiteman, M., Balka, E. B., Win, P. T., & Gursen, M. D. (1998). Drug use among Puerto Ricans: Ethnic identity as a protective factor. *Hispanic Journal of Behavioral Sciences, 20,* 241–254.

Carlson, C., Uppal, S., & Prosser, E. C. (2000). Ethnic differences in processes contributing to the self-esteem of early adolescent girls. *Journal of Early Adolescence, 20,* 44–67.

Centers for Disease Control and Prevention. (2002). Cases of HIV infection and AIDS in the United States, 2002. *HIV/AIDS Surveillance Report 2002, 14,* 1–48.

Crocker, J., & Major, B. (1989). Social stigma and self-esteem: The self-protective properties of stigma. *Psychological Review, 96,* 608–630.

Cuellar, I., Nyberg, B., Maldonado, R. E., & Roberts, R. E. (1997). Ethnic identity and acculturation in a young adult Mexican-origin population. *Journal of Community Psychology, 25,* 535–549.

Davey, M., Eaker, D. G., Fish, L. S., & Klock, K. (2003). Ethnic identity in an American White minority group. *Identity: An International Journal of Theory and Research, 3,* 143–158.

Dubow, E. F., Paragament, K. I., Boxer, P., & Tarakeshwar, N. (2000). Initial investigation of Jewish early adolescents' ethnic identity, stress, and coping. *Journal of Early Adolescence, 20,* 418–441.

Erikson, E. H. (1968). *Identity: Youth and crisis.* New York: Norton.

French, S. E., Seidman, E., Allen, L., & Aber, J. L. (2000). Racial/ethnic identity, congruence with the social context, and transition to high school. *Journal of Adolescent Research, 15,* 587–602.

Garcia Coll, C., Crnic, K., Lamberty, G., Wasik, B. H., Jenkins, R., Garcia, H. V., & McAdoo, H. P. (1996). An integrative model for the study of developmental competencies in minority children. *Child Development, 67,* 1891–1914.

Gonzales, N. A., & Kim, L. S. (1997). Stress and coping in an ethnic minority context: Children's cultural ecologies. In I. N. Sandler, & S. A. Wolchik (Eds.), *Handbook of children's coping: Linking theory and intervention.* (pp. 481–511). New York: Plenum Press.

Joiner, T. E., Perez, M., Wagner, K. D., Berenson, A., & Marquina, G. S. (2001). On fatalism, pessimism, and depressive symptoms among Mexican-American and other adolescents attending an obstetrics-gynecology clinic. *Behaviour Research and Therapy, 39,* 887–896.

Lee, R. M. (2003). Do ethnic identity and other-group orientation protect against discrimination for Asian Americans? *Journal of Counseling Psychology, 50,* 133–141.

Lorenzo-Hernandez, J., & Ouellette, S. C. (1998). Ethnic identity, self-esteem, and values in Dominicans, Puerto Ricans, and African Americans. *Journal of Applied Social Psychology, 28,* 2007–2024.

Mack, D. E., Tucker, T. W., Archuleta, R., DeGroot, G., Hernandez, A. A., & Cha, S. O. (1997). Interethnic relations on campus: Can't we all get along? *Journal of Multicultural Counseling and Development, 25,* 256–268.

Marcia, J. E. (1980). Identity in adolescence. In J. Adelson (Ed.), *Handbook of adolescent psychology* (pp. 159–187). New York: Wiley.

Marcia, J. E. (1994). The empirical study of ego identity. In H. A. Bosma, T. G. Graafsma, H. D. Grotevant, & D. J. de Levita (Eds.), *Identity and development: An interdisciplinary approach* (4th ed., pp. 281–321). Belmont, CA: Wadsworth.

Martinez, R., & Dukes, R. L. (1997). The effects of ethnic identity, ethnicity, and gender on adolescent well-being. *Journal of Youth and Adolescence, 26,* 503–516.

Negy, C., Shreve, T. L., Jensen, B. J., & Uddin, N. (2003). Ethnic identity, self-esteem and ethnocentrism: A study of social identity versus multi-cultural theory of development. *Cultural Diversity and Ethnic Minority Psychology, 9,* 333–344.

Noh, S., Beiser, M., Kaspar, V., Hou, F., & Rimmens, J. (1999). Perceived racial discrimination, depression, and coping: A study of Southeast Asian refugees in Canada. *Journal of Health and Social Behavior, 40,* 193–207.

Oyserman, D., Bybee, D., & Terry, K. (2003). Gendered racial identity and involvement with school. *Self and Identity, 2,* 307–324.

Phinney, J. S. (1990). Ethnic identity in adolescents and adults: Review of research. *Psychological Bulletin, 108,* 499–514.

Phinney, J. S. (1992). The Multigroup Ethnic Identity Measure: A new scale for use with diverse groups. *Journal of Adolescent Research, 7,* 156–176.

Phinney, J. S., Cantu, C. S., & Kurtz, D. A. (1997). Ethnic and American identity as predictors of self-esteem among African American, Latino, and White adolescents. *Journal of Youth and Adolescence, 26,* 165–185.

Phinney, J. S., & Chavira, V. (1995). Parental ethnic socialization and adolescent coping with problems related to ethnicity. *Journal of Research on Adolescence, 5,* 31–53.

Phinney, J. S., Chavira, V., & Tate, J. D. (1993). The effect of ethnic threat on ethnic concept and own-group ratings. *Journal of Social Psychology, 133,* 469–478.

Phinney, J. S., Dupont, S., Espinosa, C., Reville, J., & Sanders, K. (1994). Ethnic identity and American identification among ethnic minority youths. In M. Bouvy, F. J. R. van de Vijver, P. Boski, & P. Schmitz (Eds.),

Journeys into cross-cultural psychology (pp. 167–183). Amsterdam: Swets & Zeitlinger.

Phinney, J. S., & Kohatsu, E. L. (1997). Ethnic and racial identity development and mental health. In J. Schulenberg, J. L. Maggs, & K. Hurrelmann (Eds.), *Health risks and developmental transitions during adolescence* (pp. 420–443). New York: Cambridge University Press.

Phinney, J. S., Lochner, B. T., & Murphy, R. (1990). Ethnic identity development and psychological adjustment in adolescence. In A. R. Stiffman & L. E. Davis (Eds.), *Ethnic issues in adolescent mental health* (pp. 53–72). Newbury Park, CA: Sage.

Roberts, R. E., Phinney, J. S., Masse, L. C., Chen, Y. R., Roberts, C. R., & Romero, A. (1999). The structure of ethnic identity of young adolescents from diverse ethnocultural groups. *Journal of Early Adolescence, 19,* 301–322.

Roberts, R. E., Roberts, C. R., & Chen, Y. R. (1997). Ethnocultural differences in prevalence of adolescent depression. *American Journal of Community Psychology, 25,* 95–110.

Romero, A. J., & Roberts, R. E. (2003). The impact of multiple dimensions of ethnic identity on discrimination and adolescents' self-esteem. *Journal of Applied Social Psychology, 33,* 2288–2305.

Rosenberg, M. (1979). *Conceiving the self.* New York: Basic Books.

Scheier, L. M., Botvin, G. J., Diaz, T., & Ifill-Williams, M. (1997). Ethnic identity as a moderator of psychosocial risk and adolescent alcohol and marijuana use: Concurrent and longitudinal analyses. *Journal of Child and Adolescent Substance Abuse, 6,* 21–47.

Tajfel, H. (1981). *Human groups and social categories.* New York: Cambridge University Press.

Tajfel, H., & Turner, J. C. (1986). The social identity theory of intergroup behavior. In S. Worschel & W. Austin (Eds.), *Psychology of intergroup relations* (pp. 7–24). Chicago: Nelson Hall.

Taub, D. J. (1995). Relationship of selected factors to traditional-age undergraduate women's development of autonomy. *Journal of College Student Development, 36*(2), 141–151.

Therrien, M., & Ramirez, R. R. (2000). The Hispanic population in the United States: March 2000. *Current Population Reports* (P20–535). Washington, DC: U.S. Census Bureau.

Umaña-Taylor, A. J. (2004). Ethnic identity and self-esteem: Examining the role of social context. *Journal of Adolescence, 27,* 139–146.

Umaña-Taylor, A. J. (2005). The Ethnic Identity Scale. In K. Moore & L. Lippman (Eds.), *Conceptualizing and measuring indicators of positive development: What do children need to flourish?* (pp. 75–91). New York: Kluwer.

Umaña-Taylor, A. J., Diversi, M., & Fine, M. A. (2002). Ethnic identity and self-esteem among Latino adolescents: Making distinctions among the Latino populations. *Journal of Adolescent Research, 17,* 303–327.

Umaña-Taylor, A. J., & Fine, M. A. (2001). Methodological implications of grouping Latino adolescents into one collective ethnic group. *Hispanic Journal of Behavioral Sciences, 23,* 347–362.

Umaña-Taylor, A. J., Yazedjian, A., & Bámaca-Gómez, M. Y. (2004). Developing the Ethnic Identity Scale using Eriksonian and social identity perspectives. *Identity: An International Journal of Theory and Research, 4,* 9–38.

U.S. Census Bureau. (2000). Hispanic or Latino by specific origin [31]—Universe: Total population. Census 2000 Summary File 1 (SF 1) 100 percent data [Data file]. Retrieved June 24, 2003, from http://factfinder.census.gov/servlet/DTTTable?_ts = 74532921253

U.S. Department of Education, National Center for Educational Statistics. (2003). *The condition of education 2003* (NCES 2003–067). Washington, DC: Author.

Vazquez Garcia, H. A., Garcia Coll, C., Erkut, S., Alarcon, O., & Tropp, L. R. (2000). Family values of Latino adolescents. In M. Montero-Sieburth & F. A. Villarruel (Eds.), *Making invisible Latino adolescents visible: A critical approach to Latino diversity* (pp. 239–264). New York: Falmer Press.

Vega, W. A., & Rumbaut, R. G. (1991). Ethnic minorities and mental health. *Annual Review of Sociology, 17,* 351–383.

Verkuyten, M., & Lay, C. (1998). Ethnic minority identity and psychological well-being: The mediating role of collective self-esteem. *Journal of Applied Social Psychology, 28,* 1969–1986.

Wong, C. A., Eccles, J. S., & Sameroff, A. (2003). The influence of ethnic discrimination and ethnic identification on African American adolescents' school and socioemotional adjustment. *Journal of Personality, 71,* 1197–1232.

Yasui, M., Durham, C. L., & Dishion, T. J. (2004). Ethnic identity and psychological adjustment: A validity analysis for European American and African American adolescents. *Journal of Adolescent Psychology, 19,* 807–825.

Chapter 10

CRITICAL MENTAL HEALTH ISSUES FOR SEXUAL MINORITY ADOLESCENTS

Stephen T. Russell and Jenifer K. McGuire

Two important observations define the research on the mental health of sexual minority adolescents. First, this is a population that is in some cases at extreme risk for compromised mental health (D'Augelli, 2002); this is a critical issue. Second, there is almost no history of systematic, scientifically evaluated prevention or intervention on the topic of mental health for this population; we know very little about effective programs. What we do know is that sexual minority adolescents—those who identify as gay, lesbian, bisexual, or transgender (LGBT); those who engage in same-sex sexual behavior; or those who report same-sex attractions or desires—are a group at high risk for compromised mental health. Nearly three decades ago, scientific reports first began to suggest that LGB adolescents were at higher risk than their heterosexual peers for risk behaviors and compromised mental health (Bell & Weinberg, 1978; Hetrick & Martin, 1987; Martin & Hetrick, 1988). Through the 1980s and early 1990s, research began to confirm these concerns, showing that LGB adolescents were more likely to report mental health problems, including depression and suicidality (Hammelman, 1993; Hershberger & D'Augelli, 1995; Rotheram-Borus, Hunter, & Rosario, 1994; Russell, 2003).

The early studies were characterized by significant methodological limitations that have been described in detail elsewhere (Russell, 2003; Savin-Williams, 1994, 2001). Briefly, they include the reliance on small convenience samples, the results of which were not generalizable. In addition, most past studies were limited to LGB-identified youth, a group that may not adequately represent the range of same-sex experiences in adolescents that might include, for example, same-sex behavior, same-sex attraction or desire, or transgender identity. Adolescent transgender identity in particular has been absent from most discussions of mental health among sexual minority youth. Thus, these studies suffered from the same methodological challenges inherent in studies of youth, of gay populations, and of mental health: challenges defining and accessing the population under study and challenges measuring key constructs of interest. In addition to these methodological challenges, existing prior research has been focused predominantly on mental health problems; comparatively fewer prior studies have examined positive dimensions of mental health (such as self-esteem) or have focused on the typical developmental course of positive mental health among sexual minority adolescents. Thus, while the history of this field of research began with studies that documented risk, few models have been developed to explain the developmental course of positive mental health for sexual minority youth.

In this chapter, we synthesize what is known about mental health and same-sex sexuality in adolescence, giving attention to several dimensions of this body of research that have been underexamined in prior work: variability in mental health status among sexual minorities, including attention to the special subpopulations of homeless youth, transgender youth, and children of LGBT parents; the importance of relational contexts for understanding the mental health of sexual minority youth, including family, religion, school, and peer and romantic relationships; and finally the implications of this growing body of evidence for prevention and intervention with sexual minority young people.

MENTAL HEALTH AND SAME-SEX SEXUALITY IN ADOLESCENCE

Most past research on sexual minority adolescents and mental health has compared sexual minority to heterosexual youth; in so doing, this body of work has played the important role of documenting disproportionate risk. Much less attention has been given to the important variability that exists among sexual minority youth (Diamond & Savin-Williams, 2003). We pay special attention to work addressing the diversity within LGBT youth populations because although mental health risk is well documented, it is still the case that most LGBT youth grow up without significant impairments in mental health. This diversity in mental health experience requires more systematic study than it has received to date. Thus, it is important to distinguish possible risk among LGBT youth while avoiding the assumption that all LGBT youth are anxious, depressed, or suicidal. We review the knowledge base on adolescent same-sex sexuality and mental health and then focus our attention on subpopulations: homeless LGBT youth and transgender youth. We begin the review with suicide, the topic on which the most has been written concerning sexual minority youth.

Suicide

The existing research literature on adolescent sexual orientation and mental health began historically with a focus on suicidality (Russell, 2003). With few exceptions, studies conducted over the course of the past 30 years have consistently shown adolescent same-sex sexuality to be a strong predictor of suicidality. The risk for suicide was one of the first topics in the lives of sexual minority youth to be investigated, and suicide risk is one of the few facts about sexual minority youth to become common knowledge (for a comprehensive review, see Russell, 2003). The early studies of gay youth and suicide risk were characterized by the many methodological challenges described previously, yet from the late 1970s through the mid-1990s, multiple studies continued to provide evidence that LGB-identified youth were significantly more likely than their peers to report suicidal thoughts and suicide attempts. No existing studies have documented a link between same-sex sexuality and completed suicide; nevertheless, a prior suicide attempt or attempts is the strongest individual predictor of completed suicide. A series of published studies in the 1990s based on large-scale and representative samples of adolescents in the United States (e.g., Durant, Krowchuk, & Sinal, 1998; Faulkner & Cranston, 1998; Garofalo, Wolf, Kessel, Palfrey, & DuRant, 1998; Garofalo, Wolf, Wissow, Woods, & Goodman, 1999; Remafedi, French, Story, Resnick, & Blum, 1997; Russell & Joyner, 2001) and prospective studies from New Zealand (Fergusson, Horwood, & Beautrais, 1999) and Norway (Wichstrom & Hegna, 2003) have confirmed the prior 20 years of research while addressing many of the methodological limitations of past studies. Using large, population-based samples, these reports document a strong link between adolescent sexual minority status and suicidality.

After 30 years of documenting suicide risk among sexual minority adolescents, current efforts focus on examinations of heterogeneity among sexual minorities (why are some sexual minorities more "at risk" than others?) and on locating this risk within the broader contexts of the lives of adolescents (which we discuss in the second half of this chapter: do experiences at home, at school, or among peers help explain the disproportionate risk for suicide among sexual minority youth?). In terms of heterogeneity among sexual minorities, there are important differences based on gender and on how same-sex sexuality is measured (whether the measure is based on same-sex identity, orientation, or behavior). Historically, studies have consistently shown young gay males to be at significant risk for suicide, while the findings for young lesbians have not been consistent or strong. In fact, several studies indicate that self-identified adolescent lesbians are at lower risk for suicidality than gay males (Garofalo et al., 1999; Remafedi et al., 1997). It may be that being out as a young lesbian is an act of empowerment and resistance to heteronormativity that may be fundamentally protective for young women, while being out as a young gay man simply places young men at too great a social risk, straining their emotional health. Some support for the potentially protective quality of coming out for young women is found in a study based on same-sex romantic attraction because in that study, same-sex attracted girls and boys were equally at risk for suicidal thoughts and suicide attempts (Russell & Joyner, 2001); it is likely that many of the same-sex attracted girls had not yet self-identified as lesbians. Thus, the accumulated evidence seems to suggest that same-sex sexuality for young males, whether in or out of the closet, is a risk for suicide, but for young women, those most at risk may be those who remain silent about their emerging same-sex desires.

Other work has examined suicide risk factors among sexual minority adolescents and in doing so points to important variability among sexual minorities. Three important precursors to suicidality among sexual minority youth involve coming-out milestones, gender nonconformity, and victimization. First, coming out (Hershberger, Pilkington, & D'Augelli, 1997) and coming out at young ages (Remafedi, Farrow, & Deisher, 1991) have been linked with suicidality among LGB youth, due in part to resulting rejection from important sources of support (Hammelman, 1993; Hershberger et al., 1997; Schneider, Farberow, & Kruks, 1989). Further, coming out at a young age and having a comparatively high number of sex partners is associated with suicide attempts among gay, bisexual, and questioning males (Remafedi et al., 1991; Savin-Williams & Ream, 2003). Second, gender nonconformity has been identified as a risk factor for suicide among LGB youth (D'Augelli, Pilkington, & Hershberger, 2002); while gender nonconformity is not exclusive to sexual minority youth, the emergence of strict gender expectations in adolescence may be particularly problematic for sexual minority youth as they come of age (Olson & King, 1995). Third, not only do sexual minority youth experience more frequent and more violent victimization (Russell, Franz, & Driscoll, 2001), but the kinds of victimization they experience are qualitatively different because they are reactions to sexual minority status (D'Augelli et al., 2002). In fact, homophobia-based victimization has been shown to play an important role in suicidality among sexual minority youth (Hershberger et al., 1997). This body of work indicates that identity status and coming out, gender nonconformity, and victimization are important characteristics that may significantly impact mental health among sexual minority adolescents.

Mental Health

Given the significant attention to sexual minority youth suicidality, there has been a surprising lack of attention to standard indicators of mental health. A recent study using data from the National Longitudinal Study of Adolescent Health reports higher levels of depression among same-sex attracted youth (Russell & Joyner, 2001), and a New Zealand cohort study showed that LGB youth reported more depression and anxiety and lower self-esteem than their heterosexual peers (Fergusson et al., 1999). Several past studies based in the United States have reported that stressors due to being gay (Meyer, 1995; Rosario, Rotheram-Borus, & Reid, 1996), low self-esteem (Grossman & Kerner, 1998; Rosario et al., 1996), and victimization (D'Augelli, 2002; Hershberger & D'Augelli, 1995) are associated with compromised mental health outcomes for LBG-identified youth. On the other hand, Rosario et al. (1996) report that the urban, Black and Latino gay and bisexual males in their sample did not have elevated levels of depression or anxiety or low self-esteem when compared to baseline statistics for U.S. adolescents. In sum, while the evidence that sexual minority youth suffer from compromised mental health is somewhat mixed, most existing studies find mental health problems to be more prevalent among sexual minority youth when compared to their non–sexual minority peers.

Given the number of past studies of suicidality, it is perhaps ironic that the limited research that addresses differences in mental health among LGB youth focuses on self-esteem. These studies give attention to the role of family relationships for sexual minority youth. Independence from parents has been found to be associated with positive self-esteem for gay and lesbian youth (Floyd & Stein, 2002); specifically, independence from mothers predicted higher self-esteem for young lesbians, while independence from fathers predicted higher self-esteem for gay males. Other research focuses attention on the quality of the parent–adolescent relationship. A study of gay male youth found that perceived social support from the family contributed to positive self-esteem (Anderson, 1998); other studies have reported that parental closeness and empathy (Floyd & Stein, 2002) and satisfaction in relationships with parents, particularly mothers, is associated with higher self-esteem (Savin-Williams, 1989b). These studies report some gender differences; family acceptance was more important for the self-esteem of lesbian adolescents, while self-acceptance was central for gay male adolescent self-esteem (Savin-Williams, 1989a).

Additionally, comparisons based on urban/rural residence were examined, showing that being out to one's mother was predictive of positive self-esteem for rural youth, while infrequent contact with mother predicted positive self-esteem among urban youth (Savin-Williams, 1989b). This work demonstrates the importance of the largely unexamined role of parent–adolescent relationships (in particular the mother–adolescent relationship) in shaping the mental health of sexual minority adolescents. It also highlights important urban/rural variability.

Homeless LGBT Youth

LGBT youth and homeless youth are at risk for compromised mental health, and adolescents who are both LGBT and homeless seem to experience intensified difficulties (Cochran, Stewart, Ginzler, & Cauce, 2002; Kruks, 1991; Noell & Ochs, 2001; Yates, MacKenzie, Pennbridge, & Swofford, 1991). LGBT homeless youth engage in substance use (Cochran et al., 2002; Noell & Ochs, 2001), prostitution (Kruks, 1991; Yates et al., 1991), psychopathology (Cochran et al., 2002), and suicide attempts (Cochran et al., 2002; Kruks, 1991; Noell & Ochs, 2001) at greater levels than heterosexual homeless youth. Some evidence suggests that the life experiences that put individuals at risk for mental health difficulties also increase the risk of homelessness for LGBT youth. Specifically, LGBT homeless youth have experienced childhood physical and sexual abuse and family rejection at greater levels than their straight counterparts and continue to experience physical and sexual victimization (Cochran et al., 2002) during homelessness at greater levels than heterosexual homeless adolescents. Existing research also indicates that there are differences between gay and lesbian adolescents in life on the streets. Young women are at greater risk for sexual victimization than young men regardless of sexual minority status (Cochran et al., 2002). Yet survival sex (Kruks, 1991) is more frequently reported by homeless gay males than females. Other research shows greater lifetime drug use for homeless lesbians compared to gay males (Noell & Ochs, 2001).

Transgender Youth

Little is known about the mental health and well-being based on adolescent gender identity. This unique population of adolescents has been studied almost exclusively for the purpose of either debating the merits of allowing sex reassignment surgery (SRS; Bailey & Zucker, 1995; Bradley & Zucker, 1997; Cohen-Kettenis & van Goozen, 2002; Smith, van Goozen, & Cohen-Kettenis, 2001), or documenting the occurrence and treatment of mental illness among these youth (Cohen, de Ruiter, Ringelberg, & Cohen-Kettenis, 1997; Di Ceglie, Freedman, McPherson, & Richardson, 2002; Menvielle & Tuerk, 2002; Meyenburg, 1999; Rosenberg, 2002). While only a small percentage of children and adolescents who qualify for a diagnosis of gender identity disorder by the standards of the *Diagnostic and Statistical Manual of Mental Disorders* (4th ed.) go on to become transsexuals (Smith et al., 2001), many adolescents who display elements of gender nonconformity will face difficult reactions from parents, peers, and school personnel.

Several studies have documented higher rates of depression, general anxiety, and separation anxiety among transgender youth (Bradley & Zucker, 1997; Coates & Person, 1986; Zucker, Bradley, & Lowry Sullivan, 1996). Studies that examine mental health before and after SRS have found that SRS does not worsen the psychological profile of youth; rather, it may have some benefits for reducing the difficulties associated with gender nonconformity (Smith, et al., 2001). One study regarding the outcomes of SRS suggests that adolescents completing SRS experience positive benefits and express satisfaction with the decision to proceed through the transition (Cohen-Kettenis & van Goozen, 2002).

Adolescent Children of LGBT Parents

A small body of research has developed on the topic of the well-being of the children of LGBT parents. In many important ways, these children might face the same prejudices and discrimination as other sexual minorities, and thus their mental health has been a topic of concern in this field. In fact, much of the focus of this literature has been based on concerns that children of LGBT parents will face significant prejudice and discrimination and that these children will be more likely than their peers to become LGBT themselves. Given these issues, a final concern is that children of LGBT parents they will suffer emotionally.

First, most studies have found no differences in stigmatization based on sexual orientation of parents (Anderssen, Amlie, & Ytterøy, 2002), although two studies reported that children were concerned about the possibility of being teased more than that they actually were teased (O'Connell, 1993; Tasker & Golombok, 1997). Second, concerning the gender and sexual orientations of children of LGBT parents, several studies have found that same-sex partnerships adhere to less rigid gender roles than opposite sex partnerships, and some evidence suggests that these more open roles can impact children. Evidence across several studies exists that finds daughters of lesbians more likely to endorse both masculine and feminine activities than daughters of straight women (Stacey &

Biblarz, 2001). Yet studies of LGBT parenting are often focused on proving that having an LGBT parent does not cause children to grow up gay (Anderssen et al., 2002). Given this defensive stand, little has been done to explain the finding of increased experimentation with same-sex relationships among children of LGBT parents (Tasker & Golombok, 1997). It is reasonable to expect that it could be beneficial for LGBT children to be raised by LGBT parents, presuming that their home environments would be characterized by an acceptance of sexual diversity and same-sex relationships. Finally, a growing body of research on children of LGBT parents compares them to the children of heterosexual married or single parents and shows few or no differences in mental health, adjustment, or functioning of children of LGBT parents (Anderssen et al., 2002; Patterson, 1992, 2000).

Within LGBT headed households, there is a distinction between those who birthed or adopted young children, those who were reorganized from a heterosexual family to a family with one LGBT parent and a new LGBT stepparent, and families with a single LGBT parent. Within stepfamilies, issues related to custody, prior family conflicts, and adjustment to the divorce can be entangled with the child's response to a parent coming out. In such cases, separating the impact of having a gay parent versus the typical adjustments of family reorganization is difficult. The few studies that have explicitly addressed family structure issues continue to focus on differences between heterosexual structures and same-sex partnered families. By considering different family structures, they shed light on the ways that the variability in family structure among LGBT-headed households may affect adolescent and young adult mental health. One study of gay male stepfamilies (Crosbie-Burnett & Helmbrecht, 1993) found that some issues between the adolescent and gay stepfather (discipline, family cohesion, and adolescent self-efficacy) were not as closely linked to family adjustment as would be expected based on the literature on opposite-sex stepfamilies. However, the relationship between the adolescent and the stepparent was similarly related to family functioning. In a study comparing the offspring of single females parents and lesbian couples, greater incidence of psychiatric symptoms were reported for children of single females (Golombok, Spencer, & Rutter, 1983).

The limited research on children with transsexual parents parallels the research on children with LGB parents in that its focus is on the same three hypothetical concerns: the child will be stigmatized and social relations will be compromised, the child will be more likely to become transsexual, and the child will have more mental health problems. The few studies document that children of transsexuals are no more likely to experience gender identity issues or be transsexuals than comparison groups.

Freedmen, Tasker, and Di Ceglie (2002) compared children of transsexuals referred to a gender identity clinic to other children referred to the same clinic because they themselves were experiencing gender identity issues. The children of transsexuals reported less depression, stigmatization, and social sensitivity, even though the children of transsexuals in this sample were experiencing increased family conflict between the transsexual and nontranssexual parents. An important consideration for the children of transsexuals is that they may be more likely to have experienced conflict between parents and the difficulty of the nontranssexual parent in adjusting to the transsexual parent's physical and psychological changes. Family conflict and the resulting potential mental health concerns are important considerations for this unique population of adolescents.

THE ROLE OF SOCIAL CONTEXTS IN SEXUAL MINORITY ADOLESCENTS' MENTAL HEALTH

Mental health research generally focuses on individual-level outcomes. As a result, mental health becomes a risk status of the individual adolescent rather than a characteristic that describes a youth's contexts or experiences growing up. Prior research indicates that sexual minority youth are "at risk," but rarely is that risk considered in context, nor are the mechanisms that underlie compromised mental health the explicit focus of investigation. Yet at a most basic level, contemporary adolescents live in societies characterized by sexual prejudice. Thus, an understanding of the ontogeny of mental health problems for sexual minority adolescents must address the role of sexual stigma for these young people. Evidence of this prejudice is manifest in individual lives in the form of compromised family relationships (Herdt & Koff, 2000) or hostile school environments (Russell, Seif, & Truong, 2001). In order to understand the mental health outcomes of sexual minorities, it is essential to take into consideration the role of sexual prejudice in shaping the relational contexts, experiences, characteristics, or life statuses of adolescence.

Family

Coming out at home is one of the most difficult tasks for LGB youths, and most of the research on adolescent mental health, sexual orientation, and family life has focused on this transition. In the home, youth will typically first disclose same-sex attractions to a parent, but about 5 percent of the time they disclose to a sibling first (D'Augelli & Hershberger, 1993). Sexual minority youth face potential rejection and victimization from their parents and siblings and consequent negative outcomes such as suicide and poor mental health. Of course, not all youth choose to disclose their sexual identity at home, but such self-silencing may be detrimental to well-being. One study indicates that among LGB youth, suicidal thoughts were more common among adolescents whose parents were not aware of their sexual orientation (D'Augelli & Hershberger, 1993). Past studies have documented significant difficulties when coming out to parents and siblings for some LGB youth, including experiences of verbal threats, physical abuse (D'Augelli, Hershberger, & Pilkington, 1998), or being kicked out of their homes (Boxer, Cook, & Herdt, 1991). LGB youth typically expect that their fathers' reaction to their coming out will be more negative than their mothers'. This is partly true, but in one study lesbian youth reported more threats and physical violence from their mothers than did gay male youth (D'Augelli et al., 1998). While parent reaction to their knowledge or awareness of their child's sexual orientation is often negative (D'Augelli et al., 1998), many families of gay and lesbian children ultimately integrate their child's LGB identity into the family (Herdt & Koff, 2000). Siblings have been found to have more positive and fewer negative reactions to disclosure of same-sex attractions (D'Augelli, 1991; Savin-Williams, 1995). Very little research has been done about the reactions of extended family members except to note that some youth will first come out to extended family members that they believe to be gay (D'Augelli & Hershberger, 1993; Savin-Williams, 1998).

Beyond this research on family reactions to a youth's coming out and the research cited previously on the links between family life and self-esteem among LGB youth, there has been much less research attention to the ways that family interactions might reinforce homonegativity, thus creating emotional stress for sexual minority youth. A study by D'Augelli (2002) has shown that parental reaction to a child's disclosure of being LGB is more strongly linked to the mental health of LGB youth than is parents' knowledge of the child's sexual orientation (i.e., the way a parent reacts is more influential than the fact that the parent knows); clearly, the coming-out process is an important transition in the life of both the adolescent and the family, with important implications for youth mental health. At the same time, a recent study suggests that basic family processes may be more important than gay-specific issues for the mental health of LGB youth. This study indicates that family mental health problems, family functioning, and family stress are more important than sexual orientation or sexual orientation–based harassment for predicting internalizing and externalizing problems among LGB youth (Elze, 2002). The findings of this study suggest that existing research has underexamined and underestimated the role that normative family stressors may play in explaining the mental health problems of sexual minority youth.

Religion

Religion is an important personal experience and developmental context for young people, yet most contemporary religious groups are ambivalent or negative toward same-sex sexuality. The homophobia that characterizes the values of many faith groups may contribute to compromised mental health among sexual minorities. Specifically, a strong identification with a religious denomination that condemns or is intolerant of same-sex orientations may create a sense of dissonance between two core identities (Thumma, 1991). Religious sexual minorities may therefore experience more struggles in coming to terms with their sexual identities. In fact, religiousness has been linked with a postponed coming-out process for sexual minority youth (Wagner, Serafini, Rabkin, Remien, & Williams, 1994). The results of another study show that nearly 50 percent of all LGB youth raised in a religious faith reported having no religion (Rosario, Yali, Hunter, & Gwadz, 2003). A comparable study of non-LGB youth found that approximately 76 percent of the adolescent children of religious parents were also religious (Cnaan, Gelles, & Sinha, 2004). Thus, religious LGB persons may be more likely to resolve the dissonance they experience by rejecting their religion, by rejecting or postponing acceptance of their same-sex identity, or by attempting to integrate these identities (Rodriguez & Ouellette, 2000; Rosario et al., 2003; Thumma, 1991; Yip, 1997). Overall, these conflicts between religious and sexual identity create the context for fragile mental health (Schuck & Liddle, 2001; Sullivan & Wodarski, 2002).

The existing research on religion in the lives of sexual minority youth is small; only a few studies have directly linked religious experience to mental health. Ream and Savin-Williams (2005) report that LGB youth who had left Christianity or reported that it was difficult to believe that God loved them had poorer mental health than youth who experienced no conflict between sexual identity and religious identity or had resolved or ignored that conflict. In a study using nationally representative data, Russell, Muraco, and D'Augelli (2003) reported that while religiousness and religious affiliation did not account for the differential in mental health scores between same-sex and other-sex attracted adolescents, there were significant religious affiliation differences in depression for sexual minorities. Specifically, Catholic and Baptist same-sex attracted youth reported higher levels of depression than youth who reported no religion. Another study indicates that sexual minority girls were more troubled by their religious beliefs than were boys (D'Augelli, 2002). In sum, these studies suggest that religiousness can be a source of stress for many LGB youth and that this may vary on the basis of religious affiliation, forcing some youth to reject either their religion or their sexual orientation in order to maintain a positive self-concept (Radkowsky & Siegel, 1997; Sullivan & Wodarski, 2002; Wagner et al., 1994). Further, given strong differences in religiousness for males and females during adolescence (Wallace & Forman, 1998), there is reason to expect gender differences among sexual minority youth; yet few studies have focused on this possibly important source of heterogeneity among sexual minority young people.

School

Recent research has begun to link the negative mental health of LGB youth to challenges that they face in school, including harassment and discrimination. These challenges impede not only the students' academic performance but also their general social and emotional development. For LGBT youth, school peers may be the first people to whom they come out, and peers may also be the people from whom they receive the most harassment or victimization. In many schools, verbal abuse, graffiti, and other antigay activities permeate everyday relations among students (Smith & Smith, 1998). A recent study reported that the increased prevalence of suicidality among sexual minority youth was associated with the loss of friends due to the disclosure of sexual orientation (Hershberger et al., 1997). In another study, 69 percent of LGB youth in grades 7 to 12 reported feeling unsafe in their schools, and 31 percent reported that they missed at least one day of school in the past month because they felt unsafe (Kosciw & Cullen, 2003), compared to 5.4 percent of adolescents nationwide having skipped a day of school in the past month because of safety concerns (Brener, Lowry, Barrios, Simon, & Eaton, 2004). This pervasive homophobia in the school setting is often expressed not only by fellow students but at times by teachers as well (Human Rights Watch, 2001). Such school-based harassment has been linked with compromised emotional health that lasts into adulthood (Rivers, 2001).

Much has been written by and for school counselors to create supportive school environments and support the mental health of sexual minority students (Black & Underwood, 1998; Cooley, 1998; Dombrowski, Wodarski, Smokowski, & Bricout, 1995). In one study, school-based homophobia was associated with lower self-esteem and a higher likelihood of self-destructive behavior (Uribe & Harbeck, 1991); other work documents that gay and lesbian students come to school counselors for assistance with depression, poor self-esteem, social isolation, and elevated suicide risk (Fontaine, 1998). While many districts, schools, and individual administrators and teachers are proactive in ensuring that the school environment is free from harassment and discrimination, it remains that many schools and school personnel have limited awareness of or are not prepared or trained to understand and manage issues of same-sex sexuality or identity. School personnel often do not take sexuality-motivated harassment or victimization seriously, even for students for whom harassment and victimization are daily experiences. Some even express the belief that victims "cause" their own harassment and thereby do not support victimized youth (Human Rights Watch, 2001). However, a recent study showed that sexual minority youth with positive feelings about their teachers are significantly less likely than their peers to experience school troubles (Russell, Seif, et al., 2001). Thus, research shows that teachers can play an important role in creating supportive school environments where all youth can grow and learn. Training and support are needed to provide teachers and other school personnel with the knowledge and skills to support LGBT youth in school settings. Several studies have documented the benefits to LGBT and straight youth's well-being and sense of security in school when gay/straight alliances or similar sexual minority focused clubs are present (Blumenfeld, 1993; Russell, 2002; Snively, 2004; Szalacha, 2003).

Peer and Dating Relationships

Final contexts that we consider are peer and dating relationships. The importance of peers has been central to the discussions of school climates for sexual minority youth; past research has shown that compared to their peers, sexual minority adolescent report more fear going to school because of peer harassment and more physical threats by peers at school (Faulkner & Cranston, 1998). It has been suggested that many LGB adolescents cope with stressful peer interactions withdrawing or isolating themselves from other students (Radkowsky & Siegel, 1997). In fact, like coming out at home, coming out to peers is stressful for adolescents; telling friends about one's sexual orientation has been linked with multiple indicators of mental health (interpersonal sensitivity, hostility, phobic anxiety, paranoid ideation, and psychoticism (D'Augelli, 2002). However, not all peer relationships must be negative; Savin-Williams and Ream (2003) report that gay, bisexual, and questioning male youth who attend support groups had higher self-esteem than those who did not attend. In another study, support from LGB peers was strongly predictive of self-esteem for gay male youth (Anderson, 1998). Given the stigma and potential isolation of same-sex sexuality in adolescence, it is not surprising that friendships with other sexual minority youth may be particularly protective.

Other work has begun to explore the role of romantic relationships and dating in the lives of sexual minority youth. A growing body of research highlights the important developmental role that romantic relationships play in the lives of adolescents (Furman, Brown, & Feiring, 1999); it is through dating relationships that young people learn about trust, communication, commitment, mutuality, and their emotions (Brown, 1999). However, little attention has focused on same-sex intimacy, romance, and relationships (Diamond & Lucas, 2002; for a discussion of the role of romantic relationships in the lives of sexual minority youth, see Diamond, 2003). And while much of the existing research on adolescent romance indicates that it is associated with depression for heterosexual youth (Joyner & Udry, 2000), the negative impact of romance does not appear as consistent for sexual minority youth. For example, results from the National Longitudinal Study of Adolescent Health show that for males, having a same-sex relationship was associated with drinking alone but with less cigarette use and fewer alcohol-related problems (Russell, Driscoll, & Truong, 2002). Another report using those data shows that same-sex romantic attractions and relationships are relevant for understanding negative mental health states (anxiety and depression); sexual minority same-sex daters were not significantly more anxious or depressed compared to heterosexual other-sex daters, but they did tend to be more suicidal than their peers (Russell & Consolacion, 2003). The previously cited study that documented the protective effects of support group membership for self-esteem for gay, bisexual, and questioning males also showed that having sex with a male sex partner was linked to higher self-esteem (Savin-Williams & Ream, 2003). Finally, recent study indicates that among LGB youth, dissatisfaction with sex life was associated with all the subscales of the Brief Symptom Inventory (D'Augelli, 2003). These studies indicate that same-sex relationships are not necessarily linked to compromised emotional health but rather that gay-specific social supports—friendships and dating relationships—may be particularly important for the positive self-image of sexual minority youth, particularly young gay men.

Race/Ethnicity

There has been very little research on dual minority status (being from an ethnic minority group and being LGBT) and its relation to mental health. Among gay and bisexual Latino men, experiences of social discrimination predicted increased anxiety, depression, and suicide ideation (Diaz, Ayala, Bein, Henne, & Marin, 2001). In the Add Health study, dual minority status did not surface as a predictor of compromised mental health (Consolacion, Russell, & Sue, 2004).

PREVENTION AND INTERVENTION

There has been little systematic study of prevention and intervention efforts that specifically target the mental health of sexual minority adolescents.

A most basic step will involve integrating attention to same-sex sexuality in ongoing prevention and intervention efforts that target the general adolescent population. It is ironic that while same-sex sexuality and LGBT issues are ever present in the public discourse and in the media, few adolescents have opportunities to discuss these issues with caring adults in contexts characterized by learning or support. Existing adolescent mental health prevention and intervention programs should acknowledge the existence of same-sex sexuality during adolescence and give attention to the potential for same-sex sexuality to play a role in the mental health and well-being of the adolescents in their programs. While the integration of same-sex sexuality into existing generalized prevention and intervention efforts is an ideal, there are also important steps to be taken with programs that specifically address the mental health needs of sexual minority youth. In recent years, there has been increased attention to strategies for supporting sexual minority youth within the fields of education and health (McDaniel, Purcell, & D'Augelli, 2001; Stoelb & Chiriboga, 1998). However, studies of educators (Fontaine, 1998; Price & Telljohann, 1991; Sears, 1991) and mental health providers (Kourany, 1987) indicate that these key supports in the lives of youth are not equipped to address the needs of sexual minority youth.

The few published studies of prevention efforts for sexual minorities focus on HIV/AIDS and sexual risk. These studies show that strategies involving health care access, peer support, and education networks promote sexual health (Kegeles, Hays, & Coates, 1996; Remafedi, 1994; Rotheram-Borus, Reid, & Rosario, 1994; Rothcram-Borus, Rosario, Reid, & Koopman, 1995; Wright, Gonzalez, Werner, Laughner, & Wallace, 1998) and self-esteem (Wright et al., 1998). While unsatisfying relationships with sexual minority peers has been shown to be a risk factor (Van Heering & Vincke, 2000), social support from LGB peers has been linked to positive self-esteem (Anderson, 1998). The findings by Savin-Williams and Ream (2003) that support group membership and having sex with a male sex partner were linked to higher self-esteem are consistent with these findings.

School Climate

Emerging research on school climate interventions may provide much-needed grounding for mental health prevention and intervention efforts for sexual minority adolescents. Recent reports on sexual minority students' experiences in school highlight the roles of (1) school policy, (2) social support, and (3) school personnel in creating safer school climates. First, when schools have policies[1] that explicitly prohibit harassment on the basis of actual or perceived sexual orientation and gender, students report feeling safer, fewer instances of harassment, and stronger connection to the school (O'Shaughnessy, Russell, Heck, Calhoun, & Laub, 2004). In fact, sexual minority youth report fewer suicide attempts when they attend schools that have anti-bullying policies (Goodenow & Szalacha, 2003). Second, students who have social support from peers and adults are better able to cope with prejudice and at times harassment. In fact, when students have gay/straight alliances at their school, they report less harassment and feeling safer (Goodenow & Szalacha, 2003; O'Shaughnessy et al., 2004). When students know where to go at their school for information and support related to sexual orientation and gender identity, they report more feelings of safety and fewer instances of hearing slurs or negative comments about sexual orientation by other students (O'Shaughnessy et al., 2004).

Third, recent studies indicate that school personnel make a critical difference in creating positive school climates for sexual minority youth. A recent national study indicates that among 7th to 12th graders, sexual minority youth with positive feelings about their teachers were significantly less likely than their peers to experience school troubles (Russell, Seif, et al., 2001). There is evidence that in contexts where educators are sensitive to sexual minority issues, sexual minority youth are at lower risk; a recent study documents the importance of teacher training and sensitivity in the curriculum for LGB students. It showed that in schools with gay-sensitive HIV instruction (teacher-rated confidence, adequacy, and appropriateness of HIV instruction for LGB students), gay students reported lower sexual health risks (Blake et al., 2001). Students who report that their teachers stop slurs and harassment when they occur are more likely to feel safe, less likely to be harassed, and more likely to describe their school as safe for sexual minority or gender-nonconforming students (O'Shaughnessy et al., 2004). In addition, teacher training on sexual harassment is associated with fewer reports by sexual minority youth of being threatened or injured at school (Goodenow & Szalacha, 2003). From this work, it is evident that comprehensive education on sexual orientation and gender identity is essential for professionals in the field of mental health prevention and intervention. Together, these studies indicate that efforts based on affirming policies, training personnel, and strengthening social support will be fruitful paths for prevention and intervention for sexual minority youth.

Prevention and Intervention with Transgender Youth

The existing literature does not address the need for resources and social supports among transgender adolescents; only a very few studies have examined the support needs of transgender youth (Di Ceglie et al., 2002; Grossman, 2000; Haynes, 2004). For years, the standard of treatment for children and adolescents with gender identity disorder was to promote connection to the gender of birth and actively discourage cross-gender identification. Treatments and programs developed in this vein were rarely successful at eliminating cross-gender identification (Bradley & Zucker, 1997) and may have served to exacerbate gender dysphoria and associated symptoms (Rosenberg, 2003). In the development of prevention and intervention for transgender adolescents, the goal of intervention should not be eliminating cross-gender identity and behaviors but rather alleviating related conditions, such as anxiety or depression, that interfere with adequate functioning of the adolescent. With increasing study, it has become clear that transsexuality is not always comorbid with psychopathology (Cohen et al., 1997; Smith et al., 2001). Two studies of interventions designed to create greater acceptance of cross-gendered behavior by the adolescents themselves and their parents report decreases in anxiety and depression among the participating youth (Menvielle & Tuerk, 2002; Rosenberg, 2002).

Future Directions for Prevention and Intervention

There are many ongoing efforts to create supportive environments for sexual minority adolescents in the form of school-based and community-based programs. What is needed are better theoretical foundations to guide efforts to explicitly prevent mental health problems for these young people or intervene when mental health problems arise. Certainly, the existing research literature on adolescent mental health prevention and intervention should provide the basis for this work, but it must be complemented with approaches that acknowledge the unique needs of sexual minority adolescents. Work on minority stress among gay men (Meyer, 1995, 2003a, 2003b), "gay-related stress" among gay adolescents (Rotheram-Borus, Hunter, et al., 1994; Rosario et al., 1996), and sexual risk behavior among Latino gay men (Diaz et al., 2001) provide important theoretical starting points. This work provides the basis for an explicit understanding of the ways that homophobia, heterosexism,[2] prejudice, and stigma act as root "causes" of risk in the lives of sexual minorities. Although there are no published studies of the efficacy of mental health prevention and intervention programs that target sexual minority youth—with an explicit attention to the stigma that uniquely characterizes the process of identity development among sexual minority adolescents—this body of work creates a basis from which mental health prevention and intervention theories for sexual minority youth can be constructed.

The existing body of research on sexual minority youth and mental health indicates that negotiating coming out, gender nonconformity, and victimization will be important areas of focus for prevention. From the literature summarized in this chapter that examines critical contexts of development for sexual minority youth we know that family support, self-acceptance, and comfort with sexual identity have been linked to fewer mental health problems among LGB youth (Hershberger & D'Augelli, 1995; Hershberger et al., 1997). We know that some faith experiences are detrimental to the well-being of LGBT youth but that self-acceptance in light of religious beliefs could be protective. A growing body of research documents the multiple levels at which change in schools (at the policy, school personnel capacity, and individual student support levels) can influence student well-being. And a new body of research indicates that friendships and romantic relationships may play a crucial role in supporting sexual minority adolescents' mental health.

From this work, we can begin to develop a rough outline for focused prevention and intervention for sexual minority adolescent mental health. The best available evidence indicates that such efforts must focus on coping with stress and stigma (Hunter, 1999; McDaniel et al., 2001) by engaging young people in understanding the prejudice and discrimination that they may experience and working with them to develop the coping strategies that they may need to counter homophobia at home, in school, or among peers as well as strategies to cope with potential victimization. Attention to coming out and gendered expectations and nonconformity are crucial. Understanding pervasive social and cultural prejudice, as well as significant positive social change and sources of support, can serve as a basis for developing strategies that engage adolescents in anticipating the potentially positive and negative consequences of coming out in various contexts. Working with young people to develop these strategies will allow them to be better prepared for the range of reactions that they may receive and to anticipate the social supports that they may draw from when they decide to come out. The existing research fairly clearly points to the efficacy of peer approaches to intervention and prevention efforts for sexual minority youth (Anderson, 1998; Garofalo, Wolf, Kessel, Palfrey, & DuRant, 1998). Efforts that engage adolescents in building strategies and skills for supportive friendships with other sexual minority youth, as well as skills for positive, healthy intimate relationships, will provide them with a strong foundation of the types of support that promote the mental health and well-being of all adolescents.

NOTES

1. A policy should be well publicized and specifically include sexual orientation and gender, including gender identity, appearance, and behavior (O'Shaughnessy, Russell, Heck, Calhoun, & Laub, 2004).

2. Heterosexism: analogous to sexism and racism, describing an ideological system that denies, denigrates, and stigmatizes any nonheterosexual form of behavior, identity, relationship, or community (Herek, 1990).

REFERENCES

Anderson, A. L. (1998). Strengths of gay male youth: An untold story. *Child and Adolescent Social Work Journal, 15,* 55–71.

Anderssen, N., Amlie, C., & Ytterøy, E. A. (2002). Outcomes for children with lesbian or gay parents. A review of studies from 1978 to 2000. *Scandinavian Journal of Psychology, 43,* 335–351.

Bailey, M. J., & Zucker, K. J. (1995). Childhood sex-typed behavior and sexual orientation: A conceptual analysis and quantitative review. *Developmental Psychology, 31,* 43–55.

Bell, A. P., & Weinberg, M. S. (1978). *Homosexualities: A study of diversity among men and women.* New York: Simon and Schuster.

Black, J., & Underwood, J. (1998). Young, female, and gay: Lesbian students and the school environment. *Professional School Counseling, 1,* 15–20.

Blake, S. M., Ledsky, R., Lehman, T., Goodenow, C., Sawyer, R., & Hack, T. (2001). Preventing sexual risk behaviors among gay, lesbian, and bisexual adolescents: The benefits of gay-sensitive HIV instruction in schools. *American Journal of Public Health, 91,* 940–946.

Blumenfeld, W. J. (1993). "Gay/straight" alliances: Transforming pain to pride. *High School Journal, 77,* 113–121.

Boxer, A. M., Cook, J. A., & Herdt, G. (1991). Double jeopardy: Identity transitions and parent-child relations among gay and lesbian youth. In K. Pillemer & K. McCartney (Eds.), *Parent-child relations throughout life* (pp. 59–92). Hillsdale, NJ: Lawrence Erlbaum Associates.

Bradley, S. J., & Zucker, K. J. (1997). Gender identity disorder: A review of the past 10 years. *Journal of the American Academy of Child and Adolescent Psychiatry, 36,* 872–880.

Brener, N., Lowry, R., Barrios, L., Simon, T., & Eaton, D. (2004). Violence-related behaviors among high school students—United States, 1991–2003. *Journal of the American Medical Association, 292,* 1168–1169.

Brown, B. B. (1999). "You're going out with who?" Peer group influences on adolescent romantic relationships. In W. Furman, B. B. Brown, & C. Feiring (Eds.), *The development of romantic relationships during adolescence* (pp. 291–329). New York: Cambridge University Press.

Cnaan, R. A., Gelles, R. J., & Sinha, J. W. (2004). Youth and religion: The Gameboy generation goes to "church." *Social Indicators Research, 68,* 175–200.

Coates, S., & Person, E. S. (1986). Extreme boyhood femininity: Isolated behavior or pervasive disorder? *Annual Progress in Child Psychiatry and Child Development,* 197–213.

Cochran, B. N., Stewart, A. J., Ginzler, J. A., & Cauce, A.M. (2002). Challenges faced by homeless sexual minorities: Comparison of gay, lesbian, bisexual, and transgender homeless adolescents with their heterosexual counterparts. *American Journal of Public Health, 92,* 773–777.

Cohen, L., de Ruiter, C., Ringelberg, H., & Cohen-Kettenis, P. T. (1997). Psychological functioning of adolescent transsexuals: Personality and psychopathology. *Journal of Clinical Psychology, 53,* 187–196.

Cohen-Kettenis, P. T., & van Goozen, S. H. M. (2002). Adolescents who are eligible for sex reassignment surgery: Parental reports of emotional and behavioural problems. *Clinical Child Psychology and Psychiatry, 7,* 412–422.

Consolacion, T. B., Russell, S. T., & Sue, S. (2004). Sex, race/ethnicity, and romantic attractions: Multiple minority status adolescents and mental health. *Cultural Diversity and Ethnic Minority Psychology, 10,* 200–214.

Cooley, J. J. (1998). Gay and lesbian adolescents: Presenting problems and the counselor's role. *Professional School Counseling, 1,* 30–34.

Crosbie-Burnett, M., & Helmbrecht, L. (1993). A descriptive empirical study of gay male stepfamilies. *Family Relations, 42,* 256–262.

D'Augelli, A. R. (1991). Gay men in college: Identity processes and adaptations. *Journal of College Student Development, 32,* 140–146.

D'Augelli, A. R. (2002). Mental health problems among lesbian, gay, and bisexual youths ages 14 to 21. *Clinical Child Psychology and Psychiatry, 7,* 433–456.

D'Augelli, A. R. (2003). Coming out in community psychology: Personal narrative and disciplinary change. *American Journal of Community Psychology, 31,* 343–354.

D'Augelli, A. R., & Hershberger, S. L. (1993). Lesbian, gay, and bisexual youth in community settings: Personal challenges and mental health problems. *American Journal of Community Psychology, 21,* 421–448.

D'Augelli, A. R., Hershberger, S. L., & Pilkington, N. W. (1998). Lesbian, gay, and bisexual youth and their families: Disclosure of sexual orientation and its consequences. *American Journal of Orthopsychiatry, 68,* 361–371.

D'Augelli, A. R., Pilkington, N. W., & Hershberger, S. L. (2002). Incidence and mental health impact of sexual orientation victimization of lesbian, gay, and bisexual youths in high school. *School Psychology Quarterly, 17,* 148–167.

Di Ceglie, D., Freedman, D., McPherson, S., & Richardson, P. (2002). Children and adolescents referred to a specialist gender identity development service: Clinical features and demographic characteristics. *International Journal of Transgenderism, 6.* Available from http://www.symposion.com/itj.

Diamond, L. M. (2003). Love matters: Romantic relationships among sexual-minority adolescents. In P. Florsheim (Ed.), *Adolescent romantic relations and sexual behavior: Theory, research, and practical implications* (pp. 85–107). Mahwah, NJ: Lawrence Erlbaum Associates.

Diamond, L. M., & Lucas, S. (2002). *Sexual-minority and heterosexual youths' close relationships: Experiences, expectations, and implications for well-being.* Unpublished manuscript.

Diamond, L. M., & Savin-Williams, R. C. (2003). Explaining diversity in the development of same-sex sexuality among young women. In L. D. Garnets & D.C. Kimmel (Eds.), *Psychological perspectives on lesbian, gay, and bisexual experiences* (2nd ed., pp. 130–148). New York: Columbia University Press.

Diaz, R. M., Ayala, G., Bein, E., Henne, J., & Marin, B. V. (2001). The impact of homophobia, poverty, and racism on the mental health of gay and bisexual Latino men: Findings from 3 U.S. cities. *American Journal of Public Health, 91,* 927–932.

Dombrowski, D., Wodarski, J. S., Smokowski, P. R., & Bricout, J. C. (1995). School-based social work interventions with gay and lesbian adolescents: Theoretical and practice guidelines. *Journal of Applied Social Sciences, 20,* 51–61.

Durant, R. H., Krowchuk, D. P., & Sinal, S. H. (1998). Victimization, use of violence, and drug use at school among male adolescents who engage in same-sex sexual behavior. *Journal of Pediatrics, 132,* 113–118.

Elze, D. E. (2002). Risk factors for internalizing and externalizing problems among gay, lesbian, and bisexual adolescents. *Social Work Research, 26,* 89–99.

Faulkner, A. H., & Cranston, K. (1998). Correlates of same-sex sexual behavior in a random sample of Massachusetts high school students. *American Journal of Public Health, 88,* 262–265.

Fergusson, D. M., Horwood, J., & Beautrais, A. L. (1999). Is sexual orientation related to mental health problems and suicidality in young people? *Archives of General Psychiatry, 56,* 876–880.

Floyd, F. J., & Stein, T. S. (2002). Sexual orientation identity formation among gay, lesbian, and bisexual youths: Multiple patterns of milestone experiences. *Journal of Research on Adolescence, 12,* 167–191.

Fontaine, J. H. (1998). Evidencing a need: School counselors' experiences with gay and lesbian students. *Professional School Counseling, 1,* 8–14.

Freedman, D., Tasker, F., & Di Ceglie, D. (2002). Children and adolescents with transsexual parents referred to a specialist gender identity development service: A brief report of key developmental features. *Clinical Child Psychology and Psychiatry, 7,* 423.

Furman, W., Brown, B. B., & Feiring, C. (Eds.). (1999). *The development of relationships during adolescence.* New York: Cambridge University Press.

Garofalo, R., Wolf, R. C., Kessel, S., Palfrey, J., & DuRant, R. H. (1998). The association between health risk behaviors and sexual orientation among a school-based sample of adolescents. *Pediatrics, 101,* 895–902.

Garofalo, R., Wolf, R. C., Wissow, L. S., Woods, E. R., & Goodman, E. (1999). Sexual orientation and risk of suicide attempts among a representative sample of youth. *Archives of Pediatric and Adolescent Medicine, 153,* 487–493.

Golombok, S., Spencer, A., & Rutter, M. (1983). Children in lesbian and single-parent households: Psychosexual and psychiatric appraisal. *Journal of Child Psychology and Psychiatry, 24,* 551–572.

Goodenow, C., & Szalacha, L. (2003, August). *Which schools are safer for sexual minority adolescents?* Paper presented at the annual convention of the American Psychological Association, Toronto.

Grossman, A. H. (2000). *Transgender youth as a vulnerable population: Findings of a qualitative study.* Paper presented at the 128th annual meeting of the American Public Health Association, Boston.

Grossman, A. H., & Kerner, M. S. (1998). Self-esteem and supportiveness as predictors of emotional distress in gay male and lesbian youth. *Journal of Homosexuality, 35*(2), 25–39.

Hammelman, T. L. (1993). Gay and lesbian youth: Contributing factors to serious attempts or considerations of suicide. *Journal of Gay and Lesbian Psychotherapy, 2,* 77–89.

Haynes, R. (2004). *Towards healthier transgender youth.* New York: National Youth Advocacy Coalition.

Herdt, G., & Koff, B. (Eds.). (2000). *Something to tell you: The road families travel when a child is gay.* New York: Columbia University Press.

Hershberger, S. L., & D'Augelli, A. R. (1995). The impact of victimization on the mental health and suicidality of lesbian, gay, and bisexual youths. *Developmental Psychology, 31,* 65–74.

Hershberger, S. L., Pilkington, N. W., & D'Augelli, A. R. (1997). Predictors of suicide attempts among gay, lesbian, and bisexual youth. *Journal of Adolescent Research, 12,* 477–497.

Hetrick, E. S., & Martin, A. D. (1988). The stigmatization of the gay and lesbian adolescent. *Journal of Homosexuality, 14,* 163–183.

Human Rights Watch. (2001). *Hatred in the hallways: Violence and discrimination against lesbian, gay, bisexual, and transgender students in U.S. schools.* New York: Author.

Hunter, J. (1999). Beyond risk: Refocus research on coping. *Journal of the Gay and Lesbian Medical Association, 3,* 75–76.

Joyner, K., & Udry, J. R. (2000). You don't bring me anything but down: Adolescent romantic relationships and depression. *Journal of Health and Social Behavior, 41,* 369–391.

Kegeles, S. M., Hays, R. B., & Coates, T. J. (1996). The Mpowerment Project: A community-level HIV prevention intervention for young gay men. *American Journal of Public Health, 86,* 1075–1076.

Kosciw, J., & Cullen, M. (2003). *The GLSEN 2001 National School Climate Survey: The school-related experiences of our nation's lesbian, gay, bisexual, and transgender youth.* New York: Office of Public Policy of the Gay, Lesbian, and Straight Education Network.

Kourany, R. F. C. (1987). Suicide among homosexual adolescents. *Journal of Homosexuality, 13*(4), 111–117.

Kruks, G. (1991). Gay and lesbian homeless/street youth: Special issues and concerns. *Journal of Adolescent Health, 12,* 515–518.

Martin, A. D., & Hetrick, E. S. (1988). The stigmatization of the gay and lesbian adolescent. *Journal of Homosexuality, 15*(1–2), 163–184.

McDaniel, J. S., Purcell, D., & D'Augelli, A. R. (2001). The relationship between sexual orientation and risk for suicide: Research findings and future directions for research and prevention. *Suicide and Life-Threatening Behavior, 31,* 84–105.

Menvielle, E. J., & Tuerk, C. (2002). A support group for parents of gender-nonconforming boys. *Journal of the American Academy of Child and Adolescent Psychiatry, 41,* 1010–1013.

Meyenburg, B. (1999). Gender identity disorder in adolescence: Outcomes of psychotherapy. *Adolescence, 34*(134), 305–313.

Meyer, I. H. (1995). Minority stress and mental health in gay men. *Journal of Health and Social Behavior, 36,* 38–56.

Meyer, I. H. (2003a). Prejudice as stress: Conceptual and measurement problems. *American Journal of Public Health, 93,* 262–265.

Meyer, I. H. (2003b). Prejudice, social stress, and mental health in lesbian, gay, and bisexual populations: Conceptual issues and research evidence. *Psychological Bulletin, 129,* 674–697.

Noell, J. W., & Ochs, L. M. (2001). Relationship of sexual orientation to substance use, suicidal ideation, suicide attempts, and other factors in a population of homeless adolescents. *Journal of Adolescent Health, 29,* 31–36.

O'Connell, A. (1993). Voices from the heart: The developmental impact of a mother's lesbianism on her adolescent children. *Smith College Studies in Social Work, 63,* 281–299.

Olson, E. E., & King, C. A. (1995). Gay and lesbian self-identification: Response to Rotheram-Borus and Fernandez. *Suicide and Life-Threatening Behavior, 25*(Suppl.), 35–39.

O'Shaughnessy, M., Russell, S. T., Heck, K., Calhoun, C., & Laub, C. (2004). *Safe place to learn: Consequences of harassment based on actual or perceived sexual orientation and gender non-conformity and steps for making schools safer.* San Francisco: California Safe Schools Coalition.

Patterson, C. J. (1992). Children of lesbian and gay parents. *Child Development, 63,* 1025–1042.

Patterson, C. J. (2000). Family relationships of lesbians and gay men. *Journal of Marriage and the Family, 62,* 1052–1069.

Price, J. H., & Telljohann, S. K. (1991). School counselors' perceptions of adolescent homosexuals. *Journal of School Health, 61,* 433–438.

Radkowsky, M., & Siegel, L. J. (1997). The gay adolescent: Stressors, adaptations, and psychosocial interventions. *Clinical Psychology Review, 17,* 191–216.

Ream, G. L., & Savin-Williams, R. C. (2005). Reconciling Christianity and positive non-heterosexual identity in adolescence, with implications for psychological well-being. *Journal of Gay and Lesbian Issues in Education, 2,* 19–36.

Remafedi, G. (1994). Cognitive and behavioral adaptations to HIV/AIDS among gay and bisexual adolescents. *Journal of Adolescent Health, 15,* 142–148.

Remafedi, G., Farrow, J. A., & Deisher, R. W. (1991). Risk factors for attempted suicide in gay and bisexual youth. *Pediatrics, 87,* 869–875.

Remafedi, G., French, S., Story, M., Resnick, M. D., & Blum, R. (1997). The relationship between suicide risk and sexual orientation: Results of a population-based study. *American Journal of Public Health, 87*(8), 1–4.

Rivers, I. (2001). The bullying of sexual minorities at school: Its nature and long-term correlates. *Educational and Child Psychology, 18,* 32–46.

Rodriguez, E. M., & Ouellette, S. C. (2000). Gay and lesbian Christians: Homosexual and religious identity integration in the members and participations of a gay-positive church. *Journal for the Scientific Study of Religion, 39,* 333–347.

Rosario, M., Rotheram-Borus, M. J., & Reid, H. (1996). Gay-related stress and its correlates among gay and bisexual male adolescents of predominantly black and Hispanic background. *Journal of Community Psychology, 24,* 136–159.

Rosario, M., Yali, A. M., Hunter, J., & Gwadz, M. (2003). Religion and health among gay, lesbian, and bisexual youth: An empirical investigation and theoretical explanation. In H. S. Kurtzman (Ed.), *Sexual orientation, mental health, and substance use: Contemporary scientific perspectives.* Washington, DC: American Psychological Association.

Rosenberg, M. (2002). Children with gender identity issues and their parents in individual and group treatment. *Journal of the American Academy of Child and Adolescent Psychiatry, 41,* 619–621.

Rosenberg, M. (2003). Recognizing gay, lesbian, and transgender teens in a child and adolescent psychiatry practice. *Journal of the American Academy of Child and Adolescent Psychiatry, 42,* 1517–1521.

Rotheram-Borus, M. J., Hunter, J., & Rosario, M. (1994). Suicidal behavior and gay-related stress among gay and bisexual male adolescents. *Journal of Adolescent Research, 9,* 498–508.

Rotheram-Borus, M. J., Reid, H., & Rosario, M. (1994). Factors mediating changes in sexual HIV risk behaviors among gay and bisexual male adolescents. *American Journal of Public Health, 84,* 1938–1946.

Rotheram-Borus, M. J., Rosario, M., Reid, H., & Koopman, C. (1995). Predicting patterns of sexual acts among homosexual and bisexual youths. *American Journal of Psychiatry, 152,* 588–595.

Russell, S. T. (2002). Queer in America: Citizenship for sexual minority youth. *Applied Developmental Science, 6,* 258–263.

Russell, S. T. (2003). Sexual minority youth and suicide risk. *American Behavioral Scientist, 46,* 1241–1257.

Russell, S. T., & Consolacion, T. B. (2003). Adolescent romance and emotional health in the United States: Beyond binaries. *Journal of Clinical Child and Adolescent Psychology, 32,* 499–508.

Russell, S. T., Driscoll, A. K., & Truong, N. (2002). Adolescent same-sex romantic attractions and relationships: Implications for substance use and abuse. *American Journal of Public Health, 92,* 198–202.

Russell, S. T., Franz, B. T., & Driscoll, A. K. (2001). Same-sex romantic attraction and experiences of violence in adolescence. *American Journal of Public Health, 91,* 903–906.

Russell, S. T., & Joyner, K. (2001). Adolescent sexual orientation and suicide risk: Evidence from a national study. *American Journal of Public Health, 91,* 1276–1281.

Russell, S. T., Muraco, A., & D'Augelli, A. R. (2003, April). *Religion, mental health, and sexual minority youth.* Paper presented at the annual meeting of the Pacific Sociological Association, Pasadena, CA.

Russell, S. T., Seif, H., & Truong, N. L. (2001). School outcomes of sexual minority youth in the United States: Evidence from a national study. *Journal of Adolescence, 24,* 111–127.

Savin-Williams, R. C. (1989a). Coming out to parents and self-esteem among gay and lesbian youths. *Journal of Homosexuality, 18*(1–2), 1–35.

Savin-Williams, R. C. (1989b). Parental influences on the self-esteem of gay and lesbian youths: A reflected appraisals model. *Journal of Homosexuality, 17*(1–2), 93–109.

Savin-Williams, R. C. (1994). Verbal and physical abuse as stressors in the lives of lesbian, gay male, and bisexual youths: Associations with school problems, running away, substance abuse, prostitution, and suicide. *Journal of Consulting and Clinical Psychology, 62,* 261–269.

Savin-Williams, R. C. (1995). Lesbian, gay male, and bisexual adolescents. In A. R. D'Augelli & C. J. Patterson (Eds.), *Lesbian, gay, and bisexual identities over the lifespan: Psychological perspectives* (pp. 165–189). London: Oxford University Press.

Savin-Williams, R. C. (1998). The disclosure to families of same-sex attractions by lesbian, gay, and bisexual youths. *Journal of Research on Adolescence, 8,* 49–68.

Savin-Williams, R. C. (2001). Chapter 1: Introduction. In R. C. Savin-Williams (Ed.), *Mom, dad I'm gay: How families negotiate coming out* (pp. 3–5). Washington, DC: American Psychological Association.

Savin-Williams, R. C., & Ream, G. L. (2003). Suicide attempts among sexual-minority male youth. *Journal of Clinical Child and Adolescent Psychology, 32,* 509–522.

Schneider, S. G., Farberow, N. L., & Kruks, G. N. (1989). Suicidal behavior in adolescent and young adult gay men. *Suicide and Life-Threatening Behavior, 19,* 381–394.

Schuck, K. D., & Liddle, B. (2001). Religious conflicts experienced by lesbian, gay, and bisexual individuals. *Journal of Gay and Lesbian Psychotherapy, 5,* 63–82.

Sears, J. T. (1991). Educators, homosexuality, and homosexual students: Are personal feelings related to professional beliefs? *Journal of Homosexuality, 22*(3–4), 29–79.

Smith, G. W., & Smith, D. E. (1998). The ideology of "fag": The school experience of gay students. *Sociological Quarterly, 39,* 309–335.

Smith, Y. L. S., van Goozen, S. H. M., & Cohen-Kettenis, P. T. (2001). Adolescents with gender identity disorder who were accepted or rejected for sex reassignment surgery: A prospective follow-up study. *Journal of the American Academy of Child and Adolescent Psychiatry, 40,* 472–481.

Snively, C. A. (2004). Building community-based alliances between GLBTQQA youth and adults in rural settings. *Journal of Gay and Lesbian Social Services: Issues in Practice, Policy and Research, 16*(3), 99–112.

Stacey, J., & Biblarz, T. J. (2001). (How) does the sexual orientation of parents matter? *American Sociological Review, 66,* 159–183.

Stoelb, M., & Chiriboga, J. (1998). A process model for assessing adolescent risk for suicide. *Journal of Adolescence, 21,* 359–370.

Sullivan, M., & Wodarski, J. S. (2002). Social alienation in gay youth. *Journal of Social Behavior in the Social Environment, 5,* 1–17.

Szalacha, L. A. (2003). Safer sexual diversity climates: Lessons learned from an evaluation of Massachusetts safer school program for gay and lesbian students. *American Journal of Education, 110,* 58–88.

Tasker, F. L., & Golombok, S. (1997). *Growing up in a lesbian family: Effects on child development.* New York: Guilford Press.

Thumma, S. (1991). Negotiating a religious identity: The case of the gay Evangelical. *Sociological Analysis, 52,* 333–347.

Uribe, V., & Harbeck, K. M. (1991). Addressing the needs of lesbian, gay, and bisexual youth: The origins of PROJECT 10 and school-based intervention. *Journal of Homosexuality, 22*(3), 9–28.

Van Heering, C., & Vincke, J. (2000). Suicidal acts and ideation in homosexual and bisexual young people: A study of prevalence and risk factors. *Social Psychiatry and Psychiatric Epidemiology, 35,* 494–499.

Wagner, G., Serafini, J., Rabkin, J., Remien, R., & Williams, J. (1994). Integration of one's religion and homosexuality: A weapon against internalized homophobia? *Journal of Homosexuality, 26,* 91–110.

Wallace, J. M., Jr., & Forman, T. A. (1998). Religion's role in promoting health and reducing risk among American youth. *Health Education and Behavior. Special Issue: Public health and health education in faith communities, 25*(6), 721–741.

Wichstrom, L., & Hegna, K. (2003). Sexual orientation and suicide attempt: A longitudinal study of the general Norwegian adolescent population. *Journal of Abnormal Psychology, 112,* 144–151.

Wright, E. R., Gonzalez, C., Werner, J., N., Laughner, S. T., & Wallace, M. (1998). Indiana Youth access project: A model for responding to the HIV risk behaviors of gay, lesbian, and bisexual youth in the heartland. *Journal of Adolescent Health, 23*(Suppl. 2), 83–95.

Yates, G. L., MacKenzie, R. G., Pennbridge, J., & Swofford, A. (1991). A risk profile comparison of homeless youth involved in prostitution and homeless youth not involved. *Journal of Adolescent Health, 12,* 545–548.

Yip, A. K. T. (1997). Dare to differ: Gay and lesbian Catholics' assessment of official Catholic positions on sexuality. *Sociology of Religion, 58,* 165–180.

Chapter 11

COMPETITIVE SPORTS PRESSURES AND OUT-OF-SCHOOL LEARNING EXPERIENCES

Daniel F. Perkins and Lynne M. Borden

This study was supported by Agricultural Experimentation Stations from Penn State University (project number 3826) and the University of Arizona as well as support from the American Legion Child Welfare Foundation.

Out-of-school time is a recurring block of time full of discretionary opportunity, choice, and flexibility (Minnesota Commission on Out of School Time, 2004). It is the time that adolescents are awake and are not in school (i.e., weekends, school holidays, evenings, early mornings, late afternoons, and in the summertime). During adolescence, young people have a significant amount of this "free time" available to them. Indeed, in their comprehensive review of time use among children and adolescents around the world, Larson and Verma (1999) found that approximately 40 to 50 percent of the waking hours for high school youth in Europe and United States was spent in leisure time or free time. In addition, much of that free time for adolescents may be spent without the companionship or supervision from adults.

Out-of-school time can be either an opportunity for youth to engage in positive activities that enhance their development and foster their competencies or a time to participate in negative activities that increase their chances of yielding to social pressures to do things like engage in drug use, sex, and antisocial activities (Villarruel & Lerner, 1994). For example, crime statistics show that most acts of youth delinquency (including alcohol and substance abuse, youth crimes, and delinquent behavior) occur during after school hours when youth are unsupervised and not engaged in youth programs (Fox & Newman, 1998). Moreover,

FBI statistics indicate that 47 percent of violent juvenile crime occurs on weekdays, between the hours of 2:00 and 8:00 P.M. (Snyder & Sickmund, 1997). With this as a backdrop, the past decade has seen growing public support for more structured activities during the out-of-school hours (Roth & Brooks Gunn, 2003). In a nationwide poll of voters, 9 out of 10 believe there is a need for some type of organized activity or place where young people can go after school even though those same voters report that their states are challenged with increasing budget deficits (Afterschool Alliance, 2002).

In this chapter, youth development programs are defined as any structured learning activity offered during the out-of-school hours. They include but are not limited to sports programs, before- and after-school clubs, service clubs, faith-based organizations, 4-H Youth Development programs, Boys and Girls Club, Boy Scouts and Girl Scouts, YMCA, and those sponsored by other community and/or youth-serving organizations.

IMPORTANCE OF STRUCTURE OUT-OF-SCHOOL EXPERIENCES

Structured out-of-school programs that are youth development programs can and often do fill adolescents' discretionary time with important opportunities for socialization and learning. Youth development programs have been identified by scholars as important contexts for the promotion of crucial life skills as well as safeguards against negative behaviors (Larson, 2000; Lerner, 2001, 2004; Perkins & Borden, 2003; Villarruel, Perkins, Borden, & Keith, 2003). Numerous studies have documented that youth participation in school and community-based youth programs can contribute to a variety of positive developmental outcomes as well as increased resiliency and protective factors (Catalano, Berglund, Ryan, Lonczak, & Hawkins, 1999; Redd, Cochran, Hair, & Moore, 2002; Villarruel et al., 2003). Indeed, the seminal book by the National Research Council and Institute of Medicine (Eccles & Gootman, 2002) highlighted and provided strong scientific evidence of the value of youth's involvement in community-based youth programming in fostering positive development through the development of life skills and connections to the community.

According to Larson (2000), structured voluntary youth activities provide a rich context for "flow" activities to occur, which ultimately can foster the development of initiative. Autonomy-granting activities or experiences that are engaging, challenging, and interesting promote a range of competencies and skills; these activities were labeled "flow" experiences (Csikszentmihalyi, 1997) and involve a high level of goal directedness, concentration, and intrinsic motivation. Through participation in these experiences, adolescents engage in discovery processes about their skills, talents, and interests because they have opportunities to solve problems, make decisions, and work with others. The power of these activities comes from the "voice" and "choice" that youth are afforded within the school, youth program, and community contexts.

McLaughlin (2000) found that youth with high levels of participation in community youth programs were more likely to (1) have good grades, (2) rate their chances of attending college as "very high," (3) consider themselves as "worthy persons," and (4) express a sense of civic responsibility. There is strong evidence that time spent in youth programs can positively influence the development of young people by contributing to enhanced self-esteem, assisting in the ability to overcome adversity, increasing leadership skills, and increasing willingness to engage in efforts to help others, including involvement in political and social activities in young adulthood (Eccles & Gootman, 2002).

Participation in youth development programs has also been associated with enhanced school performance and increased aspirations to attend college as well as efforts to maintain good physical health (Barber, Eccles, & Stone, 2001; Glancy, Willets & Farrell, 1986; Hanks, 1981; Quinn, 1995; Scales, Benson, Leffert, & Blyth, 2000; Scales & Leffert, 1999). Further, some structured youth programs have been found to be critical in helping immigrant youth successfully adapt to their new culture (Roffman, Suárez-Orozco, & Rhodes, 2003). Moreover, participation in youth development programs has also been found to be negatively associated with risk behaviors (e.g., alcohol and substance use, antisocial behavior and delinquency, school misconduct and failure, and early unprotected sex) (Perkins & Borden, 2003).

While there are many benefits from participation in out-of-school experiences, there is the potential for negative outcomes especially pertaining to youth sports programs. Eccles and Barber (1999) found that youth participation in sports has positive effects on academic performance, but it also increases the likelihood of drinking and drug use. They did not find the same association with negative risk behaviors when examining other types of organized, extracurricular activities (e.g., student council, volunteering, and marching band). Further in their comprehensive literature review, Scales and Leffert (1999) found that highly competitive sports involvement has been associated with increased problem behavior in the form of alcohol use (Jerry-Szpak & Brown, 1994) and increased use of other substances (e.g., Collingwood, Reynolds, Kohl, Smith, & Sloan, 1991). In addition, Eccles and Gootman (2002) note that in two in-depth observational studies sports programs were found to promote masculine aggressive and competitive norms (Eder & Parker, 1987; Fine, 1987).

Mentoring programs, often thought as important dimensions of after-school programs, also raise concerns for youth's well-being. Rhodes (2002) noted that mentoring programs in which the mentoring relationship lasted less than six months negatively impacted the self-worth of the mentee. This example also highlights a major drawback to the out-of-school structured program arena, that is, the dosage effect of structured programs. Dosage refers to amount of program exposure participants have within a program. The amount of influence that a program has on individuals is associated with the amount of time spent within a program. For example, in the National Evaluation of the Engaging Youth, Serving Communities Initiative sponsored by the National 4-H Council, Borden (2004) found that boys with the greatest number of months in a program showed significantly more positive responses than those in the program for less time, while girls' responses did not differ significantly, depending on their time in the program. Thus, youth development programs that are not providing appropriate dosage may be doing more harm than good, such as setting false expectations among the youth participants.

Although there are some experiences that may lead to negative behavioral outcomes, there are many developmental benefits gained through participation in and engagement with youth development programs. Opportunities for participation and contribution through youth development and recognition enable youth to address several needs, including the ability to have a sense of belonging, sense of mastery, and sense of generosity and mattering (Brendtro, Brokenleg, & van Bockern, 1990; Eccles & Gootman, 2002). A sense of mattering is created when a youth is efficacious—that is, a youth has an opportunity and feels competent to do things that make a real difference in one's social world (Eccles & Gootman, 2002). For example, youth's participation in structured out-of-school experiences can provide a thread of connectedness that addresses the youth's need for belonging and recognition.

Indeed, both resiliency research and youth development research have found that opportunities to contribute or to "matter" within one's context are linked with successful outcomes in adolescence (Eccles & Gootman, 2002; Villarruel et al., 2003). For example, Werner and Smith (1992) found that resilient youth were often required to look after younger siblings or take over tasks usually done by an adult. They called this phenomenon "required helpfulness." The key is that these chores are not just to help out around the house but also are necessary for household (if not human) functioning. By engaging in acts to help others, youth gain a sense of generosity and self-worth as well as an opportunity to overcome the egocentric thinking so prevalent in adolescence. Youth involved in making contributions are reframing their self-perceptions as well as other adults' perceptions of them from being a problem to be solved and a receiver of services to being a resource and a provider of services (Bernard, 2004). Finally, the importance of mattering is nicely summarized by Eccles and Gootman (2002):

> Positive development is not something adults do to young people, but rather something that young people do for themselves with a lot of help from parents and others. They are agents of their own development. To foster development, then, it follows that settings need to be youth centered, providing youth—both individually and in groups—the opportunity to be efficacious and to make a difference in their social worlds. (p. 103)

As noted previously, young people do indeed benefit from their participation in structured out-of-school experiences (Eccles & Gootman, 2002). However, if we are to understand the influence of out-of-school experiences on the development of young people, we must better understand the influence of "selection factors" so that we can better assess the effects of participation (Eccles, Barber, Stone, & Hunt, 2003). Indeed, some youth may be more likely for a variety of reasons to "selected in" to these experiences, and/or they are subsequently more likely to benefit from and persist with activities than other youth. There are often many factors that influence a young person's decision to participate (see Borden, Perkins, Villarruel, & Stone, 2005).

STRUCTURED OUT-SCHOOL-TIME PROGRAMS CAN PROMOTE DEVELOPMENT AND PREVENT PROBLEMS

The results of numerous longitudinal and other resiliency studies have provided essential information to the field of youth development. Specifically, by identifying universal protective processes (i.e., caring relationships with nonparental adults, high expectations, and opportunities for participation, contribution, and recognition; Bernard, 2004), researchers and practitioners have gained important information for understanding what youth need in terms of opportunities and supports from various contexts for youth, including designing and implementing structured out-of-school experiences for positive youth development.

In order for youth (adolescents in particular) to become competent, contributing adult members of society, they need opportunities and support from their communities to develop important personal and social assets (see Table 11.1). These assets can be grouped into the "five Cs" identified by Lerner and his colleagues (Lerner, 2002, 2004; Lerner, Fisher, & Weinberg, 2000). These include the following:

1. Competence in academic, social, emotional, and vocational areas
2. Confidence in whom one is becoming (identity)
3. Connection to self and others
4. Character that comes from positive values, integrity, and strong sense of morals
5. Caring and compassion

However, from a community youth development perspective, there is a sixth C: contribution (Lerner 2004; Pittman, 2000). By contributing to their families, neighborhoods, and communities, youth are afforded practical opportunities to make use of the other five Cs. These six Cs helped clarify and provide some guidance to the positive youth development framework.

More recently, practitioners (Hughes & Curnan, 2000; Pittman, 2000) and researchers (Villarruel et al., 2003) have advanced the field of youth development by *integrating* positive youth development and community development to address the need for a broader, more holistic approach to increasing protective factors and thereby helping to promote resiliency. *Community youth development* (Villarruel et al., 2003) is defined as follows:

> Purposely creating environments that provide constructive, affirmative, and encouraging relationships that are sustained over time with adults and peers, while concurrently providing an array of opportunities that enable youth to build their competencies and become engaged as partners in their own development as well as the development of their communities. (p. 6)

The community youth development framework involves a two-pronged strategy for providing an atmosphere that fosters fully functioning youth. The first and most explicit strategy involves the *promotion* of universal protective processes and the six Cs. These processes and the six Cs address the personal and social assets needed by youth as outlined in Eccles and Gootman (2002; see Table 11.1).

The second strategy involves an understanding and goal within the community youth development framework that the *prevention* of risk behaviors among youth is critical; decreasing risk factors or processes in their environment is necessary if youth are to thrive. The second strategy is important and necessary; however, it is insufficient without simultaneously addressing the first strategy.

Table 11.1

Personal and Social Assets that Facilitate Positive Youth Development Aligned with the Five Cs of Positive Youth Development

Asset category (Cs of positive youth development)	Individual assets
Physical development (competence)	Good health habits
Intellectual development (competence)	Good health risk management skills
	Knowledge of essential life skills
	Knowledge of essential vocational skills
	School success
	Rational habits of mind—critical thinking and reasoning skills
	In-depth knowledge of more than one culture
	Good decision-making skills
	Knowledge of skills needed to navigate through multiple cultural contexts
Psychological and emotional development (competence, confidence character, caring/ compassion)	Good mental health, including positive self-regard
	Good emotional self-regulation skills
	Good coping skills
	Good conflict resolution skills
	Mastery motivation and positive achievement motivation
	Confidence in one's personal efficacy
	Planfulness—planning for the future and future life events
	Sense of personal autonomy/responsibility for self
	Optimism coupled with realism
	Coherent and positive personal and social identity
	Prosocial and culturally sensitive values
	Spirituality or a sense of a "larger" purpose in life
	Strong moral character
Social development (connection, caring/compassion, contribution)	A commitment to good use of time
	Connectedness—perceived good relationships and trust with parents, peers, and some other adults
	Sense of social place/integration—being connected and valued by larger social networks
	Attachment to prosocial/conventional institutions, such as school, church, nonschool youth programs
	Ability to navigate in multiple cultural contexts
	Commitment to civic engagement

Source: Adapted from Eccles and Gootman (2002).

ELEMENTS IN
STRUCTURED OUT-SCHOOL-EXPERIENCES

Youth development programs can foster positive youth development by creating developmentally intentional learning experiences. Developmentally intentional learning experiences have three main components (Walker, Marczak, Blyth, & Borden, 2005). First, opportunities are designed to build positive relationships among youth and adults and among youth and their peers. Second, the knowledge, skills, and competencies to be learned and developed are identified along with the learning methods involved. Third, the experience is tailored to the individual needs of the participating youth. In addition to providing developmentally intentional learning experiences, the positive influences that youth programs have on adolescents are dependent on several elements: (1) the focus of the program, (2) the degree of participation by youth, (3) adults involved with the program, and (4) the context in which the program takes place (Perkins & Borden, 2003).

Programs that use process-focused strategies, that is, having a dual emphasis of reducing risk and increasing assets, are more likely to have a positive influence on youth. These programs focus on the personal and social assets (Eccles & Gootman, 2002) to be developed and not problems to be managed (Lerner, 2001). High-quality youth programs are those efforts that conduct activities, establish environments, and develop sustained peer–peer and youth–adult relationships that are intentional and deliberately focused on building youths' capacity and skills.

More intense participation in youth development programs would seem to be associated with an increase in the number of experiences that youth have to build their personal and social assets or the six Cs (Borden, 2004). In her 10-year study of youth and youth programs, McLaughlin (2000), for instance, found that youth with higher levels of participation in community youth organizations were approximately 15 percent more likely to view themselves as worthy persons.

The quality of youth development programs is directly linked to the skills and competencies of adults who devote their expertise, time, and energy to youth programs (Walker, 2003; Yohalem, 2003). According to these scholars, adults who are successful at fostering positive youth development possess certain characteristics that include a strong sense of commitment to the youth, the view of youth as partners, and an orientation toward promoting youth empowerment and skill development.

According to McLaughlin (2000), the context that surrounds the youth program can either foster the success of the program or create barriers to the program's success. For example, communities that support a variety of youth programs address its diversity and acknowledge cultural and gender differences and shape youth preferences and developmental needs (McLaughlin, 2000). For example, the availability of youth symphony for youth may alter the participating youths' preferences in music.

Creating an appropriate context is crucial for fostering positive youth development. When adolescents walk in the door or onto the field of play, how they become engaged is more important than what they see (Walker et al., 2005). Therefore, programs must ensure that the context is engaging and has specific features. The following features are based on the core concepts of a positive youth development program. These elements are derived from the work of the National Research Council and the Institute of Medicine (Eccles & Gootman, 2002) and other scholars (Catalano et al., 1999; Durlack, 1998; Lerner, 2001; Mahoney 2000; McLaughlin, 2000; Roth, Brooks-Gunn, Murray, & Foster, 1998):

- *Physical and Psychological Safety.* The program provides a safe haven both physically and emotionally.

- *Appropriate Structure.* The program has clear rules, expectations, and responsibilities. Youth are involved in creating the rules, expectations, and responsibilities because generally those rules are embraced by youth when they have direct input in their development.

- *Supportive Relationships.* The program has adults involved in the activities and events that provide a vehicle for trusted connections to form and be maintained.

- *Opportunities to Belong.* The program provides activities and events that foster friendships and provide youth with a sense of a positive group experience.

- *Positive Social Norms.* The program's culture (e.g., habits and expectations) that governs behavior and daily interactions involves conventionally accepted social behaviors.

- *Support for Efficacy and Mattering.* The program provides youth, both individually and in groups, the opportunity to be useful and to make a difference in their social worlds.

- *Opportunities for Skill Building.* Through its activities and team-building experiences, the program provides youth the opportunities to build their skills (e.g., leadership skills, decision-making skills, cultural competence, communication skills, problem-solving skills, and civic responsibility).

- *Active Learning.* The program provides learning opportunities that are interactive and reflective and that engage multiple learning styles. For example, programs employ experiential learning opportunities and encourage young people to take positive risks. Whether they are successful or unsuccessful, these attempts are viewed as part of the learning process.

- *Opportunities for Recognition.* Youth are sincerely acknowledged for their contributions. The recognition conveys a positive view of youth.
- *Integration of Family, School, and Community Efforts.* The program coordinates its efforts and communicates regularly with families and schools to ensure similar norms and expectations across settings. The program offers a variety of activities and events that involve parents (e.g., social events, parental workshops, and volunteer opportunities).

No one program can address all the needs of young people or all these elements; yet one program can have many of the elements of quality programs presented here. We believe that quality programs can easily point to the previously mentioned programmatic elements within their curriculum.

SPORTS: A STRUCTURED OUT-OF-SCHOOL EXPERIENCE

Evidence-Based Benefits of Participation in Sports Programs

According to the American Academy of Orthopedic Surgeons (AAOS), half of American males and a quarter of American females, ages 12 to 21, participate in at least one sports program during the year (AAOS, 2000). Organized sports are a safe and healthy alternative to risky behaviors during out-of-school time (AAOS, 2000). Sports provide a vehicle for regular physical activity that has been linked to helping adolescents develop healthy bodies by building and maintaining healthy bones and muscles, controlling body weight and body mass, and reducing feeling of anxiety and depression (U.S. Department of Health and Human Services, 1996).

Sports are productive structured out-of school experiences in part because they address the sedentary lifestyle and physical inactivity of adolescents. According to the Centers for Disease Control and Prevention (2003), approximately 30 percent of students, ages 12 to 17, are not getting an appropriate amount of physical exercise. Moreover, numerous international longitudinal studies have found that adolescent sports participation dramatically increases the likelihood of adult sports participation and fitness (see Perkins, Jacobs, Barber, & Eccles, 2004). For example, in a recent longitudinal study by Perkins and colleagues (Perkins et al., 2004), American adolescents who participate in sports were found to be eight times more likely to participate in sports or fitness activities as adults than adolescents who did not participate in sports.

Participating in sports programs can foster socioemotional growth and development in adolescents (Le Menestrel, Bruno, & Christian, 2002). The young sport enthusiast lists having fun, learning and improving skills, being with and making friends, belonging to a team, and being healthy and fit as reasons for playing sports (Chambers, 1991). Participating on a team can also give children or youth the sense of belonging that they need (Perkins, 2003). Moreover, a quality sports programs encourages the development of a positive self-concept (Le Menestrel et al., 2002).

Many of the more than 40 million children and youth who play sports in school or within the community (Stryer, Tofler, & Lapchick, 1998) drop out of sports by adolescence. Various studies have identified a noticeable decline in physical activity as children pass through adolescence (Malina, 1996; Taylor, Blair, Cummings, Wun, & Malina, 1999). According to research, a win-at-all-costs atmosphere in a youth sports program can be harmful to a developing young person (Daniels & Perkins, 2003). Few children possess the talent to play competitive sports at the highest level; that is, most children will not grow up to be professional athletes. Therefore, our perspective is that the primary goals of sports programs are to foster the development of general physical competence and to promote physical activity, fun, life skills, sportsmanship, and good health. Youth sports programs that foster youth's personal competence are engaging them in the development of their abilities to do life planning, to be self-reliant, and to seek the resources of others when needed (Perkins & Daniels, 2004). Simply put, youth sport programs have the potential to be community youth development programs.

Integrating Community Youth Development into Sports Programs

Just as structured out-of-school experiences are a concern for the various levels of an adolescent's ecology (e.g., family, neighborhood, school, and community), youth sports are not only an individual issue or a family issue but a community issue as well. For example, in the past, researchers identified the athletic triangle model of youth sports—parents, coaches, and youth as each point of a triangle. Scholars theorized that the most important relationships involved in youth sports were among these three different categories of people. Although the athletic triangle addresses some very important participants within the youth sports arena, it overlooks another important participant—the community itself. Thus, the Athletic Square Model is needed when creating and maintaining a developmentally focused sports program (Perkins & Daniels, in press). The community is also a point in the Athletic Square Model, thereby changing the geometric shape from a triangle to a square. This model indicates that youth, parents, coaches, and the community are all responsible in creating the positive youth sports program environment needed to engender youth sports' benefits.

The Athletic Square Model integrates the principles of community youth development. As noted earlier, community youth development involves creating opportunities for young people to connect to others, develop skills, and utilize those skills to contribute to their communities that, in turn, increase their ability to succeed (Villarruel et al., 2003). Consequently, a natural process for the youth to understand and act on his or her environment is encouraged, as is a belief that youth have something to contribute to the community. Sports can provide a context for youth to contribute to the community.

Sports players have some responsibility within the sports realm. They must be willing to listen and learn, to communicate their needs, and to play with good sportsmanship and character. But the community youth development framework in relation to the Athletic Square Model indicates that youth have the right and the responsibility to contribute to the community beyond the sports program. Therefore, sports programs and the adults who organize and volunteer in them must provide meaningful opportunities for youth to contribute to the organization and community. For example, a sports program could have two youth representatives at the organization's board meeting, where both youth have equal decision-making power with the adult board members. Another example is having youth teams members host an activity day at the sports arena for a group of younger children from the local school or day care center. A more basic example would be requiring that a parent and child volunteer at a game for a different age-group, selling snacks or being the announcer. These examples build on the key components of community youth development, including building skills, giving youth a sense of belonging, and engaging youth as partners.

A community-based youth development program requires adults, in collaboration with youth, to *advocate* for opportunities and structures that provide young people with sustained positive relationships with adults and opportunities to utilize newly acquired skills in the "real-world" experiences of their communities. Finally, the following list applies the features of a positive developmental setting outlined earlier in this chapter to a sports program focused on promotion and prevention:

- *Physical and Psychological Safety.* The sports program provides safe equipment, settings, and rules of engagement that focus on protection of young people's emotional well-being.
- *Appropriate Structure.* The sports program has clear rules, expectations, and responsibilities of youth, parents, coaches, officials, and the sports

organizers. These rules are clearly visible at all sporting events. All stakeholders (youth, parents, coaches, officials, and sport organizers) are involved in creating the rules, expectations, and responsibilities. Generally, stakeholders embrace those rules when they have direct input in their development.

- *Supportive Relationships.* The sports program has adults involved in the program's activities and events. Through these activities and events, adults and youth are able to establish trusted connections. The adults are intentional about building positive relationships with the youth, and less emphasis is placed on winning.

- *Opportunities to Belong.* The sports program provides activities and events that foster friendships and provide youth with a sense of a positive group experience.

- *Positive Social Norms.* The sports program's culture (e.g., habits and expectations) that governs behavior and daily interactions involves conventionally positive social norms and good sportsmanship.

- *Support for Efficacy and Mattering.* The sports program provides youth, both individually and in groups, the opportunity to be useful and to make a difference in their social worlds. This includes helping each other during a sporting event and engaging in community service activities that extend beyond the sporting event (e.g., cleaning up the ballpark, helping little children learn the game, and refereeing games for younger children or serving as assistant coaches).

- *Opportunities for Skill Building.* The sports program develops skills and competencies through its activities and team-building experiences. The sports program provides youth the opportunity to build both their sport-related skills and their life skills (e.g., leadership skills, decision making skills, cultural competence, communication skills, problem-solving skills, and civic responsibility).

- *Active Learning.* The sports program provides learning opportunities that are interactive and reflective and that engage multiple learning styles. For example, sports programs are viewed as experiential learning opportunities, and youth are encouraged to take positive risks. Reflection and teachable moments in practice or during a game are common techniques employed.

- *Opportunities for Recognition.* Youth are sincerely acknowledged for their contributions to a sport and their team. These recognitions convey a positive view of youth that is beyond winning. Effort, improvement, and sportsmanship are recognized and praised.

- *Integration of Family, School, and Community Efforts.* The sports program coordinates its efforts and communicates regularly with families and schools to ensure similar norms and expectations across settings. The sports program offers a variety of activities and events that involve parents (e.g., social events, parental workshops, and volunteer opportunities).

CONCLUSION

Youth development programs have an essential role to play in the promotion of the six Cs and in the promotion of personal and environmental assets (see Table 11.1). They can provide settings and experiences that enable positive developmental experiences to occur if program organizers, staff, and volunteers are intentional in how they go implementing these programs. Youth need and deserve the following:

1. Early and sustained investments throughout the first two decades of life
2. Supports throughout their waking hours
3. Investments that help them achieve a *broad range of outcomes* (Tolman & Pittman, 2001)

This is a developmental imperative that calls on us to consider the full range of youth's time, particularly time spent out of school, as crucial to ensuring positive youth development. Indeed, according to Villarruel and colleagues (2003), "By engaging and providing youth with real opportunities to contribute to the communities where they live, the clubs and organizations that they participate in, and the families that they grow up in, we believe that we are ensuring the successful development of youth now and in the future" (p. 396). Addressing community youth development within structured out-of-school time experiences provides opportunities for practitioners to directly promote positive child and adolescent (youth) development.

REFERENCES

Afterschool Alliance. (2002). Afterschool alert: Poll report on findings of the 2002 nationwide poll of registered voters on afterschool programs. Retrieved March 26, 2003, from http://www.afterschoolalliance.org

American Academy of Orthopedic Surgeons. (2000). *The young athlete.* Rosemont, IL: Author.

Barber, B. L., Eccles, J. S, & Stone, M. R. (2001). Whatever happened to the "Jock," the "Brain," and the "Princess"? Young adult pathways linked to adolescent activity involvement and social identity. *Journal of Adolescent Research, 16,* 429–455.

Bernard, B. (2004). *Resiliency: What have we learned?* San Francisco: WestEd.

Brendtro, L. K., Brokenleg, M., & van Bockern, S. (1990). *Reclaiming youth at risk: Our hope for the future.* Bloomington, IN: National Education Service.

Borden, L. M. (2004). *National evaluation of engaging youth, serving community: A preliminary report of year 1.* Tucson: University of Arizona, Department of Family and Consumer Sciences.

Borden, L. M., Perkins, D. F., Villarruel, F. A., & Stone, M. R. (2005). To participate or not participate: That is the question. In H. Weiss & P. Little (Eds.), *New directions or youth development: Conceptualizing participation in out-of-school time programs* (pp. 33–50). San Francisco: Jossey-Bass.

Catalano, R. F., Berglund, M. L., Ryan J. A. M., Lonczak, H. S., & Hawkins, J. D. (1999). *Positive youth development in the United States: Research findings on evaluations of positive youth development programs.* Washington, DC: U.S. Department of Health and Human Services, National Institute of Child Health and Human Development.

Centers for Disease Control and Prevention. (2003). *Youth Risk Behavior Surveillance System: Physical activity.* Retrieved July 3, 2003, from http: apps.nccd.cdc.gov/YRBSS/

Chambers, S. T. (1991). Factors affecting elementary school students' participation in sports. *Elementary School Journal, 91,* 413–419.

Collingwood, T. R., Reynolds, R., Kohl, H. W., Smith, W., & Sloan, S. (1991). Physical fitness effects on substance abuse risk patterns and use patterns. *Journal of Drug Education, 21,* 73–74.

Csikszentmihalyi, M. (1997). *Finding flow: The psychology of engagement with everyday life.* New York: Basic Books.

Daniels, A. M., & Perkins, D. F. (2003). *Putting youth back into sports.* Brookings: South Dakota State University, Cooperative Extension Service.

Durlack, J. A. (1998). Common risk and protective factors in successful prevention programs. *American Journal of Orthopsychiatry, 68,* 512–520.

Eccles J. S., & Barber, B. L.. (1999). Student council, volunteering, basketball, or marching band: What kind of extracurricular involvement matters? *Journal of Adolescent Research, 14,* 10–43.

Eccles, J. S., Barber, B. L., Stone, M. R., & Hunt, J. (2003). Extracurricular activities and adolescent development. *Journal of Social Issues, 59,* 865–889.

Eccles, J., & Gootman, J. A. (2002). *Community programs to promote youth development.* Committee on Community-Level Programs for Youth, Board on Children, Youth, and Families, Commission on Behavioral and Social Sciences Education, National Research Council and Institute of Medicine. Washington, DC: National Academy Press.

Eder, D., & Parker, S. (1987). The cultural production and reproduction of gender: The effect of extracurricular activities on peer-group culture. *Sociology of Education, 60,* 200–213.

Fine, G. (1987). *With the boys: Little League Baseball and preadolescent culture.* Chicago: University of Chicago Press.

Fox, J. A., & Newman, S. (1998). *After-school crime or after-school programs: Tuning into the prime time for violent juvenile crime and implications for national policy.* Washington, DC: Fight Crime: Invest in Kids.

Glancy, M., Willets, F. K., & Farrell, P. (1986). Adolescent activities and adult success and happiness: Twenty-four years later. *Sociology and Social Research, 70,* 242–250.

Hanks, M. (1981). Youth voluntary associations and political socialization. *Social Forces, 60, 211*–223.

Hughes, D. M., & Curnan, S. P. (2000, Winter). Community youth development: A framework for action. *CYD Journal, 1, 7*–13.

Jerry-Spazk, J., & Brown, H.P. (1994). Alcohol use and misuse: The hidden curriculum of the adolescent athelete. *Journal of Child and Adolescent Substance Abuse, 3, 57*–67.

Larson, R. W. (2000).Toward a psychology of positive youth development. *American Psychologist, 55, 170*–183.

Larson, R. W., & Verma, S. (1999). How children and adolescents spend their time across the world: Work, play, and developmental opportunities. *Psychological Bulletin, 125, 701*–736.

Le Menestrel, S., Bruno, M. L., & Christian, D. (2002). *Sports as a hook: An exploratory study of developmental focused youth sports programs.* Washington, DC: Center for Youth Development and Policy Research at the Academy for Educational Development.

Lerner, R. M. (2001). Promotion in the development of prevention science. *Applied Developmental Science, 5, 254*–257.

Lerner, R. M. (2002). *Adolescence: Development, diversity, context, and application.* Upper Saddle River, NJ: Prentice Hall.

Lerner, R. M. (2004). *Liberty: Thriving and civic engagement among America's youth.* Thousand Oaks, CA: Sage.

Lerner, R. M., Fisher, C., & Weinberg, R. (2000). Toward a science for and of the people. Promoting civil society through the application of developmental science. *Child Development, 71, 11*–20.

Malina, R. M. (1996). Tracking of physical activity and physical fitness across the lifespan. *Research Quarterly for Exercise and Sport, 67, 48*–57.

Mahoney, J. L. (2000). School extracurricular activity participation as a moderator in the development of antisocial patterns. *Child Development, 71, 502*–516.

McLaughlin, M. (2000). *Community counts: How youth organizations matter for youth.* Washington, DC: Public Education Network.

Minnesota Commission on Out of School Time. (2004). *What is out-of-school time.* Minneapolis, MN: University of Minnesota Extension Service.

Perkins, D. F. (2003). Youth development and youth sports. In A. M. Daniels & D. F. Perkins, *Putting youth back into sports* (pp. 2–8). Brookings: South Dakota State University, Cooperative Extension Service.

Perkins, D. F., & Borden, L. M. (2003). Risk factors, risk behaviors, and resiliency in adolescence. In R. M. Lerner, M. A. Easterbrooks, & J. Mistry (Eds.), *Handbook of psychology, Vol. 6: Developmental psychology* (pp. 373–394). New York: Wiley.

Perkins, D. F., & Daniels, A. M. (in press). Athletic Square Model of youth sport. In L. Sherrod, C. Flanagan, & R. Kassimir (Eds.), *Encyclopedia of youth activism.* Westport, CT: Greenwood.

Perkins, D. F., Jacobs, J., Barber, B, & Eccles, J. S. (2004). Childhood and adolescent sports participation as predictors of participation in sports and physical fitness activities during adulthood. *Youth and Society, 35,* 495–520.

Pittman, K. J. (2000, March). *Grantmaker strategies for assessing the quality of unevaluated programs and the impact of unevaluated grantmaking.* Paper presented at Evaluation of Youth Programs symposium at the biennial meeting of the Society for Research on Adolescence, Chicago.

Quinn, J. (1995). Positive effects of participation in youth organizations. In M. Rutter (Ed.), *Psychosocial disturbances in young people: Challenges for prevention* (pp. 274–303). Cambridge, MA: Cambridge University Press.

Redd, Z., Cochran, S., Hair, E., & Moore, K. (2002). *Academic achievement programs and youth development: A synthesis.* Washington, DC: Child Trends.

Rhodes, J. E. (2002). *Stand by me: The risks and rewards of mentoring today's youth.* Cambridge, MA: Harvard University Press.

Roffman, J., Suárez-Orozco, C., & Rhodes, J. (2003). In D. Perkins, L. Borden, J. Keith, & F. A. Villarruel (Eds.), *Community youth development: Programs, policies, and practices* (pp. 90–117). Thousand Oaks, CA: Sage.

Roth, J., Brooks-Gunn, J., Murray, L., & Foster, W. (1998). Promoting healthy adolescents: Synthesis of youth development program evaluations. *Journal of Research on Adolescence, 8,* 423–459.

Roth, J. L., & Brooks-Gunn, J. (2003). Youth development programs: Risk, prevention and policy. *Journal of Adolescent Health, 32,* 170–182.

Scales, P. C., Benson, P. L., Leffert, N., & Blyth, D. A. (2000). Contribution of developmental assets to the prediction of thriving among adolescents. *Applied Developmental Science, 4,* 27–46.

Scales, P. C., & Leffert, N. (1999). *Developmental assets: A synthesis of the scientific research on adolescent development.* Minneapolis: Search Institute.

Snyder, H., & Sickmund, M. (1997). *Juvenile offenders and victim: 1997 update on violence.* Washington, DC: U.S. Department of Justice, Office of Juvenile Justice and Delinquency Prevention.

Stryer, B. K., Tofler, I. R., & Lapchick, R. (1998). A developmental overview of child and youth sports in society. *Sports Psychiatry, 7,* 697–711.

Taylor, W. C., Blair, S. N., Cummings, S. S., Wun, C. C., & Malina, R. M. (1999). Childhood and adolescent physical activity patterns and adult physical activity. *Medicine and Science in Sports and Exercise, 31,* 118–123.

Tolman, J., & Pittman, K. (2001). Toward a common vision: Naming and framing the developmental imperative. Washington, DC: Academy for Educational Development.

U.S. Department of Health and Human Services. (1996). *Physical activity and health: A report to the surgeon general.* Atlanta: Author.

Villarruel, F. A., & Lerner, R. M. (Eds.). (1994). *Promoting community-based programs for socialization and learning.* San Francisco: Jossey-Bass.

Villarruel, F. A., Perkins, D. F., Borden, L. M., & Keith, J. G. (2003). *Community youth development: Practice, policy, and research.* Thousand Oaks, CA: Sage.

Walker, J. (2003). The essential youth worker: supports and opportunities for professional success. In F. A. Villarruel, D. F. Perkins, L. M. Borden, & J. G. Keith, *Community youth development: Practice, policy, and research* (pp. 373–393). Thousand Oaks, CA: Sage.

Walker, J., Marczak, M., Blyth, D. A., & Borden, L. M. (2005). Designing developmentally intentional youth programs: Toward a theory of optimal developmental success in community-based learning experiences for youth. In J. L. Mahoney, R. W. Larson, & J. S. Eccles (Eds.), *Organized activities as contexts of development: Extracurricular activities, after-school and community programs* (pp. 399–418). Mahwah, NJ: Lawrence Erlbaum Associates.

Werner, E., & Smith, R. (1992). *Overcoming the odds: High risk children from birth to adulthood.* Ithaca, NY: Cornell University Press.

Yohalem, N. (2003). Adults who make a difference: Identifying the skills and characteristics of successful youth workers. In F. A. Villarruel, D. F. Perkins, L. M. Borden, & J. G. Keith, *Community youth development: Practice, policy, and research* (pp. 358–372). Thousand Oaks, CA: Sage.

Chapter 12

YOUTH DATING AND SEXUAL VIOLENCE

Lori A. Post, Christopher D. Maxwell, Patricia K. Smith, and Steven J. Korzeniewski

Physical and sexual violence by and against youth are significant problems affecting public health, both physical and emotional. However, physical and sexual violence among intimates of any age were not identified as social problems worthy of widespread scholarly investigation until the 1970s (Ferguson, 1998). This emphasis emerged following several developments, including Kanin's (1957) seminal study investigating male aggression in dating relationships, the women's rights movement, and the publication of Susan Brownmiller's book *Against Our Will: Men, Women, and Rape,* which launched the term "date rape" (Brownmiller, 1975, p. 3). Later, Koss, Gidycz, and Wisniewski (1987) published an important study further focusing attention on sexual violence among college-age intimate partners. Similarly, the women's rights movement began emphasizing violence against wives following Straus, Gelles, and Steinmetz's (1981) groundbreaking research reported in *Behind Closed Doors.* These early investigations suggested that both domestic violence and sexual assault were hidden problems.

While initial attention focused on violence among adults, more recent attention in this area has turned toward intimate partner violence (IPV) experienced by and against young people. Many studies have found mutual violence to be common in many adolescent and college dating relationships, even when accounting for violence perpetrated in self-defense (Archer, 2000). However, research has also demonstrated that females are more likely to suffer physical and psychological injury (Archer, 2000).

This chapter provides an overview of youth dating and sexual violence from an ecological perspective; the problem is defined, definitions and rates of youth sexual violence are enumerated, and developmental implications and consequences of this violence are discussed along with intervention and prevention efforts.

DEVELOPMENTAL IMPLICATIONS

In both adult intimate partner and youth dating relationships, there is an emotional investment in the relationship and intimacy with a significant other. Both types of relationships can be abusive, including physical and/or sexual violence as well as psychological and emotional abuse (Suarez, 1994). The victim in an abusive relationship, regardless of age, may be afraid of the perpetrator and have legitimate fears about the consequences of ending the relationship. However, youth dating violence does have significant differences from IPV experienced by adults, particularly regarding cohabiting married couples. In young people's dating relationships, there is rarely economic dependence or involvement of shared children, both of which potentially make addressing an adult abusive relationship more problematic (Flanagan, 2003). Moreover, the effects of IPV on emotional/psychological development are more significant in young people compared to adults because of the progression through developmental stages during youth and the varying levels of intimacy and responsibility experienced in adult relationships.

This difference between youth and adult IPV is rooted in the different developmental tasks of youths and adults. Throughout adolescence, important peer relationships are increasingly developed; sexual feelings, contacts, and roles are explored; and cultural/familial norms may be challenged while developing self-concept (Vander Zanden, 2000). This development occurs at an age when adolescents typically begin interacting with the opposite sex, thereby providing the opportunity to practice adult relationship roles. Suarez (1994) found that adolescents may conform to exaggerated gender roles when exploring their sexuality, however, providing an increased opportunity for relationship violence to occur. Age and gender impact the level and nature of detriment, depending on where in the developmental cycle and to whom the trauma occurs. Henton, Cate, Koval, Lloyd, and Christopher (1983) estimate that most adolescents have started dating and have already experienced violence by a dating partner by the age of 16. But what is "dating" for today's youth? And, while the general concept of physical violence in a relationship might not be difficult to discern, what do we mean by "sexual violence"?

DEFINITIONS

Sexual Violence

Sexual violence applies to a broad range of activities. In *Definitions and Recommended Data Elements for Sexual Violence Surveillance* (Basile & Saltzman, 2002), the Centers for Disease Control and Prevention has laid out the array of behaviors covered under this rubric (see Table 12.1). Any of these violations can have a profound impact on an individual's development and/or mental health. Commonly, the concept of "rape" (which is not specifically named in the definitions) involves some level of sexual penetration (see the definition of "sex act" in Table 12.1).

A key concept that determines whether something is a desired sexual activity or an act of sexual violence is the presence or absence of consent. As defined by Basile and Saltzman (2002), consent is "words or overt actions by a person who is legally or functionally competent to give

Table 12.1
Categories of Sexual Violence

Sexual violence = any of the following without a person's freely given consent

Completed or attempted (noncompleted) sex act	Contact between the penis and the vulva or the penis and the anus involving penetration, however slight; contact between the mouth and the penis, vulva, or anus; or penetration of the anal or genital opening of another person by a hand, finger, or other object
Sexual contact	Intentional touching, either directly or through clothing, of the genitalia, anus, groin, breast, inner thigh, or buttocks
Noncontact sexual activity	Activity of a sexual nature that does not include physical contact of a sexual nature between the perpetrator and the victim, includes acts such a voyeurism; intentional exposure of an individual to exhibitionism; pornography; verbal or behavioral sexual harassment; threats of sexual violence to accomplish some other end; or taking of nude photographs of a sexual nature without his or her consent or knowledge or of a person who is unable to consent or refuse

Source: Adapted from Basile and Saltzman (2002). Available at http://www.cdc.gov/ncipc/pub-res/sv_surveillance/sv.htm.

informed approval, indicating a freely given agreement to have sexual intercourse or sexual contact" (p. 9). Consent in the context of agreeing to sexual activity is active, not passive. As can be seen in the previously given definition, other factors also come into play. For example, in most states a 14-year-old is not legally able to give consent to sexual activity (see the following discussion of statutory rape). Additionally, a person must be physically able to give or refuse consent (e.g., not incapacitated because of alcohol or drugs, disability, illness, or age). "Able to give consent" is a concept that has received much media attention in the past few years with the use of the so-called date rape drugs such as GHB and Rohypnol. "Inability to refuse," however, has not received the attention it likely merits. A young person, or anyone for that matter, while physically capable of refusing unwanted sexual activity, may be unable to refuse for a variety of reasons, including "the use of guns or other non-bodily weapons, or due to physical violence, threats of physical violence, real or perceived coercion, intimidation or pressure, or misuse of authority" (Basile & Saltzman, 2002, p. 9).

"Statutory rape," while not a phrase commonly used in criminal statutes (Davis & Twombly, 2000), is a general concept regarding the legal age of consent for sexual activity that states have codified within sexual assault law. Sexual activity with a person who has not reached the statutory age of consent (which varies from 14 to 18 years, depending on the state) is a crime in all states. Some states have a two-tiered system where (1) no one under a certain age can legally take part in sexual activity and (2) young people within a certain age range can engage in consensual sexual activity as long as the age difference with their partner does not exceed specified limits. At the first level, the laws stem from the belief that, before a specified age, a young person cannot reasonably be expected to make an informed decision about participating in sexual activity. The second tier of laws was implemented to protect young people from predatory adults.

Dating

What is a date? When looking at adult relationships, it is relatively easy to identify what could be classified as falling into the realm of "date" or "dating relationship." Dates are usually thought of as noncohabiting social pairings between two persons that may be a one-time event or a long-standing relationship. Hickman and colleagues (Hickman, Jaycox, & Aronoff, 2004) discuss the complexity, however, that lies in wait for anyone attempting to define an adolescent dating relationship, which could be anything from the traditional committed boyfriend/girlfriend to one-time casual sexual events to "friends with privileges." These researchers point out that the problem of defining "date" for teenagers (relative to college aged youth and older persons) partially explains why there is little known about dating violence among young people in middle and high school.

The terms "date rape" and "acquaintance rape" are typically used interchangeably. However, as Bechhofer and Parrot (1991) point out,

> The acquaintance relationship can be any one of a variety of acquaintanceships including platonic, dating, marital, professional, academic, or familial. *Date rape* is a narrower term referring to nonconsensual sex between people who are dating or on a date. Although the two terms "acquaintance rape" and "date rape" are often used interchangeably (particularly in the lay press), they do not have the same meaning. Date rape is one form of acquaintance rape. (p. 12)

With a date, as opposed to any person someone is acquainted with, there is typically a level of intimacy or expectation of intimacy not found in other casual or formal social relationships; this intimacy may or may not be physical. Both rape and sexual violence are easier to define in nonintimate acquaintance relationships. The lines become unclear, depending on the level of intimacy in a dating relationship (physical and nonphysical). While Bechhofer and Parrot (1991) state that "acquaintance rape and lovemaking often have similar antecedents and dynamics" (p. 13), this is even truer when looking specifically at the dating subset of acquaintance relationships. There may also be differing levels of expectation between the two parties over what is permissible and what is not; how well that is communicated or heard may also vary.

Regardless of the type of relationship, however, if the sexual intimacy is unwanted or forced, it is sexual violence. While it is important for the potential victim to communicate wishes and boundaries clearly, it is even more important for the potential perpetrator to ensure that their actions are desired and welcome. Within youth dating relationships (as clearly as they can be defined for youth), both physical violence and sexual violence of all types are not uncommon, as can be seen in the next section.

PERVASIVENESS OF VIOLENCE

Physical

Estimates of the prevalence of physical aggression in youth dating relationships have varied widely. For example, Brustin (1995) estimated that 28 percent of high school and college students experience dating violence at some point. Foshee (1996) found that a quarter of their late middle school/early high school population had experienced nonsexual dating violence, while 12 percent of adolescents in a nationally representative sample reported experiencing physical violence perpetrated by a date (Halpern et al., 2001). The most recent estimate, according to the Youth Risk Behavior Survey (Morbidity and Mortality Weekly Report, 2004) is that 9 percent of teens in grades 9 to 12 have been hit, slapped, or physically hurt on purpose by a boyfriend or girlfriend. This same survey also found that the prevalence of experiencing dating violence was highest among African Americans (12.3%) and that males experienced more violence than female respondents. The wide array of prevalence estimates of physical violence can be at least partially explained by the different definitions utilized in measuring dating violence as well as the age-group and gender being studied.

Sexual Assault

Several sources of official data report on the frequency of sexual assault committed by and against youth. For instance, crime reports collected by law enforcement agencies in 12 states from 1991 to 1996 showed that youths younger than age 18 accounted for 67 percent of sexual assault victims known to law enforcement agencies (Snyder, 2000b), though they represented only 20 percent of the population (Population Estimates Program, 2001). More specifically, Snyder (2000) reported crimes that suggest that adolescents in the middle and high school age-groups (12 to 17 years old) represent 33 percent of the known sexual assault victims (and 20% of offenders), 34 percent of the known forcible rape victims (and 15% of offenders), 24 percent of the known forcible sodomy victims (and 28% of offenders), 26 percent of the known victims sexually assaulted with an object (and 20% of offenders), and 34 percent of the known forcible fondling victims (and 22% of offenders). Thus, regardless of the definition of sexual assault, adolescents are disproportionately represented among victims and offenders in incidents reported to the police.

Information from the National Crime Victimization Survey, a panel study of about 77,000 people age 12 and older from a nationally representative sample of U.S. households, also reveals a disproportionate number of sexual assaults among young people; respondents ages 12 to 17 reported twice the rate of sexual assault (2 per 1,000) compared with adults (1 per 1,000) (Snyder & Sickmund, 1999). Furthermore, high school–aged adolescents (15 to 17 years) reported sexual assault at three times the adult rate (3 per 1,000). However, among all ages, 14-year-olds (who are typically in grade 9) accounted for the greatest proportion of both sexual assault victims and offenders (Snyder & Sickmund, 1999).

Besides official data sources, a variety of studies (e.g., Jackson, Cram, & Seymour, 2000; Maxwell, Robinson, & Post, 2003; O'Keefe & Treister, 1998; Schubot, 2001) have examined the prevalence of sexual assault or sexual aggression among adolescents (13 to 18 years old). Among those studies, six measured and reported rates of sexual assaults against females. The average unweighted prevalence rate of sexual assault across these six studies was 14 percent. Maxwell et al. (2003) also found that 14 percent of their sample of females explicitly reported having experienced a rape; this rate is nearly identical to the one reported more than a decade earlier by Koss et al. (1987). The remaining studies did not specifically or separately measure sexual assault, or they reported prevalence rates that combined the sexual assault questions with other questions that may or may not capture sexual assault specifically (e.g., coerced sexual activity). These studies reported an average unweighted "sexual aggression" incidence of 24 percent. With regard to offending behaviors, only two studies reported the prevalence of sexual assault by males (2.3% and 34%), and two others reported sexual aggression rates by males (10% in one and 54% in the other) . Maxwell et al. (2003) also found that 14 percent of their sample of females explicitly reported having experienced a rape; this rate is nearly identical to the one reported more than a decade earlier by Koss et al. (1987).

These studies, like others that used college samples, uncovered more victims of sexual assault than either the National Crime Victimization Survey or the 1995 Violence Against Women Survey. Unfortunately, these studies also have several weaknesses, making it difficult to understand the exact nature of sexual aggression among adolescents. For example, several studies measured sexual assault with questions that asked whether the subjects had ever been forced into a sexual activity that they did not want. This question does not make clear what the words "force" or "sexual activity" mean. Does "force" include both psychological and physical force, and does "sexual activity" include all behaviors deemed sexual in nature, including kissing and sexual intercourse? While these studies clearly show that sexual aggression is prevalent among adolescents, the weaknesses and differences in the designs of the studies make it difficult to fully understand the nature and severity of sexual aggression in this age-group.

Youth surveys and official data also find that adolescents are often sexually assaulted by someone they know. Summary data from the National Incident Based Reporting System indicated that a majority (66%) of adolescent victims were sexually assaulted by an acquaintance, nearly half of whom were 12 to 24 years old (Snyder & Sickmund, 1999). Findings from the National Youth Survey, a longitudinal study of youth ages 11 to 17, produced an even higher proportion of adolescent rapes perpetrated by acquaintances. Victims of these rapes reported that less than 20 percent of offenders were unknown to them (Ageton, 1983). A recent study also found that sexual coercion experienced by high school students was most often perpetrated by long-term boyfriends or girlfriends rather than new partners, friends, or casual acquaintances (Jackson et al., 2000). Parties and their partners' houses were the most common settings for these incidents (Jackson et al., 2000).

Sexual assault and physical dating violence are clearly common in the lives of young people. They are complex problems arising through many different antecedents and causal chains.

YOUTH DATING AND SEXUAL VIOLENCE EXPLAINED FROM AN ECOLOGICAL MODEL

Ecological systems theory, in general, was developed by Urie Bronfenbrenner (1979) and addresses multiple factors within a child's life that may affect his or her development. To this end, we find that individuals are significantly affected by interactions among a number of overlapping ecosystems. The youth is at the center of the ecological system; around him or her are the microsystems that immediately shape human development, such as family, school, and peers. Microsystems interact in the mesosystem. The exosystem surrounds the microsystem, and contains factors such as the extended family, community services, the workplace, neighbors, and other social networks, which more indirectly influence the youth through their influence on the mesosystem and its microsystems. Influencing all systems is the macrosystem, which contains cultural attitudes, mores, and ideologies. Additionally, the chronosystem looks at the effects resulting from changes over time (Bronfenbrenner, 1979; Craig & Baucum, 2002; Trawick-Smith, 2003).

Research on mediating and moderating effects of ecological factors has focused mostly on the microsystem and youth center of the ecological system. Factors such as perceived threat, self-blame, perceived control, coping style, gender, age, maternal emotional health, and intensity and frequency of violence have been analyzed (Kerig, 1998; Kilpatrick & Williams, 1998).

A number of theorists and researchers have developed comprehensive ecological-based models for understanding the effects of exposure to IPV (including dating violence) and sexual violence. White and Kowalski (1998) modified the ecological model specifically for violence against women and White and Post (2003) more specifically for sexual violence. These models recognize the relationships between potential victims and perpetrators in various situations, representing family, marriage, social, and work networks. Each victim–perpetrator–situational network interacts with other networks and is distally affected by history, the sociocultural climate, and time. There are certain interactions between victim, perpetrator, and situational factors that lead to aggression and violence.

The National Research Council identifies ecological theory as "the framework best suited to address the causes, consequences, and treatment formulations for young victims" (Mohr & Tulman, 2000, p. 60). By looking at more than the individual, protective and risk factors can be identified, such as family, school, community, and extended family. For example, differences in behavioral problems and trauma (see the section on the relationship between violence and mental health) may be explained through the ecological model (Mohr & Tulman, 2000; Peled, 1996; White & Kowalski, 1998; White & Post, 2003). The ecological model is also consistent with the public health model, promoting prevention and positive family, community, and societal structures. Finally, ecological systems theory is perhaps the most culturally sensitive approach, focusing on the different contexts and perspectives of minority, low-income, and underrepresented groups (Bernal, Bonilla, & Bellido, 1995; Foster & Martinez, 1995; Mohr & Tulman, 2000; Trawick-Smith, 2003).

Utilizing ecological systems theory, White and Kowalski (1998) developed an approach that recognizes the importance of historical and sociocultural factors, along with the social network, dyadic relationship, situational, and interpersonal factors that affect the psychological processes (cognitive and motivational) underlying all types of male violence against women. While female-initiated violence is acknowledged, the authors felt that understanding the gendered nature of aggression and violence is critical given that the outcomes for females tend to be more severe (White & Kowalski, 1998).

The model emphasizes that an individual's behavior can be best understood by considering the impact of historical, sociocultural, and social factors across time on cognitive and motivational processes that result in aggression and gendered violence. It assumes an embedded or hierarchical perspective to categorize variables as sociocultural, dyadic, situational, and interpersonal. This perspective examines individual behavior in relationship to the specific situation in which it occurs (i.e., proximal influences as well as in relation to more distal situation/contextual influences). The model also assumes gender-related phenomena at all levels. Patriarchy is defined at the historical/sociocultural level, in turn prescribing power dynamics in terms of gender, race, class, ethnicity, and age. As a result, these power dynamics become enacted at the interpersonal level, affecting the internalization of gendered values, expectations, and behaviors.

Contextual factors exist at the cultural level (macrosystem) and reflect the shared patterns of ideas and beliefs that exist across generations (Frayser, 1989). In turn, sociocultural factors including community, and neighborhood factors (exosystem) define features of one's social networks (family, peer groups, school, and employment relations). Further embedded in these social networks are characteristics of the dyadic relationship in which violence occurs (the interaction of the microsystems and the youth). This embedded perspective argues that recognition of factors at all these levels enhances understanding of variables at the intrapersonal level, including traits, attitudes, motivations, and past history. Specifically, social and cultural influences and attitudes create the context within which men with certain personality characteristics and behavioral tendencies will likely be violent given particular social situations and dyadic relationships. Historical and sociocultural factors create an environment in which the growing child learns rules and expectations, first in the family network and later in peer, intimate, and work relationships. Early experiences define the context for later experiences. Figure 12.1 illustrates the embedded perspective and shows the interconnections between the various levels of analysis.

Time is also a critical component of the model; time indicates that effects change across time and are cumulative. The most distal influences are historical and sociocultural. Embedded in these are a number of interconnected relationships a person has, including family, social aspects, school, and work. Within each network is also embedded a relationship between two individuals—the potential perpetrator and potential victim—denoted by the circle telescoped out from each social network. These two individuals have an interaction history that will influence their behaviors in any given situation. This situation provides the proximal cues for aggression and violence. The integrative contextual developmental perspective suggests that intrapersonal variables are expressed within a cultural and social context and reflect influences from one's genetic/biological makeup, personality, attitudes and beliefs, cognitive processes, and learning history, as examined in the following section, which examines prior research in the area of youth dating and youth sexual violence.

Factors Related to Youth Dating Violence

Both accepting attitudes toward IPV and traditional gender role beliefs are related to the likelihood of experiencing IPV. Riggs and O'Leary (1989) and Yick and Agbayani-Siewert (2000) found that those who tolerate or justify the use of physical violence are more likely to use violence against their partners or be a victim. Tontodonado and Crew (1992)

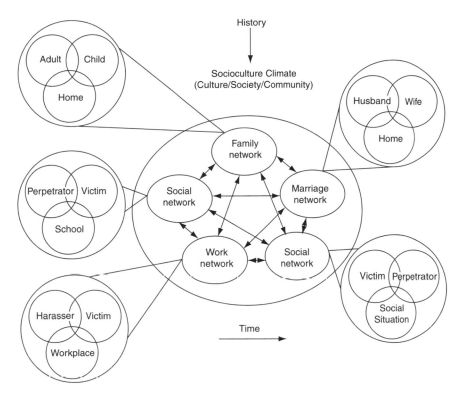

Figure 12.1 An integrative contextual developmental model of violence against women. (White, 1998; White, 2003)

quantified this likelihood reporting a threefold increase in IPV among those who could justify using IPV. Regarding gender role beliefs, both Finn (1986) and Yick and Agbayani-Siewert (2000) found that students who adhered to more traditional gender roles were more likely to deem the use of violence in relationships acceptable. Similarly, several studies (Ferguson, 1998; Thompson, 1991; Worth, Matthews, & Coleman, 1990) suggest that those males who either score higher on masculinity scales or are domineering *and* believe in traditional gender roles are more likely to perpetrate violence on an intimate partner.

A recent study by Foshee and colleagues (Foshee, Benefield, Ennett, Bauman & Suchindran, 2004) is among the first longitudinal studies to look at risk factors for serious physical and sexual dating violence victimization of adolescents, both onset of such victimization and chronic victimization. While being hit by an adult with the intention to harm was a risk factor for onset of serious physical dating violence for both genders, other victimization risk factors for males included low self-esteem and having been in a physical fight with a peer. In the multivariate analysis for chronic victimization for both sexes, additional risk factors included having a friend who was a dating violence victim, using alcohol, being white for males, and living in a single-parent household for females. The researchers also looked at risk factors for sexual dating violence victimization for females and found that both having a friend who was a victim of dating violence and depression were predictive of sexual dating violence onset. These, with the addition of gender stereotyping, were also risk factors for chronic sexual dating violence victimization.

Similarly, Howard and Wang (2003a) found that feelings of sadness/ hopelessness, suicide ideation or attempts, and fighting were highly correlated with dating violence victimization for adolescent males. For female adolescents, feelings of sadness/hopelessness, suicidal behavior, alcohol or illicit drug use, and risky sexual behavior were most strongly related to dating violence victimization (Howard & Wang, 2003b). While it is not possible to determine whether these risk factors preceded or followed being in an abusive dating relationship, some of these findings support those of Foshee and colleagues (2004). These investigations demonstrate the need to address more basic individual and social issues in adolescents' lives by going beyond classroom discussions of building positive relationships or zero tolerance of abusive relationship behavior if the incidence and prevalence of serious dating violence is to be reduced. They also point to the fact that dating violence victimization does not occur in a vacuum but is often associated with other health risk behaviors that must also be addressed.

Smith, White, and Holland (2003) found physical dating violence victimization of adolescent females to be a strong predictor of recurrent victimization once the women were in college. The researchers also discovered that physical assault by a "romantic partner" also predicted sexual assault within the same year. These findings stress the importance of focusing on preventing the first incident of violence from ever occurring.

The importance of determining a person's potential vulnerability to violence victimization and investigating means to reduce that vulnerability cannot be overlooked. However, when talking about causality, which, it is hoped, in turn leads to discussions of prevention strategies, the antecedents of *perpetration* are perhaps the most crucial factors to determine. Ultimate responsibility for violence lies with the perpetrator. Surprisingly, Bookwala and colleagues found that dating violence victimization was a strong predictor of dating violence perpetration (Bookwala, Frieze, Smith, & Ryan, 1992). Malik, Sorenson, and Aneshensel (1997) also found a strong correlation between victimization and perpetration.

Analysis of longitudinal study data by Foshee and colleagues (Foshee, Linder, MacDougall, & Bangdiwala, 2001) found that dating violence perpetration by adolescent males was predicted by attitudes accepting of dating violence. Having a friend who is a dating violence victim, alcohol use, and being a race other than white were predictive of female perpetration. Muehlenhard and Linton (1987) found factors associated with (but not necessarily predictive of) sexual aggression in dating relationships of college students to be miscommunication about sex; heavy alcohol or drug use; a power differential in the relationship as manifested by the man's initiation of the date, paying the expenses, and driving; and "parking."

Some research has also investigated the relationships between engaging in or being exposed to other forms of violence and dating violence perpetration. For example, one study found that adolescent males who perpetrated peer violence were also likely to engage in sexual aggression and dating violence (Ozer, Tschann, Pasch, & Flores, 2004). Another study found exposure to multiple forms of violence predictive of dating violence perpetration and victimization (Malik et al., 1997). While Kaura and Allen (2004) found dissatisfaction with relationship power to be predictive of dating violence use for both college-age men and college-age women, they found an even stronger predictor of dating violence perpetration to be exposure to parental violence.

The risk of physical violence for both adults and youth also increases during pregnancy (McFarlane, 1989; Silverman, Raj, & Clements, 2004). This is a serious event at any age, although the negative effects are thought be more dramatic at an earlier age because young mothers are more prone to feelings of isolation and helplessness that may be used against them by an abuser.

Factors Related to Sexual Assault Involving Youth

Five factors have been identified as associated with sexual assault involving youth cither as victims or as perpetrators. First, a preponderance of evidence suggests that alcohol and/or drug use increases the chances of sexual victimization and offending, particularly among young people who know each other. A recent national study of more than 4,000 female college students found that frequently getting drunk significantly increases the likelihood of sexual victimization and that more than 90 percent of these sexual assaults were committed by classmates, friends, boyfriends/ex-boyfriends, or acquaintances (Fisher & Cullen, 2000). Another recent national study of college students showed that alcohol use by both the victim and the offender significantly increases the severity of sexual victimization (Ullman, Karabatsos, & Koss, 1999).

Even among samples too young to consume alcohol legally, research reveals that drinking is still a significant risk factor for sexual assault.

Maxwell et al. (2003, p. 472) found that one in four girls reported having sex when they were "very drunk, stoned or unconscious," and, surprisingly, 50 percent of the boys reported having sex with a "very drunk, stoned or unconscious" girl. Yet another study found that drinking alcohol was one of the most common reasons given by high school seniors for engaging in unwanted sex (Jackson et al., 2000).

According to the National Crime Victimization Survey data, offenders under the influence of alcohol commit 183,000 rapes and sexual assaults in a typical year, or approximately 30 percent of all rapes or sexual assaults (Greenfeld, 1998). Ageton's (1983) analysis of the National Youth Survey data also revealed that about 70 percent of offenders reported drinking or taking drugs before the assault. Finally, in a youth survey of high school students, substance abuse was found to increase the likelihood that both males and females would inflict dating violence, a measure that includes physical violence and forced sexual activity (O'Keefe, 1997).

Adolescents' dating and sexual history is also related to the likelihood of becoming either a sexual offender or a victim of sexual violence. Vogel (2000) found that males entering college who self-reported aggressive and/or illegal sexual behavior started having sex at an earlier age and reported having more sexual partners than did nonaggressive males. Hall and Flannery (1984) found that rape victimization among adolescents was significantly related to membership in a sexually active peer group. Another study reported that high school seniors engaged in unwanted sex because they believed their friends were doing it (Jackson et al., 2000). Other research finds that the number of dating partners, dating frequency, and previous sexual intercourse increases the risk of sexual victimization among female adolescents (Bergman, 1992; Maxwell et al., 2003; O'Keefe & Treister, 1998; Schubot, 2001; Silverman, Raj, Mucci, & Hathaway, 2001). This research suggests that as dating and sexual experiences increase, so too does the adolescent's risk of victimization or proclivity for offending.

A third factor that has emerged in some research is the relationship between academic achievement and sexual offending. For example, Fehrenback et al. (1986) found that only 57 percent of their sample of adolescent sex offenders were placed in the appropriate grade level. Adolescent sex offenders have also been found to have high rates of learning and/or behavioral difficulties at school; 71 percent of sex offenders compared to 46 percent of the delinquent controls have only remedial education (Awad, Saunders, & Levene, 1984). In a comparison of adult rapists who had adolescent sex offender records versus adult rapists who did not, Knight and Prentky (1993) found that those who began offending as adolescents had less education.

In a sample of high school students, Bergman (1992) found that the likelihood of severe violent victimization (both sexual and physical violence) decreased as students' self-reported grade-point average increased. Similarly, Maxwell et al. (2003) found that the likelihood of victimization increased sixfold if the female student reported having no college plans.

A fourth factor that has emerged from past research provides consistent evidence that many adolescents hold rape-supportive attitudes, which may increase the likelihood of perpetration or victimization. Surveys of adolescents typically find that between 25 and 50 percent blame the victim for their sexual assaults, usually by identifying styles of dress or behaviors by the victim believed to provoke sexual violence (Elliott, Ageton, Huizinga, Knowles, & Cantor, 1983; Kershner, 1996; Maxwell et al., 2003). Kershner (1996) found that many students ages 14 to 19 considered forced sexual intercourse acceptable under certain circumstances. Approximately half the students strongly agreed that most women fantasized about rape (52%), that some females encourage rape by the way they dress (46%), and that some women provoke men into raping them (53%). Both male and female high school seniors were more likely to interpret a vignette as a date rape when the victim was dressed conservatively or no information was provided about her attire than when the victim was dressed provocatively (Cassidy & Hurrell, 1995). Another study found that many high school students believe that rapists commit rape for sex (73%), that victims can prevent rape (41%), that females claim rape to get back at men (42%), and that rape is sometimes the victim's fault (42%) (Proto-Campise, Belknap, & Woolredge, 1998).

Building on prior attitudinal research, one study investigated the predictors of victim-blaming attitudes among adolescents. For both male and female adolescents, acceptance of traditional gender roles led to greater levels of rape myth acceptance, and males had higher levels of rape myth acceptance when they self-reported participating in violent acts (Marciniak, 1998). Together, these studies suggest that sex roles, attitudes, and cognition may play important roles in the etiology of sexual aggression.

Extant research has also revealed a high level of unfamiliarity with what behaviors fall within the legal definition of rape, which may also be related to adolescent sexual violence. In a large-scale survey of teenagers in Los Angeles, Goodchilds, Zellmann, and Giarusso (1988) found that the label "rape" was reluctantly applied by the students. Two factors affected the likelihood that nonconsensual sex would be perceived as rape: the amount of force used in the incident and the type of relationship between the victim and offender. As the force to gain victim compliance increased, students were more likely to perceive the incident as rape.

Even if great force was used, however, the students were less likely to label the act as rape if the couple had previously dated. This study also found that most females and males believe that forced sex is acceptable when the boy spent money on the girl, the girl led the boy on, the girl went to the boy's house, or the girl had a bad reputation.

Overall, this research illustrates that high school females are equally, if not more, at risk for sexual victimization than college students. High school males are also at risk for offending. Male students' adherence to beliefs that promote sexual aggressiveness and their willingness to blame their coercive and violent behaviors on their victims are important to note.

Not surprisingly, while both sexual assault and dating violence may have serious physical consequences for youth, perhaps less well understood are the mental health consequences to young people.

RELATIONSHIP BETWEEN VIOLENCE AND MENTAL HEALTH

Psychological Responses

A very common yet often misunderstood diagnosis of posttraumatic stress disorder (PTSD) has been strongly identified as a possible outcome for adolescents who are victims of violence (Shavers, 2000). Findings revealed that school-age children exposed to violence and trauma were more aggressive and more inhibited and had somatic complaints (i.e., stomachaches or headaches), cognitive distortions, and deficits that reflected learning difficulties and trouble concentrating in school (Burgess, Hartman, & Clements, 1995; Green, Wilson, & Lindy, 1985; Osofsky, Wewers, Hann, & Fick, 1993). This is further complicated by the fact that not all survivors of extremely stressful events meet the diagnostic criteria for PTSD (Pynoos, Sorrenson, & Steinberg, 1993). For purposes of this chapter, psychological responses are conceptualized as a group of characteristic symptoms that develop following exposure to a stressful situation or series of events that are outside the normal range of experience (Campbell, 1989). The fourth edition of the *Diagnostic and Statistical Manual of Mental Disorders* of the American Psychiatric Association (1994) has defined PTSD in six parts as an informational guide for studying the phenomenon of PTSD and the antecedent childhood traumatic stressor(s).

Emotional Responses

Adolescents' emotional responses and behavioral patterns reflect the interaction of their temperament and inherited personality, the history of their experiences, and the particular nature of each situation (Wolraich, 1997). Adolescents exposed to violence and trauma may also internalize their feelings and emotions (Shavers, 2000). Studies have shown that the internalization of emotions may result in anxiety and depression and the presence of symptoms of PTSD (Davies & Flannery, 1998; Horwitz, Weine, & Jeke, 1995; Singer, Anglin, Song, & Lunghofer, 1995).

Behavioral Patterns

In a study investigating the degree to which violence exposure and symptoms of psychological trauma are related, researchers found that anger was the most important trauma symptom in predicting violent behaviors for both male and female adolescents (Song, Singer, & Anglin, 1998). However, as previously mentioned, the clinical assessment of the overall impact of stressful events on the behavioral patterns of adolescents experiencing violence appears to be multicomplex and multifaceted. Behavioral patterns can be thought of as any action or response by an individual, including observable activity, measurable physiological changes, cognitive images, fantasies, and emotions (Barker, 1995).

Academic Performance

Adolescents experiencing violence may experience symptoms that may impair their ability to learn at school (Davies & Flannery, 1998). In addition, it is also possible that an indirect result of exposure to violence is lower student achievement. Finally, parents and guardians along with adolescents are considered to be the most important sources of data about children's competencies and problems (Achenbach, 1988, 1998; Achenbach, McConaughy, & Howell, 1987).

FROM A DEVELOPMENTAL PERSPECTIVE

Trauma

Childhood developmental tasks or developmental trajectory and transition to adulthood may be negatively affected by violence and acts related to violence (McFarlane & deGirolamo, 1996; Pynoos, Sorenson, & Steinberg, 1993). Terr (1991) has proposed, as a result of extensive clinical research in the area of trauma, that there are two basic types of adolescent trauma and that each one has its own specific behavioral characteristics. Type I occurs as a result of one sudden shock and includes full, detailed memories, "omens," and misperceptions. Type II trauma is identified as precipitating by a series of "external blows" that may result in the adolescent developing coping and defense mechanisms that will help to protect the mind and the body. The defense and coping behaviors recognized in the type II trauma include massive denial, repression, dissociation, self-anesthesia, self-hypnosis, and identification with the aggressor and aggression turned against the self, often leading to profound character changes in the young child (again, this depends on the age at which the adolescent experiences violence).

Antecedent Childhood Traumatic Stressors

Antecedent childhood traumatic stressors are viewed as a reported event or experience that violates the child's existing way of making sense of his or her reactions, structuring of perceptions regarding other people's behavior, and creating a framework for interacting with the world at large (McFarlane & deGirolamo, 1996); however, information on the mental health effects associated with this victimization is lacking.

Often, adolescents have romanticized views about love and relationships. One of the roles practitioners can assume is that of an educator. Programs targeting healthy, unhealthy, and abusive relationships with a client or facilitating a group about relationships may raise the level of awareness and challenge sex role views.

CONCLUSIONS

Sexual violence research commenced in 1957; however, dating and sexual violence did not truly begin to draw mass attention until the 1970s. Initially, research focused on demographics, risk factors, and developmental implications; recently, attention has been directed toward assessing the efficacy of youth relationship violence prevention programs. The theoretical basis supporting this youth-centered focus comes from the application of ecological theory embedded within the conceptual framework of the integrative contextual developmental perspective. Ecological theory posits that youths are at the center of an overlapping system of ecosystems; thus, in order to exhibit sustainable changes in the cumulative ecosystem, that core must be influenced. The integrative contextual developmental perspective supplements this theory by eliciting awareness of the unique context of IPV among youths. Specifically, the model focuses on historical, sociocultural, and social factors across time said to influence the processes and results of sexual aggression in that group. Unfortunately, the recent attention on prevention has yielded few applicable results, perhaps because of several methodological flaws in past research and development of interventions.

Specifically, the appropriateness of study designs, along with inconsistent methods of measuring independent/dependent variables and the lack of direct behavior measurements, is thought to have slowed the understanding of youth sexual violence. The severity, prevalence, and societal impact of such violence have been adequately investigated; however, an effective form of remediation has been much more elusive. Past sexual/dating violence literature suggests that interventions must occur earlier, in middle school–aged children and earlier, if they are to have a positive influence on the developing concepts of gender and sexual roles. The importance of associated factors, including drugs and alcohol, has been emphasized along with the role of past relationship experience, although previously mentioned methodological flaws prevent strong individual conclusions or any cumulative assertions about sexual violence in nonadult populations. Thus, a new line of research focusing attention on testing youth-based interventions targeting both healthy and unhealthy behavior armed with sound methodology and an emphasis on replication is strongly needed. The prevalence of sexual violence is staggering among youths; without proper intervention, the incidence is likely to remain stable or rise (either is unacceptable), leading to continued devastating emotional/psychological effects.

REFERENCES

Achenbach, T. (1988). *Child Behavior Checklist.* Burlington: Center for Children, Youth and Families, University of Vermont.

Achenbach, T. (1998). *Manual for the Child Behavior Checklist/4–18 and 1991 Profile.* Burlington: Department of Psychology, University of Vermont.

Achenbach, T., McConaughy, S., & Howell, C. (1987). Child/adolescent behavioral and emotional problems: Implications of cross-informant correlations for situational specificity. *Psychological Bulletin, 101,* 213–232.

Ageton, S. S. (1983). *Sexual assault among adolescents.* Lexington, MA: Lexington Books.

American Psychiatric Association. (1994). *Diagnostic and Statistical Manual of Mental Disorders* (4th ed.). Washington, DC: Author.

Archer, J. (2000). Sex differences in agression between heterosexual partners: A meta-analytic review. *Psychological Bulletin, 126,* 651–680.

Awad, G., Saunders, E., & Levene, J. (1984). A clinical study of male adolescent sexual offenders. *International Journal of Offender Therapy and Comparative Criminology, 28,* 105–115.

Barker, R. (1995). *The social work dictionary* (3rd ed.). Washington, DC: National Association of Social Workers Press.

Basile, K., & Saltzman, L. (2002). *Sexual violence surveillance: Uniform definitions and recommended data elements.* Atlanta: National Center for Injury Prevention and Control, Centers for Disease Control and Prevention.

Bechhofer, L., & Parrot, A. (1991). What is acquaintance rape? In A. Parrot & L. Bechhofer (Eds.), *Acquaintance rape: The hidden crime* (pp. 9–25). New York: Wiley.

Bergman, L. (1992). Date violence among high school students. *Social Work, 37,* 21–27.

Bernal, G., Bonilla, J., & Bellido, C. (1995). Ecological validity and cultural sensitivity for outcome research: Issues for the cultural adaptation and the development of psychosocial treatments with Hispanics. *Journal of Abnormal Child Psychology, 23,* 67–82.

Bookwala, J., Frieze, I., Smith, C., & Ryan, K. (1992). Predictors of dating violence: A multivariate analysis. *Violence and Victims, 7,* 297–311.

Bronfenbrenner, U. (1979). *The ecology of human development: Experiments by nature and design.* Cambridge, MA: Harvard University Press.

Brownmiller, S. (1975). *Against our will: Men, women, and rape.* New York: Ballantine.

Brustin, S. (1995). Legal response to teen dating violence. *Family Law Quarterly, 29,* 331.

Burgess, A. W., Hartman, C. R., & Clements, P. T., Jr. (1995). Biology of memory and childhood trauma. *Journal of Psychosocial Nursing and Mental Health Services, 33,* 16–26.

Campbell, R. J. (Ed.). (1989). *Pediatric dictionary* (6th ed.). Oxford: Oxford University Press.

Cassidy, L., & Hurrell, R. M. (1995). The influence of victim's attire on adolescents' judgments of date rapes. *Adolescence, 30,* 319–323.

Craig, G. J., & Baucum, D. (2002). *Human development* (9th ed.). Upper Saddle River, NJ: Prentice Hall.

Davies, W. H., & Flannery, D. J. (1998). Post-traumatic stress disorder in children and adolescents exposed to violence. *Pediatric Clinics of North America, 45,* 341–353.

Davis, N., & Twombly, J. (2000). *State legislators' handbook for statutory rape issues.* Washington, DC: U.S. Department of Justice, Office of Justice Programs, Office of Victims of Crime.

Elliott, D. S., Ageton, S. S., Huizinga, D. H., Knowles, B., & Cantor, R. (1983). *The prevalence and incidence of delinquent behavior: 1976–1980. The National Youth Survey* (Vol. 26). Boulder, CO: Behavioral Research Institute.

Fehrenbach, P. A., Smith, W., Monastersky, C., & Deisher, R. W. (1986). Adolescent sexual offenders—Offender and offense characteristics. *American Journal of Orthopsychiatry, 56,* 225–233.

Ferguson, C. U. (1998). Dating violence as a social phenomenon. In N. A. Jackson & F. C. Oates (Eds.), *Violence in intimate relationships: Examining sociological and psychological issues* (pp. 83–118). Boston: Butterworth-Heinemann.

Finn, J. (1986). The relationship between sex role attitudes and attitudes supporting marital violence. *Sex Roles, 14,* 235–244.

Fisher, B. S., & Cullen, F. T. (2000). Measuring the sexual victimization of women: Evolution, current controversies, and future research. In D. Duffee (Ed.), *Measurement and analysis of crime and justice* (pp. 317–390). Washington, DC: U.S. Department of Justice, Office of Justice Programs, National Institute of Justice.

Flanagan, A. Y. (2003). Teen dating violence. Retrieved November 28, 2004, from http://www.nursingceu.com/NCEU/courses/dating/

Foshee, V. A. (1996). Gender differences in adolescent dating abuse prevalence, types of injuries. *Health Education Research: Theory and Practice, 11,* 275–286.

Foshee, V., Benefield, T., Ennett, S., Bauman, K., & Suchindran, C. (2004). Longitudinal predictors of serious physical and sexual dating violence during adolescence. *Preventive Medicine, 39,* 1007–1016.

Foshee, V., Linder, F., MacDougall, J., & Bangdiwala, S. (2001). Gender differences in the longitudinal predictors of adolescent dating violence. *Preventive Medicine, 32,* 128–141.

Foster, S. L., & Martinez, C. R. (1995). Ethnicity: Conceptual and methodological issues in child clinical research. *Journal of Clinical Child Psychology, 24,* 214–226.

Frayser, S. G. (1989). Sexual and reproductive relationships: Cross-cultural evidence and biosocial implications. *Med Anthropology, 11,* 385–407.

Goodchilds, J., Zellmann, P., & Giarusso, R. (1988). Adolescents and their perceptions of sexual interactions. In A. W. Burgess (Ed.), *Rape and sexual assault* (Vol. 3, pp. 245–270). New York: Garland.

Green, B. L., Wilson, J. P., & Lindy, J. D. (1985). Conceptualizing post-traumatic stress disorder: A psychosocial framework. In C. R. Figley (Series Ed.), *Trauma and its wake: Vol. 4. Brunner/Mazel Psychosocial Stress* (pp. 53 69). New York: Brunner/Mazel.

Greenfield, L. A. (1998). *Alcohol and crime: An analysis of national data on the prevalence of Alcohol involvement in crime.* Washington, DC: Bureau of Justice Statistics.

Hall, E. R., & Flannery, P. J. (1984). Prevalence and correlates of sexual assault experiences in adolescents. *Victimology, 9,* 398–406.

Halpern, C. T., Oslak, S. G., Young, M. L., & Kupper, L. L. (2001). Partner violence among adolescents. *The Brown University Child and Adolescent Behavior Letter, 17*(11), 5–6.

Henton, J., Cate, R., Koval, J., Lloyd, S., and Christopher, S. (1983). Romance and violence in dating relationships. *Journal of Family Issues, 4,* 467–482.

Hickman, L. J., Jaycox, L. H., & Aronoff, J. (2004). Dating violence among adolescents: Prevalence, gender distribution, and prevention program effectiveness. *Trauma, Violence, and Abuse, 5,* 123–142.

Horwitz, K., Weine, S., & Jeke, J. (1995). PTSD symptoms in urban adolescent girls: Compounded community trauma. *Journal of American Academy Child and Adolescent Psychiatry, 34,* 1351–1361.

Howard, D., & Wang, M. (2003a). Psychological factors associated with adolescent boys' reports of dating violence. *Adolescence, 38,* 519–533.

Howard, D., & Wang, M. (2003b). Risk profiles of adolescent girls who were victims of dating violence. *Adolescence, 38,* 1–14.

Jackson, S. M., Cram, F., & Seymour, F. W. (2000). Violence and sexual coercion in high school students' dating relationships. *Journal of Family Violence, 15,* 23–26.

Kanin, E. J. (1957). Male aggression in dating-courtship relationships. *Journal of Sociology, 63,* 197–204.

Kaura, S., & Allen, C. (2004). Dissatisfaction with relationship power and dating violence perpetration by men and women. *Journal of Interpersonal Violence, 19,* 576–588.

Kerig, P. K. (1998). Gender and appraisals as mediators of adjustment in children exposed to interparental violence. *Journal of Family Violence, 13,* 343–363.

Kershner, R. (1996). Adolescent attitudes about rape. *Adolescence, 31,* 29–33.

Kilpatrick, K. L., & Williams, L. M. (1998). Potential mediators of post-traumatic stress disorder in child witnesses to domestic violence. *Child Abuse and Neglect, 22,* 319–330.

Knight, R. A., & Prentky, R. A. (1993). Exploring characteristics for classifying juvenile sex offenders. In H. E. Barbaree, W. L. Marshall, & S. M. Hudson (Eds.), *The juvenile sex offender* (pp. 45–83). New York: Guilford Press.

Koss, M. P., Gidycz, A., & Wisniewski, N. (1987). The scope of rape: Incidence and prevalence of sexual aggression and victimization in a national sample of higher education students. *Journal of Counseling and Clinical Psychology, 55,* 162–170.

Malik, S., Sorenson, S., & Aneshensel, C. (1997). Community and dating violence among adolescents: Perpetration and victimization. *Journal of Adolescent Health, 21,* 291–302.

Marciniak, L. M. (1998). Adolescent attitudes toward victim precipitation of rape. *Violence and Victims, 13,* 287–300.

Maxwell, C. D., Robinson, A. L., & Post, L. A. (2003). Nature and predictors of sexual victimization and offending among adolescents. *Journal of Youth and Adolescents, 32,* 465–477.

McFarlane, J. (1989) Battering in pregnancy: The tip of the iceberg. *Women and Health, 15*(3), 69–84.

McFarlane, A. C., & deGirolamo, G. (1996). The nature of traumatic stressors and the epidemiology of posttraumatic reactions. In B. A. van der Kolk, A. C. McFarlane, & L. Weisaeth (Eds.), *Traumatic stress: The effects of overwhelming experience on mind, body, and society* (pp. 129–154). New York: Guilford Press.

Mohr, W. K., & Tulman, L. J. (2000). Children exposed to violence: Measurement considerations within an ecological framework. *Advances in Nursing Science, 23,* 59–67.

Morbidity and Mortality Weekly Report. (2004). Violence-related behaviors among high school students—United States, 19912003. *Morbidity and Mortality Weekly Report, 53*(29), 651–655.

Muehlenhard, C., & Linton, M. (1987). Date rape and sexual aggression in dating situations: Incidence and risk factors. *Journal of Counseling Psychology, 34*, 186–196.

O'Keefe, M. (1997). Predictors of dating violence among high school students. *Journal of Interpersonal Violence, 12*, 546–568.

O'Keefe, M., & Treister, L. (1998). Victims of dating violence among high school students. *Violence Against Women, 4*, 195–223.

Osofsky, J. D., Wewers, S., Hann, D. M., & Fick, A. (1993). Chronic community violence: What is happening to our children? *Psychiatry, 56*, 35–44.

Ozer, E., Tschann, J., Pasch, L., & Flores, E. (2004). Violence perpetration across peer and partner relationships: Co-occurrence and longitudinal patterns among adolescents. *Journal of Adolescent Health, 34*, 64–71.

Peled, E. (1996). "Secondary" victims no more: Refocusing interventions with children. In J. L. Edleson & Z. C. Eisikovits (Eds.), *Future interventions with battered women and their families* (pp. 125–153). Thousand Oaks, CA: Sage.

Population Estimates Program, P. D., U.S. Census Bureau. (2001). Resident population estimates of the United States by age and sex: April 1, 1990 to July 1, 1999, with short-term projection to November 1, 2000. Retrieved October 11, 2001, from http://www.census.gov/population/estimates/nation/intfile2-1.txt

Proto-Campise, L., Belknap, J., & Woolredge, J. (1998). High school students' adherence to rape myths and the effectiveness of high school rape-awareness programs. *Violence Against Women, 4*, 308–328.

Pynoos, R. S., Sorenson, S. B., & Steinberg, A.M. (1993). Interpersonal violence and traumatic stress reactions. In L. Goldberger & S. Breznitz (Eds.), *Handbook of stress: Theoretical and clinical aspects* (pp. 573–587). New York: Free Press.

Riggs, D. S., & O'Leary, K. D. (1989). A theoretical model of courtship aggression. In M. A. Pirog Good & J. E. Stets (Eds.), *Violence in dating relationships: Emerging social issues* (pp. 53–71). New York: Praeger.

Schubot, D. B. (2001). Date rape prevalence among female high school students in a rural midwestern state during 1993, 1995, and 1997. *Journal of Interpersonal Violence, 16*, 291–296.

Shavers, C. A. (2000). The interrelationships of exposure to community violence and trauma to the behavioral patterns and academic performance among urban elementary school-aged children (Doctoral dissertation, Catholic University of America, 2000). *Dissertation Abstracts International, 61*(4-B), 1876.

Silverman J. G., Raj, A., & Clements, K. (2004). Dating violence and associated sexual risk and pregnancy among adolescent girls in the United States. *Pediatrics, 114*, 220–225.

Silverman, J. G., Raj, A., Mucci, L. A., & Hathaway, J. E. (2001). Dating violence against adolescent girls and associated substance use, unhealthy weight control, sexual risk behaviors, pregnancy, and suicidality. *Journal of the American Medical Association, 286,* 572–579.

Singer, M., Anglin, T., Song, L., & Lunghofer, L. (1995). Adolescents' exposure to violence and associated symptoms of psychological trauma. *Journal of the American Medical Association, 273,* 477–482.

Smith, P., White, J., & Holland, L. (2003). A longitudinal perspective on dating violence among adolescent and college-age women. *American Journal of Public Health, 93,* 1104–1109.

Snyder, H. N. (2000a). *Juvenile arrests 1999.* Washington, DC: U.S. Department of Justice, Office of Justice Programs, Office of Juvenile Justice and Delinquency Prevention.

Snyder, H. N. (2000b, July). *Sexual Assault of Young Children as Reported to Law Enforcement: Victim, Incident, and Offender Characteristics.* Washington, DC: U.S. Department of Justice, National Center for Juvenile Justice.

Snyder, H. N., & Sickmund, M. (1999). *Juvenile offenders and victims: 1999 national report.* Washington, DC: U.S. Department of Justice.

Song, L., Singer, M. I., & Anglin, T. M. (1998). Violence exposure and emotional trauma as contributors to adolescents' violent behaviors. *Archives of Pediatric and Adolescent Medicine, 152,* 531–536.

Straus, M.A., Gelles, R.J., & Steinmetz, K. (1981). *Behind closed doors: Violence in the American family.* New York: Anchor Books.

Suarez, K. E. (1994). Teenage dating violence: The need for expanded awareness and legislation. *California Law Review, 82,* 423–471.

Terr, L. C. (1991). Childhood traumas—An outline and overview. *American Journal of Psychiatry, 148,* 10–20.

Thompson, E. H. (1991). The maleness of violence in dating relationships: An appraisal of stereotypes. *Sex Roles, 24,* 261–278.

Tontodonato, P., & Crew, B.K. (1992). Dating violence, social learning theory, and gender: A multivariate analysis. *Violence and Victims, 7,* 3–14.

Trawick-Smith, J. (2003). *Early childhood development: A multicultural perspective* (3rd ed.). Upper Saddle River, NJ: Merrill/Prentice Hall.

Ullman, S. E., Karabatsos, G., & Koss, M. P. (1999). Alcohol and sexual assault in national sample of college women. *Journal of Interpersonal Violence, 14,* 603–625.

Vander Zanden, J. W. (2000). *Human development* (7th ed.). Boston: McGraw-Hill.

Vogel, B. L. (2000). Correlates of pre-college males' sexual aggressions. *Women and Criminal Justice, 11*(3), 25–47.

White, J., & Kowalski, R. M. (1998). Violence against women: An integrative perspective. In R. Green & E. Donnerstein (Eds.), *Perspective on human aggression* (pp. 205–229). New York: Academic Press.

White, J. W., & Post, L. A. (2003). Understanding rape: A metatheoretical framework. In C. B. Travis (Ed.), *Evolutionary models and gender* (pp. 383–412). Boston: MIT Press.

Wolraich, M. L. (1997). Addressing behavior problems among school-aged children: Traditional and controversial approaches. *Pediatrics in Review, 18,* 266–270.

Worth, D. M., Matthews, P. A., & Coleman, W. R. (1990). Sex role, group affiliation, family background, and courtship violence in college students. *Journal of College Student Development, 31,* 250–254.

Yick, A., & Agbayani-Siewert, P. (2000). Dating violence among Chinese American and White students: A sociocultural context. *Journal of Multicultural Social Work, 8,* 101–129.

Chapter 13

THE IMPORTANCE OF PEERS

Darrell Meece and Robert D. Laird

As children transition into the adolescent years, their social worlds become increasingly complex and diverse. Researchers have investigated how significant close relationships—including families, peers, and romantic relationships—may contribute to the underpinnings of adolescents' mental health. The bulk of early research in social relations across children's development focused primarily on parent–child interaction, with adolescence viewed as an extension of childhood. Traditionally, the transition to adolescence was framed as a period of "storm and stress" during which parents were replaced by peers as the most significant individuals in adolescents' social worlds. However, researchers have come to recognize that parent–child relations remain important throughout adolescence. As such, researchers have moved away from viewing parents and peers as competing sources of influence. Instead, much of the current research on parent and peer relationships in childhood and adolescence seeks to understand how multiple domains of social interaction may function to enhance or derail the lives of youth (Collins & Laursen, 2004).

While acknowledging the continuing importance and contributions of parent–adolescent relations, this chapter focuses primarily on social relationships with same-age peers and, more specifically, on how these relationships may be associated with aspects of adolescents' mental health. By and large, a long history of research suggests that problematic peer relations predict maladaptive outcomes for adolescents (see Coie, Dodge, & Kupersmidt, 1990; Deater-Deckard, 2004; Rudolph & Asher, 2000). Because individuals working from different research traditions have tended to study different aspects of adolescent adjustment, this chapter will consider mental health broadly rather than focusing on specific etiologies. In addition, it is important to note that peer relations do not suddenly emerge when children enter adolescence. Adolescent peer relations are a continuation of and build on earlier peer experiences. We will begin with two preliminary sections. The first will discuss four models offered to account for links between adolescent peer relationship experiences and adolescent mental health. The second will review four conceptualizations of peer relationships as contributors to and indicators of social competence. The two preliminary sections will provide the necessary foundation to review empirical research on peer relationships and mental health. To conclude this chapter, we will consider social-cognitive process as potential mediators and parental monitoring as a potential moderator of peer relationship influences on mental health before offering a general summary and directions for future research.

PEER RELATIONSHIP CONTRIBUTIONS TO MENTAL HEALTH

In a recent review, Deater-Deckard (2004) concludes that strong evidence exists connecting aspects of adolescent peer relationships to psychopathology. Rudolph and Asher (2000) review four models that have guided research examining links between peer relationships and psychopathology. The first model, which guided early research on peer relations, was based on an "incidental" model (Parker & Asher, 1987). This model viewed difficulties in peer relationships as a "detection system" or marker for underlying disorder. This view assumes that negative child behavior disrupts peer interactions, and therefore tangential associations between peer interactions and later adjustment difficulties are obtained. Based on this view, problematic peer relations are useful as predictors of later adjustment but do not contribute to disorder.

The second model described by Rudolph and Asher (2000) views psychopathology as the result of difficulties in peer relationships, assuming that peer relationship problems can cause later maladjustment. According to this view, the inability to establish positive peer relationships prevents children from developing skills or problem-solving abilities that would usually be acquired or practiced in peer-based contexts. Thus, experiences in peer relationships contribute directly to later maladjustment.

A third, more contemporary model to account for links between peer relationships and adjustment presented by Rudolph and Asher (2000) focuses on the interaction between qualities of the individual child and experiences in the peer domain. In this view, unique pathways to adjustment difficulties result from the interaction of internal child characteristics and their environments. This type of model suggests that peer relationship difficulties are associated with the most negative outcomes for children who already possess characteristics or qualities that predispose them to maladjustment. Thus, child characteristics may moderate—exacerbate or buffer—the impact of peer relationship difficulties, and thus similar peer relationship experiences could produce substantially different outcomes.

Finally, transactional models of links between peer relationships and adjustment (see Rudolph & Asher, 2000) have arisen from recent research and theory. These models posit that characteristics of individual children—and the environments that they experience—interact through reciprocal feedback loops across development. The broad focus of transactional models is in articulating the processes through which children and their environments influence each other. One example is Crick and Dodge's (1994) reformulation of social information processing theory. According to this theory, over time, stimuli from the environment (e.g., peer-based experiences) encourage the development and organization of social cognitions that, in turn, lead to changes in peer-based experiences. This transactional process results in some children experiencing a trajectory propelling them toward adjustment difficulties.

CONCEPTUALIZATIONS OF PEER RELATIONS AND SOCIAL COMPETENCE

Social interaction is a complex process. Accordingly, theorists and researchers have emphasized different aspects or features of peer relations in their conceptualizations. Likewise, social competence is a broad term used to describe a wide range of studies of children's social interaction and, in particular, interactions with peers. Definitions of social competence typically involve effectiveness in interpersonal interaction in terms of reaching a desired goal. Rose-Krasnor (1997) offered four categories of operational definitions of social competence: social skills approaches, peer status approaches, relationship approaches, and functional approaches.

Social skills approaches are based on attempts to identify specific behaviors or sets of behaviors that are thought to constitute social competence. Typically, research examines individual differences in children's performance of these skills. Social skills approaches to the study of children's peer relations benefit from focusing on behaviors children display, but these approaches are limited in that there is little consensus from study to study about which behaviors are most salient and informative for understanding children's social competence. Furthermore, it is important to note that social skills approaches place the locus of social success on the individual rather than viewing social competence as the result of interactions between individuals (Rose-Krasnor, 1997). Research consistent with the social skills perspective is uncommon during adolescence, as a greater emphasis is placed on social skills development in young children.

Peer status approaches typically rely on sociometric methods in which children are given a list of peers (typically classmates) and asked to nominate peers that meet certain criteria (e.g., especially like to spend time with, behaves aggressively) or to rate each peer along some dimension of social behavior. One unique feature of peer status approaches is that this approach assesses social competence from the perspective of the child's peers instead of adults. Each child is assigned a score based on the combined judgments of their peers. For example, children who receive primarily positive (e.g., like, fun to play with) nominations or ratings are termed "popular," while those who receive primarily negative (e.g., dislike, not fun to play with) nominations or ratings are termed "rejected." "Neglected" children appear to go unnoticed by peers and receive few positive or negative nominations or ratings. Although these strategies have proven very useful for identifying children who are viewed by peers as possessing or lacking social competence, they do not reveal the nature or source of children's difficulties in social interactions as do social skills approaches (Dodge, 1985; Rubin, 1983).

Relationship approaches to social competence are based on the child's ability to form positive relationships. In terms of peer relationships, studies that have taken this approach often focus on friendships. One common technique for identifying friendships stems from the sociometric approach (and the ability to reanalyze existing data sets that include sociometric data); individuals who mutually nominate each other positively or who rate one another highly are considered to be friends. A more informative approach evaluates the quality of the relationship from one or, preferably, both of the relationship partners (Rose-Krasnor, 1997). Commonly assessed qualities of friendships in late childhood and adolescence include support, intimacy, help, and companionship as well as lack of conflict (Parker & Asher, 1993).

Functional approaches to assessing social competence focus on identifying children's social goals and evaluating the processes that children use to attempt to achieve the desired outcome. From this view, the social outcomes are viewed as a joint product of the actions of the individual and the responses of others (Rose-Krasnor, 1997). One limitation of this approach is that evaluation of the outcomes, in terms of success or failure in obtaining one's social goals, is a judgment that requires not only knowledge of the child's goal but also a recognition that there are often competing social goals in a given situation.

The heuristic offered by Rose-Krasnor (1997) offers a useful way of organizing research that has examined links between adolescents' peer relations and aspects of their mental health. We will begin with a brief overview of the development of peer relationships in early childhood and present evidence that these relationships provide the foundation for adolescent peer relationships and contribute to adolescent mental health. Next, we will review research from the sociometric tradition, which emphasizes the social skills and peer status approaches to social competence. Sociometric research focuses primarily on the middle childhood and early adolescence age-groups. We will first review research that has focused on the behavior and mental health correlates of different sociometric status classifications before moving on to research on victims and bullies. Research on victims and bullies also relies primarily on sociometric interviews and thus is heavily influenced by social skills and peer status approaches to social competence. In the next section, we will discuss research on adolescent peer groups relying heavily on Brown's (1990) distinction between cliques and crowds. Research on cliques and crowds dovetails with peer status approaches but also incorporates elements from the relational and functional approaches to social competence. In the final section, on peer relationships, we will focus on research that has considered the mental health implications of dyadic relationships, such as friendships and romantic relationships. Research on dyadic relationships is heavily influenced by the relational approach to social competence.

PEER RELATIONSHIPS

Peer Relations in Early Childhood

Interaction with same-age peers begins very early in life—children as young as six months demonstrate interest in other children (Vandell & Mueller, 1995). Individual differences are apparent in the social behavior of children as young as 14 to 24 months, and toddlers at 18 months of age have been observed imitating other children and even playing simple games, such as peek-a-boo or look-for-the-toy, with other children (Howes & Matheson, 1992). During the toddler years, young children begin to demonstrate evidence of preferring some play partners over others (Ross & Lollis, 1989), and many three- to six-year-olds have at least one mutually nominated friendship (Lindsey, 2002). Preschool-age children are described as being egocentric, meaning that they are not able to take another's perspective and instead think only of their own side of the relationship. Thus, these early friendships are not truly "mutual" in the sense that a child attempts to match their behavior to the other child's needs.

Nonetheless, young children's social competence and peer acceptance show moderate stability over the preschool years (Ladd & Price, 1987). Moreover, measures of young children's social competence and peer acceptance predict children's adjustment during the transition to kindergarten and elementary school (Ladd & Price, 1987; Ladd, Price & Hart, 1988; Olson, 1992). Aggressive and prosocial behavior in early childhood has been linked to behavioral adjustment in middle childhood (Howes & Phillipson, 1998; Ladd & Burgess, 1999). In one study, children rejected by peers in kindergarten were either consistently high in behavior problems or showed strong increases in behavior problems over middle childhood and into adolescence. In contrast, children who had not been rejected by peers in kindergarten showed decreases in behavior problems over the same time period (Keiley, Bates, Dodge, & Pettit, 2000). These findings suggest that continuity exists in the peer experiences of children as they transition from childhood to adolescence and that those early difficulties in peer relationships impact later adjustment.

Sociometric Status Classifications

A great deal of research that has examined children and adolescents' relations in peer groups has been based on peer status approaches in which individuals have been categorized into sociometric classes (e.g., popular, rejected) based on information provided by peers. To date, there has been more investigations of social status among school-age children than among adolescents because the stable classroom membership characteristic of most elementary school classrooms is more amenable to sociometric methods. Therefore, we have included some studies of children in the 8- to 12-year range in our review of findings from the adolescent years (for a broader review of the childhood peer relations literature, see Coie et al., 1990). There is general agreement that children who are popular or well liked seem to be those whose peers view them as cooperative in group situations. Likewise, popular children and adolescents are typically helpful to peers and generally follow the rules. Similarly, teachers rate sociometrically popular individuals as high in prosocial behaviors such as interpersonal sensitivity and rule following. Peers and teachers describe those individuals rejected by the peer group as aggressive and disruptive. Direct observational studies of school-age children suggest that rejected children have fewer positive interactions with their peers and teachers and more negative interactions, particularly aggressive and argumentative interactions, than do other children. Rejected children initiate interaction as frequently as other children do but are rebuffed at higher rates than other children. The methodology of some studies makes it impossible to discern neglected children from rejected children (i.e., the study focused on popular vs. nonpopular children). However, children classified as neglected have been found to be very nonaggressive, and this is one behavior that distinguishes the rejected and neglected groups. Direct observation of neglected children suggests that they spend more time in solitary activities than other children, make fewer attempts to initiate interaction, and display fewer aggressive acts (Coie et al., 1990). Similarly, there is a link between social withdrawal and peer rejection; however, peer-rejected children do not differ from sociometrically average children in shyness or social assertiveness (Coie et al., 1990). Based on these findings regarding the characteristics of sociometric groups, this chapter will first examine peer rejection and aggression, followed by withdrawal from the peer group.

Aggression and Rejection from the Peer Group

Peer rejection involves the active exclusion of an individual's social participation by their peers, often in response to aggressive acts committed by the individual. Aggression can be proactive, in terms of an unprovoked, deliberate aggressive behavior aimed to achieve a specific goal, such as coercion, or reactive, in terms of defensive or retaliatory behavior that is the result of a provocation or perceived provocation from a peer (Price & Dodge, 1989). Researchers also have differentiated between overt and relational aggression. Overt aggression—aggression through physical violence or the threat of physical violence—has received a tremendous amount of attention from researchers. Overt aggression may be either physical, such as hitting, kicking, or slapping, or verbal, in that words are used to threaten physical harm or to verbally insult the victim. In the past decade, researchers also have become increasingly interested in relational aggression, in which harm is inflicted on another through manipulation or through controlling their social relationships (Crick, 1997; Crick & Grotpeter, 1995). In contrast to overt physical or verbal aggression, in which the goal of the aggressive act is to cause physical or psychological harm, relational aggression is covert or indirect in that the goal is to harm the targeted individual's relationships with others. Examples of relational aggression include spreading rumors and other attempts to damage one's social reputation, threats of removal of friendship (e.g., in an attempt to control the victim's behavior), or other forms of social exclusion. Xie, Swift, Cairns, and Cairns (2002) further differentiated covert forms of aggression, noting that reputational aggression, which attempts to damage the reputation of another, was distinct from relational aggression, which attempts to use social relationships to cause harm to another. Xie and colleagues (2002) reported that reputation aggression was most often used in the initiation of conflict, whereas relational aggression was more often used during retaliation, maintenance, and escalation stages of conflict.

Research has demonstrated that rates of overt aggression are significantly higher for boys than for girls (Berkowitz, 1993), although data suggest that the gap between boys and girls in the rate of overt aggression acts may be decreasing (Crick, 1997). Because of this, a great deal of the research that has examined overt aggression has focused on males, although this has begun to change in the past decade (Crick, 1997). Unlike overt aggression, girls exhibit significantly higher rates of relational aggression than do boys (Crick & Grotpeter, 1995). Owens, Shute, and Slee (2000) identified several forms of aggression among adolescent girls, including aspects of relational aggression such as gossiping and spreading rumors, nonverbal aggressive acts such as glaring or gestures, indirect harassment (telephone calls, threatening notes), as well as overt verbal and physical aggression. Interestingly, Crick (1997) found that both boys and girls (9- to 12-year-olds) whose peers reported that they participated in high amounts of non–gender-normative aggression (e.g., overt aggression for girls and relational aggression for boys) had significantly higher rates of adjustment difficulties than did children who engaged in gender-normative aggressive behaviors or few aggressive behaviors.

Research has consistently linked peer rejection to aggressive and externalizing behavior problems in adolescence. For example, a longitudinal study (Woodward & Fergusson, 1999), reported that peer relationship problems among nine-year-olds predicted subsequent risk for externalizing but not internalizing behavior problems at 18 years of age. In a review of the literature documenting the link between peer rejection and aggression and externalizing problems, Deater-Deckard (2004) describes a developmental process consistent with a transactional framework. First, children who display externalizing and aggressive behavior are rejected from the peer group because children who are aggressive are more likely to be avoided by their peers than are other children. The experience of rejection from the peer group maintains the aggressive behavior by limiting the child's opportunity to learn alternative modes of interaction through positive social exchanges with same-age peers.

There appears to be two distinct categories of individuals participating in antisocial behavior: (1) those who engage in antisocial behavior in nearly every stage of life and (2) a larger group of persons temporarily involved in antisocial behavior during the adolescent years (Moffitt, 1993). Researchers have suggested that peer-rejected children tend to frequently interact with each other, and therefore antisocial individuals tend to interact frequently with one another (Patterson, Reid, & Dishion, 1992). This suggests that, at least for some children, antisocial peer involvement in adolescence follows peer rejection in middle childhood, as peer rejection leads children to form a network of antisocial peers that serve to reinforce or facilitate antisocial behavior. This trajectory may account for early-onset antisocial behavior typical of individuals who display lifetime persistent antisocial behavior. On the other hand, late-onset, adolescent-limited delinquency may result from mimicry of antisocial peers (potentially either lifetime persistent or adolescent limited) during the adolescent years (Moffitt, 1993; see also Lynam, chapter 6 in this volume).

Although the link between peer rejection and aggression and externalizing behavior is well documented, researchers also have identified other clusters of individuals. An investigation that employed cluster analysis of teacher ratings identified a subgroup of adolescents who were both popular and aggressive (Rodkin, Farmer, Pearl, & Van Acker, 2000). Rodkin and colleagues (2000) labeled these adolescents as "popular-toughs" because they were viewed by peers as having reputations of being athletic, antisocial, and "cool." In further work in this area, Prinstein and Cillessen (2003) used peer nominations to assess tenth graders' peer-based popularity as well as rates of overt, relational, and reputational aggression. Findings revealed that high rates of relational and reputational aggression uniquely predicted peer popularity, whereas high rates of overt aggression predicted low levels of peer preference. Further, the victims of reputational aggression also were high in peer status. These results fit well with the work of Xie et al. (2002), who concluded that adolescents who were well connected in peer groups were most likely to use reputational aggression effectively. Together, these findings suggest that high rates of aggression are associated with adolescents' peer-based popularity reputations among peers, but not necessarily with likability, or peer acceptance. In other words, the effective use of relational and reputational aggression may require that adolescents enjoy high status and visibility among peers; however, using aggression does not result in being well liked by peers. In a second longitudinal study conducted by Prinstein and Cillessen (2003), high rates of peer-based popularity and low rates of peer preference predicted higher rates of all forms of aggression over a 17-month period. Together, these findings suggest that links between aggression and peer status among adolescents are complex and that high-status peers may use more sophisticated forms of aggression, perhaps in efforts to maintain their peer status.

Peer Withdrawal and Isolation

As noted previously, some studies of children's and adolescents' sociometric status have focused on "low social status" children and thus were unable to distinguish between rejected and neglected children. As also mentioned earlier, there is some evidence that rejected children are more likely to be withdrawn from the peer group, but rejected children do not appear to differ from average children in shyness or social assertiveness. In a review, Coie and colleagues (1990) suggest that children who are rejected from the peer group may withdraw from the peer group in reaction to the peer rejection rather than being rejected by the peers because they are withdrawn.

In a series of studies focused primarily on early childhood, Rubin and his colleagues (see Rubin, Burgess, & Coplan, 2002) define withdrawal as a cross-situational display of solitary behaviors in the company of familiar or unfamiliar peers—in other words, individuals isolating themselves from peers. These researchers have identified subtypes of withdrawn behaviors that help to further illuminate the concept. "Passive withdrawal" is the term used to describe the individual's withdrawal from the peer group, whereas "active isolation" is the term used to describe the individual being actively isolated by the peer group. The term "reticence" is used to describe displays of solitary, wary behavior and appears to be a reflection of shyness and social wariness. Reticent individuals watch others interact, appear to be interested in interaction and motivated to participate socially, but seem to be challenged by anxiety or fearfulness (Hart et al., 2000). Reticence may be the result of a conflict between social approach and social avoidance motivations (Asendorpf, 1990). Reticence is contrasted with solitude, which seems to reflect a lack of interest in social interaction or social immaturity. "Solitary active" is the label applied to individuals who actively avoid interaction with peers whether actively rejected by peers or not. The solitary active individual may be present during group interactions but acts alone, which may be viewed by peers as disruptive or nonnormal. The term "solitary passive withdrawal" is used to describe observed solitary behavior, such as quietly doing constructive activities alone (Rubin et al., 2002), and is thought to represent low social approach and low social avoidance motivations (Asendorpf, 1990). This form of withdrawal is not linked to psychopathology, and it seems that individuals displaying this type of withdrawn behavior are simply not interested in high levels of social engagement. The clinical terms "social phobia" and "social anxiety disorder" are used to describe a fear that speaking or interacting with others will result in embarrassment and appear to be consistent with extreme withdrawn behavior (Rubin et al., 2002). The onset of social phobia often begins during adolescence.

According to Rubin and colleagues (Rubin, Bukowski, & Parker, 1998), children who actively avoid peer-based interaction (regardless of peer-based rejection) are most prone to developing internalizing disorders and depression. Withdrawn behavior appears to be stable over time and contexts (Schneider, Younger, Smith, & Freeman, 1998). Withdrawn behavior is not highly associated with peer rejection during early childhood but becomes more strongly associated with peer rejection during middle childhood and adolescence (Rubin, Bukowski, et al., 1998). It is important to distinguish between individuals who are rejected by their peers because of aggressive behavior from those individuals who are both rejected and withdrawn. It appears that, rather than either peer rejection or withdrawn behavior alone, it is the combination of withdrawn behavior and peer rejection that promotes feelings of social isolation and loneliness (Deater-Deckard, 2004; Rubin, Bukowski et al., 1998). For instance, Hecht, Inderbitzen, and Bukowski (1998) examined associations between peer status and depression among 1,687 students in fourth, sixth, seventh, eighth, ninth, and eleventh grades. No associations were obtained between peer rejection and depressive symptoms when all rejected children were included as a single group. However, findings suggested that rejected individuals who displayed higher rates of aggression reported more interpersonal problems, whereas rejected individuals who were also withdrawn displayed higher ratings on some depressive symptoms.

Bullies and Victims

In addition to research that has focused on associations between social status groups and outcomes, such as peer rejection and aggressive and externalizing behavior, and withdrawn and internalizing behavior, researchers have examined the more specific peer relationships of bullies and victims (for a review, see Pellegrini, 1998). Research on bullies and victims will be reviewed next because although the terms "bully" and "victim" imply a complementary dyadic relationship, bullies and victims are often identified using sociometric nomination approaches. In general, bullies receive many nominations in response to descriptors such as "picks on other kids," whereas victims receive many nominations for items like "is picked on by other kids." Bullying may involve overt physical aggression toward an individual or using objects, verbal attacks (such as name-calling or threats), or relational aggression (such as spreading rumors) (Mynard & Joseph, 2000). Boys report being the victim of overt bullying more often than do girls (Crick & Bigbee, 1998; Crick & Grotpeter, 1996; Storch, Brassard, & Masia-Warner, 2003). Individuals who bully others display higher levels of aggression and conduct disorders than do others, and a history of bullying behavior is associated with adolescent delinquency and antisocial behavior (Baldry & Farrington, 2000).

It appears that the role of victim is somewhat stable and is most associated with internalizing disorders, such as high rates of anxiety and loneliness

(Crick & Bigbee, 1998). Hodges and Perry (1999) found that, over the course of a one-year period, peer-based victimization predicted increases in internalizing symptoms, which in turn predicted increases in victimization. Hawker and Boulton (2000) conducted a meta-analysis of studies examining links between peer victimization and maladaptive outcomes, including depression, loneliness, anxiety, and low self-esteem. Among studies that did not control for method variance (e.g., self-report data from the adolescent for both peer victimization and outcomes), as much as 20 percent of the variance in maladaptive outcomes were accounted for by peer victimization. Among those investigations that did control for method variance, as much as 9 percent of the variance in outcomes was associated with peer victimization. Being the victim of both overt and relational aggression has been linked with the fear of negative peer evaluation, social avoidance, loneliness, depression, externalizing problems, and lower levels of self-esteem (Storch et al., 2003), suggesting that adolescents who experience multiple forms of victimization may be at greater risk than those experiencing a single type of aggression. In their study of 383 ninth and tenth graders, Storch and colleagues (2003) also found that prosocial behaviors from peers moderated associations between victimization and loneliness in that victimized adolescents who received prosocial behaviors from peers were moderately less lonely than other victimized adolescents.

Several studies have demonstrated that bullies and victims are not completely distinct groups and that bullies are often victims themselves. Haynie and colleagues (2001) identified patterns of behavior consistent with three distinct groups—bullies, victims, and bullies who were also victims. In their study of 4,263 middle schoolers, 30.9 percent were identified as victims, and 7.4 percent were identified as bullies. Note that more than one-half of the middle schoolers identified as bullies also were classified as victims. It appears that those bullies who are also victims are at the highest risk for maladaptive outcomes; this group scored more negatively than either the bullies or the victims in self-reported problem-solving behaviors, attitudes toward deviance, peer influence, depressive symptoms, school-related problems, and perceptions of parenting. Furthermore, Schwartz (2000) examined differences between four subgroups of school-age children: aggressive victims, nonaggressive victims, nonvictimized aggressors, and a normative comparison group. Findings suggested that children in the aggressive victim group were more likely to experience academic failure, peer rejection, and emotional distress and had more difficulties with emotional and behavioral regulation than were children in other groups. These studies suggest that it is important not to think of "bullies" and "victims" as distinct groups of adolescents but rather to recognize that bullies are often the victims of aggression themselves and thus are likely to suffer the consequences associated with both roles.

Adolescent Peer Groups: Cliques and Crowds

The following sections review research that breaks from the classroom-based sociometric interview tradition. Studies that have examined associations between the peer relations of adolescents and adolescent adjustment have most typically focused on either the examination of dyadic relationships (e.g., friends or best friends) or the study of adolescents' interactions in larger peer groups (e.g., cliques, crowds, or friendship groups; see Brown, 1990). The preponderance of studies that have examined either dyadic relationships or peer group relations suggest that adolescents' behavior, such as delinquency, smoking, drinking, and drug use, tends to reflect the behavior of their close friends and peer groups (e.g., Tolson & Urberg, 1993). Research on peer group relations will be reviewed before moving to a discussion of dyadic relationships.

One aspect of adolescents' peer group relations that has been of interest to researchers is friendship networks, or cliques. Building on Dunphy's (1963) description, Brown (1990) identified cliques as a small group of individuals who are friends with one another. Degirmencioglu, Urberg, Tolson, and Richard (1998) classified the friendship network roles of middle and high school students as clique members (i.e., dense network of friendship nominations), loose group members, dyad members, isolates, and remainders, based on friendship nomination patterns during the fall and spring of the school year. Results indicated moderate stability in dyadic friendships—best friends as nominated in the fall were likely to be a close friend or best friend in the spring. There also was stability among friendship groups, particularly for clique members, and this stability increased with age (Degirmencioglu et al., 1998). In contrast to friendship networks, social crowds are defined as reputational labels that describe stereotypical behaviors and personality traits of the members of the crowd (Brown, 1993). The "crowd" label is given by adolescents to their peers; the stereotypes associated with a given crowd vary according to the crowd membership of the person doing the stereotyping. For example, crowds that have been labeled by researchers include jocks, preppies, brains, normals, druggies, nerds, and so on. A jock might hold the stereotype that preppies are friendly, for example, whereas a druggie might hold the stereotype that preppies are stuck up. Brown (1993) suggests that crowd membership is based on reputation in the peer group rather than an individual's active participation, and so crowd membership does not require friendship among crowd members.

Based on the idea that crowd membership is based solely on reputation among peers, Brown and colleagues have assessed crowd membership by asking expert peer informants to identify crowds. Urberg and colleagues have reported that there is reasonable congruence between self- and other-nominated crowd memberships, suggesting that adolescents are able to accurately self-identify their crowd memberships (Urberg, Degirmencioglu, Tolson, & Halliday-Scher, 2000). Findings from this study also suggest that both self- and other-nominated crowd membership is related to delinquency, substance abuse, and grade-point average.

The hypothesized function of crowds is to "channel" adolescents toward friendships. This is based on the idea that we tend to choose friends similar to ourselves and supporting data that suggest that friendship selection is based on similarities in levels of substance use (Kandel, 1978), school-related variables (Epstein, 1989), and sexual activity (Billy & Udry, 1985). Brown, Mory, and Kinney (1994) suggest that crowd membership indicates to adolescents whether another adolescent would be similar enough to them to be a potential friend in that knowing another individual's crowd membership helps in making quick judgments about potential similarities. Adolescents are most friendly toward members of their own crowd and have a higher proportion of friends from their own crowd or similar crowds than would be expected by chance (Urberg et al., 2000).

Adolescents' adjustment may be linked with adolescents' feelings of belonging to a peer group, how connected adolescents feel to the peer group, their level of involvement with the peer group, and how important the adolescent feels the peer group is (Brown, 1990; Laird, Pettit, Dodge, & Bates, 1999). In fact, associations between adolescents' drinking, smoking, and drug use more closely match their peers when the adolescents spend more time with the peer group and feel more attached to the peer group (Agnew, 1991).

DYADIC RELATIONSHIPS

Researchers who have studied the dyadic relationships of adolescents have focused largely on close friendships and romantic relationships. Collins and Laursen (2004) suggest that during the past two decades, researchers have come to realize that the close relationships (e.g., family, friends, and romantic relationships) of adolescents are different from those experienced during childhood and that adolescents of different ages differ in their participation as partners in close relationships. During early adolescence, same-sex friendships begin to take on higher levels of intimacy, self-disclosure, and support. According to Hartup (1993), most adolescents during this period report extensive involvement with friends.

These relationships take an increasingly important role, relative to family relationships, during the early adolescent years. Because these are the first intimate, nonfamilial relationships that adolescents experience, they may be vitally important in setting the stage for future close peer relationships (Connolly, Furman, & Konarski, 2000).

As youth progress through the adolescent years, there is an increase in participation in opposite-sex friendship dyads, and the more high-status members of a peer group or crowd are usually the first to engage in romantic dyadic relationships (Collins & Laursen, 2004; Dunphy, 1963). It is important to note that modern teens often do not follow traditional patterns of "dating," and this has proven challenging for researchers to distinguish between opposite-sex friendship dyads and romantic partners (Connolly & Goldberg, 1999). According to Collins (2003), most teens have participated in a romantic relationship by mid-adolescence, and by late adolescence most are participating in ongoing romantic relationships.

The social support provided by friendships may serve as a protective factor. In one study (Goodyer, Herbert, Tamplin, Secher, & Pearson, 1997), having a difficult relationship with a friend at the onset of an episode of depression was associated with the maintenance of mood disturbance over a nine-month period. The presence of a best friend reduces the probability that an individual will be victimized and also seems to reduce the potential negative outcomes associated with being victimized (Cowie, 2000). Hodges, Boivin, Vitaro, and Bukowski (1999) found that victimization led to increases in internalizing symptoms and that internalizing disorders in turn led to further victimization; this association was not found, however, among those who had a best friend.

According to Furman (1996), dyadic friendships that are characterized by companionship, support, closeness, security, and a lack of conflict may provide adolescents with social support that serves as a buffer from stressors. Additionally, dyadic friendships characterized by these four qualities may allow opportunities for adolescents to practice peer-based problem-solving techniques and thereby valuable social problem-solving skills. In fact, research has linked these qualities of adolescent friendships with higher ratings of self-esteem and lower rates of delinquent behavior, hostility, school problems, and psychiatric symptoms (Hirsch & DuBois, 1992).

The friendships of early adolescents who display more antisocial behavior have been found to be of lower quality than the friendships of other early adolescents (Dishion, Andrews, & Crosby, 1995), and interactions between two antisocial friends are more likely than other friendships to include talk about deviance and deviant talk (e.g., swearing) and to be more conflict ridden (Dishion et al., 1995). Pleydon and Schner (2001) compared the friendships of delinquent and nondelinquent high school–age females. The friendships of the two groups did not differ in terms of reported companionship, conflict, help, security, loyalty, trust, and closeness with their best friend. However, consistent with the findings of other researchers (Henggeler, 1989), the delinquent group reported higher rates of perceived peer pressure. These findings suggest that, although quality of friendship may be an important predictor of adjustment, the behaviors of the friend may also be important. Peer pressure, whether constructive or destructive, plays a role in all friendships, and female adolescents appear to conform more to peer pressure than do males (Gomme, 1985).

Across age ranges, we tend to have friends who are similar to ourselves, and antisocial children are more likely to have antisocial friends than are other children (Hartup & Stevens, 1999). Several studies have established that associations between adolescent behaviors and the behaviors of their peers result from friendship selection processes as well as peer influence processes (e.g., Dishion, Patterson, & Griesler, 1994) that probably operate in tandem. For instance, Aloise-Young, Graham, and Hansen (1994) investigated adolescent smoking and the smoking behavior of their peers. Results suggested that smoking predicted the formation of friendships but not the breakdown of dyadic friendships and friendship groups. These authors conclude that adolescents might modify their behavior to make friends or to enter a friendship group or may select friends on the basis of similarity in smoking behaviors.

Laird and colleagues (1999) examined correlations between adolescent antisocial behavior and adolescents' perceptions of their best friends' and peers' behavior among a longitudinal sample of 431 12- and 13-year-olds. Adolescents who perceived their friends and peer groups as participating in antisocial behavior were themselves rated higher in self-reports and teacher reports of antisocial behavior. For both males and females, the association between an adolescent's own antisocial behavior and their best friend's antisocial behavior was moderated by the quality of the friendship; antisocial behavior was most strongly associated with the antisocial behavior of the best friend's behavior when the friendship contained high levels of help, companionship, and security. Among females, a similar moderating effect was obtained for peer group friendships, such that females' antisocial behavior was most strongly associated with the antisocial behavior of the friendship group for females who reported high-quality relations with the friendship group. Thus, although close, supportive peer relationships are often thought of as potential buffers from risk, these sorts of relationship qualities may also afford adolescents with the opportunities and social support for engaging in negative behaviors.

Peer Relationships Summary

Research has documented clear links between adolescents' peer relations and the adolescents' adjustment. Although the nature of peer relations may change as children transition into the adolescent years, evidence exists that there is at least some stability in peer experiences from early and middle childhood to adolescence and that early peer interaction influences an individual's peer relations during adolescence. Active rejection from the peer group has been consistently linked to aggressive behavior and externalizing problems. Though the literature on peer withdrawal is not as large as the literature on peer rejection, it seems that adolescents who actively avoid peer interaction are at greater risk for internalizing disorders and depression.

An area of research that has received growing attention involves the roles of bullies and victims. Bullying behavior has been linked with antisocial behavior and delinquency, and being a victim of bullying is linked with internalizing disorders, anxiety, and loneliness. There is also some overlap between bullies and victims, and those adolescents who are both bullies and victims may be at most risk. Research has demonstrated that having a close friend may reduce the impact of peer victimization (Cowie, 2000; Owens et al., 2000), and further research is needed to better understand linkages between the bully and victim roles and adolescents' relations in the larger peer group, in close relationships, and in family relations. As with research on aggression, which has identified different aspects of aggression such as overt and covert behaviors, future researchers may seek to more fully understand bullying behaviors, focusing on the impact of behaviors such as sexual harassment on the peer relationships and mental health of adolescents.

Although not nearly as elaborate as research on sociometric status, research on adolescent cliques and crowds has shown that clique membership and crowd affiliation have implications for adolescents' mental health. One the one hand, clique membership provides feelings on inclusion and belongingness, which may bolster resilience and mental health. However, research clearly shows that the behavior of clique members and the behavioral profile of affiliated crowds have mental health implications as well. It appears that the negative developmental correlates of affiliation with a deviant clique offset any positive developmental repercussions (Laird et al., 1999).

A similar pattern has emerged in research on dyadic relationships. Having a close friend may serve as a protective factor for some adolescents in that the deleterious effects of negative experiences in the peer group, such as peer rejection, may be buffered by experiencing a close friendship. However, friendships may also have a "negative" side in that adolescents who view their friends and peer groups as participating in antisocial behavior are more likely to participate in those behaviors themselves. This may be especially true when adolescents for adolescents who feel very close to the friend or group who is perceived to engage in the antisocial behavior.

SOCIAL-COGNITIVE PROCESSES AND ADOLESCENTS' PEER RELATIONS

Researchers interested in the precursors of individual differences in adolescent peer experiences have identified several cognitive mechanisms that may guide or constrain an individual's social behavior and may serve as mediators between peer relations and adolescent adjustment. Such social-cognitive mechanisms can be categorized as discrete (or online) processes, which are situation-specific responses to a given social cue, or as latent cognitive representations, which are more global cross-situational cognitive structures reflecting children's feelings and beliefs about peer interaction. In either case, the basic assumption is that the way individuals think about and process social information impacts their behavior with peers, which in turn impacts the peers' behavior toward the individual, and in a recursive fashion the behavior of peers impacts the manner in which individuals think about and process social information (see Crick & Dodge, 1994).

Discrete social-cognitive processes involve children's cognitions about immediate and specific social events. This body of research primarily has been inspired by social-information-processing models (Crick & Dodge, 1994) and models from the social-learning perspective (Ladd & Mize, 1983), both of which describe sequences of cognitive events thought to guide behavior in a particular social exchange. Discrete processes include detection (or encoding) of social cues, interpretation of social cues (often referred to as attributions of intent), and generation of social strategies in response to social cues. A bias among aggressive children toward attributing hostile intentions to others has been well documented among second-though eighth-grade children (e.g., Feldman & Dodge, 1987). This hostile attribution bias has been demonstrated through studies in which children are presented with a hypothetical social provocation in which the intention of the provocateur is ambiguous; aggressive and peer-rejected children are more likely to attribute hostility as the intention than are other children. In addition, aggressive children are more likely than other children to view aggressive behavior as an appropriate and effective manner to achieve social goals. In a clinic-based sample of 6- to 15-year-old boys, those diagnosed with conduct disorders generated more aggressive responses to social problems (Dunn, Lochman, & Colder, 1997).

In addition to discrete social cognitions, theorists and researchers from multiple perspectives have posited that deeper, more generalized cognitive representations of relationships may influence social behavior. The distinction between discrete processes and latent representations of relationships is that discrete processes represent relatively brief cognitive events that influence immediate social behavior, whereas latent representations of relationships are seen as more enduring, trait-like conceptualizations of others and the self in relation to others. Burks, Laird, Dodge, Pettit, and Bates (1999) reported that hostile knowledge structures predicted aggressive biases in discrete social-cognitive processing. Moreover, more hostile knowledge structures were associated with higher ratings of aggressive and externalizing behavior and accounted for some of the stability of aggressive behavior during childhood and adolescence.

Associations also have been noted among perceptions of the self, perceptions of peers, and depression. Among a sample of 1,725 sixth through twelfth graders, perceived difficulties in peer domains, including perceived appearance, peer likability, and athletic competence, were associated with elevated rates of symptoms of depression (Harter & Whitesell, 1996). Kistner, Balthazor, Risi, and David (2001) asked high school students to predict the peer ratings they expected to receive from peers. Female adolescents for whom the difference between the expected and received scores were greatest (e.g., viewed themselves most negatively compared to peers) reported the highest dysphoria on a self-report depression measure. These findings suggest that one's perception of their relationship to the peer group, not just one's actual standing, may be important in understanding adjustment.

PARENTS AND ADOLESCENTS' PEER RELATIONS

As noted at the beginning of this chapter, researchers are seeking to understand how parent and peer relations converge to influence development. One example of this work is in seeking to understand how parents can protect their adolescents from the maladaptive outcomes associated with certain peer relationship experiences. Evidence suggests that parents who are more aware of their adolescents' whereabouts and activities may be in a position to prevent and protect their adolescents.

Although there is some debate as to the source of parents' knowledge and thus resistance to the label "parental monitoring" because it implies an active parent role, two decades of research has consistently shown that adolescents are better off when their parents know where they are, who they are with, and what they are doing. Lack of parental knowledge is a key predictor of adolescents' association with antisocial peers (Patterson et al., 1992). Pettit and his colleagues (Pettit, Bates, Dodge, & Meece, 1999) computed the amount of unsupervised time that early adolescents (sixth graders) spent with peers through adolescents' reports of how and where they spent their time on two after-school afternoons. Unsupervised time with peers was associated with increased teacher-rated externalizing behavior problems both concurrently and at a one-year follow-up. The association between unsupervised time with peers and externalizing behavior problems varied as a function of parental knowledge and parents' perceptions of neighborhood safety. Young adolescents who lived in the least safe neighborhoods and whose parents reported the lowest levels of knowledge were at the greatest risk. Parental knowledge was most important as a buffer for risk for those early adolescents who lived in unsafe neighborhoods.

Laird, Pettit, Dodge, and Bates (2005) tested the hypothesis that high levels of parental knowledge disrupts the peer influence and selection processes that result in escalating delinquent behaviors. Results indicated lower levels of antisocial peer involvement in grade 9 and less similarity in levels of adolescent and peer antisocial behavior among the high-knowledge group as compared to the low-knowledge group. Moreover, among the high-knowledge group, increases in delinquent behavior were less likely to co-occur with increases in antisocial behavior during the high school years, and antisocial peer selection processes were weakened. These findings suggest that monitoring-related knowledge may protect adolescents from becoming involved with antisocial peers as well as from the negative associations of that involvement.

Adolescent gender may play an important role in understanding the protective role of parent–adolescent relations. For example, Crosnoe, Erickson, and Dornbusch (2002) report that, although having a delinquent friend is a significant risk factor for participating in delinquent behavior for both male and female adolescents, it is a significantly greater risk factor for males than for females. Moreover, the pattern of findings from this study suggest that family- and school-based protective factors may differ in importance for boys and girls, with academic achievement and school orientation being a significant protective factor for both boys and girls but household organization being a significant protective factor only for boys. Kim, Hetherington, and Reiss (1999) found that associations between parental knowledge and externalizing behavior varied by the gender of the adolescent as well as family structure. Low rates of maternal knowledge were associated with increased rates of externalizing behavior for boys in stepfather families and for girls in nonstepfather families.

FUTURE DIRECTIONS

To date, peer relations research in childhood and adolescence has focused primarily on describing peer interactions and establishing links between peer experiences and outcomes. It is likely that these avenues of exploration will continue to expand with the consideration of a broader range of peer experiences and outcomes. Individuals are finding ever more creative ways to analyze peer nomination data. Recent studies have used nomination data to identify mutual friends and enemies (i.e., based on reciprocated positive and negative nominations, respectively; Abecassis, Hartup, Haselager, Scholte, & Van Lieshout, 2002), and researchers have broadened the peer relationships domain to incorporate romantic relationships and sibling relationships, which share some attributes with same-sex peer relationships while also having some unique attributes with relevance for mental health in adolescence. As researchers expand the scope of peer relationship research, it will become important to examine contributions form multiple relationships and multiple types of relationships in combination and simultaneously. For example, Gest, Graham-Bermann, and Hartup (2001) show that the number of friends an individual has, the individual's centrality to the peer network, and peer rejection contribute to the prediction of a range of social behaviors. Other work has taken a more developmental focus to consider how peer experiences in one domain relevant to a particular developmental era are linked to experiences in another domain more relevant to a later era (Laird et al., 2005). Future research may contribute by continuing to articulate the peer ecology and by further developing our understanding of the unique and overlapping contributions of different conceptualizations of peer experiences.

Although many studies have linked peer relationship experiences to aspects of adolescent mental health, the mechanisms that account for such links have not been fully explicated. A body of research has demonstrated that differences in social cognitions are associated with differences in social behavior and peer acceptance and that perceptions of peer relations are linked with adolescent mental health. Further work is needed to develop models in which social cognitions may play a role in accounting for linkages between adolescent peer relations and mental health. In addition to social cognition, the interpersonal processes that may connect peer experiences and outcomes remain understudied. A notable exception is Dishion's (e.g., Dishion, Spracklen, Andrews, & Patterson, 1996) work on influence processes at work in antisocial dyads, which shows that highly antisocial adolescents influence one another, in part, by discussing and engaging in rule-breaking behavior, which serves to articulate a set of shared norms and expectations. More attention to the interpersonal and experiential processes that link peer experiences with mental health is necessary to develop and carry out interventions to improve the lives of children and adolescents.

It is likely that efforts to understand such processes will benefit from an explicit consideration of a continuing thread in peer relationships literature—the direction of effects with regard to mental health and peer relationship experiences. For example, among the models offered as a framework for understanding processes linking peer rejection and maladaptive outcomes is the possibility that peer rejection is a developmentally relevant proxy for the mental health difficulties that are formally recognized at a later time (Coie et al., 1990; Parker & Asher, 1987). Thus, to identify processes that link peer relationship experiences and mental health, it will be helpful to first understand whether the peer relationship experiences are a symptom of difficulties, whether the peer experiences contribute to the difficulties, or both as articulated by the transactional and goodness-of-fit models.

Finally, as with nearly all social science research, one major challenge is to understand both the generalizability and the limitations of current research to diverse populations. Much of the peer relationships research has been conducted with white, middle-class samples. In contrast, many studies of peer relationship outcomes, particularly negative outcomes, have been conducted with high-risk samples (e.g., low socioeconomic status, males, inner city). It is important to determine both whether the structure of peer relationship experiences is different in more diverse communities and whether peer relationship experiences carry similar consequences in low-risk settings. Researchers are challenged to determine both whether current knowledge is applicable and relevant to other populations and whether diverse peer subcultures offer different or additional types of experiences that should be evaluated for their relevance to adolescent mental health. Crick's (1997) research on relational aggression is a powerful example of how research may be well served by considering peer relationship experiences more common to, or even limited to, a particular subpopulation that has been overlooked. Although overt aggression may predict maladjustment for girls just as it does for boy, Crick's work clearly shows that limiting research to overt aggression severely restricts our understanding of peer aggression and its association with mental health among girls.

Further work is necessary not only to investigate the role that ethnicity, gender, and other contextual factors such as socioeconomic status may play as moderators of associations between aspects of peer relations and adolescents' mental health but also to more fully understand the meaning of these different contexts to developmental processes. In one study in this area, Laird and colleagues (2005) investigated patterns of early-onset and late-onset antisocial behavior among adolescents in four groups: European American boys and girls and African American boys and girls. In their analysis, these researchers found that the overall pattern of associations among externalizing behavior problems during early childhood, peer relationship experiences during childhood and middle adolescence, and delinquent behavior in adolescence was very similar for each of the four groups. Further research is necessary not only to include other groups of adolescents but also to more fully understand the *meaning* that different peer-related risk factors and protective factors may have in different cultural groups and the impact that this may have on adolescents' mental health. For example, the concept of family and the attitudes concerning parental monitoring of peer relations are likely different for diverse groups, and these behaviors may have a differing impact on mental health for adolescents of diverse groups. Similarly, the ways in which boys and girls are addressed by family and peers may differ cross-culturally, and the variation in meaning of behaviors may lead to different patterns of associations with mental health. Cultural differences in attitudes toward peer relations and academic/school issues may also prove to be important. Finally, it is likely that researchers in this area will further investigate biological underpinnings associated with peer-based behavior and mental health, and awareness of culture will be vital in understanding interactions between biological mechanisms and environment.

REFERENCES

Abecassis, M., Hartup, W. W., Haselager, G. J. T., Scholte, R. H. J., & Van Lieshout, C. F. M. (2002). Mutual antipathies and their significance in middle childhood and adolescence. *Child Development, 73,* 1543–1556.

Agnew, R. (1991). The interactive effects of peer variables on delinquency. *Criminology, 29,* 47–72.

Aloise-Young, P. A., Graham, J. W., & Hansen, W. B. (1994). Peer influence on smoking initiation during early adolescence: A comparison of group members and group outsiders. *Journal of Applied Psychology, 79,* 281–287.

Asendorpf, J. (1990). Beyond social withdrawal: Shyness, unsociability and peer avoidance. *Human Development, 33,* 250–259.

Baldry, A. C., & Farrington, D. P. (2000). Bullies and delinquents: Personal characteristics and parental styles. *Journal of Community and Applied Social Psychology, 10,* 140–153.

Berkowitz, L. (1993). *Aggression: Its causes, consequences and control.* New York: McGraw-Hill.

Billy, J. O., & Udry, J. R. (1985). Patterns of adolescent friendship and effects on sexual behavior. *Social Psychology Quarterly, 48,* 27–41.

Brown, B. B. (1990). Peer groups and peer cultures. In S. S. Feldman & G. R. Elliot (Eds.), *At the threshold: The developing adolescent* (pp. 171–196). Cambridge, MA: Harvard University Press.

Brown, B. B. (1993). The meaning and measurement of adolescent crowd affiliation. *Journal of Research on Adolescence, 7,* 7–9.

Burks, V. S., Laird, R. D., Dodge, K. A., Pettit, G. S., & Bates, J. E. (1999). Knowledge structures, social information processing, and children's aggressive behavior. *Social Development, 8,* 220–236.

Brown, B. B., Mory, M. S., & Kinney, D. (1994). Casting adolescent crowds in a relational perspective: Caricature, channel, and context. In R. Montemayor & G. R. Adams (Eds.), *Personal relationships during adolescence* (pp. 123–167). Thousand Oaks, CA: Sage.

Coie, J. D., Dodge, K. A., & Kupersmidt, J. B. (1990). Peer group behavior and social status. In S. R. Asher & J. D. Coie (Eds.), *Peer rejection in childhood* (pp. 17–59). Cambridge: Cambridge University Press.

Collins, W. A. (2003). More than myth: The developmental significance of romantic relationships during adolescence. *Journal of Research on Adolescence, 13,* 1–24.

Collins, W. A., & Laursen, B. (2004). Changing relationships, changing youth: Interpersonal contexts of adolescent development. *Journal of Early Adolescence, 24,* 55–62.

Connolly, J., Furman, W., & Konarski, R. (2000). The role of peers in the emergence of heterosexual romantic relationships in adolescence. *Child Development, 71,* 1395–1408.

Connolly, J., & Goldberg, A. (1999). Romantic relationships in adolescence: The role of friends and peers in their emergence and development. In W. Furman, B. B. Brown, & C. Feiring (Eds.), *Contemporary perspectives on adolescent romantic relationships* (pp. 226–290). New York: Cambridge University Press.

Cowie, H. (2000). Bystanding or standing by: Gender issues in coping with bullying in English schools. *Aggressive Behavior, 26,* 85–97.

Crick, N. R. (1997). Engagement in gender normative versus nonnormative forms of aggression: Links to social-psychological adjustment. *Developmental Psychology, 33,* 610–617.

Crick, N. R., & Bigbee, M. A. (1998). Relational and overt forms of peer victimization: A multi-informant approach. *Journal of Consulting and Clinical Psychology, 66,* 337–347.

Crick, N. R., & Dodge, K. A. (1994). A review and reformulation of social information-processing mechanisms in children's social adjustment. *Psychological Bulletin, 115,* 74–101.

Crick, N. R., & Grotpeter, J. K. (1995). Relational aggression, gender, and social-psychological adjustment. *Child Development, 66,* 710–722.

Crosnoe, R., Erickson, K. G., & Dornbusch, S. M. (2002). Protective functions of family relationships and school factors on the deviant behavior of adolescent boys and girls: Reducing the impact of risky friendships. *Youth and Society, 33,* 515–544.

Deater-Deckard, K. (2004). Annotation: Recent research examining the role of peer relationships in the development of psychopathology. *Journal of Child Psychiatry, 42,* 565–579.

Degirmencioglu, S. M., Urberg, K. A., Tolson, J. M., & Richard, P. (1998). Adolescent friendship networks: Continuity and change over the school year. *Merrill-Palmer Quarterly, 44,* 313–337.

Dishion, T. J., Andrews, D. W., & Crosby, L. (1995). Antisocial boys and their friends in early adolescence: Relationship characteristics, quality and interactional process. *Child Development, 66,* 139–151.

Dishion, T. J., Patterson, G. R., & Griesler, P. C. (1994). Peer adaptations in the development of antisocial behavior. In L. R. Huesmann (Ed.), *Current perspectives on aggressive behavior* (pp. 61–95). New York: Plenum Press.

Dishion, T. J., Spracklen, K. M., Andrews, D. W., & Patterson, G. R. (1996). Deviancy training in male adolescents' friendships. *Behavior Therapy, 27,* 373–390.

Dodge, K. A. (1985). Attributional bias in aggressive children. In P. C. Kendall (Ed.), *Advances in cognitive-behavioral research and therapy,* Vol. 4 (pp. 73–110). San Diego: Academic Press.

Dunn, S. E., Lochman, J. E., & Colder, C. R. (1997). Social problem-solving skills in boys with conduct and oppositional defiant disorders. *Aggressive Behavior, 23,* 457–469.

Dunphy, D. (1963). The social structure of urban adolescent peer groups. *Sociometry, 26,* 230–246.

Epstein, J. L. (1989). The selection of friends: Changes across the grades and in different school environments. In T. J. Berndt & G. W. Ladd (Eds.), *Peer relationships in child development* (pp. 158–187). New York: Wiley.

Feldman, E., & Dodge, K. A. (1987). Social information processing and sociometric status: Sex, age, and situational effects. *Journal of Abnormal Child Psychology, 15,* 211–227.

Furman, W. (1996). The measurement of friendship perceptions: Conceptual and methodological issues. In W. M. Bukowski, A. F. Newcomb, & W. W. Hartup (Eds.), *The company they keep: Friendship in childhood and adolescence* (pp. 41–65). New York: Cambridge University Press.

Gest, S. D., Graham-Bermann, S. A., & Hartup, W. W. (2001). Peer experience: Common and unique features of number of friendships, social network centrality, and sociometric status. *Social Development, 10,* 23–40.

Gomme, I. M. (1985). Predictors of status and criminal offences among male and female adolescents in an Ontario community. *Canadian Journal of Criminology, 27,* 147–159.

Goodyer, I. M., Herbert, J., Tamplin, A., Secher, S. M., & Pearson, J. (1997). Short-term outcome of major depression: II. Life events, family dysfunction, and friendship difficulties as predictors of persistent disorder.

Journal of the American Academy of Child and Adolescent Psychiatry, 36, 474–480.

Hart, C. H., Yang, C., Nelson, L. J., Robinson, C. C., Olsen, J. A., Nelson, D. A., et al., (2000). Peer acceptance in early childhood and subtypes of socially withdrawn children in China, Russia, and the United States. *International Journal of Behavioral Development, 24,* 73–81.

Harter, S., & Whitesell, N. R. (1996). Multiple pathways to self-reported depression and psychological adjustment among adolescents. *Development and Psychopathology, 8,* 761–777.

Hartup, W. W. (1993). Adolescents and their best friends. In B. Laursen (Ed.), *Close friendships in adolescence* (pp. 3–22). San Francisco: Jossey-Bass.

Hartup, W. W., & Stevens, N. (1999). Friendships and adaptation across the life span. *Current Directions in Psychological Science, 8,* 76–79.

Hawker, D. S. J., & Boulton, M. J. (2000). Twenty years' research on peer victimization and psychosocial adjustment: A meta-analytic review of cross-sectional studies. *Journal of Child Psychology and Psychiatry, 41,* 441–455.

Haynie, D. L., Nansel, T., Eitel, P., Crump, A. D., Saylor, K., Yu, K., & Simons-Morton, B. (2001). Bullies, victims, and bully/victims: Distinct groups of at-risk youth. *Journal of Early Adolescence, 21,* 29–49.

Hecht, D. B., Inderbitzen, J. M., & Bukowski, A. L. (1998). The relationship between peer status and depressive symptoms in children and adolescents. *Journal of Abnormal Child Psychology, 26,*153–160.

Henggeler, S. W. (1989). *Delinquency in adolescence.* Thousand Oaks, CA: Sage.

Hirsch, B. J., & DuBois, D. L. (1992). The relation of peer social support and psychological symptomatology during the transition to junior high school: A two-year longitudinal analysis. *American Journal of Community Psychology, 20,* 333–347.

Hodges, E. V. E., Boivin, M., Vitaro, F., & Bukowski, W. M. (1999). The power of friendship: Protection against an escalating cycle of peer victimization. *Developmental Psychology, 35,* 95–101.

Hodges, E. V. E., & Perry, D. G. (1999). Personal and interpersonal antecedents and consequences of victimization by peers. *Journal of Personality and Social Psychology, 76,* 677–685.

Howes, C., & Matheson, C. C. (1992). Sequences in the development of competent play with peers: Social and social pretend play. *Developmental Psychology, 28,* 961–974.

Howes, C., & Phillipson, L. (1998). Continuity in children's relations with peers. *Social Development, 7,* 340–349.

Kandel, D. B. (1978). Homophily, selection, and socialization in adolescent friendships. *American Journal of Sociology, 84,* 427–436.

Keiley, M. K., Bates, J. E., Dodge, K. A., & Pettit, G. S. (2000). A cross-domain growth analysis: Externalizing and internalizing behaviors during 8 years of childhood. *Journal of Abnormal Child Psychology, 28,* 161–179.

Kim, J. E., Hetherington, E. M., & Reiss, D. (1999). Associations among family relationships, antisocial peers, and adolescents' externalizing behaviors: Gender and family type differences. *Child Development, 70,* 1209–1230.

Kistner, J., Balthazor, M., Risi, S., & David, C. (2001). Adolescents' perceptions of peer acceptance: Is dysphoria associated with greater realism? *Journal of Social and Clinical Psychology, 20,* 66–81.

Ladd, G.W., & Burgess, K.B. (1999). Charting the relationship trajectories of aggressive, withdrawn, and aggressive/withdrawn children during early grade school. *Child Development, 70,* 910–929.

Ladd, G. W., & Mize, J. (1983). A cognitive-social learning model of social skill training. *Psychological Review, 90,* 127–157.

Ladd, G. W., & Price, J. P. (1987). Predicting children's social and school adjustment following the transition from preschool to kindergarten. *Child Development, 58,* 1168–1189.

Ladd, G.W., Price, J.P., & Hart, C.H. (1988). Predicting preschoolers' peer status from their playground behaviors. *Child Development, 59,* 986–992.

Laird, R. D., Pettit, G. S., Dodge, K. A., & Bates, J. E. (1999). Best friendships, group relationships, and antisocial behavior in early adolescence. *Journal of Early Adolescence, 19,* 413–437.

Laird, R. D., Pettit, G. S., Dodge, K. A., & Bates, J. E. (2005). Peer relationship antecedents of delinquent behavior in late adolescence: Is there evidence of demographic group differences in developmental processes? *Development and Psychopathology, 17,* 1–18.

Lindsey, E. W. (2002). Preschool children's friendships and peer acceptance: Links to social competence. *Child Study Journal, 32,* 45–156.

Moffitt, T. E. (1993). Adolescence-limited and life-course-persistent antisocial behavior: A developmental taxonomy. *Psychological Review, 100,* 674–701.

Mynard, H., & Joseph, S. (2000). Development of the multidimensional peer-victimization scale. *Aggressive Behavior, 26,* 169–178.

Olson, S. L. (1992). Development of conduct problems and peer rejection in preschool children: A social system analysis. *Journal of Abnormal Child Psychology, 20,* 327–350.

Owens, L., Shute, R., & Slee, P. (2000). "Guess what I just heard!": Indirect aggression among teenage girls in Australia. *Aggressive Behavior, 26,* 67–83.

Parker, J. G., & Asher, S. R. (1987). Peer relations and later personal adjustment: Are low-accepted children at risk? *Psychological Bulletin, 102,* 357–389.

Parker, J. G., & Asher, S. R. (1993). Friendship and friendship quality in middle childhood: Links with peer group acceptance and loneliness and social dissatisfaction. *Developmental Psychology, 29,* 611–621.

Patterson, G. R., Reid, J. B., & Dishion, T. J. (1992). *A social learning approach, Vol. 4: Antisocial boys.* Eugene, OR: Castalia Press.

Pellegrini, A. D. (1998). Bullies and victims in school: A review and call for research. *Journal of Applied Developmental Psychology, 19,* 165–176.

Pettit, G. S., Bates, J. E., Dodge, K. A., & Meece, D. (1999). The impact of after-school peer contact on early adolescent externalizing problems is moderated by parental monitoring, perceived neighborhood safety, and prior adjustment. *Child Development, 70,* 768–778.

Pleydon, A. P., & Schner, J. G. (2001). Female adolescent friendship and delinquent behavior. *Adolescence, 36,* 189–205.

Price, J. M., & Dodge, K. A. (1989). Reactive and proactive aggression in childhood: Relations to peer status and social context dimensions. *Journal of Abnormal Child Psychology, 17,* 455–471.

Prinstein, M. J., & Cillessen, A. H. (2003). Forms and functions of adolescent peer aggression associated with high levels of peer status. *Merrill-Palmer Quarterly, 49,* 338–341.

Rodkin, P. C., Farmer, T. W., Pearl, R., & Van Acker, R. (2000). Heterogeneity of popular boys: Antisocial and prosocial configurations. *Developmental Psychology, 36,* 14–24.

Rose-Krasnor, L. (1997). The nature of social competence: A theoretical review. *Social Development, 6,* 111–135.

Ross, H. S., & Lollis, S. P. (1989). A social relations analysis of toddler peer relationships. *Child Development, 60,* 1082–1091.

Rubin, K. H. (1983). Recent perspective on social competence and peer status: Some introductory remarks. *Child Development, 54,* 1383–1385.

Rubin, K. H., Bukowski, W., & Parker J. G. (1998). Peer interactions, relationships, and groups. In W. Damon (Series Ed.) & N. Eisenberg (Vol. Ed.), *Handbook of child psychology, Vol. 3: Social, emotional, and personality development* (5th ed., pp. 619–700). New York: Wiley.

Rubin, K. H., Burgess, K. B., & Coplan, R. J. (2002). Social withdrawal and shyness. In P. K. Smith & C. H. Hart (Eds.), *Blackwell handbook of childhood social development* (pp. 329–352). Oxford: Blackwell.

Rudolph, K. D., & Asher, S. R. (2000). Adaptation and maladaptation in the peer system. In A. J. Sameroff, M. Lewis, & S. M. Miller (Eds.), *Handbook of developmental psychopathology* (pp. 157–175). New York: Kluwer/Plenum Press.

Schneider, B. H., Younger, A. J., Smith, T., & Freeman, P. (1998). A longitudinal exploration of the cross-contextual stability of social withdrawal in early adolescence. *Journal of Early Adolescence, 18,* 374–396.

Schwartz, D. (2000). Subtypes of victims and aggressors in children's peer groups. *Journal of Abnormal Child Psychology, 28,* 181–192.

Storch, E. A., Brassard, M. R., & Masia-Warner, C. L. (2003). The relationship of peer victimization to social anxiety and loneliness in adolescence. *Child Study Journal, 33,* 1–18.

Tolson, J. M., & Urberg, K. A. (1993). Similarity between adolescent best friends. *Journal of Adolescent Research, 8,* 274–288.

Urberg, K. A., Degirmencioglu, S. M., Tolson, J. M., & Halliday-Scher, K. (2000). Adolescent social crowds: Measurement and relationship to friendships. *Journal of Adolescent Research, 15,* 427–445.

Vandell, D. L., & Mueller, E. C. (1995). Peer play and friendships during the first two years. In H. C. Foot & A. J. Chapman (Eds.), *Friendship and social relations in children* (pp. 181–208). New York: Wiley.

Woodward, L. J., & Fergusson, D. M. (1999). Childhood peer relationship problems and psychosocial adjustment in late adolescence. *Journal of Abnormal Child Psychology, 27,* 87–104.

Xie, H., Swift, D. J., Cairns, B., & Cairns, R. B. (2002). Aggressive behaviors in social interaction and developmental adaptation: A narrative analysis of interpersonal conflicts during early adolescence. *Social Development, 11,* 205–224.

INDEX

CONTRIBUTING
AUTHORS AND EDITORS

EDNA C. ALFARO, M.S., is a doctoral student in the Department of Family and Human Development at Arizona State University. She completed her undergraduate studies in Psychology at St. Mary's University-San Antonio, and obtained a Master's degree in Human Development and Family Studies from the University of Illinois at Urbana-Champaign. Her primary research interests focus on Latino adolescents' academic success.

LAURA BATES, M.A. is a research associate for University-Community Partnerships & the Institute for Children, Youth, and Families, at Michigan State University. She has extensive experience managing community research projects and developing university-community partnerships, including statewide afterschool programs and programs for families with 0–5 age children. Ms. Bates has published extensively on topics related to the factors associated with successful outcomes among preschool children born to low-income adolescent mothers. Before coming to the university she had 20 years of experience in program development and management in the areas of early childhood and youth development.

LYNNE M. BORDEN is an Associate Professor in the School of Family and Consumer Science and Extension Specialist with an emphasis in youth development at the University of Arizona. Dr. Borden received a Ph.D. in Human Resources and Family Studies from the University of Illinois at Urbana-Champaign in 1997. Lynne's research focuses on youth development specifically on community youth development, community programs that promote the positive development of young people, and public policy. Her research concentrates on the assessment of the influence of youth programs on the development of young people with a specific emphasis in understanding why young people chose to participate or not participate in youth programs.

MARK E. COURTNEY is Director of the Chapin Hall Center for Children and an Associate Professor at the University of Chicago School of Social Service Administration. His current work includes studies of the adult functioning of former foster children, experimental evaluation of independent living services for foster youth and the impact of welfare reform on child and family welfare. He has served as a consultant to the federal government, state departments of social services, local public and private child welfare agencies around the country, and the foundation community. Dr. Courtney has an M.S.W. in Management and Planning, as well as a Ph.D. from the School of Social Welfare at the University of California, Berkeley.

BRANDON COVALT is a doctoral candidate in Human Development and Family Studies at the University of Wisconsin-Madison. Ms. Covalt obtained a dual B.S. in Human Development and Family Studies/ Psychology and an M.S. in Human Development and Family Studies at Colorado State University. Her Master's Thesis was a qualitative examination of the welfare-to-work phenomenon among Colorado women, and her doctoral dissertation research, currently being conducted under the tutelage of Dr. Stephen A. Small, is aimed at understanding decision-making processes in adolescence. Minoring in Child/Family Policy and Prevention/ Intervention Science, Brandon has extensive training in the arena of "bridging the gap" between research and action, including program development and evaluation, family-school-community partnerships, and positive youth development.

DEBORAH J. JOHNSON, Ph.D. is Professor of Family and Child Ecology at Michigan State University. Her interests focus on status-based, race, and culturally--related development, parental socialization and parent/child relations in early and middle childhood. Much of her work has been in the area of racial/ethnic identity development and racial socialization in varying context including child care principally among African-American and other ethnic children and families, but also internationally with Zimbabwean and Indigenous Australian children and families. She has a Visiting Professor Fellowship at Edith Cowan University in Western Australia, and is an Honorary Fellow at the Telethon Child health Research Institute in Western Australia.

STEPHEN J. KORZENIEWSKI is both a research associate at Michigan State University and a public health consultant for the Michigan Public Health Institute. He is involved in several research initiatives including sexual assault and suicide surveillance/prevention, as well as investigating disproportionate juvenile minority contact within the Michigan legal system.

He has earned a the Master of Science degree from the Department of Epidemiology in the College of Human Medicine and a Master of Arts degree from the Program in Health Communication within the College of Communication Arts and Sciences at Michigan State University.

ROBERT D. LAIRD is an Associate Professor in the School of Human Ecology at Louisiana State University. His research interests center on the contexts in which children develop social and behavioral competencies with an emphasis on parent-child and peer relationships. Dr. Laird has authored articles focusing on poor quality peer relationships and affiliation with antisocial peers as contributors to children's and adolescents' maladjustment. The goals of the project are to identify developmental changes in parental monitoring knowledge and psychologically controlling parenting during the childhood to adolescence transition and to elucidate the interpersonal and relationship processes that afford and maintain parents' knowledge of their children's whereabouts and activities.

TOM LUSTER is a Professor in the Department of Family and Child Ecology at Michigan State University. He joined the faculty at MSU in 1985 after completing his doctoral program in the Department of Human Development at Cornell University. His research has focused primarily on three areas: (1) risk and resilience; (2) adolescent mothers and their children; and (3) influences on parenting behavior. His latest research includes: (1) a nine-year longitudinal study of adolescent mothers and their children in Flint, Michigan, and (2) an ongoing study of the Sudanese refugees known as the "Lost Boys" who lived for most of their lives in refugee camps in Ethiopia and Kenya without contact with their parents.

DONALD R. LYNAM is Professor of Psychology at the University of Kentucky. His research interests include developmental models of antisocial behavior, the role of individual differences in deviance, the early identification of chronic offenders, and psychopathy and the juvenile and adult levels. He is a recipient of the 2002 Distinguished Scientific Award for Early Career Contribution to Psychology in the area of Psychopathology from the American Psychological Association.

RUBY J. MARTINEZ is an Associate Professor and Director of the Student Services and Diversity Office at the CU School of Nursing. Dr. Martinez earned her PhD from the University of Colorado Health Sciences Center in Denver in 1995. Dr. Martinez studies Latino health, attitudes toward people who abuse substances, seclusion and restraint, personal safety of runaway teenagers and cultural differences in pain expression in older adults. Currently, Dr. Martinez holds the office of President in the National Latino Behavioral Health Association, where she is a founding member. She was commissioned by President Bush's New Freedom Commission on Mental Health to serve as a consultant in the area of cultural competence in mental health.

CHRISTOPHER D. MAXWELL is Associate Professor in the School of Criminal Justice at Michigan State University and is Associate Research Scientist in the Institute for Social Research at the University of Michigan where he is also the Director of the National Archive of Criminal Justice Data. Dr. Maxwells research interests include testing for the benefits and costs of sanctions and therapeutic treatments for spouse abusers, the impacts of police and court services on victims of domestic violence, the epidemiology of violence against women by intimates, and the extent and correlates of sexual assault by and against adolescents. Dr. Maxwell earned his M.A. (1994) and Ph.D. (1998) degrees in criminal justice from Rutgers University.

JAMES J. MAZZA is an associate professor in the School Psychology program at the University of Washington. He received the masters degree in 1990 and his Ph.D. in 1993 from the University of Wisconsin—Madison. His current research interests focus on the area of adolescent mental health and the identification of youth who are at-risk for suicidal behavior, depression, posttraumatic stress symptomatology and exposure to community violence. His research consists of identification of at-risk youth through self-report mental health surveys and clinical interviews. Results from his research are used to better understand adolescent mental health problems and to examine the complex relationship between mental health problems and precipitating risk and protective factors.

JENIFER K. MCGUIRE Jenifer McGuire is currently a post-doctoral research associate in the division of Family Studies and Human Development at the University of Arizona. Jenifer's background is in applied research on adolescent sexuality: Including sex education, sexual behavior, romantic relationships, and sexual orientation. Her research experiences include quantitative research with large, representative datasets as well as local community based studies and program evaluations that examine a how social contexts interact with adolescent sexuality.

DARRELL MEECE is an Assistant Professor in the Department of Family and Child Ecology at Michigan State University. His main research interests are childrens peer relations, particularly social cognition and the impact of contextual factors, such as out-of-home care experiences, on children's peer relations. Dr. Meece has co-authored articles and presentations that focus on concurrent and subsequent correlates of children's out-of-home care experiences, and on continuity in children's care experiences from early childhood through adolescence. Dr. Meece is conducting studies of infant care in low-income families and in migrant farm working families, and of informal care of preschoolers in low-income families.

DANIEL F. PERKINS, Ph.D., is an Associate Professor of family and youth resiliency and policy in the Department of Agricultural and Extension Education at The Pennsylvania State University. Daniel received a Ph.D. in Family and Child Ecology from Michigan State University. His scholarship involves the integration of practice and research into three major foci: (1) Positive Youth Development—decrease risks and increase skills and competencies of youth; (2) Healthy Family Development—increase resiliency through strength-based educational programming; and (3) Community Collaboration—promote strategies for mobilizing communities in support of children, youth, and families.

LORI A. POST is Director of Interdisciplinary Research and Outreach in the College of Communication Arts and Sciences, Research Fellow at MSU Outreach and Engagement, and Assistant Professor in the Department of Family Child Ecology at Michigan State University. Her research focus is on Violence Against Women which she approaches from a public health perspective. Currently, Dr. Post is the Principal Investigator on a grant aimed at testing the impact of creating a standardized background check system for persons with direct access to long term care populations such as nursing homes. This project involves changing and evaluating the legislation to better protect our must vulnerable populations from abuse, neglect, and exploitation.

DESIRÉE BAOLIAN QIN received her doctoral degree from Harvard Graduate School of Education and is currently a Postdoctoral Fellow at Steinhardt Graduate School of Education at New York University. Her research focuses on immigration, adolescent development, and education. Her dissertation study explored how gender interacts with home- and school-level factors in Chinese immigrant children's educational and psychosocial adaptation. In her current research, she is examining psychological adaptation and development of Chinese immigrant adolescents, particularly parent-child relationships at home. She is co-editor (with Marcelo Suárez-Orozco and Carola Suárez-Orozco) of the six-volume series titled *Interdisciplinary Perspectives on the New Immigration* (Routledge, 2001) and co-editor (with Marcelo Suárez-Orozco) of *Globalization: Education and Culture in the New Millennium* (UC Press, 2004).

STEPHEN T. RUSSELL is Associate Professor of Family Studies and Human Development in the John & Doris Norton School of Family and Consumer Sciences. He completed his Ph.D. in sociology at Duke University in 1994 with a concentration in life course studies and demography. Stephen is a William T. Grant Foundation Scholar (2001-2006), and a Visiting Distinguished Professor of Human Sexuality Studies at San Francisco State University. Stephens research focuses on adolescent ethnic and sexual identities, sexuality development, and sexual health. He conducts research on adolescent pregnancy and parenting, and on the health and development of sexual minority youth.

MARC SCHINDLER, J.D. is General Counsel for the Department of Youth Rehabilitation Services in the District of Columbia's cabinet-level juvenile justice agency. He is a graduate of the University of Maryland School of Law and Yale University. Marc served as a Staff Attorney with the Youth Law Center (YLC) from 1997 to 2005. While at YLC Marc was involved with training, technical assistance, law reform litigation, and legislative and administrative advocacy on legal issues related to children, with particular emphasis on improving the conditions of confinement for institutionalized children and addressing racial disparities in the justice system. Marc served as co-chair of the national Juvenile Justice & Delinquency Prevention Coalition in Washington, DC, and currently is a member of the ABA's Juvenile Justice Committee.

LOU ANNA KIMSEY SIMON, Ph.D. is the 20th President of Michigan State University. Prior to assuming the role of president, she was provost and vice president for academic affairs at Michigan State University, and provost of the Michigan State University College of Law. She is regarded nationally as a powerful advocate of a research-active, student-centered university that is an engaged partner with society, in the land grant tradition. Dr. Simon is deeply committed to the development of effective university-community partnerships that focus on solution-based approaches to the problems of children, youth, and families. Most recently, she co-edited with Maureen Kenny, Karen Kiley-Brabeck and Richard Lerner, *Learning to Serve: Promoting Civil Society Through Service Learning* .

STEPHEN SMALL is a professor at the University of Wisconsin-Madison. He holds faculty appointments in Human Development and Family Studies, Educational Psychology, Social Work, Nursing and with the University of Wisconsin Cooperative Extension. He received his Ph.D. in human developmental from Cornell University in 1985. Dr. Small works with communities across Wisconsin and the nation to help them understand and address the concerns, aspirations, and positive and problematic behaviors of young people and their families. This program of research and action has addressed a range of issues including adolescent risk-taking, positive youth development, mental health, sexuality, drug use, parent-child relations, and building organizational and community capacity.

PATRICIA K. SMITH, M.S., R.D., is the Violence Prevention Program Coordinator for the Injury & Violence Prevention Section of the Michigan Department of Community Health. She has worked in injury prevention and control at the state level in Michigan for the past fifteen years. She was the Director of the Department's Violence Against Women Prevention Program for 11 of those years. She has Bachelor degrees from Eastern Michigan and Michigan State Universities, and received her Masters degree from Michigan State.

CAROLA SUÁREZ-OROZCO, Ph.D is Associate Professor of Applied Psychology and Teaching & Learning at New York University's Steinhardt School of Education and Co-Director of Immigration Studies. Her research focus in recent years has been on the intersection of cultural and psychological factors in the adaptation of immigrant and ethnic minority youth. She has published a number of articles and chapter on such topics as academic engagement, the role of the "social mirror" in identity formation, immigrant family separations, the role of mentors in facilitating positive development in immigrant youth, and the gendered experiences of immigrant youth among many others.

SHERRI TERAO is a licensed psychologist in private practice in the Bay Area. A doctoral degree in Counseling Psychology was completed in 1999 at the University of the Pacific, Stockton, CA. S has conducted numerous forensic evaluations on parents involved in the child welfare system. In addition, Dr. Terao had an academic appointment and researcher position at the Chapin Hall Center for Children at the University of Chicago where she directed a project on youth "aging out" of the foster care system in three states. Dr. Terao is currently a member of the American Psychological Association (APA) and the American Professional Society on the Abuse of Children (APSAC).

IRINA TODOROVA works on issues related to psychosocial aspects of health and well-being, migration and health, social change and health, and health disparities. She has received her degrees from Sofia University and the Bulgarian Academy of Sciences and has been a post-doctoral scholar at the Department of Human Development and Psychology, Harvard University. She is the Director of the Health Psychology Research Center in Sofia, Bulgaria. Her research interests also cover the topics of Social change in Eastern Europe and implications for health. Todorova is Board member of the European Health Psychology Society (EHPS), newsletter editor for the EHPS, as well as a member of the working group on Research collaborations.

ADRIANA J. UMAÑA-TAYLOR is an Assistant Professor of Family and Human Development at Arizona State University. She received her PhD in Human Development and Family Studies from the University of Missouri-Columbia. She obtained her M.A.degree in Child Development and Family Relationships and her B.A.degree in Psychology, both from the University of Texas at Austin. Her research interests include adolescents' ethnic identity formation, familial socialization processes, and psychosocial functioning. Although her research includes adolescents from a variety of ethnic groups in the U.S., the majority of her work focuses on Latino adolescents and their families.

FRANCISCO A. VILLARRUEL is a University Outreach Senior Fellow and a Professor of Family and Child Ecology at Michigan State University. He is also a senior research associate with the Institute for Children, Youth, and Families and with the MSU's Latino research institute—the Julian Samora Research Institute. Villarruel is author of *Lost Opportunities: The reality of Latinos in the US Criminal Justice System,* which is available from the National Council of La Raza. He is co-author of the nation's first report that focuses on analysis of disproportionate and disparate treatment of Latino and Latina youth by the U.S. justice system, *¿Dónde Está la Justicia? A Call to Action on Behalf of Latino and Latina Youth in the U.S. Justice System,* and the forthcoming volume, *The crisis in adolescent mental health,* scheduled for release in the Fall of 2005 (Greenwood Press), and co-editor of *Making Invisible Latino Youth Visible: A Critical Approach to Latino Diversity,* and *Community Youth Development: Programs, Practices and Policies.*